Making Lemonade With Ben:
The Audacity to Cope

By Katherine J Perreth

ISBN: 1477665161
ISBN-13: 9781477665169
LCCN: 2013902922
CreateSpace Independent Publishing Platform
North Charleston, South Carolina

This is a work of nonfiction. Many names and identities have been changed.

The author is grateful for use of the following:
The excerpt from chrisdraftfamilyfoundation.org is used
by permission from Chris Draft.
T-shirt quote is reprinted by permission from Snorg Tees, snorgtees.com.
Scripture taken from the Holy Bible, NEW INTERNATIONAL VERSION®.
Copyright © 1973, 1978, 1984, 2011 by Biblica,
Inc. All rights reserved worldwide. Used by permission.
Simplesnails font, for reproduction of the author's mother's note, used with
permission from Poemhaiku (Le Thi Thu Huong – haikuume@gmail.com).
Celtic Trinity/Heart chapter heading design inspired by a pendant created
by Claddaghstore.com, Dublin, Ireland, and used with permission.
Photograph of Institute of Museum and Library Services National Medal Ceremony
is provided by IMLS. All other images provided by the author, the primary family
photographer. (Because she's the mom.)

Cover image of Ben: Taken when he still had the proper use of his right side, by
JoAnne Elsa, the author's mother. (Because she really was The Mom.)

Back image of Ben and Katherine in DC: Taken by Martin from Manchester,
England. Cheers!

For Ben-tachi

Dan, Sam, and Sarah, but mostly for Ben who said, "This book's total yin and yang, Mom. I'd give you a double thumbs up if I could."

CONTENTS

Chapter 1

Do Not Go Gentle

"He's going to die soon...I'm sorry," concluded the barely audible chief neurosurgeon. "We could try to operate...but his chances of surviving surgery are...slim. What do you want to do?"

4:00 a.m. Saturday, January 20, 1996. The whitewashed sterile innards of the University of Wisconsin Hospital were deserted, mirroring the frozen stillness of sub-zero deep winter outside, matching my heart's plummeting iciness.

Chief Neurosurgeon had not been with us during the previous five hours of repeated CT scans, and one angiography. Just before his appearance, three of us sat hushed, awaiting news: my husband, Dan, one of our pastors, and I. Or rather the two men sat in receptionists' chairs, while I prostrated myself on the floor, staining the carpeting with salt water, continuing to implore Deity for our deeply comatose boy. Voice strangled in the pre-dawn dark, my internal words repeated relentlessly. In my mind, only One understood our seven-year-old son's brain, only One comprehended the turmoil, terror, and confusion entombed inside me, only One could answer my unvocal screams for help.

When Chief Neurosurgeon walked through the scan unit doors, I rose and stood with Dan and Senior Pastor, worriedly anticipating we-knew-not-what from this middle-aged doctor. Introducing himself, he calmly, quietly, resignedly asked us to sit with him. Cognizant of nothing but this man's face: not my breath, not my presumably pounding heart, not Dan, nothing.

A large gathering of doctors had conferred throughout the night, debating what to do, he explained, misty-eyed. (He did not mention what we heard days later; at least one surgeon had considered the case hopeless, no point operating. One by one, apparently, expert surgeons had weighed in throughout the night until reaching the top of the food chain – UW's Chief of Neurosurgery.)

The second CT, conducted at 3:30 a.m., had revealed that the massive bleeding inside Ben's head was growing, forcing their hand. Unknown cause. It could be a tumor. Regardless, the bleeding would shortly kill our firstborn.

"What do you want to do?"

Whether Dan spoke, I do not remember. My mind commanded full attention. In a split second, images appeared of another tow-headed dying boy, this one only two, unable to lift his head from his father's shoulder, the little neighbor I had babysat for as a girl. His brain tumor, the chemo, his thin, wracked body, then death. A tiny, glossy, baby blue coffin slowly descending into the ground. Would surgery save my son now only for him to face death again soon, next time awake? Instead of a losing brain cancer battle, I preferred letting Ben escape now, sparing him pain and fear, flouting Dylan Thomas' injunction, allowing Ben to fade comparatively gentle.

"What will happen if we don't operate?" I suddenly asked, snapped out of reverie. I don't know why. The man had just said my son was dying. But I found so much that night difficult to grasp the first time around.

"Death...," he spoke softly, pausing, "...or possibly he could remain comatose."

My vibrant, radiant, loquacious boy stilled for life in some kind of freeze-frame existence? "Operate," I firmly whispered, one horror-choked breath later, looking at Dan for confirmation.

Dan nodded agreement.

"Can we say good-bye to him?" I blurted in agony.

"Of course," murmured our saddened surgeon as he stood to go prepare for his task.

"Could I pray for you?" Senior Pastor quietly interjected. Much appreciated, he had not spoken a word through the doctor's explanation. Indeed, he had barely made a peep during the entire excruciating night.

Melting back down into his chair, relief flooded the powerful surgeon's weary face, the pinnacle of his field, yet only a man.

We three laid our hands upon his while Senior Pastor succinctly asked for God's help. Oddly, it did not seem impertinent, or intrusive, to touch a stranger's hands at that moment of empowerment, solidarity, and sorrow.

While we prayed, others wheeled Ben into the hallway on a gurney, and when the momentary prayer finished, I ran to my son. One doctor "bagged" Ben, rhythmically squeezing a manual respirator every three seconds to keep him alive. This doctor, one of the first we met in the ER, had stayed by Ben's side for five hours.

Leaning over the gurney, "It's Mommy, Ben," I whispered to my boy's closed eyes. "I love you. If you need to keep sleeping and go to heaven, you should." Kissing Ben's cheeks and forehead, wetting them with anguish, repeating my motherly final instructions several times, I felt it important to give him permission to go. Unable to control myself any longer, I raced back to the chair sobbing, my head in my hands, while Dan stayed by Ben's side, having his tender moment, singing softly *Jesus Loves Me* – one of Ben's favorite songs, and the other, *Benjamin's Song*.

Benjamin's Song, the love song Dan and I had sung for seven and a half years to this child. The melody a borrowed show-tune, the lyrics my husband's own: banal, redundant, and true. And I'd commandeered Dan's song for Ben on a nightly basis, while tucking our boy in bed. Each of our three children had their own song.

"*Oh! Sammy!*" Throwing my head back like a she-wolf, ejaculating my second son's name heavenward, razor-sharp shards cracked for his loss. Unaware now that his big brother "slept" on a gurney instead of the futon beside him, Sam, only five, would awake in a few hours to his hero's permanent absence. Perhaps preferable only to waking next to a cold, dead brother.

Abruptly, an uncontrollable urge drew me to my feet, catapulting me to Ben's side. *Benjamin's Song* must be sung one more time. For the last time, and with a cracking voice, I trilled his lullaby. Then granted permission again for my beautiful, blond boy to sleep on.

My good-bye to my comatose son was as complete as it ever would be.

The silent ER doctor bagging Ben remained perpetually twelve inches away from our faces during my farewell performances. I can't imagine watching a parent commit a child to death. Perhaps the ER doc was accustomed to it.

They wheeled Ben away.

Chapter 2

Nanoseconds

The evening before, on Sarah's first birthday, smoke rose from the blown out candle on the rainbow cake. Big brother Ben struck again.

A human ATV since six-months-old, Ben exuded irrepressible impulsivity. He dominated our home life with his fearless, unbounded energy, rabid, unchecked curiosity, unfettered joie de vivre, and gregarious chatter and laughter. His mind brimmed with a constant stream of ideas that translated directly into action, bypassing even a typical young boy's judgment. Ben kept Dan and me continuously on our tippy toes.

We nicknamed him Mr. See-Do. If it could be thought, it could be done, it could be said, and it was. Giving us daily cause for embarrassment, pride, fear, and awe, often in equal measure. But perhaps the best description of Ben comes from German philosopher Friedrich Nietzsche, "You must have chaos within you to give birth to a dancing star."

Holes were Ben's specialty. Darkly mysterious, holes could contain anything. His fingers found their way into many during his short seven years: moving fans, trees, pipes, rocks, ground. Sometimes the unknown critter inside fought back with a sting, a bite, a pinch – that from a crab in Nagasaki, Japan. We lived there from 1990 to 1993, while Dan taught English at two women's colleges, during Ben's ages twenty-one-months to almost five.

Twice Ben really scared me. The first in Nagasaki, at age four, when he announced of my friend, "Mama, next time she comes I'm gonna find out what's down that hole." He referred to the tip-top of her cleavage, never having seen any before. The second time, at age five, after our return to the States, when he declared his temptation to put his hand down the new whirring gizmo he called the "gurgler." The garbage disposal. I convinced him on both counts it would not be prudent.

His second love, climbing, tied only with building in order to destroy, tied only with ingesting whatever lay about. As a preschooler in Nagasaki, he once drank milk from a saucer left out for stray cats in a park. I knew he would, but being eight months pregnant with Sam, I wasn't quick enough on my feet. A problem I often had even without a babe in the womb. Ben threw up, fortunately. Throwing up frequently occupied his earliest years.

Besides atypical, Ben's off-the-Richter-Scale outgoing ways occasionally shook me up. He struck up heartfelt conversations in men's rest rooms, on planes, trains, and airport shuttle buses, in shopping areas, and on the street. We regularly watched him, lost in conversation with others. Ben waxed eloquent on entomology, and could've been lured by anyone, anywhere, with the promise of viewing an interesting insect.

When Ben cocked his head as a six-year-old, thoughtfully eyeing our living room/kitchen wall, chills went up my spine. When he climbed a defunct dog's kennel wearing a real construction worker's hardhat (my prescience), and sat on makeshift rope scaffolding, his brother tried to follow and nearly hung himself. The mark on Sam's neck didn't last too long.

None of us could keep up with Ben. Parenting this boy kept me, as his stay-at-home mother, perpetually on high alert, never allowing him out of sight for long. His hands, fingers, arms, and legs were not safe, and neither was anything within a ten-foot radius. Although, fortunately, by age seven, Ben had mellowed – at least women had nothing to fear.

Because of the precocious, outlandish statements and ideas he came up with, his head seemed only wondrous to me. Indeed, the boy wrote before he could print his name, commanding me to provide captions for his illustrations in his ongoing "Tiger versus Ootooderman" superhero story, "Mama, write this down!"

I never dreamed the inside of Ben's head wouldn't physically be safe.

Exactly two years younger, wired completely opposite, Sam embodied ninja-like stealth skills as a contented, cautious, quiet snuggler of mighty few words. He learned quickly from his occasional lapse in judgment, from mistaken adventures with Ben, retreating never to attempt that again, or anything even remotely similar. Most often it sufficed for Sam to vicariously watch Ben in action. As for Sarah – their baby sister just taking her first tentative steps – time would tell.

So that evening – Friday, January 19, 1996, after Sarah's birthday dinner and first taste of frosting celebration – it seemed out of

character for Ben to allow his Grandma Jo to wrap him tightly in her arms, holding him still and close, cuddling. We all sat on the floor with Sarah, watching her lackadaisically unwrap her presents. Ben, always eager to help anyone unwrap anything, anytime, seemed subdued. Grandma Jo, besides loving her grandkids to death, played zone defense, a strategy the adults in Ben's life employed frequently. Man-to-man wore us all out.

A welcome relief, Ben's tamped down mood. Rarely did I catch a break from pairing those two syllables, those two words reigning supreme in my spoken lexicon: "No, Ben!"

Grandma Jo and Grandpa Syrup (a moniker a la Ben, so named for making golden brown sourdough pancakes, then drowning them) left for their home in the country. We put the kiddies to bed, Sarah at 7:00, the boys at 7:30. Parents dropping exhausted onto the couch.

It was time for our quiet reading habit. Mysteries, *Sports Illustrated*, classic literature, poetry, humor, satire, biography, historical fiction, the Bible, novels, I read them all. (I credit voracious reading with maintaining my vocabulary during our years in Nagasaki; at that time I had spoken fluently in only preschooler English and toddler Japanese.)

On the couch, decked out in my warmest flannel nightgown, I first read the sports page before grabbing my book. Only six days before, Green Bay Packers wide receivers' coach Gil Haskell had been seriously injured on the sidelines by a player's momentum. His brain injury, resulting from his head violently cracking on the artificial turf overlaying concrete, could've been lethal. Reggie White, a defensive end, and an ordained minister, had led a team prayer for Haskell, and I prayed too. I kept up with Haskell's medical reports in the paper.

About 9:30 p.m., I heard some kind of cry, or moan, or whimper coming from the boys' room. Except as a toddler in Japan, when he routinely attempted to get up with the nation's rising sun at 4:30 a.m., Ben usually slept like the dead through the night. No nightmares, no wakening. His body demanded complete cessation of movement for half the day, presumably to recover from the thirty-six hours of living he jam-packed into every twelve-hour span. As his mother, I so appreciated his body's complicity in preserving my sanity.

Lying down next to him, I held his left hand as he lay on his back. His right hand swiped across his forehead. I whispered to him softly, but could not get any response. Then his legs thrashed, his right arm moved jerkily, and he moaned. I spoke again, louder, "What hurts, Ben?" No response. "It's okay, Ben, Mommy's here."

All quiet. At one point his left hand squeezed mine tightly and I felt his body stiffen alongside mine, as his breathing changed. I didn't think anything sinister occurred, only an uncommonly bizarre, deep dream. When his breathing sounded regular and his body relaxed, I left.

I left.

At 9:55 I sought bed, finished with the freezing day and night. Typically, it takes up to thirty minutes for me to fall asleep, this night no exception. Fifteen minutes after I left Ben, more noises came from the boys' room across the hall, just twenty feet from our bed. This time Ben sobbed. Leaping out of bed, I threw on the hall light and raced to his side, into the unmistakable aroma of vomit. Not sobbing.

"Guess I'll be in here off and on tonight," I sighed. Earlier in the week, I'd fought a bug. It seemed about right for another family member to start puking. No matter the cause, Ben followed the same vomit patterns: about every twenty minutes for the first hour or more, then slowly tapering. What a night it would be.

Ben still lay dangerously on his back, lava-like vomit emitting from his lips. How strange. My kids never slept through vomiting. Hollering for Dan to bring a bowl, yanking away the bedclothes, I grabbed Ben to sit him up and remove his pj top.

His torso buckled, totally limp. His head lolled and rolled as though his neck had liquefied. Panicky and sickened, I screamed for Dan. Within seconds he appeared by my side, flicking on the light in the boys' room. He took Ben by the shoulders and we yelled point blank at our son, speaking words never before used. "Wake up! Ben! Wake up!" No response. We hesitantly slapped his face, something else we'd never done. No response. Horrified, I ordered Dan to support Ben's head while I flew the seven stairs down to the kitchen phone. My fingers clumsily dialed our clinic. The answering service assured me a doctor would return my call soon.

"I need one now!" I cried, hanging up. Had I taken one second to explain my boy's condition, I would've received direction.

Coincidentally, we attended the same church as our pediatrician, Dr. Dots. (Sam, at age three, unable to pronounce her name, had first called her that. With blood copiously running from Sam's eyebrow, the three of us had met over his stitches. I thought Sam yelled for his dad that day, but he'd clarified impatiently, "I want Gaahhd!")

Shaking, I looked up Dr. Dots' home number in the church directory. I knew she wouldn't be mad at me, not for a suddenly Raggedy Andy, unrousable child.

"Ben's throwing up and he won't wake up!"

"Is he blue?"

"*Is he blue*?" I bellowed up the stairs.

"*No!*"

"Take him to the ER or call 911," Dr. Dots directed.

911. I had never dialed 911 before. Not unless you counted the time in Nagasaki when I called the cops in the middle of the night, speaking in jerky and broken Japanese, to report the domestic battery occurring in the apartment below ours. The thug was beating his wife, or so I imagined from her screams and the crashing. I'd seen her once before on our stairwell, hiding a black eye. The cops came. The abuser stood roaring on his doorstep, "Dare!?" (Who!?) Which of his neighbors had called the cops? I don't imagine he ever suspected me,

the stupid woman gaijin (foreigner). But the emergency number in Japan is 119, not 911.

911. Emergencies only. My brain hadn't yet understood the fact that unresponsive noodle-neck vomiting constituted an emergency, but it managed to latch on to an order.

The dispatcher calmly verified my name, address, and Ben's condition. An ambulance would come. According to records I called at 10:17, they left at 10:18, and the ambulance arrived at 10:20.

By 10:00 p.m. the temperature had fallen to one degree, the day's wind abated. I should know. After turning on the porch light, in my flannel nightie I stood on our stoop, anxiously listening for the sound of sirens, barefoot and pregnant with worry. That is, when not running circles in the living room, frantically flapping my arms, squeaking inaudibly, "God Almighty! Jesus Christ! Do something! Help! Help Ben! Help me do this right! Help! God Almighty! Help!"

As my prayers went in those days, one of my shortest and most redundant, but I think I got to the crux of the matter.

Three minutes elapsed from phone call to ambulance appearance, incredibly fast in real time. But a mere 180 seconds? Not good enough. Nanoseconds. Since a nanosecond is one billionth of a second, one nanosecond is to one second as one second is to 31.7 years. Much better. I waited interminable eons; the world does not contain enough paper to print the zeros.

I wonder now how Dan's mind occupied his painstaking eons, presumably longer than even mine. I spent my minutes galvanized into action while Dan held his barfing son's flopping head up. Odd, we have never discussed it.

Finally, I heard and saw it. Lights and siren. Screaming past the intersection, then down a street one away from mine (going past?), coming back, pulling up at the curb (not in the empty driveway?), disgorging an army of help.

Sheer chaos commenced. Four EMTs strode purposefully into the house, up the stairs, into the boys' room, shocked into an adrenaline-fueled head rush at the sight of Ben. Or at least they gave the impression Ben's condition was freak-out-worthy worse than they had expected. I didn't care if they joined me in panic, as long as help had arrived. They rushed, dragging equipment, vociferously swearing, raucously commanding, clomping boots tearing up and down the stairs, bless their hearts, they rushed. The noise was fit to wake the dead...but neither Ben nor his brother.

From his futon, lying side by side on the floor next to Ben's, I scooped up Sam, carrying him to our bed. I had actually forgotten about my sleeping second son until I feared he'd be crushed underfoot in the pandemonium. He never woke up, never made a sound. Not when his brother cried out and vomited. Not when we slapped and yelled. Not in a fully lit room with six clamoring adults charging in and out.

Irish mystic Lorna Byrne, author of *Angels In My Hair*, believes angels can keep people asleep. It seems as good an explanation as any for how a five-year-old managed not to stir during the twenty minutes all hell broke loose two feet from his head.

Through her closed bedroom door, contained in her crib, I heard Sarah cry out once. But, otherwise engaged, I ignored her.

Calm intelligence in a crisis, Dan disappeared downstairs, pragmatically calling my parents and a pastor. Grandma Jo would return. While Dan phoned, most of the EMTs worked on Ben, while one worked on me. He asked numerous questions about drugs, poisons, Ben falling on his head. I knew all the answers.

Much earlier that day, wind-whipped Wisconsin's overnight icy temps had fallen, gifted by Canada. By 7:00 Friday morning, the temperature had been just below zero, the wind chill sending it well below. No school. Breathing single digits, negative or positive, hurts; no one wanted frostbitten children. But I could not have been happier, with my second-grader and kindergartner home on Sarah's first birthday. Since it was obviously too cold to play in the snow, Ben and Sam had contented themselves with playing in the basement, playing with their sister in the living room, and helping make her layered cake. The rainbow frosting had been Ben's idea.

Despite his propensity to ingest weird edibles, I knew where the boy drew the line. Besides keeping his hands out of the gurgler, and cleavage, he'd proven responsible with medicine. He would never take something out of the drug closet. Ditto for poison. He steered clear of Mr. Yuk.

Thank goodness it wasn't summer, when Ben regularly played outside and he might have eaten a new, albeit poisonous, insect. Partial to sampling ants, the variety of insects safely consumed in different cultures and by wilderness survivalists intrigued him. Or, on a whim, he could've chewed some neighborhood flora I hadn't dreamed I needed to warn him about. The ever-growing cautionary category of things I failed to instruct upon, things not in the realm of ordinary living, frustrated. Hindsight superseded my foresight way too many times.

But no, Ben had not swallowed anything odd this day. And I knew he hadn't climbed something and fallen either. With his brother, or me, all day long, a spill in the basement on the concrete floor wouldn't have gone undetected. We spent the day of Sarah's first birthday pleasantly tear-free. Ben home from school and indoors. What a relief to be absolutely positive about what hadn't happened.

Wracking my brain to answer the EMT, dinner was the only culprit I could think of. Yet irrationally, as we'd eaten coq au vin many times, without this incredible consequence. The alcohol in the wine should have been boiled away, I explained anxiously, afraid that somehow, unbelievably, my cooking had caused this terrible thing to happen. The EMT assured me it wasn't the dinner.

They loaded Ben onto a stretcher in his bedroom. As they were moving Ben through the hallway, he threw up again. Snowmelt from their boots had puddled, making the wood stairs slippery, and while attending to vomit, they slid. Ben nearly tumbled all the way off the stretcher. Dan hovered at the bottom and would've caught him, if needed. Our adored, noisy rescuers hauled Ben, clad only in his jammie bottoms, out to the ambulance.

Motherhood Common Sense wondered if he'd catch his death of cold or be frostbitten. She would never have taken a half-naked boy into sub-zero weather. Regular common sense overruled. Ben was fine as far as that went.

The whirlwind left at 10:31 according to records, eleven minutes after they arrived. Another eon, this one action-packed. Dan went with them, riding shotgun, while I shivered bewildered in the cold.

Chapter 3

What's The Frequency?

Late summer 2011, or early fall, depending on which air mass on any given day won the tug-of-war over the great state of Wisconsin, found me in a new season of life. Delighted, but not overly so, just contentedly so, well, strong, at peace, in a life of my choosing. With a new walking habit embraced and an old paradigm laid to rest.

For once I could say, "I am happy," without furtively looking over my shoulder wondering when the next salvo would fall. Since Ben's survival, his rebirth in January 1996, waiting for the next proverbial shoe to drop had never taken long. My burning question: Exactly how many shoes were there? The kid's medical charts measured in feet. For years I had lived resigned to the flight-or-fight lifestyle stemming from the myriad repercussions of Ben's surviving a massive brain hemorrhage. But recently, the repeated traumatic events had hit a lull, granting me respite. Hadn't Ben been well enough for fifteen months and counting? Hadn't I also been the same? Every day of gifted wellness counted disproportionately, exponentially, prompting thankfulness.

Ben's acceptance, at age twenty-two, in a mental health program called Yahara House (YH), provided dignity, structure, and pride.

And relieved me of my title Case Manager Mom, a badge I'd worn with increasing despair for fourteen years.

Ben also volunteered very part-time at Madison Children's Museum (MCM). Juggling one-handed, handling Earl the Eastern Milk Snake (especially thrilling, as he had given up his childhood dream of becoming a herpetologist), caring for chickens on the museum's rooftop, and interacting with the general public and their children. Ben had found home, delivering one-liners to a steady stream of strangers, making them smile.

The near-simultaneous combination of becoming part of the YH community, and volunteering at MCM, had proved a rescuing one-two punch, knocking out Ben's hopelessness, fear, uncertainty, low self-esteem, and a host of other negatives. Taking one arm each, they had hoisted him to his feet, and his mother along with him.

On Saturday, 9/10/11, I pondered our new lives while on one of my endorphin-seeking walks. Returning, I saw messages from the evening before flashing on the answering machine. I routinely miss messages left in the evenings.

Okay, and the daytime too. What can I say? The answering machine is in Ben's old room, now the junk room, the one making my three kids wonder if I'm turning into a hoarder. I'm not, only now that I've embraced choice in my new life, why would I spend time cleaning and sorting the past? Some day I'll get around to it – the box loads of psycho-spiritual angst and enlightenment written since The Words started unleashing themselves in 2008 regarding the profound and permanent effect Ben's traumatic life wreaked on every aspect of our family's existence and my own identity – reams of my vignettes, blackened humorous anecdotes, pseudo-manuscripts, especially one called *Magnum Opus*, all the... oh, right. Later.

One message perkily communicated, "Hi, this is Eric, the Volunteer Coordinator from Madison Children's Museum. I'd like to talk to you about Ben. Please call me, I'll be around Saturday from noon until five."

For 5,700 days, phone calls regarding Ben had often meant trouble of sorts. This one didn't sound bad; Eric sounded upbeat. And Ben had recently interviewed for a paid position at the museum. He thought the interview went well. But why would staff call me? Breathe.

"Hi, this is Ben's mom, Katherine Perreth. I'm returning your call."

"Hey, great, thanks! Well, I just want to tell you the Broncos are playing Tuesday night at five."

"Umm, the...?"

"The football game. It's Tuesday, at five, so if you – "

"Football game?" I interrupted.

"Yeah, the Broncos' game is Tuesday night, at five."

How could this be? Sure, the NFL season just kicked off on a Thursday night, but at last look they didn't play Tuesdays. Besides, I'm a Packer Backer through and through, residing in Packerland, why would I care about the Broncos this early in the season? Were we even playing the Broncos this season? I didn't think so. If this wasn't about professional football, what game was it about? And why? Suddenly, I felt kindred spirit with poor news anchorman Dan Rather the night of his mugging in the 1980s. His attacker repeatedly demanding, "Kenneth! What's the frequency!?"

Only no one was hurting me. Shaking cobwebs from my head, I stammered, "I'm... Ben's mom?" (Since I knew perfectly well Ben was my son, what was the reason for that question mark?) "And he's...uhh ...what?"

"Yeah, your son, will you be driving him to the game?"

"Is this something I'm supposed to know about?"

For the first time Eric hesitated. "Uhh, the game? If you could have your son at the field by five?"

(Something definitely has to be done about this conversation, Kenneth.) "Listen, I'm really sorry. I have absolutely no idea what you're talking about. I'm Ben's mom, Katherine Perreth, and I thought you wanted to talk about something to do with the children's museum?"

"Oh, man! I'm sorry. You're that Ben's mom? I just started coaching a team of eight and nine year olds..."

Now that we inhabited the same planet, I assumed the conversation would clarify.

"So, what I wanted to talk to you about is the, uhh, award. The museum, uhh, well it's involving the mayor, uhh, and libraries and service. So it's a very high honor. Michelle Obama will be, uhh, presenting it, and the Executive Director, Ruth, will be going to the, uhh, White House."

(Kenneth, what the hell's the frequency?)

"Yeah, so if you could uhh, write a letter on Ben's behalf? Part of the award is, uhh, about how the children's museum has changed somebody's life, and uhh, Ruth asked if I could call you and see, uhh, if you could write a letter for Ben?"

"Sooo, umm, you want me to..."

A brief pause ensued while Eric-Kenneth explained he needed to park his car. At least I finally understood the reason for his stuttering sentence structure. Once parked, fully regaining his command of English, he made a wee bit of sense.

"Yeah, see, I know Ben really, really, really wants to work here, and he knows everybody and everybody loves him, and Ruth thought of Ben as someone whose life has been changed by the museum."

(Bingo! Now we're back in orbit.)

"She'll be going to the White House to accept the award, and a person whose life has been changed gets to go too. Ruth thought if Ben went, maybe his mom would go along?"

Whoopa! Tripped up on Saturn's rings. My voice suddenly gone from mystified, to non-existent, to choked. "Kenne-er...sorry, Eric,

I'm a bit emotional here...if Ben...if Ben is chosen to go to the White House I can tell you right now his mom will definitely go with him." (Wild horses.)

"So, could you write a letter on Ben's behalf? Explaining how the museum has changed his life, so the committee can decide later this week or next?"

(Oh yeah, Kenneth, I've got that frequency covered!) "Eric," I declared, "this is a far cry from the Broncos play on Tuesday. I can't believe this. I just...I just told Ben...I'm sorry I'm emotional. I told Ben ten days ago...if he kept on...no matter what...being faithful, responsible, professional, cheerful, and hardworking he would be rewarded some day. Even if he doesn't get chosen, just to be considered, what an honor."

"We didn't tell Ben about it, because we didn't want to get his hopes up and then disappoint him. Ruth is also considering him for a paid position."

"Unbelievable! Thanks so much for not telling him, and I won't breathe a word." Since Ben is overly acquainted with squashed dreams, their thoughtfulness pleased me.

After we hung up, I took leaps and bounds to inform Dan, vaulting myself to the backyard corner of refuge. Prefacing my disjointed speech with, "These are good tears!" as opposed to the vast majority flooding my world since 1996, I ended with, "Nobody leads the life I do, nobody."

"Forrest Gump," Dan deadpanned, adding a congratulatory smirk.

"Dang, that's brilliant. I can't believe I didn't figure that out. And know what? If this happens, it's the framework for The Book!"

"Huh? You just gave up on that idea a month ago, when you left the book writing group."

"I know! But if a book jumps up and bites me in the butt, I've got to write it!"

The Book had been a hot topic of conversation for several years. In 2008, skeptical Dan had played devil's advocate with me over my intended audience, "hurting women over forty." (I figured they'd get my humor better than anyone.) Since then, the man had jumped heartily on board, but still wondered about my genre: real-life-tragedy-black-humor-with-a-spiritual-twist. Sort of Level One Trauma, meets Moses, meets ersatz Nora Ephron. But I thought it might work.

In his tale *The Siege of London*, Henry James wrote, "There was no doubt whatever that she was several women in one, and she ought to content herself with that sort of numerical triumph...it was stupid of her to wish to scale the heights."

Nope! Although acrophobic, heights here I come. Not knowing what I'm doing has never stopped me before!

Mrs. S, my kindergarten teacher, once beautifully attested to that fact. The woman nailed me at the tender age of five, and I have proof. My mother's handwriting clearly explains her first ever parent-teacher conference, in October 1966. Had my mother learned anything new? I know I did as an adult, yelping in alarm, the day I found the yellowed piece of paper with the shortlist of my character: "Intelligence – academically above, impressed with her collection of Zs; patrol – won't cooperate; doesn't play well with other children – do it her way and other kids keen on it; plays with boys better than girls – needs improvement in this area; loud voice and carries; just a little S. accent; outspoken – volunteers stories; flighty."

(In my defense as a Wisconsinite, these days I say "y'all" infrequently and always by vernacular choice. I like to mix it up with British idioms from the 1940s.)

Unbelievably, forty-six years later I reunited with my kindergarten teacher. Debating if I should bring up the memorized sheet enumerating my flaws, flighty and outspoken won out. But Mrs. S explained all, either neutralizing or spinning each into a positive. In her sweet, mild-mannered way she concluded these traits had served me well in adulthood. Thinking it over later, I agreed. Since I know the trick is to be aware of, and balance, our double-edged swords, why hadn't I been able to apply that to my list of kindergarten shortcomings? Mrs. S. taught me yet again.

Life also taught me: pay attention, expect the unexpected, and forge ahead. You never know if you'll get another lightning bolt from heaven, like the phone call from the Madison Children's Museum. It left me practically bursting at the seams, marveling that the astonishing, confusing, and triumphant conversation had only been possible because I did the initial spadework in 2010. I gave myself props for the MCM idea, and pats on the back for getting Ben connected. Trained to "Give God the Glory" by accepting blame and rejecting credit, I now believed my work fully counted.

"Well done, you!" I applauded myself. "Be happy you helped create good." But mostly, "Well done, son!"

I could not wait to tell Ben the double great news. "Oh! I can't. How'm I gonna sit on this?"

Chapter 4

A Long, Strange Trip

It took six hours, over the course of two days, to finish my advocating summary letter, my motherly PR pitch, to MCM. Had I succinctly covered Ben's past fifteen years with emotional details sure to grip? Carbonated breath bubbling through my veins, my finger hovered, then pushed, "Send." My words flew skyward, attached to one thousand imaginary colorful balloons, putting me squarely on pins and needles.

Not trusting a virtual letter of such magnitude to make it through the ether, I requested being informed of its receipt. A response came in less than an hour from a delighted woman, heaping praise upon Ben, giving the time frame for nominee review.

"The next ten days," I thought, "will be some of the longest of my life." But if anyone had waiting down to a fine art, I did. I'd be okay.

I would be wrong. I only excelled at negative-in-nature waiting. Perceived good coming down the pike had been all too infrequent. A whole 'nuther animal, it danced wild polkas and jigs in my guts the way dirges of despair never did – maybe because of the contrast.

Hope was hard to handle. Spared hope, spared sharper disappointment. Sometimes it seemed easier to live hopeless.

But once, spring of 2008, I had dared trust the good I saw coming, the launching of my fledgling freelance writing career: tooting the horns of my fellow townspeople for our hometown newspaper, the *Middleton Times Tribune*, circulation 3,000. What a ride! My own version of *It's a Small World*, but way less scripted.

Full-time, inflexible employment had never been an option for Ben's mom, either on call, or in recovery from call, 24/7/365/15. When not gracing medical facilities with our black-hued comedic tandem, I spent much of my life post-1996 alone in my home, either staring into space, or reading, or thinking, sometimes simultaneously. Scientifically proving inertia is indeed a property of matter, especially when one is perpetually emotionally felled. And attempting all things domestic demigoddess: laundry, cleaning, cooking nightly dinners, and managing a household of five. Chaperoning school trips, and volunteering in classrooms and at church, had rounded out my life.

Yet, now, I balanced three part-time, flexible jobs, a puzzle I put together in the late 2000s. Besides writing exclusively upbeat features for the weekly paper, I adored my administrative gopher role at Wisconsin English as a Second Language Institute (WESLI), the ESL school Dan directed. Working behind the scenes in promotion, supplies, and incidentals, indirectly I aided people from all over the world as they built a firm English foundation for their mountain high dreams. And, for twenty days each year, I facilitated a group of sixty-to-ninety-year-olds as they wrote the stories of their lives. I dubbed those women of a certain age, and our lone man, the Renegade Reminiscence Writers (3Rs). Their stories, capturing pert near 1,500 years of collective wisdom, should be mandatory high school reading.

The critical, peace-inducing practices of yoga and tai chi, instituted about the same time as the jobs, fleshed out the rest of my daily schedule.

But how long would this allotted lifestyle and respite last? Suddenly, as it always seemed to be, an odd phone call sent me reeling, jerked around in my emotions, back to living life on a precipice. Albeit, Saturday's phone call from Eric had contained the words "award," and "White House," in one sentence. Not "doctor," and "hospital."

Could it possibly be true? After receiving nomination letter confirmation, I surfed the web and up it popped, last year's award ceremony. December 2010. The First Lady resplendently presented the Institute of Museum and Library Services National Medal to five museums and five libraries. The backdrop a coniferous tree decorated in blue for the holidays. Had the ceremony been held in the Blue Room of the White House? I shook my head, surely not hallucinating.

In my backyard, up where I often look at the half-century-old towering trees I grew up with, from his perch among the verdant needles and leaves all tangled up in blue, hovered Father Goodness. Cheering me on, thrilled with my strength and this good fortune, and conducting the symphonic canopy. To FG's bouncing baton the ash applauded, murmuring "ahhh," the pine swayed, counseling "shhh," the maple nodded approval, humming "hmmm," and the quaking aspen shimmied, rippling with trilling laughter.

As if on FG's cue, a huge sales packet from Kohl's arrived. One of the peel-off 15, 20, or 30% discounts, this time announcing a semi-annual sale of men's suits, shirts, accessories, and shoes. Removing the sticker, I chanted under my breath, "Be a 30, be a 30, be a 30... for Ben."

30%. I glanced upward at Blue-Green in thanks.

The next day, first day of the sale, I rearranged my work schedule to natty-up Ben. At age twenty-three it was about time he owned a suit, "for weddings and such," I explained. True. Funerals too, I thought. In the past few years he'd been suit-less to enough of them, two of them suicides. If nothing came of the nomination to represent the museum in DC, at least Ben would have proper death duds.

As we pulled into the Kohl's parking lot, Ben airily mentioned, "I talked to Kenzie yesterday, and she said, 'Nothing but good news tomorrow.'"

"Who's Kenzie?"

"She's the one who interviewed me for the position." Ben's first chance to be paid in the currency of the realm. His life heretofore overwhelmed by survival and school.

"Tomorrow? Nothing but good news?" I danced victoriously in the parking lot, emitting minor whooping.

"Mom, stop it!" he laughed. "You're acting like me. It's scary!"

"Didn't I tell you a few days ago that I thought something good would happen?"

"Yeah," he said, "you did."

"And when the 'something good' happens tomorrow, I want you to call me first."

"Weelll, Janet at Yahara House wants to know."

"Janet? She's only been helping you for a year! I've been with you for twenty-three years and – "

"Twenty-four," he said smirking, counting in utero, yanking his mother's chain.

I continued to wildly dance my way through the doors, high on oxygen. The only obvious difference between Kristen Wiig's character "Aunt Sue" and me, I bit down harder on my tongue about the surprise.

"It's about time you had some good, Ben. What goes around comes around. You've done a lot of good."

"Is it karma?" he asked, laughing.

In the virtually empty store, we found a suit, dress shirt, tie, and the mandatory two pairs of shoes to make one, sizes 11½ and 13. The large one courtesy of Ben's right foot encased in a plastic leg brace, a smiley-face, ankle-foot orthosis (AFO).

I knew we'd have great shoe luck; we always had. Throughout Ben's childhood, Kohl's provided reasonably priced, quality shoes.

Something I especially appreciated the year, early in middle school, when his AFO foot grew to men's, leaving Ben's other foot firmly in boys'. Crumpled in a shoe aisle meltdown, a saleswoman found me, and then found men's tennies fairly similar to the boys' pair. Black and white they both were. For a long time, we stayed with that color scheme hoping kids would not notice the difference between one shoe and the other. Ben's limping gait, withered and spastic arm, and unique speech already provided enough ammo. Fortunately, most kids did not tease him. But I will never forget the image of a high school kid, mocking Ben's gait and arm while I silently watched from afar. If icy looks could kill, that teen would've melted like the Wicked Witch of the West.

A ton of weight lifted the year both Ben's feet hit men's, removing another proverbial last straw from my life.

Light as a feather on this day, as Ben sat tight outside the men's dressing room, clad in suit pants and a deep purple dress shirt, I repeatedly flitted between suit and shoe departments. Peripherally spying a flash of bright color, I pulled up sharply. Jerry Garcia ties. Totally Ben. I grabbed two. The ties sported various shades of purple, gray, blue, and aqua. Trying them on, Ben declared the aqua, "Out there. Too bright."

Too out there, for him? Was he growing up or something? The other tie wouldn't do for a funeral, but it would look darn good at the White House! I danced a wee jig. Ben thought the Grateful Dead tie coloration caused my exuberance. Our cart loaded with success, I dragged Ben away from five more strangers-to-well-wishers he'd made.

Dropping my son at Yahara House for the afternoon, I drove the few blocks to my admin job at WESLI. The emotions kept choking me as I stuffed thousands of language brochures with applications. The mindless, calming, paper-pushing job used up nervous energy, but allowed thoughts to wander, emotions to well, and tears to fall.

Occasional hyperventilation occurred, a routine job hazard with my son, and I talked myself down. "You're going to stuff these Korean brochures, then Spanish, then Chinese. Breathe."

Dan worked in the office next door with a thin wall between us. As always (outside of watching the Packers), he maintained composure. Even after I hissed earnestly, sotto voce, "Ben says Kenzie says, 'Nothing but good news tomorrow!'"

"There is no reason to get all excited and then get a kick in the ass," Dan advised. "I'm waiting. If there's good news, then we'll pop the champagne. Keep in mind the language issues Ben has. Maybe Kenzie was talking about something else completely."

Perhaps rock solid Dan had not remained stoically unworn from the past fifteen years? Had hopelessness ingrained too? He knew how to wait for good. Just don't believe it. But I had fielded Eric's phone call, written the nomination, and listened to our son happily expect good news because he was told to. Dan hadn't experienced the benefit of direct communication. This time, I dared to hope for good.

In our respective offices we sat, a complete psychological study. Dan choosing to ignore hope, while I nearly finished casting for the movie.

"Ben would play Ben, of course," my brain instructed itself as my hands mechanically stuffed brochures, "at least the older Ben. Sandra Bullock for me. People say we kind of look like each other, except for my rapidly graying hair, green eyes, freckles, and er, a few minor body parts. But that shouldn't be a problem. And Johnny Depp. He'll have to be in the mix somehow. We couldn't possibly do a movie without him. His 4:00 a.m. hug partly kick-started my new life. Could he play Dan?"

I didn't know. Could Johnny Depp play a family man with no obvious character quirks, whose pseudo-stoic demeanor belied his insides? Johnny once played a math teacher from Wisconsin. What about an ESL teacher? It would have to be broached. Or, Matt Damon, perhaps he could? Were either free in, say, 2015?

On second thought, with the complete exception of our Grande Dame Meryl, Hollywood rarely seemed able to fully portray the nuances of real-life trauma, unlike European filmmakers and actors. Perhaps because Europe's descended, collective psyche embodies bloodied soil containing so many of her citizens?

Colin Firth, then? Emma Thompson? Two of my favorite seasoned British actors, but too old to play mid-thirties parents? Dames Judi Dench and Maggie Smith were unfortunately out of the question. Unless, of course, one played Grandma Jo!

So much to think about while stuffing ESL promo brochures. And waiting.

(In May 2012, taking a break from writing, I rented *Extremely Loud & Incredibly Close* and *We Bought a Zoo*. Sandra and Matt just might work!)

Chapter 5

Light Thickens

When a situation is beyond EMTs' ability or licensing, they call for help. Immediately upon roaring away with Ben and Dan, the Middleton ambulance crew requested mutual aid from Madison Fire Department paramedics. (Middleton abuts Madison.) En route to a West Side car fire, the MFD crew diverted to meet Ben's ambulance, the rendezvous occurring in a church parking lot about one mile from our home – the church Dan and I had married in, ten years before. Paramedics hopped into Ben's ambulance. Throwing it into warp speed, they left the church at 10:36, arriving at the hospital in three minutes, flying down 3 ½ city miles.

But I didn't know that then, as I stood frozen, watching lights and siren speed away with my unconscious son. A police car crunched in the frozen snow, stopping in front of the house across the street. My neighbor, Carol, came out her front door and crossed the street with the officer. Carol had become my mother's second pair of eyes in 1966, when we moved from Oklahoma back to my place of birth. I grew up playing Mother May I, Freeze Tag, and Kick Ball with her children. (Decades later, Dan and I purchased the home I'd grown up in.)

On this night, Carol's son, Officer K, pulled duty. As they escorted me back inside my home, Officer K's walkie-talkie buzzed to life, announcing a change of destination. Ben now headed for UW Hospital. It boasted Madison's only Pediatric ICU (PICU).

Jodie, a neighbor I also knew from church, arrived. A pastor, thinking of me and for me, had called her right after Dan had called him. Carol and Officer K planned to stay until my mother arrived from the country, while Jodie drove me to the hospital.

So much confusion and activity – and past my bedtime too.

But I was ready. Then one of my caregivers suggested I change out of my flannel-wear, and put on some socks and shoes. Throwing on jeans, a sweatshirt, and my winter coat and mittens, I jumped into Jodie's car and we left for UW ER at 10:45.

Jodie and I arrived twenty minutes after Ben had. Soon, staff let me see him in an ER bay. His eyes were partially open, but unaware. Knowing that hearing is the last sense to slip away before death, I spoke comforting words. An IV drip supplied medication, I thought, and a machine clicked over, providing respiration. Manual bagging, to keep Ben breathing, commenced whenever they transported him for testing that night.

Once, before they wheeled him away, it seemed I made momentary contact with my boy through one eye-slit. Seizing the chance, I loudly told him I loved him; I was there with him. And then the awareness evaporated. The brief sense of cognition, even if untrue, greatly comforted me during the next two weeks of Comaland. When I wondered where my boy went, wondered if he thought he was alone, wondered if he wanted his mother, but couldn't find her.

Two pastors stayed with Jodie in the ER waiting room. But Dan and I were not with our supporters for most of the night, first sequestered, then allowed to follow in Ben's wake. Traipsing through many brilliant-white, long hallways, while pulling an all-nighter in shock, blurred the nightmare. However, contending with a multitude of professional questioners really rattled.

Over and over, I recounted to various staff how I'd twice found my son. Eager to help, never omitting one detail, I hoped the wealth of information would clue just one person on how to fix my boy. As soon as one finished with me, it seemed another replaced, and the siege started all over again, "Tell me, what happened tonight?"

The incessant retelling of the story ingrained it deeply. Soon, whenever I narrated finding Ben on his futon, his head flopping, I stuttered on every "f."

But my attentive and persistent interrogators were nothing compared to what Dan endured, when he mentioned he and the boys "roughhoused" after dinner.

"How hard did you hit him?" they wanted to know.

Despite my UW-Madison Social Work degree, and twenty-five years of digesting millions of whodunit words, it never dawned on me that staff initially considered us prime suspects. A medical professional told me years later.

Since I prostrated myself before God in the ER waiting room, and continued to do so sporadically throughout the night, perhaps staff thought guilt from harming my son motivated me, instead of sheer terror. Perhaps they thought I begged forgiveness, instead of my boy's life. Perhaps they thought I was crazy, crazy with fear not too far off.

Sometime after the first CT scan, the questioning ceased, staff understood we were not to blame. The undiagnosed mass in Ben's head proved it. (It would not have been remiss then, if someone had attended to electrified parents. Years later, warm blankets packed around me in another medical facility did much to alleviate my mother-of-patient distress. I have learned well the value of warm linen.)

Doctors required more detailed information, so we followed through the labyrinthine building, to angiography. Crouched on the hallway floor with Dan outside the closed doors, I sang hymns softly, not my habit outside Sunday mornings. But the hymns comforted, and gave me something else to communicate besides "Help!"

Restless, I shuffled to an alcove, away from the doors and Dan, away from the risky test on Ben's brain. Picking up a magazine, an article caught my eye. I skimmed a woman's account of losing her husband to brain cancer, wondering if maybe it was an omen, preparing me for Ben to die. Indignation warred with resignation as I tossed the magazine down, holding onto hope. Was God listening, as I assumed? Would he act?

Staff then conducted one more CT scan, and Senior Pastor found us as we awaited results, just before Chief Neurosurgeon appeared and asked, *"What do you want to do?"*

After the four of us prayed together, Chief Neurosurgeon left to prep, and Senior Pastor left to send our remaining ER waiting room supporters home with the dismal news. Ben's emergency craniotomy – death probable.

Dan and I wept our good-byes to Ben, and staff escorted us one last time. The winding route led to elevators whisking loved ones up, up, up to the Pediatric ICU.

Just before the PICU entrance, across the hall from the nurses' station, beckoned a small, private room complete with shuttered window blinds and a closing door. An oasis. As if shutting out the rest of the hospital could make misery vanish. Here we were told to wait. Staff warned the surgery might take up to eight hours, but assured us someone would call this room every ninety minutes with an operating room (OR) report.

Senior Pastor joined us in the private room. Hear no evil, see no evil, speak no evil, the three of us sat separately, lost in our own thoughts, utterly spent, awaiting news of Ben's death. About 5:00 a.m., the first OR phone call communicated the surgery was underway.

Next to the low-lit lamp, on the corner table, sat a rotary dial phone. I found this ancient phone astonishing in 1996. A few months later, I bought a touchtone, remedying the problem. No more shaking parents struggling to stab fingers seven, or more, times in correct number holes. Spinning the rotary like a roulette wheel, perhaps with even better odds than those of their child. If offered for sale, my replacement would've been equipped with a direct line to God. Just push the big, red button once.

The softly ambient room, a calming baby blue, held soothing chairs and a coddling couch, designed to comfortably uphold the bodies of those dealt a parental visceral blow. A quilt hung on one wall, and an inspirational poetic plaque adorned another, "In Memoriam." Meant to comfort, it disturbed; I averted my gaze.

Prayed-out, one last time I asked silently for help for the surgeon, then mused briefly about Ben's funeral. I felt hands-open acceptance of Ben's impending death, strangely at peace, and wondered if I should start planning with Senior Pastor. Ever the practical multitasker, it would be a good use of time.

But I did not. Instead, in the Little Blue Room, I soothed myself by thinking about Ben's last day on earth, a good one, pleased he left his mark on his final day, as if it could be any other way with him. Playing well with his brother, creating the rainbow cake frosting, singing *Happy Birthday* to his sister for the first time.

And the last.

For about four hours we kept quiet vigil, occasionally broken by the OR's jangling phone calls. Once I spoke into the silence. Lying back on the couch, confused by my peaceful mental state, I murmured, "How can you tell the difference between exhaustion, throwing in the towel, and peace?"

"You can't manufacture peace," counseled Senior Pastor with quiet confidence.

Besides this answer, and his earlier request to pray for Chief Neurosurgeon, during the whole saga he spoke only one other sentence forever inscribed on my soul, "Little boys should be outside making snow angels." A poignant truth. I couldn't have agreed more, and his simple statement screamed empathy. Rocklike, Senior Pastor's near-soundless presence that night, the best anyone could do.

With each call from the OR, my astonishment increased. For hours I expected "our surgeon" to tap gently on the door of the Little Blue Room, tentatively enter, bloodied and bowed, sympathizing with our loss. But the OR called for the last time around 9:00 a.m. to report the finished surgery. Ben would be coming up to a private PICU room.

One more bolt in the unending night's scraggly, electric storm.

"Our surgeon" did come, neither visibly bloodied nor bowed. Not jubilant either –cautious, cautioning. Chief Neurosurgeon described the operation as "a surgeon's worst nightmare, ferociously bleeding," impeding visibility. Then, as he worked, the bleeding ceased. He could not remove the cause of the massive hemorrhage, but was almost positive it wasn't a tumor. He suspected something we'd never heard of, an arterio-venous malformation (AVM). The next week to ten days would be crucial, he explained. Ben still walked a critical fine line between life and death. He would be kept in a coma, "buying him some time." Minimizing the swelling in Ben's brain, the next hurdle to jump.

I blurted, "We've been praying for you all night!"

"You'll never know how much I appreciate that," he softly replied. And then he left to give orders to the PICU staff.

Peace fled, my heart soared, and my hands went from open acceptance to clenched fists, fists of victory – fists to fight like hell for Ben's life, to do whatever I could to nurse him back to health.

Divine marching orders were handed me. Noblesse oblige. I felt the Merciful One had delivered, extending Ben's life. As Warrior Mother, I prepared myself for battle. Not perhaps as much to fight against as ancient Boudicca, Queen of the Celtic Iceni, but enough. I only needed to sack an AVM, not Roman Londinium.

Chapter 6

Comaland

Right after Chief Neurosurgeon left us to brief PICU staff, I saw a pediatrician I knew from church striding purposefully past the open door of the Little Blue Room. For years I had cared for her children, twins Ben's age and in his class at school.

"Oh! She's looking for me." Dashing out the door, I yelled, "Sue!"

She spun around in utter confusion, "What are you doing here?"

"Ben had brain surgery *and he didn't die*!" I trumpeted. She had only been doing her rounds. We had catching up to do.

Soon after, nurses brought Ben up from the OR. When we first glimpsed our post-op son Saturday morning, wheeled on a bed through the PICU hallway, the volume of gadgetry attached to Ben stupefied me. So did the incongruity of the pristine white turban swathing his head. Surreal. He was intubated, a large machine breathing for him. Two cranial drainage tubes, multiple monitoring wires, medication IVs, and catheter lines protruded from his puffy body. Three poles carried most of the life-support equipment. He looked like a science experiment gone haywire.

Chief Neurosurgeon explained to Dan exactly what they had done to Ben. As was to be my way, for the most part I avoided attention to technology, methodology, and gory details, focusing only on what things meant for my boy: Are you a good witch or a bad witch? Dan, on the other hand, loved the details, reveled in understanding the machines, the numbers, the brilliant wisdom of Chief Neurosurgeon and PICU staff, and the bloody facts. (Late in Comaland, he asked to watch when they removed tubing from Ben's left ventricle, but missed out on the right.) For Dan, detailed knowledge relieved stress, offered a way to own some control. For me, a load I could not even bear to hear.

Surgeons had cut a long swath of Ben's scalp, temple to temple along his hairline, and rolled the flap back, exposing his skull, then drilled three holes. Playing connect-the-dots, they sawed a circular cork and removed it, gaining access to the hemorrhaging area. Chief Neurosurgeon had lowered instruments into Ben's brain. Ben's skull, a battlefield, the front line, the AVM.

An AVM, he explained, was a congenital defect of abnormal blood vessels lacking capillaries. Drawing a plane between the ears, and straight back through the nose, Chief Neurosurgeon diagrammed the AVM's deep location at the intersection: a "thalamic, hypothalamic, and chiasmatic AVM," alongside the controls for sight and many basic bodily functions.

Chief Neurosurgeon explained Ben's initial deep, natural coma, barring surgical intervention a sure path to death, would now lift. Hopefully. But doctors would augment Ben's state with drugs, to keep him still. They did not even want his eyelids to twitch, as every movement would increase the pressure in his brain, the Intracranial Pressure (ICP). Meds paralyzed Ben, machinery kept him alive.

Besides the unknown severity of brain damage inflicted by the rupturing AVM, ICP dictated what would remain of Ben's functions, if he lived. Sustained high brain pressure causes damage, crushing tissue, cutting off blood supply, and is often fatal. Both the hemorrhage and surgery had caused swelling, and thus, increased pressure. Enveloped by a hard skull, the swollen brain has nowhere to go. To relieve some pressure, surgeons had drilled two ventricular blowholes to drain fluid out the top of Ben's skull.

The turban mostly covered the blowholes, fifty-two industrial strength staples, and many stitches. Ghastly to look at, days later when the bandaging came off, I requested gauze cover the long line of hairline staples. Of course, for Dan, they were a source of fascination. The day a resident neurosurgeon removed them, Dan stood by, cheering Ben on. And then Dan counted them. And saved them. The staples were the precursor to Ben's mega-scar.

The next phase, Comaland, consisted of waiting, waiting, waiting, and fear, while Ben walked a tightrope between life and death. Doctors didn't know how long Ben might remain comatose. Favorite Nurse warned us it would be for some time, probably close to four weeks. We should expect valleys of trouble, she counseled – notably, spiking ICP. Bedside-stationed, PICU nurses constantly monitored Ben's ICP, vital signs, various draining fluids, and other mysteries.

For Dan and me, the ICP numbers became the sole focus of attention, the first topic of conversation as we tag-teamed keeping vigil, and the bane of our existence. Those dreaded numbers! They popped up occasionally, but prolonged high periods were few. Usually, they elevated overnight while Dan "slept" in a PICU provided bunk bed, in a room only slightly wider. Once they did so while I took night watch.

Twenty-four hours after I'd found Ben in a coma on his futon, I laid my head upon his PICU bed. Closing my eyes, holding his hand, silently praying, my major organs clenched with my teeth, as the ICP numbers rose dangerously. Two nurses seated on the other side of my son held a low conversation. One came to relieve the other, and the new night nurse questioned the numbers. Something seemed off. I wanly smiled inwardly, in hope, desperately willing and praying for her to be right. After Dan took my place, and I left for home, the night nurse adjusted the machine. She was right, she explained to Dan, as the false numbers lowered. Full of accolades for Chief Neurosurgeon, to Dan she marveled at the surgeon's skill, courage, and wisdom in using less fluid during surgery to help prevent high post-surgery ICP.

Weeks later, a nurse, not one of ours, sought me out, telling me she'd seen me that first night. She explained, after the things she'd witnessed on the pediatric floor, not much caused her to cry anymore. But the scene, presumably of a sleeping mother holding her comatose son's hand in the PICU, kicked in her lacrimal glands.

We didn't know it then, but Ben was to become medically famous. His case a doozer even within a mammoth building accustomed to the uncommon.

Dan spent some of the first PICU night in a room around the corner from Ben, but ejected from his bunk bed as an alarm screamed over the loudspeakers at 2:00 a.m. "PICU Code Blue." Dan's frantic appearance startled Ben's night nurse. Why had he raced to Ben's side in the middle of the night? Oh. Right. But it wasn't Ben dying.

Sorry.

On Sunday, thirty-six hours after the bleed, people came in droves: family, of course, and local friends, and pastors. And a good college friend in Illinois who had suffered a car accident as a teen, requiring brain surgery himself. And my boys' elementary school principal, now our district's Assistant Superintendent. Pastors, family, and friends I understood, but the sight of our young principal walking toward me in the PICU on Sunday afternoon, his face etched with care and concern, crystallized our new reality. I fairly dissolved at his feet, my arms held out in supplication, touched beyond words. He became more than a principal then, as he enveloped me in his arms. Super Principal remains our staunch friend and ally to this day.

That afternoon, my sister-in-law, up from Chicagoland, proved invaluable. Organizer extraordinaire, Anne nearly single-handedly whipped practical care into shape. Senior Pastor wondered what the church could do to best help, knowing we were going to be inundated by do-gooding. Already abuzz, folks in the several-hundred-parishioner church wanted, needed, to do something.

I had nothing.

Anne, her husband, and Senior Pastor brainstormed and implemented. My contribution was vacuous attendance and nodding an obtuse "yes" or "no."

Anne suggested a phone hotline, one number anyone could call to hear a recorded update on Ben's condition. (We didn't own a computer, a cell phone, or even an answering machine.) This would eliminate most calls to our home, streamline our ability to communicate with literally hundreds, and greatly help my mother, steadfast at her post with our other two children. Already the lone kitchen phone rang incessantly. Grandma Jo kept a notebook of messages for me, but my mind contained no wits to comprehend, my body no energy to attend.

And so it would happen. Early each morning, from the hospital Dan called in two reports, first to me, then to Pastor M, who left an update on his home answering machine. Genius Anne. She also thought point people should coordinate needs, one for meals, another for everything else. What else did we need? A whirling dervish of emptiness, I had no idea.

Later in the week, when the physical therapist (PT) insisted Ben wear high top tennies to keep his ankles stable and toes pointed upright, someone from church donated to our cause. But the shoes weren't high enough, so I ventured out to Kohl's for coma accessorizing. Eeyore-like, I explained the dire situation, mumbling dejectedly, "Can you show me what you've got for little boys in a coma?"

With hushed tones the stunned clerk helped me choose a pair, and sent me shuffling off with wishes of wellness, her eyes leaking concern.

Anne's point person system also coordinated rotated dinner preparation between groups of people. For months, people delivered home-cooked meals to our door. Occasionally we used one of the many restaurant gift cards given to us. Meals came from our faith community, the Japanese community of which we were a part, Dan's co-workers, our neighbors, family, friends, and elementary school staff.

And the gifts wouldn't stop. The barrage of tangible support came by snail mail, or in-person delivery: cards stuffed with money, boxes filled with stuffed animals and toys for Sam and Sarah, pictures drawn by children for Ben's hospital room, letters from his second-grade playmates, get-well wish banners and murals made by his classmates, church Sunday school kids, and by kids in another school who heard of Ben's trouble. Christmas arrived daily, but brought me only numb gratitude, no smile.

Hospital staff were blown away by the overwhelming care rendered by our extended circle of life. It seemed everyone we knew, scattered around the United States, even on other continents, went all in for us. We heard later about the network of unknown people, friends of our supporters, pulling for us, praying for us, hoping for us. Later, I stuck labels on US and world maps to show Ben where his cheering section lived.

Three families, in Nagasaki, banded together to fold one thousand tiny, origami cranes, stitching them together in nineteen yard-long strands. The colorful, paper waterfall is a painstaking symbol of wishes for long life. Annually, Japanese schoolchildren fold and string thousands of paper cranes, sending them to the Peace Parks in Hiroshima and Nagasaki. The enormous, vibrant mounds represent wishes for world peace. Sometimes presented in personal dire circumstances, it is unusual for a Japanese family to own a thousand paper cranes. I daresay we are one of few Western families to receive such a gift. To this day, the outpouring of love shown by those three Nagasaki families is our treasure, hanging in Ben's old room. Many times, I carefully transported it to our school district's third grade classes, during the unit on Japan, making *Sadako and the Thousand Paper Cranes* come alive. During my kimono-wearing, seventy-five-minute traveling show, referred to as "The Japan Lady" by the children, I routinely required the tissue tucked in my kimono sleeve. Lifting high my son's thousand paper cranes, my eyes always blinked rapidly while my throat constricted.

Besides fashioning the origami cranes, our friends in Japan also prayed, joining the throng. For over two weeks, people from church filled 'round-the-clock prayer time slots, every hour on the hour during the days of Comaland. One family set an alarm for 3:00 a.m. We heard of others around the globe, in the Philippines, Russia, Papua New Guinea, Australia, and Kenya, who heard of Ben's plight. They prayed in their respective time zones, covering most of the US night shift. God must've been working overtime, his ears red, ringing with "Ben!" Or, in Japan, "Ben-kun!" Little Ben.

The whirlwind of activity remained mostly outside my awareness, partly by choice. Only once do I remember answering our doorbell during Comaland. Then wishing I hadn't. A woman on the doorstep, dropping food off, proceeded with questioning. "Was it a stroke?" Then ticked off the several people she knew who died of similar causes, concluding with, "Was it congenital?"

"No!" I yelped, more in answer to her peppering presence than her questions, nearly shoving her out the door. But I knew she didn't intend to be discouraging.

I hid from people, but not only because I had nothing to say. I shunned questions, unsolicited advice, spiritual/God's will/he'll be okay platitudes, and even gentle commiseration, fearing hugs. An introvert at heart, I gain energy from going within, energy I use for zippy extrovert purposes. (With very few people, I am able to hang out one-on-one until the cows come almost halfway home, still a moderately extended time in Wisconsin. And I do make brazen forays into energy-draining larger groups. But then I must withdraw for long periods to recharge.) During Comaland, I could barely handle just myself. Fragile, significantly in need of energy, others' speech and hugs only sucked me dry.

Later, when I could read them, I found extremely valuable the letters and cards conveying simple statements of affirmation, "This must be so hard for you. I am thinking of you/praying for you/standing with you. I love you."

Even better was the presence of a handful of people, silently sharing my sorrow, especially Dan. Curriculum for Grief 101, the three Bs. Be there. Be sorry. Be silent. But the very best, solitude with my Creator, solace from the Spirit.

Dreamlike, I scarcely took in what the army of do-gooders on earth did for us, even those in my midst. Someone's frequent flier miles whisked Ren, my friend since college, to my side. Her two small boys accompanied. The boys' tickets had "been taken care of," explained Pavilion, Dan's best bud since they were eight. Ren and crew came exactly one week after the craniotomy, to provide some comic relief for Sam. He spent his mornings at half-day kindergarten, but found post-school afternoon rough, without Ben.

By the third day of Comaland, Sam had missed his brother so much he even said so. That night Binky, his trusty blanket, called Ben at the hospital. Apparently exercising superpowers just like Linus's.

Ren's presence was priceless, and her boys playing with Sam, balm. She lived in our home for about a week, but I wouldn't talk to her, couldn't talk to her. Gone early morning during the second week of the coma, home in the early evening, I quickly disappeared into my bedroom, barely acknowledging her. She wondered at my distance, we two who rarely fell quiet for more than a minute whenever together. She offered to listen. Cut off at the knees, with a hemorrhaging heart, I managed to sit mutely with her one evening for a little while. Then I left for bed.

As with Ren, I remained silent with my mother. She moved in for six weeks. Probably we briefly discussed logistics. Undoubtedly, she gave newsy reports on Sam and Sarah, which I could not grasp. Saint Grandma Jo, surrogate mother to my other two children, gentle warrior, holding her flank, providing stability as she took my place. Known for her addiction to picture taking, she chronicled Sarah's first steps. Keeping notes on Sarah and Sam's activities, she dutifully filled in the spaces on Sarah's baby calendar. But Hallmark had been lax. Between the stickers for "Stands Alone," and "Walks," much later I inserted, "Ben in coma/AVM/Grandma moves in." Grandma Jo managed the meal deliveries, worked with the point people, and saw to everything else. Most important, she gave the loving attention I could not. I trusted no one on earth more to mother my kids.

Only once did she lose her temper, if it can be called that. Nearly forty-eight hours after she'd arrived from the country on that bitter cold Friday night, in exasperation Sunday evening, Grandma Jo stamped a verbal foot, "I want to see my grandson! Everyone else has."

She was right. From then on, she made sure she got in to see him regularly.

Grandma Jo. Superglue in my shattered Supernova world.

Through Comaland, Dan and I fell into a changing-of-the-guard routine. I came mid-morning, unable to kick Dan out of his role as sentry until late morning. Her Majesty The Queen of England couldn't have asked for a better watch. Dan left under duress, but he soldiered on, playing heavyhearted with Sam and Sarah each afternoon, eating dinner with them and Grandma Jo, and then switching with me. (Dan's employers gave him compassionate leave for as long as required, and he missed teaching an entire seven-week session at WESLI.) Early in Comaland, I returned to the PICU after eating dinner by myself and putting the children to bed, leaving the hospital late. But I couldn't keep up that pace for long, so Dan took the evening shift along with the night. A steady stream of men came through to encourage him.

Including my father. He brought the morning newspaper to Dan each day, invariably asking how he could best help. He worked at the adjacent VA Hospital, so could provide some early morning respite, kicking Dan out to get himself food. For a long time, my dad's car stayed in the mix, too, our one car not enough.

Switching gears each day wore heavily upon both Dan and me. When I entered the hospital in the morning, a dark fog descended upon me, wrapped thickly around my heart, and held me close, stifling me, growing darker, and weightier, as I rode the elevator up. As I walked into the PICU room, glimpsing afresh my little one's unchanged stillness, the black sank its talons deep in my body and set me crying. Searching for breath, I slowly adapted to Ben's new visage and body. After washing my hands, kissing my son, and speaking tenderly to him, I didn't have much to do during my seven or eight hour shift. This allowed time to stare vacantly lost, read without focus, or pray.

My prayers continued their redundant themes, wisdom and help for the doctors and nurses, protection of Ben's mind and his comfort, the Merciful One to deliver him intact, banishment of evil, heavenly reinforcements, and above all, to keep those ICP numbers low. As in the biblical story of Adam and Eve's ejection from Eden, I pictured a mighty angelic sentinel guarding Ben's room, keeping harm at bay with a flaming sword. It helped. I fought for hope of recovery with any tool I thought I held, seeking the saving of my son for the Merciful One's name's sake. Wrestling with the idea of Ben surviving a "surgeon's worst nightmare" only to die now? Unthinkable!

When my turn ended, Tag, Dan's It, and I left for home wiped out. But even when I was there, I wasn't. Sarah became my Teddy Bear, her babyhood pudginess my comforter. She tolerated my desperately mute clutching only so long, squirming to be released. Food didn't interest me, I couldn't engage, didn't talk, alternated facially between blank or crumpled, and lost weight rapidly. Clothes drooped on my frame, as I diminished from thin to skinny. The decade of not caring enough for myself had begun.

I spent whitewashed, sterile days at Ben's side, the silence broken by beeps and whistles when one machine, or another, needed attention, or if staff took Ben away for a CT scan. The ordeal required unhooking his special, inflated, sore-prevention bed. It then sounded like a vacuum cleaner on steroids. Numerous staff accompanied Ben on his journeys, to bag him for respiration, contend with his three poles, and steer. I watched quietly as they wheeled my comatose Ben away from me.

My boy and I, we remained mute together during Psalm 23's "valley of the shadow of death." Every day the same image emerged, unbidden. From my watching place high atop a cliff, I could not go to him. He could not come to me. Towering, steep walls lined a narrow, deep, rock-strewn valley where death lurked. Inkiness pervaded, gray fading to black, as the valley curved desolately out of sight. I could not tell where the valley ended, if it ended. No way to see where a foot could be firmly set between sharp, precarious rocks, no way to warn Ben of pitfalls, even if illumination were possible.

But he was not alone. Someone carried him through danger. Someone sure-footed and careful, omniscient, all-powerful, a Shepherd called Sacrificial Love. Terrified, yet I trusted the Carrier to bring my flaccid boy back to me.

The frozen beginning and tail end of Comaland colored those two weeks. The January 19 deep freeze stayed with us, driving temperatures to well below zero. Three of the last four days of Ben's coma, daily highs ranged between *minus* 14 and 0 degrees. Fahrenheit. Dead of winter. But Wisconsin's frigidity is sustained only with clear skies – the nights star-studded, the days blindingly sunny, and Ben's window faced east, morning sun streaming in. His room was warm, cheery, unless one's gaze lingered too long upon his monstrously wired frame, his hideous head, and completely stilled, diminishing body.

UW doctors and nurses conducted a curious circus act during Comaland, complete with magical juggling and legerdemain. Staff minimally shrank Ben's brain by hyperventilation, drained cerebral fluid, and drugs. They gave him enough fluid to remain alive, while sucking him dry to hinder swelling. Thiopental, a high-powered drug, kept his brain in a coma without doing further damage. They balanced wasting away to nothing with minimal nutrition because his stomach and bowels were shut down. And, because the paralyzing meds didn't allow Ben to cough, they prevented pneumonia from aspiration by vibrating his chest to keep it loose, while avoiding unnecessary stimulation that would raise brain pressure.

Staff made plans, then re-configured and adjusted on the flying trapeze. The skills of PICU nurses and doctors, and neurosurgeons, walking the high wire in imperfectly perfect unison, astounded. The medical army waged a great battleship campaign on Ben's sea of recovery.

"Whispering Only" read the sign taped on the outside of Ben's door. Favorite Nurse made and enforced it, as chief sentinel in Ben's room. His ICP perked up with the smallest of noises, especially conversation, and later in Comaland, especially with his father's voice. Dan took vows of silence during the worst.

When we weren't there, Favorite Nurse once kicked out family members when they became too chatty, and barred a praying couple from entering Ben's room. She took her role in saving our boy's life seriously, and we loved her for it. Favorite Nurse helped me hone my junkyard dog skills. Following her lead, I boldly shushed other nurses when she wasn't there. Once I ordered a nurse to wash her hands before she touched my son. We badly missed Favorite Nurse on her days off.

We also adored two expert night nurses for their curiously strange interest in caring for children with head injuries through the dead of night. Their calm and professional demeanors reduced Dan's fears.

Day five, PICU Doc gave Dan a double thumbs-up. Ben was still critical, and had a low-grade fever, yet all staff agreed the numbers looked great. The day's EEG and chest x-ray showed stable. Docs stopped the paralyzing drugs, but kept Ben's brain medicinally comatose, so his body remained unchanged, immobile. Chief Neurosurgeon declared himself "privately optimistic."

Habitually, during the night Dan awoke and checked on Ben. That night, the nurse started bathing Ben at 2:00 a.m., allowing Dan to help. Bathing occurred regularly in the small hours. Dan's detailed Comaland notebook reads, "I got to see and touch Ben all over. It was really special to touch my Ben and feel his life." The thinness of Ben's legs, usually covered by thick, white support hose, surprised Dan, but his boy's warm torso comforted my man. "I am shocked by Ben's vulnerability and how skinny he is," Dan wrote days later, after another bath.

Chief Neurosurgeon sat us down halfway through the first week, explaining his upcoming absence for a conference. Our Hero leaving made us anxious. We'd become quite attached to the man.

When Chief Neurosurgeon left, it seemed disaster struck for the second time in a week. First, PICU staff and the substitute neurosurgeon didn't see eye-to-eye regarding the timing of the next CT. Regularly conducted scans monitored brain swelling and proved the AVM wasn't re-bleeding. Favorite Nurse put her bet on PICU staff, proceeding slower with a CT than neurosurg wanted. We had understood from Chief Neurosurgeon that the next CT would wait for his return. Dan raised the topic. Staff compromised, after phoning the chief, but a CT would occur in his absence.

On Thursday morning, day seven, Dan wrote, "Looking to God for a great day today, especially regarding CT, starting lightening, and starting feeding through an NG tube." Additionally, the right blowhole shunt might be taken out of Ben's brain.

The noon CT road trip did not spike the ICP as per usual. A major victory! But mid-afternoon, the juggled chainsaws began dropping, and continued to do so for twelve hours. The day brought no shunt removal, reduction in coma-inducing meds (lightening), or feeding through a tube snaking down Ben's nostril to his stomach.

Staff became quite concerned about Ben's decreased urine output. Then the CT results revealed more swelling than one conducted at the crack of dawn three days before. And for six hours Thursday evening the ICP numbers raged. (Behaving in a gentleman-like manner, they waited to rise until after I left.) Late that night, Ben's brain fluid, regularly tested for infection, showed positive. A resident didn't believe it, used his teeth to pop off the cap of a syringe, and withdrew another sample from a cranial drainage tube for re-testing. (Threat of bacterial infection particularly unsettled us. In 1992, we had fought sepsis for Sam's life in a Nagasaki hospital PICU.)

Dan recorded the understatement, "numb, scared, and tired." And alone. He would not call me during the night with all the terrible news.

We knew a large number of UW doctors through church, and they often checked on us, reviving our PICU spirits, upholding the Hippocratic oath. After concluding a heart transplant operation at 12:15 a.m., seasoned Dr. Love stopped by Ben's room at the opportune moment, when Dan's morale had hit its nadir.

"Is there any hope?" Out of his wits with fear, Dan awaited bacterial testing results, with ICP numbers on a rampage.

"Yes, there's a lot of hope," Dr. Love comforted, calling Ben's surviving surgery "miraculous," and giving Dan the gift of courage. Dan calls the encounter one of the most significant twenty minutes of his life.

At 3:00 a.m. the bacterial test came back negative, no infection. And the ICP numbers slowly subsided. "I saw this as a basketball game," Dan wrote, "and we are getting deep into the second half on the seventh day."

Then Dan rested from his work.

The next morning, Friday, Dan encouraged me to stay home a few hours, explaining he could "handle the shocks better" at the hospital than at home. The ICP numbers were still up to their tricks, and so was he, something I appreciated later.

The first week of Comaland ended with 13.4 inches of snow and communion. As Wisconsinites understand, the snow didn't stop any of us. Grandma Jo jumped in her Subaru and drove through the drifts to visit her grandson. (I wonder now if she reminisced about another such day, bound for a hospital through twelve inches of snow only the year before, that time bringing her two grandsons to visit their newborn sister. I wish I could ask her – along with about a million other things.)

Late Friday afternoon, Senior Pastor met Dan and me at the hospital, bringing some comfort with him in the bread and the wine. I had requested communion, wanting more to a relationship with my Creator than begging. I wanted to refocus; I wanted tangible thankfulness. The three of us sat alone again, this time in the hospital chapel. After communion, Senior Pastor mentioned his plan to preach on the silence of God. Employing my junkyard dog skills, I reproached him, "God is not silent. He speaks to me every day."

My hope, strength, and affirmation came from written words. While Dan went directly to biblical stories and verses he knew would uphold him, every day I played biblical Russian roulette, opening the book anywhichway. New or Old Testaments, I didn't care. Something always leapt off the page, sometimes astonishingly so, paralleling my reality. St. Luke's account of Jesus seeing a grieving woman, going to her aid unsought, resurrecting her dead son, and giving him back to his weeping mother. St. Mark's account of Jesus healing a boy who looked so corpse-like bystanders had declared him dead. Poetry in Isaiah described the author walking in the dark, without a gleam of light, trusting his God.

But the most remarkable conversation came the weekend that turned out to be mid-way through Comaland. When I hit the wall, brokenhearted, beseeching God to shorten unbearable Comaland. Just before bed Saturday night, I begged, "I miss my husband, I miss my family, please make it like it was before!"

Then I flipped open my Bible, landing in Jeremiah 33. Having hacked off the rulers with dismal national prophecies, Jeremiah languished in confinement. But his God continued to speak to him, first with more on the horrific future of Jerusalem. (Par for Old Testament prophets.) Then, "'Nevertheless, I will bring health and healing to it; I will heal my people...and will rebuild them as they were before.'"

I sat dumbstruck, staring at the words I'd just sobbed. Then dropping my gaze, I continued reading, "You say about this place, 'It is a desolate waste....'"

"Yes, I do say that! I say the PICU room, with all its beeping machines and flashing ICP numbers that terrify, is desolate. And I am desolate!"

Yet again, I continued to read, "'...there will be heard once more the sounds of joy and gladness...For I will restore the fortunes of the land as they were before,' says the LORD."

I went to bed that night feeling seen, heard, and understood.

Sunday morning, immediately upon waking I grabbed my Bible, finding Jeremiah. Had I dreamed those words, given to me as if via neon highlighter? Hallucinated? Invented? No. And just after the promises of restoration, rebuilding, and making "as they were before," in verse thirteen, something I'd missed, "'In the towns of the hill country...in the territory of Benjamin...flocks will again pass under the hand of the one who counts them,' says the LORD."

My hope hung web-like upon those courage-inducing words, fragile yet strong.

The next morning, Sunday, Dan dutifully recorded, "Pooped! A big one! The first!" Never so fecally focused since Ben's infancy, we celebrated each. Then Ben "coughed, on his own, three times!" And, when they suctioned him, his eye twitched as well. All without prolonged high ICP numbers.

Chief Neurosurgeon returned that morning, and ordered another CT. He believed we were beyond the peak swelling, buoying Dan, who called me. I remained at home while Dan waited for CT results. After two hours, PICU Doc entered Ben's room, smiling with the news. The swelling was down, the brain more defined. Euphoria reigned, despite PICU Doc cautioning the future could still hold infection. Dan sucked up his strong emotions, repressing his tearful joy until he reached home to tell me in person. Desiring to run and jump off our deck into the deep snow in celebration, instead he barreled through the front door crying, terrifying me: *Ben was dead!*

"The swelling is down!" Dan managed through sobs, as we clung together.

After putting the children to bed, while my mother visited Ben, I deflated Dan with my attitude, courtesy of Jeremiah that morning. Even though my resolve had dissolved immediately at the sight of my crying man, I remained (almost) positive the Life Giver foreshadowed Ben's recovery. Not intentionally smug, yet also not affirming the work of lonely, sleep-deprived agony Dan had endured for days.

The traumatic hospital life caused the English teacher to write at a fifth grade level. "We are dealing with this very differently at different times. Seems to be opposite at times. This can be good, but is very hard at times. We are both very tired, very numb, at times nothing matters. Other times, heavy sobs, others peace, etc., etc. We are really tired, too, and struggle at times to be patient with each other. We need lots of grace in the coming weeks. Ben could be pretty wacked out for a while."

And that, in a nutshell, would be the rest of our lives.

Back with Ben Sunday night, Dan wrote about his friend, "Pavilion and I chatted about a bunch of stuff: my emotions, next week, how people can help, and lots of football. It was fun. It's nice to joke with guys occasionally. This place is jammed with females." (Just like the ESL profession.)

Pavilion, coincidentally an elder at our church, also counseled Dan, "God doesn't need a twenty-four hour prayer vigil from you and everybody else to save Ben."

But better than football, or his wife's earlier spiritual prognostications, Dan witnessed Ben's first movement in nine days.

"When I was singing at 10:45 p.m. I felt Ben move his finger!" he wrote. It would be the first night he didn't get up to check on Ben.

Dan slept.

Chapter 7

Roll Out The Barrel

WESLI, where Dan and I work, is located right across the street from the state Capitol, and beautifully situated on Madison's isthmus. I'm not the only one who thinks so. There, in May of 2008, I first ran across the filming of *Public Enemies*. Literally. A break in lights, camera, action! and Security lifted the tape, allowing us commoners to go about our business. That day, WESLI's staff and students smashed their faces up against the school's windows, peering out onto the sidewalk. Period actors strolled by, pretending to look into our "shop." I caught movie fever pretty badly too, the Universal Studios' trucks completely turning my head. Cameramen filmed several scenes in and around Madison's epicenter. (Much more later. I pinky promise.)

From the Capitol Square, diagonal spokes shoot out four corners, all but one leading down to large lakes on either side, Mendota and Monona. The rebel spoke angles where it should, eight blocks down State Street, to the UW campus, my alma mater.

The first mascot I ever fell in love with was Pistol Pete of the Oklahoma State University Cowboys. When we left him in our rearview mirror, and returned to the land of Bucky Badger and the Packers, I warmed to Bucky quickly. (It would take decades for me to love the Packers – no mascot.) Furry, black, and white, Bucky wore a red and white sweater on his barreled chest, and looked like he meant business.

In first grade music class we learned the songs of Wisconsin. The best of them all, *If You Want To Be A Badger*. The catchy, upbeat tune, simple repetitive lyrics, and easy, dynamite hand actions got us first graders up out of our seats, lustily singing.

Unlike most of my schoolmates, I was privileged once each year to practice the song while watching the real Bucky in action. Taking my mother's seat for UW men's basketball games, I sat with Dad in the Field House, close to the UW pep band. I endured the game, and my father's loud clapping, while rooting in my heart for Bucky and the percussion section. The mascot and those drums....Yes, Bucky, I do wanna be a Badger!

Now, I drive through my alma mater on the way to and from work.

WESLI is only a few yards away from the three-way intersection on the square's northwest spoke, home of Madison Children's Museum, UW Credit Union, and YWCA. The corner also contains one of the coldest areas in the city. Wind races around the square, brutally builds momentum, claps crescendo, and rips down the diagonal street to Lake Mendota. Or, more often out of the north, the barreling wind donated by our Canadian cousins streams uphill, eh. Nothing polite about this air, however. Some windblown, bent-over days it's enough work to walk up the hill to WESLI. Other days I am propelled.

But I shudder to think what the wind must be like at the top of our fair, white granite Capitol, just three feet shy of the Nation's and just a touch less majestic. There, atop the dome and towering above the peasantry, stands our state's gilded heroine, "Wisconsin." That is her formal name, but she prefers to go by Miss Forward, or Ms. Forward, as it were, since our state prides itself as Progressive. "Forward" is our state's motto, and I'd love to attribute my outspoken ways to being reared under Ms. Forward's far-reaching shadow. But, according to my kindergarten teacher, they arrived with me from Oklahoma.

Ms. Forward faces southeast, odd, really, since most of our grand state stretches Up North. However, the nod represents our union with another forty-nine states. With one arm raised, Ms. Forward hails DC and blesses us with her royal wave. Her other hand holds an orb topped by an eagle, spreading his wings. Her toga, or cloak, falls in gentle folds, and her yoga toes poke out from beneath. She stands in Mountain, belly firm and chest lifted. As she gazes down upon her subjects, she also wears the mien of a golden-hued Blue Man Group: frozen, serious, and slightly bewildered. As she well might be. For it is her captivating headdress that really rules Wisconsinites. The Brits' outrageous hats and fascinators never were as fascinating as the fierce badger perched on Ms. F's helmeted up-do. Ever since lead miners in the 1800s lived in dug out holes in hillsides, Wisconsin has been nicknamed "The Badger State." The omnivore on the head of our Sister Golden Hair, our own Ms. Forward Wisconsin, proves it.

Wisconsin's Capitol can be seen from the interstate linking Milwaukee to Minneapolis. I drove that stretch many times after college, following the sharp turn of the highway as it curved past Madison. Each time, Bucky snarled, and Ms. Forward's beckoning call grew louder, "Come back, come home, come home!"

Like a boomerang, I did. Now, I am privileged to work at WESLI, the school at Ms. Forward's feet.

It was there I sat the afternoon Nothing-But-Good-News Thursday arrived, the day I expected Kenzie and MCM to change Ben's life. The Bucky Badger/Ms. Forward stories above are excellent examples of the kinds of things I think when mindlessly stuffing brochures. But not on the Thursday Ben met with Kenzie, then I couldn't think anything but "Call me, call me, call me, Ben!"

He didn't. He volunteered at the museum Thursday afternoons until 4:00. I gave him until 4:25, walked impatiently out of the school, stood toe-tapping thirty yards from where I expected my son had received phantasmagoric news, and couldn't stand it any longer.

"Hey, Mom." At least he answered his cell.

"Where are you?"

"In the bank."

"The bank? I'm coming in!" He meant the credit union. Striding through the doors, I saw my boy schmoozing with a teller. Grabbing his bionic left arm, the arm he's used to do nearly everything since age seven, I pulled him over to a corner.

"Well? Good news?"

"No, she was too busy today."

"*What?*"

"She said to come next Tuesday, at 12:30, and it would be only good news."

"Next Tuesday? At 12:30?" Five whole days.

"Yeah, she wants to talk about the guidelines for Visitor Guide. That's the name of the position, not Gallery Guide –"

"Wait! She wants for you to come and talk about the guidelines for the job?" My excitement messed with my English. "Did she offer you a job?"

"No, Mom! She wouldn't say if I had a job. I asked her. She said to come Tuesday, and it would only be good news."

"Sooo, d'ya think she'd have made an appointment with you to talk about job guidelines if she wasn't going to give you a job?"

"Mom! I. Don't. Know. It's not your ultimate, it's not my ultimate, now you just go and think about something else. You're worse than me."

"You call me, ASAP after 12:30, on Tuesday!" I ordered. "Right away! Y'hear?"

"Don't worry, Mom. You'll be one of the first I call." My twinkly-eyed imp laughed. Happily waiting.

I decided to take my wise son's advice. My brain owed it to my guts, to at least try. During the next five days I found plenty to keep myself occupied. Tried tracking down my town's rumored, retired astronaut for a feature story. Went to two yoga and two tai chi classes. On long fast-walks, trying hard not to picture my son at the freakin' White House. (*The Freakin' White – Stop it!)* Breathed. Out with friends for dinner, where I kept my mouth shut. Edited the 3Rs' class submissions. Made scones and packed a picnic dinner for Dan's birthday. Stuffed more language brochures at WESLI. (*The Freakin' White – Stop it!)* Breathed. Finished reading a mystery. Did laundry. Watched Sarah march and trumpet at Friday night's halftime show. Picked a peck of fruit and veggies at Dad's farm. Made pear sauce with Dad's pears. (*The Freakin' White – Stop it!*) Breathed. Watched British mysteries. Spoke with my editor about the mysteriously hidden astronaut. Made chicken fried rice. Thought of more news stories. Made up a new cole slaw with Dad's cabbage; we hate cole slaw. Sent out feelers for aforementioned stories. (*The Freakin' White – Stop it!*) Breathed. Continued transcribing conversations.

Emotional leaks occurred. How could they not? The glowing phone call from the museum did not make up for the previous long string of precarious calls. They'd make a great title, *From The Psych Ward to The White House: In Fewer Than 700 Days.*

No wonder my guts embodied a wildly swinging pendulum. (*The Freakin' White – Stop it!*) Marveling again on the strange animal called my life, I scrolled through the writer's Bible: who, what, why, where, when, and how. Indeed. Anyone care to flippin' explain?

"Oh, Father Goodness! Oh, Father Goodness!" was about all I could muster. I think he knew what I meant, as he trembled in the green, in the warm, golden sunshine of Wisconsin's early-autumn-late-summer azured breezes, a smile playing upon his lips.

Beauty in strength. I felt it in my body, mind, spirit, and soul. My guts returned to normal, my jumpiness abated, as I focused on what

I could reasonably control, the gift we all have been given. Beautiful, beautiful, peace-inducing breath.

As I breathed, and time ticked nonchalantly, Nothing-But-Good-News Tuesday finally came. What to wear, what to wear? And I wasn't even going to be there with my son at the meeting with Kenzie. Nevertheless, a mom will help in any way she can, including wearing celebratory clothing just to move things along, dontchaknow. Against my sports physical therapist's instructions, I seriously considered wearing my second-hand high-heeled Mootsies Tootsies, knees-be-damned. It was an M-T banner day! (I hoped.) Naw, be sensible. I put on my sports PT-approved Mary Jane's.

Anne, up from Chicagoland, was visiting my mother-in-law, and stopped by WESLI to see Dan and me. As she and I left the school for a quick walk, we saw Ben arriving early for his 12:30 meeting with Kenzie.

"Good luck, son. Call me!" I yelled.

"Thanks, Mom. I will."

Since Anne had never visited Frank Lloyd Wright's famously designed Monona Terrace, we took the grand promenade from the Capitol to the terrace rooftop, walking in the opposite direction from where my heart headed with my son. I gave Anne a four-minute inside tour, listening to her marvel at the merger between building and lake as we descended to the shoreline. I hoped we'd make it back to WESLI by the time Ben called.

At 12:35 my cell rang. "Mom. I got the job." Ben stated it so matter-of-factly, unemotionally, and I received it, surprisingly, the same.

"Ben, that is just so wonderful. That is fantastic news. Congratulations," I monotoned anticlimactically, and hung up. Huh? Why no dancing and jumping for joy? Why no tears of happiness and relief? All the nervous energy from the week before, where had it gone? I felt numb, not excited. Maybe the morning's tai chi had helped? Or perhaps we both felt as pre-celebratory runners initially feel at the end of a marathon? Thank God that's over.

Synapses functional, the news connected. My boy, struggling through life for so long, finally found his place! My son, with myriad disabilities, the person with the biggest heart I know, got his first job. *The perfect job.* All by himself! I spoke this to Anne, and then shouted to the sky for the benefit of the local citizenry and my own self worth, "And because his mother kicks ass!" Kick-box complimentary.

I decided to wait to congratulate Ben in person. Running from Lake Monona, across the isthmus, to Lake Mendota seemed impractical, even if wearing my sensible shoes. (But I knew I could do it. Numerous years, I had carried my half of canoe across the isthmus for Madison's Paddle and Portage, although in reverse lake order. Alternately jogging, walking, and dragging my feet, depending on incline and cheering crowd support.)

Since it would be unprofessional to run into a museum and tackle my son, after his volunteer shift I strolled over from WESLI. "Well done, Ben. I am so proud of you."

"Thanks, Mom." Then he added with a grin, "It was really funny to see you so stressed out. And with one word I could smash it all away!"

Glad someone thought my nervous state humorous. Undoubtedly he enjoyed making his mother better. He increasingly understood the toll the years had taken.

I told him to call people – family, friends – after all, it was his great news. But I couldn't control myself, and sent out email missives, inviting folks to do a little polka in their hearts with me. My creative Wisconsinite friends responded with "*Full* Beer Barrel Polka" and, "In Heaven There *Must* Be Beer."

It was good.

Still in delirium, alone at home the next morning, I decided a mother's thanks were due.

Dear MCM Staff,

Ben's mom here. Overstepping her bounds. But can you hear me whooping in Middleton? It's not customary for moms to thank their children's employers, but thank you so very much! As I said in my nomination letter, if Ben's great hope of being employed by MCM ever happened, the revolution of his life would be complete. This has meant the world.

Within fifteen minutes, an unexpected response came from Executive Director Ruth.

Dear Katherine,

Your happiness is matched by our own. Ben has been a terrific addition to our volunteer corps, and we're even more delighted to have him on staff. I have to commend Eric and McKenzie, and the Visitor Services team, for their encouragement of Ben and his remarkable growth in the MCM family.

We have additional good news, but I prefer to share that with you and Ben in person. Sometime soon, could we grab a few minutes to chat?

Many thanks, and congratulations again to Ben, and YOU for your indefatigable support as a loving mom.

I made it most of the way through in rapid eye movement silence, but then the last two paragraphs leapt off the page. Additional good news!? I forgot to breathe, eyes flying wide open. On the all-caps "you," and "indefatigable support," the floodgates opened. But they were not happy tears. They hurt. They were the mournful, grieving tears to which I was so accustomed. I admonished myself, "But these are happy tears!" knowing immediately the untruth. But why? Why crumpled in fetal position, crying again? When I thought I'd only be dancing, why was I balled up wailing?

Sudden revelation, what my indefatigable support had cost. This is what happens when a mother's shattered heart is partially put back together. The ragged edges don't quite fit anymore, the years of scar tissue impeding. The joy of this moment behaved so strangely because of the depth and longevity of repeated trauma, exultancy connected deeply to anguish. As so often has been the way, I did not see this coming. I found it sobering. And just a titch bit scary as the roiling emotions oscillated between laughing and mourning. Breathe. I emailed my psychotherapist, just in case the emotions started running functional interference.

Substantially calmed, skimming the email again, two things became apparent:

1. Ben's Kenzie must be *Mc*Kenzie.
2. There was more for me to do.

Chapter 8

Get What You Give

Ruth and I tentatively scheduled the meeting just before Ben's next volunteer shift, exactly forty-eight hours after his first job offer. This begged the question: Would Ben and I be able to handle this much good news, this fast? And would I settle into pure, undiluted joy, without co-mingled sorrow?

I reminded myself of Ben's color-splashed Jerry Garcia tie hanging in the closet, ready to wear to *The Freakin' White – !*

While the trees of my backyard clapped their hands, Father Goodness laughed his head off amongst the breeze-blown branches, head tilted back, chortling with gusto.

After another dose of tai chi, with wandering mind and tears of disbelief rolling down my cheeks, I wondered how to get into Ruth's office with Ben without tipping him off. Or worse, scaring him into thinking something already went wrong – the direction our minds naturally gravitated. Ruth suggested I tell Ben she wanted to personally congratulate him on his new position. With his mommy in tow? It'd have to do. It was his first job. Maybe he wouldn't quite catch on to the strange ploy of Executive Director wants to meet newest-employee's-mom? I called Ben.

"Hi, Mother-Of-Mine!"

"Hey! I've got your passport, you said you needed it for the job, and the desk lamp you wanted for your roomie. I'll be downtown tomorrow at noon." Ben lived with a revolving door of male students from Saudi Arabia, one after another, as they completed WESLI studies and moved on.

"Okay."

(Here goes.) "And, uh, your executive director emailed me, and she'd like to see you and, uh, me tomorrow in her office."

"O...kaaayyy???"

"To, uh, congratulate you on getting the job!"

Laughter, then hesitant, "Is that...great news?"

"Yeah, it's great. Weird, but great. Could we meet at 12:30, before your shift?"

"Sure. That's tomorrow?"

"Yep. 12:30. So, we can meet outside just before 12:30?" Drilling the time (or any piece of information) into his hit-or-miss-memory usually worked.

"Okay, like 12:20?"

"12:20. Sounds good. Do you need anything else from home?"

"Just love and hugs and not drugs."

"Yeah, we got plenty of that. Love and hugs and just a few drugs," I giddily replied.

"*What?*"

"Well, just the ones we both need."

"Mom, that's not drugs, that's medication."

Ben asked no questions regarding the oddity of our meeting with Ruth. His life, already so full of abnormal, allowed him to take things in stride. A valuable lesson I could learn myself some day. Perhaps. I congratulated myself there had been no give-away tone in my voice. Poker face, poker voice, poker life, going for that Oscar. Besides, before calling Ben I had wisely employed strategy.

Upon returning from tai chi, I'd blown the next ten minutes in the garage expelling pent up everything. Tai chi couldn't contain these forty-eight hours. Caterwauling in my little car, driver's seat dancing to The Beach Boys' *God Only Knows,* Train's *Drops of Jupiter,* and New Radicals' *You Get What You Give.* All were part of the "You 'n Me" fifty-song CD set I'd put together for Dan, in celebration of our twenty-five years of marriage, our twenty-nine years of dating, his fifty years of living.

Trauma had not won. Subsequent depressions and suicidal tendencies had not won. And I had safely landed after metaphorically looking for myself, whole again and free, with a fully recovered identity. Now, completely sliced and diced, Ben'sMom-cum-CaseManager had bisected blissfully to "Ben's mom." But finding my voice had taken trial and error, and a certain amount of creative chutzpah.

Belly dancers, Celts, and scribes: Are you my people?

Doubtful. I could not bear watching an uncoordinated walking stick attempting to swivel. And I tried. Just as I had tried at age seven to follow the smooth tap dancing feet of my best friend. Neither of my feet had cooperated then. My terpsichorean lineage had obviously skipped a generation. Then my arms had rebelled at age fourteen when I attended cheerleader tryouts and wound up in tears. In vain, willing one arm to go up while the other went out. As an adult, still lacking coordination, while dancing with my father, mother, Beloved Aunt, and Dan, they'd routinely accused, "You're leading again."

Not intentionally, I assure you. Unless we polkaed. As best I can tell, polkas are simply glorified hopping. Once acquiring the knack late in childhood, I had always considered myself a decent, even a lead-worthy, hopper. Too bad belly dancing involved more. Given a lifetime and unlimited funds, I would never master the art of locating and simultaneously controlling multiple muscle groups. (Never-say-die, I kept my jingles just in case coordination suddenly appears in my fifties.)

Celts, kinda. Such great craic (fun) tossing beads and candy with Ben and Sarah, while representing each branch of our Irish heritage in the St. Paddy's Day parade.

Scribes, absolutely! Writers, you are my people.

During my searching, Dan had wondered if my wandering ways would lead me far from him. Like The Depressions left him wondering if he would come home to a pre-catatonic wife or a corpse. No, I had not been led away, and never would. Leave plain ol' Jane Dan? The man who still provided laughter every day of my life? Whose tender care held our family up and together? Who kept me on the planet when I'd threatened to leave, irrevocably? The man who gently held me tethered to the ground while I inspired him to fly? Together we made the best no-foam, extra-hot, soy chai tea latte I ever had.

So of course, directly after receiving Ruth's email, I called my man. "Babe, listen to this!"

"Congratulations." Dan replied with as much inflection as his evenly keeled personality could muster. "That's great!"

"Are you free then tomorrow, at 12:30?"

"But this is your deal."

"It's only my deal because of you. I want...you...there," I sniveled. I wanted Dan to reap the rewards, to see joy with his own eyes, and hear it with his own ears. The man deserved it. He had once run that miracle mile with me at 4:00 a.m., saying good-bye to comatose Ben.

Dan had always seemed like granite, but his recently developing post-firey fissures were only to be expected. He was man, not igneous rock. Perhaps Dan needed to simply become Ben's dad, and not the family's RockDad?

Anticipation of the highly emotional day, even though positive, meant I couldn't fall asleep that night. (Watching a British spy movie before bed hadn't helped.) Would I really hear the words "First Lady" and

"Ben"? And while hearing them, what shoes should I wear? Black heels?

"How silly of me!" I chided, in my best British English. "Tomorrow is a shiny day, like no other." Of course, my patent ruby red slippers were the only possible choice. Weren't we celebrating a type of going home? Low-heeled, my knees would be happy, my sports PT happy, and my heart happy. Deep maroon, shiny Dorothies, even without glitter, click, click, click.

I woke up early. That's what nerves will give you, pleennty of time. That, and what some of my relatives aptly call "havin' the shits."

I...took...it...slow. Read the paper, drank cups of Irish tea, and as sixteen-year-old Sarah left for school, danced around like a maniac in front of her face, making mysterious statements causing her to correctly use the word "like."

"Mom, stop it! It's like you're in *The Matrix* or something," she giggled. (Well, okay. Technically that's not right either. She should've said, "It's *as if* you're in *The Matrix* or something." But she's her mother's daughter.)

Ready? Ready! Lots of spare time, time to...relax? Breathe? Get grounded? Sure, I'm into yoga and tai chi, but I'm not that balanced yet. Instead, I played air drums and sang, wearing long pants and a short jacket, dancing to *Short Skirt/Long Jacket,* by the band Cake. Inspired, I sent a lyrical teaser email to a group of women, describing Ben's employment and expected great news as a chocolate cake so decadent that the thick, chocolate, butter cream frosting on top made it a double cake. (My friends are used to moody, cryptic me. They know sooner or later I will probably make sense. Or if not, I'm usually worth a laugh, either with me or at me.) I didn't mention Dan deemed the Cake lyrics an accurate description, as many a time he'd watched me deftly cut through bureaucracy. However, he questioned the burning ember eyes. Mine occasionally shot sparks at him from blow-torchy pupils.

Pleased with my missive to my posse of women, I watched my fingers flying over the keyboard. No sparkle. On such a day as this, the nails must match my Dorothies – to shine with justice, just like Cake's lyrics.

Quickly now, two layers of Bing Cherry polish, omygoshlo okatthetime,andmynailsnotdry...Oh*No!*Gottausethefacilities... don'tsmearyourpolish...watchoutforthe,toolate,notonmyfing!... whatamess!...scrub,scrub,scrub...can'tbuttonpantswithwetnails...grabloosemoneycreditcardcheckbookpassportandstuffinpurse,grab3Rsbag,backpack,lamp,tea...outthedoor!

I drove safely, only my mood and the heater on high, blasting my damp nails.

Striding quickly into the building where 3Rs class meets twenty Thursday mornings each year, my left Dorothy stuck in a crack. She wouldn't come out. I tugged. No good. Removing my foot, I yanked and pleaded, "C'mon! I need this shoe today!"

Flighty, I led the group of sixty-to-ninety-year-olds with one finger smelling strongly of disinfectant, a bunch of banged up Bing Cherry nails sorta shining, my pants modestly buttoned (I'd fixed them in the parking lot), and both shoes on my feet. You can dress her up, but you can't take her anywhere.

As always, the 3Rs women beautifully modeled how to age as a learner. Sitting at their feet, I gleaned life-altering bits of wisdom, as well as old wives' tales. During class that day I learned you could throw the hormone card to get out of cooking. Eons ago, one woman's mother-in-law refused to let her near food prep when she learned of her "menses condition." It had naught to do with hygiene and all to do with hormonal imbalance. But maybe mum-in-law simply followed pragmatism, not superstition? Maybe MIL thought it unwise at that moment to mix knives and her daughter-in-law?

Three hours later, I parked between the UW Credit Union and MCM. Ben needed my help before the meeting. Yesterday, late in the afternoon, he had called.

"Mom, I have serious trouble!"

Holy cannoli. Serious trouble, of exactly what nature this time, son? AFO issues? Depressive issues? Medication? Hot head and dizziness? Had he fallen and hurt himself again? Lost something important again? Forgotten someth – gasp! Had he been fired? A new one. The possibilities seemed nearly endless to an overly active, negatively trained brain, ticker taping themselves as neon exclamation points across my forehead. (But I didn't mention them.)

"I don't have any money! The credit union says I'm $93 below. Can you help?"

Thus, into the credit union I flew, wrote a check, and called Ben's landlord to fix the mistake, not even Ben's fault.

Machete wielded, red tape sliced, fingernails ablaze.

Stepping outside, I saw Dan through the window of the museum with Ben by his side. Standing stock still, I breathed deeply, intentionally. Here goes, Dorothies take me inside. Exquisite timing, my cell registered a text, "Thinking of you." From Ren, who still lived several states away as she did when she flew to my side during the silent days of January '96. In I went, knowing my posse of women accompanied in spirit.

We rode the elevator together, only to get hit by surreal at the top. Much later, with thinking reinstated, I thought, "No matter how many times I do surreal, I don't seem to get any better at it." Bad surreal, good surreal, everything becomes blurred. How could it not with the world spinning off-kilter? We passed the office of Volunteer Coordinator Eric, the man who'd first requested I drive Ben to the Broncos' football game. Shaking his hand, I couldn't resist.

"Hi, Eric. Nice to finally meet you. Did the Broncos win on Tuesday?"

The heads of Dan and Ben swiveled, their faces registering, "She's flipped."

“Hey! I’m sor –” but I gave Eric the universal ssshhh, finger-to-lips and a wink, so he swallowed his words, changing to gurgling laughter.

Yep, Mom has lost her mind again, and apparently this time it’s contagious. “Don’t worry, guys, we just speak a secret language,” I burbled. Eric laughed harder while I Elsa Snorted. (These nasal noises, punctuating hilarity, come with my ancestral gene pool on the matricide – no sorry, that would be the maternal side.)

Then Eric ushered us into Ruth’s office. Many things happened next. What they were, I can hardly say. The most extraordinary string of words came out of Ruth’s mouth. Certain phrases lodged in one or the other of my lobes, clinging to neuron cliffs for dear life: “prestigious award,” “presented by the First Lady,” “Federal government will pay,” “White House,” “one member from the community,” “enthusiastically unanimous decision” – and the complete sentence kicker, “Ben, we’ve chosen you.”

My misting eyes laser beamed on my son through Ruth’s entire explanation. Ben looked, understandably, confused. Ruth made it clear – as clear as astonishing words could ever be. The First Lady will present an award to MCM in DC, and the museum would like him to be the community member representative.

“First Lady? I get to meet Hillary Clinton?” Ben couldn’t have been more thrilled. He once dressed as Hillary for Halloween.

“No, Ben! The President’s wife! Michelle Obama!” we all chimed in, laughing. Who could blame him? Secretary of State HRC, certainly a top DC female.

Ben stretched his strong left arm over the desk to shake Ruth’s hand, while I buried most of my face in my hands, eyes still boring into my son.

“Is this a dream? Thank you, thank you! Is this a dream? Thank you!” Ben repeated.

But Ruth hadn’t finished. She professionally continued, “I will be going to Washington DC with you to receive the award, and the federal government will allow you to take one person along, so we're wondering who –"

"Sorry, Dad!" Ben immediately turned in his chair, fully outstretching his muscular left arm, pointing at me. Overwhelmed, I buried my face in my hands, sobbing. My Dorothies wanted to do a tap dance, or at the very least, a polka, but my legs were lead.

"Mom, are you okay?"

"No! Yes!" I stood up and Ben opened his arms for a big hug. I wept upon the shoulder of my twenty-three-year-old. "It's like the universe shifted and all the planets have been rearranged," I choked.

Ruth continued speaking, her phrases embedded in my brain: "embargo on this news," "press conference October twenty-fifth," "write a bio," "First Lady's schedule," "between November and March," "bio due October third," "one page, double-spaced," "Your mom can help, she's your PR department."

Ben grasped the essentials. "So, what is said in this room stays in this room, just like in Las Vegas?" he asked innocently.

"Yes, Ben, like that," Ruth agreed. "Until the press conference."

"Press conference?" Okay, most of the essentials.

Ruth explained media, television and newspapers, would come for the museum's announcement. And there would be local VIPs speaking. And the press would want to talk to Ben too.

A flicker of fear passed over his face, along with confusion. Then the inkling of an idea occurred. The real potential for significant negative impact this weighty news could have on my son. It had not entered my mind, so intent was I on Ben receiving his props, and my basking in his joy. What person, even without memory, cognitive language processing, and mental health issues, gets his first job offer at age twenty-three on Tuesday and is invited to the White House on Thursday? If I was having trouble assimilating, what about Ben? But the thought didn't fully develop, as I wallowed in the rich moment.

Ben sought clarification. How could this possibly have happened?

"They asked me to write a letter a few weeks ago, on your behalf," I crowed. "Explaining why you'd be a good choice. So, I did!"

"Thank you, Mom!"

Intentionally trying to lighten the mood, I sneakily asked, "What are you going to wear to the White House?"

"Ahh, she knows," the light bulb went on. "She took me to get a suit."

"Yeah," I hollered, "and a Jerry Garcia tie! The Grateful Dead at Kohl's! Who knew?" I do not know how many Elsa Snorts accompanied this pronouncement. Boisterous hilarity, and that was it for me, the last of my linguistically correct sentences for the next four hours. Neurotransmitters officially on holiday, synapses left staring across vast chasms, alternately giddy or numb, my scrambled brain incapacitated.

My two guys went out in the hallway after the meeting and I stayed with Ruth. "*Oh!*" I began. I said a lot more, who knows what.

Days later I recalled with a cringe, at one point I'd picked up my foot, commanding Ruth to, "Look! My fingernails match my Dorothies! Because we're going home! I hardly ever wear fingernail polish!" Frenzied laughter had accompanied. Yoiks. A good thing Ruth had previously read my logical, cogent, succinct-yet-wordy, 1,000-word advocacy pitch.

"Validation," Ruth had concluded while giving me a bear hug. "For you, as his mom too."

Didn't I know it? But *The Freakin' White House!?* Way over the top validation.

Chapter 9

God Put A Smile

Nurses warned us about "the crazies," as staff would be "lightening" Ben – weaning him off the induced-coma meds. As Ben slowly regained consciousness, strange things might happen, or be said. Could it be any stranger than the past ten days?

I asked Favorite Nurse to explain. She recounted two stories, one about a boy whose intellect remained intact except for forgetting the word "clock." The other concerned a teenage girl in a car accident. Glass still entangled in her luxurious hair, Mom chopped it off, unable to bear the sight. Post-coma, the furious girl chewed her mother out after seeing herself in a mirror, bemoaning the loss of her locks.

To me, Favorite Nurse told only bolstering, ironic, inspiring stories but to more inquisitive Dan she explained the withdrawal symptoms that could occur, irritability, repetitive picking, and, most concerning, an increased heart rate. Favorite Nurse understood she really cared for more than one patient in the room. She was *good.*

Beginning eleven days after the initial coma, Ben's utter stillness lifted. His eyelids twitched, but his ICP did not spike. As Ben successfully lightened, I lightened, Dan lightened. We all lightened.

Eyes remaining shut, Ben slowly found his body, slightly moving his head, shoulders, left fingers, arm, and leg. But in his weakened state, he struggled to move at all. His arms and hands, encased in splints to prevent his hands curling, and his feet, wearing high top tennies, added extra weight. Whenever freed of its splint, his left hand searched. One night it found the big respirator tube stuck in his throat, and was rewarded by being tied down. None of that, not yet. The next day, he grabbed the chest vibrator – with a surprisingly strong grip.

As best he could, with a respiration tube taped to his face, he grimaced, flinched, and cried during certain procedures, oddly uplifting my heart. The nurse and Dan took notice that occasionally I even laughed.

Picture taking is genetic and I inherited a heavy dose from both parents. A few days before Ben fully came out of the coma, smelling life, I brought my camera. Sick, right? I have never regretted it; embarrassed to admit it, sure, but never regretted. Much later, the pictures helped Ben assimilate what happened. (In the future, I would avoid opening that album.)

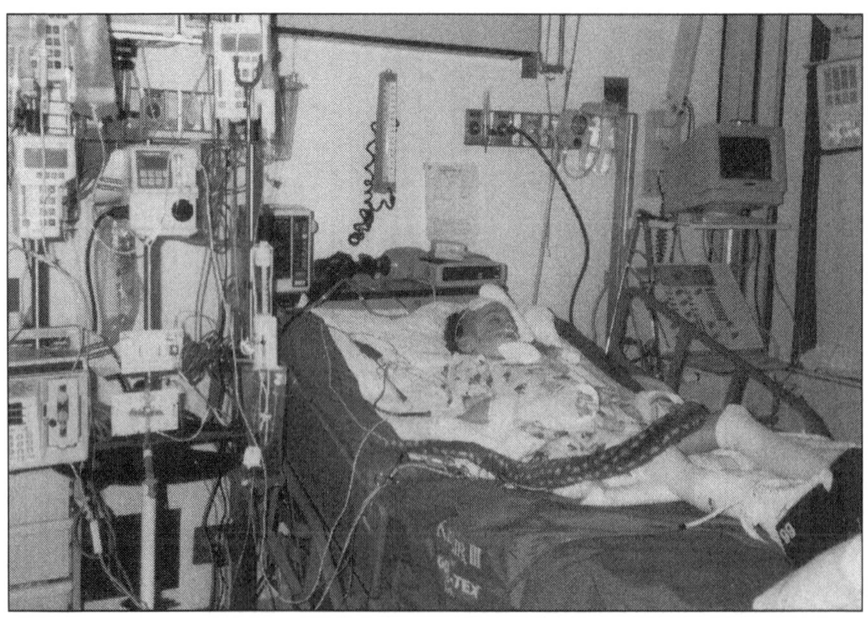

Comaland day thirteen started a string of mammoth days; each day Ben victoriously climbed a new mountain peak. Dan's notebook filled with exclamation points. "He yawned three times!" "Thiopental off at 12:02 p.m. Wednesday!" "Started feeding Pedialyte through a tube and it worked!" "Moved right arm some for his mom!" "Blinked eyes at nurse's request!" "Moved fingers for me!"

Ben's right eye opened more than his left, which remained at half-mast. We were overjoyed, since not even a smidgeon of his mega baby blues had been visible for nearly two weeks. What's more, Ben seemed to attend to Dan and me. He didn't say anything; how could he with a large tube in his mouth breathing for him? But his partially open eyes followed us around the room, and we experimented on our son, to see if he could follow commands to move body parts.

Dan's last entry, day thirteen, "Another CT road trip at 7:00 p.m., but no results until morning. Pediasure feeding started at 10:00 p.m.! (Favorite Nurse) said she thinks we as a family have done remarkably well."

In the morning, a neurosurgeon resident visited Dan before 7:00 a.m., remarking that the CT remained unchanged. But later, Chief Neurosurgeon explained the improvement. Never send a boy to do a man's work. A lesson I would learn well.

Dan's notebook continues, "This morning (Favorite Nurse) said to wave bye to Grandpa Syrup and Ben did! Grandpa went over to him and Ben reached for his tie and shirt, it seemed. I went over, and he reached again and grabbed my neck and pulled. I put my head on his chest. I think he needed a hug and was giving me one."

Ben's affectionate ways were well known, even as a tyke in Nagasaki. Trying to hug and kiss in a culture that bows. But he had soon learned well to nod his head with a Japanese "haahdato," American preschooler for "arrigato." (Thank you.)

After our return to the States, Ben had once interrupted Senior Pastor's children's sermon. Senior Pastor held two large action figures in his hands, their arms extended forward, as though, he said, they were going to engage in battle. A no-fight lesson.

"Maybe they're just going to hug," volunteered our son loudly. From that day forward, the entire church of a few hundred knew Ben. By then, we were used to it. In Nagasaki, people had referred to us as Ben-tachi. Ben and the rest of 'em. Ben et al. Even as a preschooler, Ben had defined us as a family.

Another true sign that Ben was surfacing from Comaland as Ben, he yanked his hospital support hose down a few inches, trying to get it off. Since babyhood he constantly removed his socks, and later, kept his infant brother barefoot, presumably thinking he was doing Sam a favor. We had perpetually played Sam Socks On/Socks Off.

Ben pulled at the diapers too, trying to remove them. Favorite Nurse gave him permission to poop in them, and he did. Unbelievably satisfying for us all.

"Tremendous progress today," Dan's entry ends. "Nurses very encouraged. Even (Chief Neurosurgeon) seemed happy according to one nurse." Our Hero constantly wore a thoughtful, some might say grave, look on his face. I suppose full-out smiles are rare in his business. Yet, as the ICP numbers finally became a non-issue, the PICU chimed with a chorus of optimistic voices.

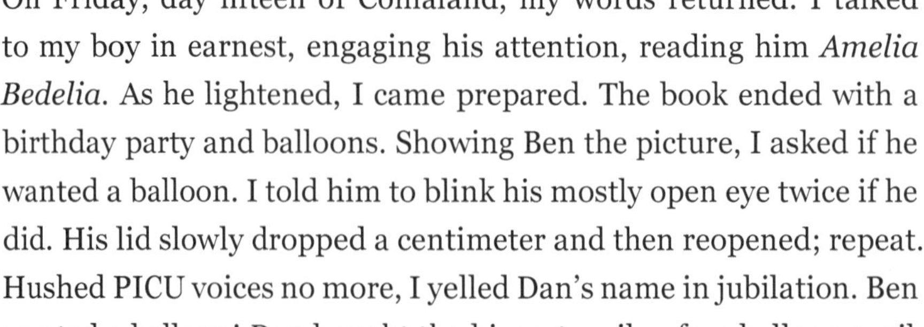

On Friday, day fifteen of Comaland, my words returned. I talked to my boy in earnest, engaging his attention, reading him *Amelia Bedelia*. As he lightened, I came prepared. The book ended with a birthday party and balloons. Showing Ben the picture, I asked if he wanted a balloon. I told him to blink his mostly open eye twice if he did. His lid slowly dropped a centimeter and then reopened; repeat. Hushed PICU voices no more, I yelled Dan's name in jubilation. Ben wanted a balloon! Dan bought the biggest smiley-face balloon available in the hospital gift shop, with a printed mop of rainbow hair on top. All Friday I asked Ben "yes/no" questions, and he blinked his eye to answer. At first PICU staff seemed skeptical, but I knew my boy communicated as I intently watched his eye.

With Ben now aware, some of the necessary procedures hurt to watch. While hooked up to the respirator, staff regularly suctioned Ben's nose and throat, especially when the tube made him cough, as it increasingly did. Ben clearly hated suctioning. But before he could be extubated, he had to attain a certain level of independent breathing. Staff slowly reduced the machine's oxygen level to encourage Ben's lungs to function. Friday night, four hours of torturous coughing, suctioning, and re-taping the tube indicated Ben's ICP didn't like suctioning either. It distressed all of us, not as badly as the Friday night two weeks before, but Ben hadn't been conscious then.

Saturday's entry begins, "Ben is down to one pole for drips, meds, etc. He's come so far in two weeks! He was still in surgery two weeks ago."

That day, we learned Ben could still count. I asked him to hold up one, two, three, and five fingers on his left hand. He received an A+ on his home school test.

But around 5:00 p.m., Ben began coughing heavily again, and the ICP numbers rebelled. He fought the tube, and wouldn't relax. Coughing and suctioning kept up for an hour, concerning me. I did not want a four-hour repeat of the previous night, so I spoke to PICU Doc. If staff wanted to prevent ICP spikes, how were hours-long coughing fits achieving the goal? Docs had hoped to take him off the respirator that morning, but didn't. Could they do it now?

I expected Dan to relieve me at six, so put on my coat and mittens, pre-warming in preparation for starting my father's car in the minus-thirteen-degree darkness.

"They're going to extubate him!" Dan blurted upon entering Ben's room.

Whipping off my red woolen mittens, I stood by. Once they made the extubation decision, PICU staff hustled. One nurse hovered with another intubation kit ready. If things didn't go well, they'd have to re-intubate fast. A respiratory therapist and the doctor expertly removed the tubing. I couldn't bear to watch, but as they hauled the big tube out of Ben's throat I yelled encouragement using our favorite Japanese word, "ganbatte!" (This command, combining "go for it," "hang in there," and, "try your best," became well known to therapists.) The whirring respirator fell silent to shouts of success. Ben breathed!

Thirty minutes after extubation, sitting in the frozen car as the engine warmed, I sang at the top of my lungs. Spiritual songs of triumph, deliverance, and thankfulness, my Tin Man creaky voice came alive as Ben rejoined the living. Counting, communicating, and breathing! Initially expecting death, after two weeks of minimal change, these changes staggered.

Dan's last entry on Saturday night reads, "After extubation, Ben slept from 6:30 then was awake from 9:30 to midnight. I asked him to high five and he did. Then I did 'up high,' he did; 'down low,' he did; then as I was moving away and saying 'too slow' he chased my hand with his and kept hitting it. We did this two, or three times. Then he kept messing with my hand. I didn't get it for a while. Then I figured it out – he wanted to thumb wrestle. We did this a bunch of times. He was fairly strong and showed a bit of a smile one or two times. Then I showed him the football and 'passed' it to him. He 'caught' it with his left hand and then 'passed' it to me three times. Then he slept well."

His playful football buddy back, undoubtedly Dan did too.

Sunday morning dawned with smiles. On our faces and the faces of PICU doctors and nurses, neurosurgeons, rehab therapists, and family and friends. Ben's weak smile muscles couldn't do much, but a smile by any other name would still be as sweet.

We thought it finally safe to bring Sam. That morning, as soon as Ben saw me walk through the door with his brother, his face lopsidedly lit up.

Then, officially, I received my seven-year-old son back from the dead. PICU staff decided Ben should get out of bed. They wanted to exchange the inflated bed for a normal one. And he'd been lying on his back for 380 hours, therapists stretching his inert arms and legs.

I sat in a rocking chair while nurses lifted him, placing him gently in my lap. He cried a little – moving pained him. For the second time in our lives I held and rocked my newborn, supporting the head he could not lift. If possible, it felt more miraculously profound the second time around. Ben, never this still since infancy, allowed me to cuddle him all I could.

As I held a one-sided conversation with him, Ben's head rested near my mouth. I didn't understand why he didn't reply, thought perhaps his newly-extubated throat hurt too much to talk, but didn't really care. It was enough to hold my boy in my lap. With a little chuckle, I muttered, "Ben's probably wondering why I'm talking so loud. 'Gee, Mom, I'm not deaf.'"

Dan saw him smile a bit at my joke. I quit shouting in Ben's ear.

Like his sister on her first birthday two weeks before, Ben got his first taste of rebirth day sugar, apple juice. He was unable to suck through a straw because his muscles weren't working, so we gave him a cup. He grabbed for it constantly, lefty (for the first time in his life), taking sips. When we offered him a chocolate milkshake, we joked he'd turn it down. He smiled, but wouldn't blink an answer. No milkshake? Had he forgotten "milkshake," or "chocolate," "vanilla," and "strawberry?"

When Dan left for home with Sam, I questioned Ben about Sarah's birthday party. "Do you remember the rainbow cake?" He smiled. I took that as a "yes."

My humor intact, I kept up a steady stream of amusing anecdotes, causing my boy's smile to widen, and his body to wiggle slightly, as if laughing without sound. Humor, my first defense, from that day forward became my primary weapon of offense, determined to lead the way laughing, as much as crying, through whatever came.

If we thought we'd exhausted the multitudinous hospital staff involved since Ben's ambulance arrival in the ER, we were wrong. Ben's room became ringside, Ben center ring in the rehabilitation show. Speech Therapist evaluated his swallowing ability. Surrounded by people staring at him while he attempted to drink, then to eat, Ben's mischievous ways kicked in, more clown-like than ever before. His mouth twisted in an embarrassed grimace, his left eye squinched as he tried rolling his right. He sighed, seeming to deride the hawk-eyed focus on his swallowing mouth. Dan said he thought Ben wouldn't eat with everyone watching him. But Ben had to, to prove he could.

The evidence of higher-level thinking delighted us: understanding jokes, registering dislike and humiliation, rebelling against food minders. And he smiled, silently, at the people around him, just as he had as an infant. From four months of age, when we would visit someone's house in the evening, I'd place Ben on his blanket on the floor to fall asleep. Two hours later, we would pick him up ever so gently, bundle him, and put him in the car seat to go home. Invariably he'd wake with a smile on his face, happy to see people any time of day or night. True to form, Ben came out of Comaland smiling.

Dr. Dots, Ben's pediatrician, visited the day after extubation. It seemed years ago that I had called her home to inquire correct protocol for an unresponsive, limp child.

"Now comes the hard part," she murmured with a sympathetic sigh, as she readied to leave Ben's PICU room. The hard part? As opposed to the excruciating part? The terrifying part? The unbearable part? Flabbergasted, I did not ask what she meant. Years later, I fully understood.

Told during Comaland that if Ben survived we were in for a very long haul, Dan didn't tell me, keeping up my spirits. Oblivious of the arduous rehab road of recovery ahead, I only knew my blue-eyed young son had returned to me, carried thousands of miles past Bob Dylan's mouth of a graveyard.

Chapter 10

Hard Rain

"Everyone is very excited about Ben's progress," reads Dan's PICU notebook on ordeal day eighteen. "Our pediatrician called him a miracle boy, a new resident doctor said the same, and Dr. Love said this is nothing short of miraculous!"

Staff were well aware of the spiritual support our family received, and some thought it helped Ben recover quickly. During the next few weeks post-Comaland, his recovery rate astonished everyone. But Ben's survival, amazingly with his mind and personality pretty much intact, bought him Life and a world of Trouble.

Our Curious George explored his new condition. His left hand moved his right arm manually, while his eyes implored his father. Dan explained the right arm and hand were weak, but we'd help them strengthen. Then Ben's fingers found the long line of acme-size staples on his head, touching them gingerly. He had a "bad ouch," Dan explained. Ben seemed dazed, and didn't smile much that day.

That evening, our last in the PICU, I reminisced with Ben's initial ER "bagger," the doctor who'd stayed by Ben's side for five hours. On that night of familial infamy, this doctor had worked Ben's breathing, just inches from our farewells. Although we presumed him to be an ER doc at the time, he turned out to be PICU Doc, brought down to help the ER. Doctors even require mutual aid. Misty-eyed, PICU Doc vowed he'd never forget that night, either. He wasn't accustomed to watching parents commit children to death, as I had supposed.

"When he arrived, your son wasn't going to be breathing on his own much longer," he explained.

I marveled again at finding Ben on his futon in time, granted that second chance to understand the danger to Ben's life. He would have died in his sleep, probably even before midnight. Embracing while thanking him, I told PICU Doc I thought the God of second chances, unlimited second chances, had returned Ben to me.

At 2:30 the next afternoon, on PICU day nineteen, the passing of the Ben-baton parade began, our son the Grand Marshal supine on his hospital bed. We followed in his wake, as congratulatory PICU staff stood by. Nurses from the older children's unit, Big Peds, wheeled pole-free Ben out of the PICU, past the Little Blue Room, down the hallway and around the corner, to his new room.

"Stick!" we used to say in my track and field days. Baton, safe.

We brought no candy to throw that day, or petals to strew before him, yet in our A. E. Housman hearts "we chaired (Ben) through the market-place; Man and boy stood cheering by, And home we brought (Ben) shoulder high." Staples and stitches topped the "early-laurelled head," of this athlete not dying young.

The Big Peds room felt abysmal, facing inward, nothing visible but brown building walls, a stone-strewn rooftop, and the insides of other patient rooms and offices. No sky. We traded the sunny, warm PICU room, where Ben walked through the gray valley of the shadow of death, for real-time murky.

(To be fair, the renowned UW Hospital-connected American Family Children's Hospital opened in 2007. I have never seen such a colorfully textured, whimsical medical facility, and that's just the lobby. I have no intentions to view the rest of its glories, unless I need inpatient hospitalization in the future and they waive the age limit.)

But in 1996, we heavily decorated Ben's dismal walls, creating a colorful and cheery environment with pictures, letters, murals, and gifts given during Comaland. What seemed like a zillion balloons filled the room. When people heard Ben had blinked for a balloon, inflated bouquets came. In addition, the hospital "picture lady" came by regularly with choices of posters to brighten the room. We made space for one poison tree frog.

Favorite Nurse warned us to be prepared for much less nursing. Accustomed to bedside 24/7 nineteen days of care, a scarified jolt took up residence in our guts. Left alone with Ben, in a room several doors away from the nurse's station, with only a beeper at our disposal to summon a nurse, the response time seemed in slow motion.

Knowing Ben would remain inpatient for some time, I requested a room where we could see the sky – as much for my own sanity as his. Within a few days we moved to a room across from the nurse's station, a room with a view. The cold snap lifted, and with it went the clear skies. For the next three weeks the sun took a vacation, but the leaden sky in her place improved upon the brown brick, and miseries of others.

"It was sad saying good-bye to Favorite Nurse and PICU. Strange? It's lonely in Big Peds," wrote Dan the first afternoon. "No one has come."

We were off the grid. Not quite. Dan, downgraded from his private PICU bunk bed, slept on an uncomfortable, faux leather and wood chair-bed in Ben's new room. Someone came the first night, "every two hours for meds, neuro checks, vitals, etc. and a blood draw at 5:45 a.m. Blood guy comes and tries three times, unsuccessfully, to get blood. Left for an hour and then got some on other side. Ben obviously hated it."

Ben's ridiculously hard-to-find veins plagued the next decade of his life.

RehabDoc heard Dan's complaints. If Occupational Therapy (OT), Physical Therapy (PT), Speech, and Rehab Psych expected Ben to work his arse off all day long, how could he be at his best recovery strength when disturbed every two hours during the night? She quickly fixed the problem with her colleagues, earning our undying love, stretching out the checks to every four hours, and consolidating blood draws. The impressive woman also always knelt or crouched on the ground, even in a dress, to get at Ben's eye level. She would do so for years.

Ben gave blood, unwillingly and frequently, to monitor the anti-seizure meds in his system. Regular, routine blood draws became part and parcel of his new existence, for pharmacologic and other reasons. We soon had our favorite phlebotomist, One Stick Nani, whom we often requested. Blood draws quickly became nothing to Ben. As opposed to Sam, who, for years, could not bear to even look at the door through which his brother always passed for outpatient blood-letting.

Ben's powerful anti-seizure meds made him groggy and interfered with his rehab. RehabDoc wanted him switched to a less powerful drug as soon as possible. But the doc in charge of anti-seizure meds saw "activity" in Ben's brain. Dr. Sure wanted it controlled at maximum strength every second of every day, and refused to switch fast, although he agreed change was necessary. Any seizure, he explained, could cause the AVM to bleed again, which "would be devastating." (The mother of understatement, I felt.) No gaps allowed in anti-seizure drug coverage whatsoever, as one replaced another – not on his watch. We heartily concurred.

The further Ben's removal from the concatenation of Comaland, the easier docs rested. Soon, staff successfully switched Ben's meds.

wI found the first week out of PICU tough, drawing out my mama grizzly claws. Ophthalmology sent people with boatloads of equipment to perform in-depth, lengthy testing on Ben's vision, fearing damage to his sight from the AVM rupture. The bright flashing lights upset Ben, and the timing wasn't optimal – naptime, something I took seriously as all the rehab therapies easily exhausted him. Not to mention the bone-weariness caused by the previous weeks' intense stress upon his body. I held naptimes sacred, an important puzzle piece in Ben's recovery.

One ophthalmologist spoke, as if Ben weren't there, about future loss of sight. Disturbed, I asked him to step out into the hallway to speak to me privately. Discovering that the testing results would have zero impact on Ben's current rehab program, I kicked them out, insisting they discontinue testing that day. It worked, oddly enough. Perhaps they had enough information to go on. As it turned out, Ben did have visual field cuts, and trouble with peripheral vision, right out of the coma, but with further testing months later, docs deemed his sight normal – enough. (However, difficult neuro-ophthalmology testing continued for years, each appointment with a specialist taking about four hours.)

At the end of the first week, another crew came by with equipment for EEG testing, insisting it wouldn't hurt. Apparently they hadn't experienced emergency craniotomies as children. Attaching twenty-two wires to Ben's scalp, gluing with stinking epoxy one small, metallic disk for each wire, they poked sharply into each disk. Ben screamed every time, needles in my heart. It took a long time to get all twenty-two properly attached.

Lying still, a bright light shone in his eyes for part of the testing. For the other segment they allowed him to sleep. When they removed the wiring, Ben's pockmarked head showed where points had been driven into his scalp. Tiny scabs formed.

In fury, I wondered about ophthalmology and EEG testing within seven days post-coma. Was it necessary, right then? Yet this first week out of PICU mildly foreshadowed Ben's future.

Then a surprise CT occurred. Ben's first while fully cognizant. Staff couldn't believe Ben did so well without the sedation typically used for children. Before the procedure, Dan explained the machine was a big camera, perfect for camera-hog Ben.

Good things happened too. Ben learned from OT and PT how to lift up his butt, a first step in movement, tried to pull himself, and figured out how to hook his right foot on the bed bar to slide sideways. His right leg had more strength than his right arm. A lefty now, he tried to pull socks off and on, and pants off to pee. OT taught him how to brush his teeth, wash his face, and stab and scoop food. Although it took him up to an hour to eat, even the IV disappeared.

Ben, unplugged!

Back in the land of the living for a week, during breakfast, Dan recorded, "Ben got mad and smashed his brown sugar into his eggs," protesting onlookers while he ate. "It's good for rehab staff to see Ben has limits to what he'll put up with."

Besides all the rehab therapists, Ben's perpetual stream of visitors included family, friends, pastors, church elders, Super Principal (with a book, of course), and nurses and doctors – and doctors and doctors and doctors. Ben's PICU nurses would visit from time to time as well. All adults, except for that lone, short visit with five-year-old Sam.

Soon after Ben's release from slumbering in that dreadful poppy field, we brought both Ben's siblings. Sarah reached for her brother, sweetly laid her head next to Ben's, then showed off her new trick. She had learned to walk during his coma. Keeping up with a one-year-old would become his high motivation.

The Twins, his school chums, and their parents accompanied Ben on his first wheelchair ride. An attached tray supported his right arm. We guessed correctly his favorite destination would be the window looking out upon the emergency Med Flight chopper-landing pad. But he could handle only short trips in the wheelchair.

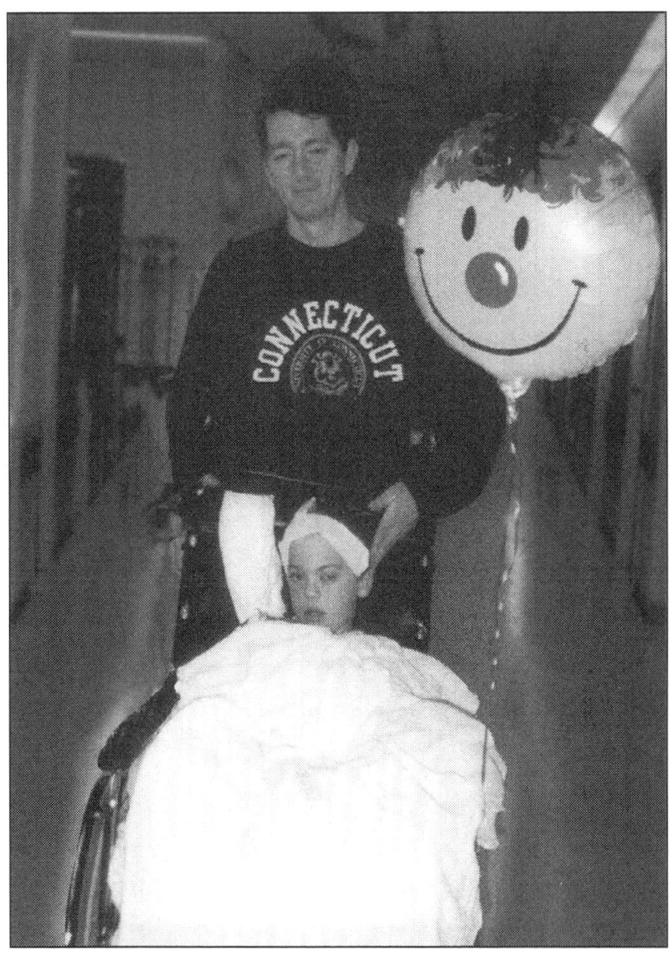

Dan With Ben, First Time In Wheelchair

While Ben struggled to regain his life, Dan and I strove to maintain our relationship. "We talked for twenty minutes on the phone today," Dan wrote, three weeks out from the start of Comaland. "Today was the first time in a long time we'd talked at length – we really need to – but she's very tired by 6:30 p.m. and I am by 11:00 a.m."

We took Dan's concern seriously. The next afternoon, Pavilion stayed with Ben, giving Dan and me a date. Dan drove us the short distance to the campus dorms where we had fallen in love and established our habit of heartfelt conversation. How odd to sit sadly in a freezing car at the beach, near the Lake Mendota paths we had often walked as good college friends. On our first date in November 1981, we had debated the nature of love. (I would've married him then and there.) Now, we sat as seasoned friends and lovers, no energy to walk, this time debating the nature of suffering. Dan's questions tended toward, Why Ben? Mine toward, How Long? Neither of us had any answers.

We also discussed the stories trickling in regarding how "God was using" Ben's tragedy in many ways in people's lives. At first we felt novel encouragement; it appealed to our pride, flattering us. Then it wore. I didn't want to be a cosmic guinea pig, held up as an example, lesson, or object of learning, and started to resent all the "Yay God! Look what God's doing!" commentary. It seemed to diminish the hardship of our reality.

"Of all the kids in Wisconsin, why Ben?" Dan wrote. "Will we ever know? Why the double whammy of rehab and an unresolved AVM? It's great that God is using this, but why Ben? Not so interested in how God is using this. I just want Ben back."

The notion of "God using" our repetitive, cumulative trauma now seems harsh. Victimized by The Ruler, like the Great Oz pulling the strings. It took time to waffle through and undo my erroneous thinking. Redeeming Spirit coming alongside, weeping for me, and strengthening so I could eke good from horrific, but never God using. Semantics? Is this part of what he meant by not taking his name in vain? These thoughts were not in my mind then, however, as Dan and I held each other in a freezing car on a mid-winter's darkening Saturday afternoon.

Back at the hospital, that evening Ben slowly, barely audibly, spoke my name, "Ma...ma," dripping golden honey into my soul.

Ben's obvious improvement uplifted my countenance, and Bucky helped too. Sunday afternoon, the UW men's basketball team suddenly appeared to perk up the floor. The UW coach and three of his players came into Ben's room, along with a little girl accompanying Coach. She exclaimed, "You're Ben! We pray for you every day!" She spoke of her class at a private elementary school.

"Bless you, son," said Coach, after I briefly explained Ben's ordeal and faith.

But mischievous Ben grabbed the Minnesota Gopher ball cap he'd received the previous Christmas. In the heart of the University of Wisconsin Hospital, in front of brawny Big Ten Badgers, he put it on his head, delighting them all with his chutzpah. Mutely talkin' smack to the big boys, more evidence Ben remained Ben.

Born in a Minneapolis suburb, living there for a whopping first two months of his life, Minnesota claimed Ben's undying Gopher allegiance. Every year, someone paraded a small, cardboard Paul Bunyan's Axe around our home after the rival Badger-Gopher football game. (Ben vs. the four of us.)

UW Badger doctors tried for years to convert Ben, with limited success. As an adult, he roots for Wisconsin sports every game they don't play the Gophers. The Vikings, however, never once threatened his loyalty to the Packers. Uncannily knowing the exact proximity to any line that should never be crossed.

On Monday, ten days after winning Comaland, Ben sat on the edge of the bed by himself for five minutes, twice pulled himself up to sit, and orthotics casted and fitted him for a metal, right leg brace. All milestones to celebrate. Then he indicated he had to pee, and peed all over everything, laughing, just as in infancy. He had routinely and intentionally tried to spray us during diaper changes, giggling when he accomplished his goal.

At fifteen months old, able to walk around the doctor's office during a check-up, he didn't. He ran. Buck-naked, he had toured the room, peeing in each corner. The surprised nurse asked if I'd considered potty-training him.

His antics, so exasperating in the past, now only thrilled us. Even better, that evening on the phone I heard his tinkling laughter and sweet voice, "Ma...ma...nigh."

Yet, Dan and I both felt such sweet sorrow.

Dan grieved the apparent loss of two of Ben's greatest strengths, talking about anything with anyone, and his athleticism. I focused on Ben's mental capacities, as well as lack of words. We rehabbed Ben accordingly. Dan played stationary wheelchair hoops and catch, and I read books and played easy board games.

RehabPsych thought Ben's problem-solving skills remained intact, although Ben couldn't distinguish between red and orange. Color confusion I could've cared less about. But incorrectly pointing to which card read "queen" vs. "three," or "happy" vs. "sad," concerned me, as well as the "short term memory weirdness" recorded by Dan. Asked to pick out cards illustrating words like "chair" or "circle," Ben missed easy ones.

Dan chronicled sorrow comingled with pride, seeing his son so helpless, yet trying so hard. "It's clear Ben can't talk very much if at all. Very hard on me to watch him struggle to even say 'aa.' I was quite saddened by this. Ben is trying to talk – frustrated by it, but keeps working at it. The words are in his head, they just don't come out."

Ben learned to say "aii," haltingly putting his first sentence together, many seconds between each sound: "aii...ah...nah" and "aii... oh...ah...nah." (I wanna. I don't wanna.)

"Ben's so strong and courageous. Everybody compliments him on how hard he works and how upbeat he is. He never gives up, never complains, never whines. He's my hero, no joke," wrote Dan.

When a doctor removed the last of the fifty-two staples in Ben's head, he didn't flinch. Dan tried to give Ben the nickname Mr. Courage, but he shook his head "no." He had few words, but his smiling face and attitude spoke for his heart.

February would fill with all kinds of heart.

On Valentines Day, but not because of it, my father stayed the night with Ben. Dan slept at home with me for the first time in twenty-six days. Someone leaked our plans to Super Principal, and suddenly school staff delivered money, flowers, and a gift card to a restaurant. We didn't use the gift card for seven months, until our eleventh anniversary, preferring to simply stay home.

Just after Valentine's Day, doctors granted Ben a tentative weekend pass. But while weaning him off one anti-seizure drug as another reached therapeutic levels, vomiting became a serious issue. Staff quickly spirited Ben away for a CT to monitor the AVM. Was it bleeding again? Negative. Docs then assumed the culprit to be the amount of strong drugs in Ben's system. The puking frequency dictated if, and when, we could use our pass. Friday evening, at 7:00 p.m., they extended the scepter.

Exactly four weeks after Ben left our home in an ambulance, he returned in our car. We bundled him up as best we could by stuffing his weak arm, hand, and leg in winter wear, and loaded him into the car, along with a big bag of meds, Chux pads, diapers, and other medical supplies. And a wheelchair.

Gloriously, triumphantly, jubilantly, frightfully terrifying!

That first brief weekend together, our family of five entered the crucible of intense bonding as Team Ben, family dynamics forever changed. Previously rambunctious Ben now needed propping up with pillows to simply sit. We carried him on our backs everywhere in our tri-level home, upstairs to the bedrooms and bathroom, downstairs to the TV room and basement toy room. The wheelchair stayed on the main floor, rolling through the L-shaped living room/dining room, and kitchen. He ate off his wheelchair tray and used a Tippy Cup, like Sarah.

Dan shaved Ben's head that weekend, the hair that wasn't removed by OR staff during craniotomy prep. Post-surgery, Ben's super-sensitive scalp prevented us even cutting off the EEG epoxy chunks. As his father gently shaved, Ben sat in his wheelchair watching his reflection in the mirror, grinning his approval. Clearly delighted to resemble a naked mole rat, with bits of glue still stuck to his scalp here and there. (One of Ben's favorite *Bill Nye the Science Guy* episodes featured the creatures with faces only a mother and God could love.) Afterward, Ben took his first bath, Dan in the tub with him, holding him up, pads from EKG wiring still attached to Ben's chest.

More of Ben's abilities kicked in at home that weekend, pleasantly shocking us. A favorite part of the boys' lives, roughhousing with their father after dinner, continued. Albeit curtailed. Wheelchair-bound Ben threw a left-handed spiral with a small Nerf football. While I performed Ben's right arm, hand, and leg stretching exercises on the floor, he moved his right arm on his own, for the first time lifting it from his side to his stomach, elating himself. At bedtime, he gestured as if going to chase Sarah on the futons, giving her giggles. With my prompting, he hugged and kissed Sarah, sending her off to bed as always. Then, relatively quickly, clearly, and strongly, he said, "Nigh... nigh...Sawah."

But we didn't sleep too well that weekend, courtesy of sole nursing responsibility and potential nocturnal vomiting. During the first night, Ben cried out twice and I bolted up in fear. He only required being carried to the bathroom. We took turns, both on high alert for any noises coming from the boys' room, just like with newborns. Back then, I couldn't sleep with Ben in our room, startling with every tiny baby noise he'd made, and Dan couldn't sleep either, startling with every silence. Now, we knew noises could herald disaster, and feared silence as well. We were more electrically wired to this child than ever. Back then we put him in his baby basket, six feet around the corner from our room for relief. Now?

Sarah seemed least affected by Ben's changed presence. Although, her baby calendar three days after Ben's hospitalization reads, "At breakfast, pointed at Sam and said, 'Beh.'" She had noticed the absence of her in-your-face brother. Ben's first weekend home, they mutely exchanged many sweet looks and smiles.

But Sam, only five and a half, blew our minds. At dinnertime he asked Ben how to do the napkins and silverware, quickly figuring "yes/no" questions the best way to go. His big brother could still nod. After dinner, spontaneously taking a tiny, green, plastic fighter jet in each hand, he flew one around Ben's head, landing it on the wheelchair tray. Ben slowly picked it up, trying to make jet engine noises like Sam. Crooked smile on one face, a welcome home smile on the other, they piloted together once again. Then Sam put Legos on Ben's tray, and the boys built together, Ben holding a piece, Sam attaching another. Sam kept up a running patter for both. I knew then our family would be all right, as Sam led the way with kindness, thoughtfulness, and amazingly, words.

Two-year-old Sam, mostly still silent, had spoken his first sentence under duress in the Nagasaki Pediatric ICU in 1992. We feared losing him to a freak, systemic, raging bacterial infection. The blood poisoning brought him dangerously close to septic shock, a 50/50 life or death proposition. Powerful, broad-spectrum antibiotics weren't working, and between the language barriers, Japanese and Medicalese, we were fearfully confused. From his PICU hospital bed, where Dan and I had alternately sat and slept with him for two weeks, Sam whimpered, "Head...hurt...tummy...hurt," repeating it ad nauseam for days.

Sam's 1992 served as dress rehearsal for Ben's 1996.

With Ben's words now shut off at the tap, stealthy Sam spoke volumes. He explained every sport's respective, potential cause for pain: falling, hit with a ball, hit with a puck, hit with a stick, hit with a club, hurt.

"Hurt" became more than a part of his vocabulary. Ben's condition drilled it deeply into our second son's psyche. So deep in fact, it took anesthesia for wisdom teeth removal to reach it. The words his five-year-old voice couldn't express, his teenage heart uttered a decade later through a drooling, bloody mouth. Coming out of the ether Sam wailed, "Why? Why does Ben have to have so much pain?"

Sam was the perfect sibling for a rehab patient. But the toll began Sunday evening, our last dinner together before Ben and Dan returned to live at the hospital, fracturing our family yet again. Sam wouldn't eat. His tummy felt sick, so he sat on the couch with a bowl. Sure enough, he barfed then, and later in bed. Virus? Physical response to emotions? Or worse? It took a long time before I could look at puke in the same light I had prior to January 19, 1996. Indeed, I feared Sam and Sarah had explosions hiding in their heads, especially Sarah, who looked so much like Ben. I wanted to conduct CTs on both, but knew Ben's condition was not genetic.

The mirage-like oasis dissipated, and back we went to the rehab grind of Big Peds.

A few days later, staff granted Ben a special, dinner-only, mid-week pass for my thirty-fifth birthday. Both of my sisters, Koo and Boo, flew in, Koo with her girls in tow. (Koo's nickname, for no reason. Boo, for Mr. Radley, as we swore her flawless porcelain skin never saw the light of day.)

I blew candles out with my dad, as his birthday is two days before mine. I needed the lung help, anyway. Another family picture taken, this time Ben in his wheelchair, the four of us surrounding him. My three kids looked happy; Dan and I like Bogey on the Paris train station platform in *Casablanca*, as if someone had kicked out our guts.

Just after my birthday, I received a wonderful present. A rehab doc, subbing for RehabDoc, checked on Ben one evening. He messed with Ben's legs a while, suddenly declaring, "Well, I can tell you right now this boy's gonna walk."

No one had said anything like that!

The last weekend in February, staff granted our last home pass. One thing became crystal clear. Suddenly acquiring a child with special needs does not exclude a family from normal life. Years later, I whined to my friend Phoebe, "It should be a law: no flu, no colds, no strep, no hand-foot-mouth, no croup, no shingles, no ear infections, no pneumonia, no falls and fractures, no stitches, no normal kid sickness."

She knew what I meant, having a child of her own with extraordinary challenges.

Our second weekend home visit felt like Country & Western, minus the dead dog. Dan battled diarrhea every hour on the hour through the night. Then Ben's kicked in. Grandpa Syrup's truck died – we had been using it. Sarah bit off the top of liquid meds, dribbling red translucence all over the futon and herself, down her chin, in her mouth, and down her throat. I called Poison Control while Dan frantically tried to determine how much she might have ingested. Then she pinched her finger in a door. Returning to the hospital Sunday night for the last stretch of inpatient hospitalization, Dan locked immovable Ben in the car, with the keys still inside. Ben, with his daddy's encouragement, raised the lock on the door.

"Our Hero!" wrote Dan. "Asleep by 8:00 p.m."

I think he meant both.

The next morning, Chief Neurosurgeon ordered an angiography to check on the size and blood volume of Ben's AVM. It would be Ben's second round of anesthesia while aware. The previous October, he'd undergone an adenoidectomy and had trouble recovering from anesthesia-induced dizziness and nausea. We weren't sure what to expect after all his body had been through since then. Lying flat for seven hours after the procedure, he did quite well, smirking, making faces, and sipping apple juice.

On February 28, the day after the angiography, staff discharged Ben from living at the hospital. Doctors and nurses congratulated and flattered us – surprised Ben could leave inpatient care so soon. They variably chalked up his fast recovery to Ben's character, good parenting, and prayer. A neurologist called Ben "one tough kid."

The five of us triumphantly marched through Big Peds on our way out, Ben wheeling himself a little, one-handed. Sarah, giggling, her chubby, wobbling legs carrying her away from her brother in his big, black, rolling thing. In slow-mo pursuit he followed his sister down a long, white, cement hallway. "Aii...oh...ah...*ih*...ooo!"

Ben perfectly intoned "I'm gonna get you!"

A smile radiated from my heart, lifted my lips, and trickled into my eyes. Would it be the way it was before?

Ben's forty days in the wilderness, completed. Dan's forty days sleeping at the hospital completed. Would that they had been enough.

Chapter 11

Circle The Wagons

Ben went directly from being invited to represent the museum in DC to his three-hour volunteer shift, slightly more ebullient than usual. (Bet that was some fun for the museum's visitors.) Dan and I walked back to work at WESLI. But I couldn't. Not even to stuff language brochures. Crashing after the sweet sugar high, I couldn't focus, and stared at the wall I shared with Dan. It was white.

"Babe, I'm done. I gotta go home."

Deciding he could work from home, he drove us. And I soberly thought about our son and the weight of his sudden employment and White House news. They posed a new set of problems. Could we sail smoothly through good?

Two out of the past three autumns caused so much negative stress for Ben that he'd presented with late December weeklong stays in the UW Hospital psych unit. (In fifteen years, it seems we've covered every department but oncology. Shh, don't tell cancer we're hiding.) If the years taught me anything, stress, good or bad, is still stress. Fight, flight, freeze, I didn't want to live yet again in any of those states. I had worked so hard to get out. And I certainly didn't want an over-stressed Ben back in the hospital.

"Well, you," I silently pep-talked myself, "you're back on familiar ground, a ridiculously abnormal life where you exert one of your roles as Mom: circler of wagons, controller of damages, container of messes. You know what to do."

But before I could call Ben from home, he called me. His tiny voice nearly whimpered, "Mom?"

"Hey, how're you doing?"

"Umm, I'm screaming inside and trying to be calm on the outside."

Me too. We both had difficultly absorbing the news. Not to mention digesting the request to remain quiet about it, for a month, until the press conference.

"Yeah, I'm all bottled up!" he agreed.

Reminding him to use his tools for good mental health, I taught him the idiom circle the wagons. "So, how would it be if you got in to your psychotherapist ASAP? And how about if we meet tomorrow with Janet at Yahara House? You can tell her everything. Ruth gave me clearance for that; Janet's vowed confidentiality as a staff worker. We can make a list of people you want to tell, people to invite to the press conference, and then decide what we can say, and when."

He sounded better when he called again twenty minutes later. "Mom, I laid down and did deep breathing just like you said. I feel less bottled."

"Good. And tomorrow you get to start telling people, one by one."

Day one of the news, managed. Now for the next however-long. Sometime between November and March we'd go to DC, Ruth thought. Six months from now? Management, finesse, I might need to be significantly on board again in Ben's life. Well, the fifteen-month span of normalcy provided by psychotherapy, medication, life-affirming habits, and the very intentional support of YH and MCM, not necessarily in order of importance, had felt great while it lasted.

Day two, Ben and I created fun. We found Janet on duty in YH's buzzing cafeteria. A small group of people was meeting at one of the cafeteria tables, while members and staff worked the lunch counter as folks came in to eat.

All have equal footing at YH. Members and staff contribute to the running of the building and its programs, serving people with significant mental illness like severe depression, schizophrenia, post-traumatic stress, bipolar, and psychotic disorders. The motto? "Yahara House Works!" And it does. According to 2011 YH stats and information, Clubhouse membership significantly increases employment, and reduces psychiatric hospitalizations and suicide rates. For eight consecutive years, no YH members had committed suicide. YH provides members with teamwork, support, and opportunity for employment, in other words, dignity and hope.

The National Registry of Substance Abuse and Mental Health Services Administration (SAMHSA) has ruled International Center for Clubhouse Development (ICCD) Clubhouse Models hold Evidence-Based status – meaning their methods work. In addition, ICCD has been granted Consultative Status with the United Nations. ICCD Clubhouse Models for mental health recovery and treatment, such as Yahara House, have a proven track record of excellence. Around the planet, ICCD Clubhouses improve the quality of life for those with mental illness.

"Hi, Ben's Mom!" one man in the cafeteria greeted me enthusiastically. "I remember you from last year."

That's right, I remembered too. Over a string of highly emotional days, Ben and I had testified with the man on behalf of YH. Staff thought it would be powerful for Ben and me to give back-to-back speeches imploring local elected officials not to cut YH funding. My speech outlined Ben's traumatic life. He followed with what YH had done for him. For each of our six-minute state speeches, we spoke into a camera with only a handful of onlookers. Still, partway into my speech the film crew rounded up a box of tissues for my running nose. Thankfully, I have never seen my dripping movie debut. (I don't know why I even bothered with mascara.) The county budget hearings the next evening only allowed for three minutes, but in front of hundreds, including forty officials. (If my mother had thought my girly hands shook during annual enforced piano recitals, held in the tiny living room of my teacher, with only eight parents on hand....)

The evening meeting's emcee instructed the audience in the cavernous, warehousey Alliant Energy Center to hold applause, or we'd be there all night. Because of Ben's disabilities, we were allowed to speak early in the evening. Armed with tissues clenched in my fist, I ended my speech with a twist on the old African proverb.

"It takes a village to raise a child? For people like us, it takes a village, a city, a county, a state, and even a nation. We need extra help from the community in order to productively give back to it."

Then I sat, tear-stained, and violently trembling, the room remaining hushed. Ben stood at the podium, utilizing his best dramatic voice, complete with pregnant pauses, and drove the point home. When he finished, the place erupted.

I couldn't get out fast enough, trotting blindly for the door, about one hundred yards away, or maybe even a mile. A few female elected officials left the meeting to come hug us in the lobby. We rocked the house, one said. I just blubbered.

"Mom, why did they clap for me when they were told not to?"

"Haven't you ever heard of Cinderella Story, kid? They couldn't help it; they had to. We kicked ass in there, Ben!"

"It was easy, Mom. Just like a play."

My weeklong shaking mess, a small price to pay for pride.

YH is filled with pride too, for those able to carry on lucid conversations, and write and read speeches like the man at the cafeteria table, and for those working the cafeteria that day, some walking as if in a dream world. All portray the dignified faces and abilities of mental illness.

Ben, Janet, and I found a table off to one side, away from others. Then Ben leaned toward Janet, softly whispering, "We gotta talk slowly...and low."

(Oh, this should be good. I leaned back in my chair for the ride.)

"The government is getting a plane, and putting me and my mom on it, and flying us to the White House, so I can get an award from the First Lady!"

To Janet's credit, her face registered mostly belief and joy, along with just a hint of apprehension. With a big grin on my face, I nodded my head vehemently, "He's almost right! The museum is getting an award and he's been asked to go to DC, and I get to go too!"

Just as with Janet, over the next few days I accompanied Ben while he leaked the news to his short list of men, tagging along purely for backup. Naw. That's a lie, backup and basking. Ben dubbed the news Code Cheese. What else would a Wisconsin-bred Packers fan choose? While I Elsa Snorted, he snickered and routinely took to high-fiving me at odd moments. His mantra became, "Today we'll tell (so and so) about Cheese!"

Meeting in parking lots with some of the guys made the surreptitious drama even better. In our element, Ben said we were black ops, I countered with cland ops. Ben said we met with guys in ghost corners, like in *Bourne* movies. I proclaimed we'd tell people strictly on an eyes-only, need-to-know basis. Ben explained three levels of government security: confidential, secret, and top secret. Code Cheese he deemed confidential, as opposed to the hunting down of Osama bin Laden, which Ben declared had clearly been top secret. But, Ben always finished by whispering to his guys, "This is still a matter of federal government security."

When Pavilion replied, "I'm a vault," Ben went into Secret Service orbit.

When we met my father en route to a UW Badgers football game, Ben began by asking, "Grandpa, do you know the White House?"

"Yeah, there's the one you grew up in."

I only heard key words, "government," "flying," "First Lady," and, "White House," too busy studying my dad's face. His looked like Janet's had: slack, with a confused, questioning look around the forehead. (I think it's technically called, "Wha-?") I got in my dad's face, whispering hoarsely, "Can you believe this?"

"No, no I can't!" His head would not stop shaking back and forth.

Ben swore him to secrecy, invoking the three-tiered federal government security levels, and invited him to the press conference.

That left Ben's siblings as the last family members to inform. We planned to tell Sam, away at college, the next evening. Sarah knew only that she wouldn't be going to school on October twenty-fifth.

"Mom, it would really help if I knew why I have to miss school, you know."

"Yeah, but, and here is the question: Can you keep your mouth shut for a month? Not tell (and here I listed her five closest friends and her boyfriend)?"

"I can keep secrets, Mom! Is Ben going to give us a museum tour or something?" She intoned teenage insouciance.

"Nope, gotta think bigger than that."

"*Hey!*" she shrieked, thinking way bigger, "That gives me a six day weekend!" Her fall break fell just after the twenty-fifth.

"Not exactly. You can go to school in the afternoon."

"Oh."

"Trust me. You'll want to go to school then. You'll have news to tell." She usually wanted to anyway. It's where her 1,900 peeps hung out during the day. In addition to eyes and dimples, she resembled her eldest brother more than she admitted.

After Ben explained Code Cheese, Sarah's sixteen-year-old eyebrow shot up, "Serious?"

"Yep!"

"So, can I post this as my Facebook status?" she snarked. But her telltale, capacious dimples proved her excitement.

"Good job, Ben," Sarah complimented seriously. "So, who else knows?"

"Grandpa. We told him yesterday in a parking lot."

"You told Grandpa in a parking lot? Like that isn't sketch?"

Before dinner, Ben prayed as we held hands, as always my left hand joining his curled, withered right hand, "Heavenly Father, thank you for our love and your love. Amen."

Simple. Grateful. Perfect. A prayer even I could still pray.

Later that night, just before falling asleep, maybe because I'd been missing my mother something fierce that day, from its deep recesses my mind curiously dredged up one wee factoid: Sparkling Bling. I had forgotten all about the fiftieth birthday gift I'd purchased myself. Courtesy of my long-deceased mother's inheritance, I owned teensy Sparkling Bling, representing my family of five. I could wear it in DC. Mom would come with me! Sort of. Not really.

Some people think of the dead as gone, turned to stardust or energy, some think of them as gone, but watching, and sometimes even directing what goes on below, some think of them as still here, walking invisibly along, and some think they're here, but in a different form, reincarnated. None of those interested me. I had not seen my mother for twelve years. I wanted my visibly healthy, flesh and blood mother, softly warm to the touch. I wanted her holding my hand gently while I told her Ben's great news, then enveloping me, hearing her whisper tenderly, "Oh, honey. That's so great!"

It is great, isn't it, Mom?

The next day, Ben came home for dinner again. Two nights in a row, almost like the olden days. In fine fettle, her homework completely finished within school hours, a juiced Sarah goofed with her eldest brother. The first and third born, although different genders and six years apart, have in common personalities the antithesis of subdued and reserved. Boisterously playing foosball, screechily imitating raptors, the house rocked.

It was good. Into the soul, good.

As arranged, the four of us contacted Sam, via Skype, in his dorm room. The racket continued, each sibling happily imploring the other to shut up.

Sam sat at his desk, occasionally popping a cheese puff with the flick of a finger, silently waiting for the tumult to die down, a grin plastering his face.

"Can't we make Sam any bigger?" I complained. I loathed using reading glasses to see my son on the computer.

Dan complied.

"And can't we get Muhammad Ali off the screen?" I whined. "What's he doing there, anyhow?" The massive boxer bugged me. He was, like, in the way.

"*Mom*! It's a poster on Sam's wall!" Sarah corrected, giving all three kids fits, while Dan deadpanned, "Technology."

(Sigh. I hate it when I give them more ammo.)

Ben gave his spiel.

Barely audible, Sam murmured, "Cool." Cheese puff pop. Grin.

"So what do you think about that?" Ben asked.

"Exciting." Grin. Cheese puff pop. "So, can I post it on Facebook?"

A minute later, when Sarah's chatter died down, Ben asked again, "So what do you think of this?"

"I already said it was exciting." Grin. Cheese puff pop.

"Couldn't you tell?" I asked smarmily. "There was this split-second pause between cheese puff popping that showed his excitement for you."

"Ha, ha, Mom."

Sam is so his father's son, although he has my green eyes and chestnut hair.

I left to cook dinner, while the pseudo-quiet siblings went back to the basement to raise ruckus. Dan and Sam virtually decompressed together for a few minutes. (Must be rough to be emotionally outnumbered.)

Ben prayed at dinner again, as we held hands, embellishing the previous night's prayer, "Heavenly Father, thank you for this berserky family and our love, and your love. Amen."

Even better.

Ben's 2010 State And County Testimonial

My name is Ben Perreth and I have been a member of Yahara House for eight months. I want to tell you that, for me, and not only for me, Yahara House works! For all the unfairness of life I've gone through, the pain, the suffering, and then, years later, I blindly find this place called Yahara House.

It all began when I first went there with my mom in January of this year. At that time I was drugged with medicine and was pretty out of it. I was like a new seed, very small and vulnerable, but full of potential. I was greatly surprised by the enormous kindness, welcome, and guidance throughout, by a tour guide that did the job flawlessly. At this point I had no idea that she was a member who has a mental illness just like me! It was almost impossible for me to focus and even walk, yet I was shocked at how friendly all the people were to me. My curiosity got me and I wanted to find out more about this rare place.

My life at that point was a hazy fog of confusion to me. I had just gotten out of the psych unit at UW Hospital for the second time in two years. I had been attending college for 3 ½ years. My counselors, teachers, and parents were all telling me to take a break. I knew they were right but I felt a great loss. Going to school was one of my worlds and it was taken away from me. Where would I go? I didn't know.

Despite the overwhelming odds, here I am, telling you, that because I found Yahara House my life is *COMPLETELY* different from then. There are over ten skilled jobs I've been doing for the last eight months I've been at Yahara House. Some of them are: reporting for the daily newspaper, *The Chronicle*; video taping, anchoring, and editing for the weekly YH Video News; outreach calls to other members; writing plays for our cultural competence efforts; and creating birthday and get well cards for YH members. All thanks to the staffers and the members who now are my good friends that I trust.

I feel so alive because I'm enjoying life. My self-esteem is flying high, with bounds of colors. I'm one of the countless seeds here and across Wisconsin that got water, sunshine, and good soil to grow. Please, don't rip my roots out and cast them away.

Chapter 12

Save A Life

Dan and I took Ben out to lunch to celebrate and to brainstorm on the one page, double-spaced bio requested by MCM and the Institute of Museum and Library Services (IMLS). Ben's few ideas included mentioning his mental health struggles.

"I'm so proud that you want to say you have mental illness," I complimented. "Lots of folks would want to keep it quiet. There's a stigma, you know."

"I know, Mom."

"But Madison is a very accepting place. Heck, a national organization for mental illness started here," I continued. "It's called NAMI."

The National Alliance on Mental Illness, founded in Madison in 1979, had flourished. Perusing the national NAMI website once, I read that mental illness can occur in those leading ordinary lives, or be triggered by traumatic stress. I believe they are quite correct.

"NAMI's having a walk next Sunday," I added.

"Let's do it, Mom!"

"Well...okay, let's." It would be good – for both of us. We'd built our internal resources enough during the past fifteen months to be able to, I thought. Both of us reaped the fruits of our labor, enjoying the lull, freedom from the medical black hole.

Women my age enter menopause. I entered Benopause.

Arriving early to yoga as usual on Sunday morning, forehead to mat, arms curled backward cradling my body in Embryonic Child's Pose, I got small, breathing deeply.

Breathing did not make it onto my to-do list until midlife. I had considered it the one thing I didn't need to worry or think about. But as a ten-year-old, visiting my grandparents, I had received my first lesson. An ancient man perched on a shaded park bench, sunlight dappling through leaves. The stifling high summer heat of St. Louis shimmered off the pavement around him. His hands rested upon his cane. Long, slow, deep inhales and exhales, his only movement. Upon finishing, he opened his eyes and saw me standing before him, staring. In heavily accented English he told me every day he took ten breaths like that. "It's good for you. You should do this," he instructed. For over three decades I thought him crazy; then I thought him an oracle.

In my forties, yoga taught me to breathe.

On my mat, I went inside to hide before my big day – walking for NAMI and helping Ben compose his bio. Our regular yoga instructor had been out on maternity leave, but that day, exactly three weeks after giving birth, Sweet Melissa returned. I was astounded because three weeks after each of my kids' births I still rode the wild hormonal roller coaster. Our class is mainly composed of womenfolk, and some chattered loudly before class in anticipation of our yogini's arrival. They sprinkled their baby talk with Badgers, Packers, and Brewers. Many Wisconsin women equally love their babies and world-class teams. Then word spread, "She's here! With pictures!"

The clucking, I'm sorry but there really is no better word, moved out into the hallway without me. Yoda-like newborns rarely did it for me. Sleep, allow you I will not. Puke, on you I will. Eat, rely on you I must. When infants could reward with coos and smiles, my love affair began. But when the little ones could use words, humor, and then play board games, I became forever rapturously besotted.

Class started and Sweet Melissa gently took us to the now in our bodies, as we focused on breathing, engaging our restful parasympathetic nervous systems, the antidote to flight or fight. She encouraged us to become aware of what we needed in class that day, and to listen to, and honor, that need. Pose modifications are not bailing.

Only once had Sweet Melissa significantly interfered with my listening to myself during yoga. But when I stopped laughing, I quickly forgave her. On the morning of Super Bowl Sunday 2011, when the Packers were prepping for XLV, Sweet Melissa had instructed us to, "Hold your plank for twelve breaths."

(Twelve? Weird numb-)

"Because, today, a certain man will take the field."

It worked. Aaron Rodgers and the Pack over the Steelers.

I find steel often accompanies yoga. Standing strong in the Warrior II and Tree poses, I feel especially empowered. Once, in Warrior II, a virtual pencil materialized in my outstretched hand. It is how I always envision myself now, Warrior Mother, Pencil In Hand (keyboard too unwieldy). In Tree, leg rooted, face upturned, my arms uplift to my Creator in supplication, gratitude, and thanksgiving.

About forty minutes into this Sunday class, within the first notes of a certain song, in seconds I went from Down Dog to just down. As I lay prone, Sweet Melissa's instructing voice faded quickly, droning softly in the background. The Fray took me with them, forcing me front and center into, yet again, contemplating *How to Save a Life*. It never mattered where I was, or what I was doing, from the very first time I heard the song. A javelin through my heart regularly pinned me to earth, and I stood, sat, or as on this day, Child's Posed my way through the next few minutes, riveted, motionless, barely breathing. No other song has this exact effect. Talk about grounding. The haunting refrain contains years of my sorrow, and loss of all kinds. For my son, my self, and all the attempted and successful suicides I've ever known. There were too many. Not to mention my own bitterness of soul, losing sight of its Friend along the way. The mish-mash of emotions streamed out of my eyes and nostrils, as Isaac Slade relentlessly crooned.

A three-Kleenex blow, I had to wait until Otis Redding partially finished wastin' his time dockside before I could actually up and get to the class tissue box. Kicking myself for never purchasing stock in a solid Wisconsin-founded company, Kimberly-Clark, I took pity on the class and removed my soggy self. One of the reasons I am always in the back, behind a pillar if possible, in a corner on the fringes of class, attempting introverted invisibility: sometimes I must eject myself.

Only a handful of times in five years' worth of yoga had *How to Save a Life* played. How dare The Fray intrude on my calm-inducing time before such a big day? I adored the song, but not out of its proper place and time. As class continued, The Words in my head came to life and refused to wait, lining themselves up in grammatical order. By the time I walked home, showered, and drove off to get Ben, the above had been set in stone. Or gray matter. Or virtual, screen ink. Or whatever.

While we drove the few miles from Ben's apartment on the shore of Lake Mendota, to the shore of Lake Monona (where Mr. Redding had met his demise in 1967, I am sorry to say), we planned our day.

"One giant step for the Perreths, one small step for mankind," my son announced, laughing. Not too far off the mark, I thought.

A large group turned out to walk on the early October day, another warm one. No hard freeze had yet hit southern Wisconsin, eerily glorious.

Walking up to the registration table, I saw Tanker, a friend from high school. His daughter, sadly, had been the last suicide to impact my life, and Ben's.

We bear hugged. "I've been thinking about you a lot recently," I barely squeaked. I'd had so much good recently, and I wanted that for my former homeroom chum.

"Are you with our group?" he asked.

"No, we're here by ourselves."

"Well, you are now! Grab a t-shirt!" Tanker and Co. had brought an entire fleet of t-shirts, all sizes, aqua, the color of Lindsey's smiling eyes, proclaiming "Lindsey's Love." On the back, balloons floated free with "NAMI Walks" printed underneath. Tanker took his girl's suicide public – vivacious Lindsey, a victim of mental illness. As Tanker had said at the visitation, "It was like cancer, came and went, grew and took her."

Before the walk, a photographer took group pictures, but I doubt Lindsey's crowd completely fit in the photo. Someone yelled, "Say 'cheese'!"

"Ben," I Elsa Snorted in glee, "Say '*Cheese*'!" earning myself an elbow in the ribs. Ben took his Code Cheese Secret Service gig seriously. A Wisconsin mom couldn't even make a dairy joke.

We walked from Olin Park to the Monona Terrace, and back. A grand 5K parade led by taiko drummers. Ben recognized folks from Yahara House, I saw an ex-neighbor, and many others whose faces I couldn't place. Community, my community, joining together for the day's motto, "taking a bite out of stigma," by advocating for mental health issues "one step at a time." The day's weather wasn't the only glorious thing.

As we walked, I asked my man-boy about his first, paid, five-hour shift at MCM.

"The first three hours were great. I took a break, you get to for fifteen minutes."

"Yeah, it's a law." At least for those covered by the Americans with Disabilities Act (ADA). Employers must make allowances for ADA protectees.

"The next two hours were hard, but I was happy," Ben continued. "On my break I went up to the roof and held Cheddar, the calming chicken."

"Good for you, Ben."

From his pocket he pulled out a surprise for me. "Look, Mom!" Proudly, he held out a lanyard with his nametag attached, "Ben P." (The volunteer badge he'd worn previously had read "Care Bear.")

"I made it!"

"You mean you made the nametag, or...?" I asked with a grin.

"No, Mom, I *made* it!" he exclaimed, giving me a high five and a kiss, leaving no doubt. "It's dignity, humility, and happiness together," he added. "And they won't turn into gray!"

Afterward, we sat on a secluded bench by the beach. Reading the first draft of Ben's bio aloud, I edited. Most of the words were his, even "neurosurgeon." Only I changed it to the plural.

"More than one thought you were going to die," I explained. "I know at least one didn't even want to try and operate."

"What? That's news to me! Is there more you haven't told me?"

"Ben, there's a whole ton you don't know, probably. You haven't exactly been in a place you could handle hearing it all, you know. For a long time you were a child, then teen, then young adult, just trying to survive. You've had enough dark on your plate. Besides, I don't know what you do and don't know, at this point."

He was glad to hear I hadn't totally intentionally been hiding his life from him.

"Can I read the letter you wrote to the children's museum?"

Earlier, I'd told him he could read it after we worked on his bio. I hadn't wanted my language interfering with his. But, I hesitated. "There's stuff in it you might not...um, like. Tell me if you find some."

While he silently read my nomination letter, I kept editing the bio, adding only two simple sentences. After ten minutes, he cocked his head at me and complimented, "You're a skilled writer, Mom."

"Why, thank you, Ben."

He read another chunk, suddenly laughing about our speechifying on behalf of YH, "Yeah, you were a shaking mess that day!" When he reached the end he asked, "Why did you think I would be angry?"

"Well, is there anything in there that made you feel...small?"

"No, it made me happy! I mean it was really sad and depressing, but you said it the way it was. The way it is. It's all true."

"Yes, it is, but I didn't know if some of the way I said it would hurt your feelings. And, it's all there in one chunk, in your face. I didn't want it bringing you down."

"Mom. It's in my face every day."

Touché. His mother is allowed to forget.

"The children's museum isn't in the first paragraph of the bio," he observed. "I feel kinda bad about that. But, it's better this way."

"I think so," I agreed.

"Because, you have to see where I've been, and then it's...like light!"

"Yeah, Ben, it's like a beacon."

Just like this grand, community-wide, glorious beacon of public de-stigmatization on an early October day, in Wisconsin.

May 2012, Ben wore his "Lindsey's Love" aqua t-shirt, standing on Observatory Drive at the top of Bascom Hill, and then near Liz

Waters dorm, cheering on his 10K father and other runners. He brought smiles to their faces as he stood in his smiley-face AFO, yelling, "C'mon! You can do it! I'm juggling balls with one hand and you've got two legs! I think I can, I think I can, I think I can, I knew I could, I knew I could, I knew I could!"

Chapter 13

Mortality Or Morbidity?

We hoped for a second miracle in 1996. If late February's angiography revealed a vanished AVM, Ben wouldn't need further treatment. Voila! No decision-making necessary. Unfortunately, not to be.

Neuroradiology doctor, RadDoc, briefly discussed AVM treatment options with Dan. RadDoc's guys specialized in coil and bead placement – jamming the vessels feeding the AVM, preventing blood flow. Technically, this clogging is called embolization. If blood couldn't reach the AVM, it couldn't re-bleed. Simple, if it worked. But RadDoc thought in Ben's case it wouldn't.

Chief Neurosurgeon sat us down for a sobering meeting of bewares, turn backs, and squalls up ahead. "There are some doctors out there who will tell you, 'I can remove that AVM surgically.' Well, I could, too," explained Our Humble Hero. "But what Ben would be left with, in terms of mental and physical abilities, would be minimal at best."

As if we two, shell-shocked parents in our mid-thirties were ever going to seek a second opinion and choose it over his. Not simply a brilliant neurosurgeon spoke, but a caring father. Limpet-like, Dan and I attached to Chief Neurosurgeon – you save our son we love you for life. We hung on his words. What did Paean, wise physician to the Greek gods, think we should do? Radiate. In California or Massachusetts.

At that time in the US, two facilities were equipped with the highest-precision radiation possible: proton beam. Loma Linda University Medical Center (LLUMC), near LA, owned one machine, partnering with Stanford for preparation. The other resided on the East Coast – in NYC for the prep and Massachusetts for the procedure. Both coasts required two trips each, with three or four weeks between.

But even Stanford, AVM treatment mecca, had only seen three or four referral cases of Ben's magnitude. Docs categorized Ben's AVM, at best, as a Spetzler-Martin Grade Four, out of five. (Reminding me very much of the Fujita scale for tornadic rating. Anyone living even close, like we do, to Tornado Alley, understands. We get the strays. Plenty of Toto-we're-not-in-Kansas destruction.) Spetzler-Martin AVM gradation allots points according to size, location, and vein drainage. Ben's AVM, located deeply in an extremely significant area of the brain, precluded further surgery. Chief Neurosurgeon had only operated in the first place because of imminent death. Radiation seemed the only viable option for further treatment.

Or we could do nothing, leaving the AVM ticking away, large and poised to blow, a 2-4% chance annually of a re-bleed. Partially obliterating itself when it erupted in January, still an awful lot remained. Chief Neurosurgeon advised late spring radiation.

RehabDoc helped solidify our decision to radiate, "You have the choice between mortality and morbidity." Death or damage. (Couldn't there be a door number three?)

East Coast or So Cal, for radiation? All things being equal, as any Northerner will understand, we chased sun and warmth after the Hellacious, long, and frigid winter. Besides, Mickey Mouse beckoned.

The letter from our insurance company confirmed Mickey Mouse by stating we'd been cleared for "proton bean (sic) radiation." (Navy? Lima? Garbanzo?)

Once in contact with the radiation prep docs at Stanford, it became clear a third embolization option existed, not beads or coils. A non-FDA approved substance, made in Germany, would have to be smuggled in from Canada. Okay, not smuggled, just given special dispensation by FDA/US Customs for a Canadian distribution company to ship across the border. But it must jump through bureaucratic hoops. Would our government let Superglue for brain vessels cross?

A dicey prospect. I'd had my own run-in on the northern border once, in 1984, the summer I moved to St. Paul. Camping in Northern Minnesota with heart-of-my-heart, Ren, I learned she'd never visited Canada. I insisted we go. After staying for less than a minute, we attempted to regain entry into the good ol' US of A. At the time, I drove a 1973 red Dodge Dart, dubbed The Flintstone Mobile for its low-rider tendency.

"How long have you two been in Canada?"

"About fifteen seconds," I answered, snickering, proving the brain does not possess fully developed judgment, even for females, until at least age twenty-five.

"Didn't you see us?" I continued, bubbling. "We just drove past a minute ago." That tiny bit of border humor cost us a boatload of time. (And this was way pre-Homeland Security.)

Accused, "What have you girls been smoking?" we laughed even harder. Ordered out of the car, our stuff strewn about, a full-scale search sent us into doubled-over gales. We owe our prominently placed Bibles for getting us off with a warning. I think. Or maybe he'd taken all he could of just-out-of-college female humor.

Would the contraband glue for Ben's brain make it across the border in less time than Ren and I had?

Crossing all the Ts, dotting all the Is, and attending to every other letter in the alphabet, I worked closely with Stanford's Neuroradiology Nurse Coordinator, BlueEyesNurse. (So nicknamed soon after we met her.) We spent what seemed like hours on the phone in preparation for the California trips. Her listening care, and concern for me, as well as for Ben, went above and beyond. I could hardly wait to meet her.

While stacks of paperwork on our behalf got the California ball rolling, Dan returned to teaching at WESLI, and my mother moved out. Ben's recuperation increased with the restored normalcy of sleeping in his own room with Sam and eating dinner as a family. So did mine. After dinner, while he played with his dad and siblings, I blissfully washed dishes as usual. (We first lived without a dishwasher in Nagasaki, and have never seen the need for one ever since. Saving the planet one fork at a time, dontchaknow.)

One evening, Dan propped Ben in the basement's yellow beanbag. Sam kicked goals at Dan, Ben mutely reffed, and Sarah toodled around, while Enya blared. I joined to watch the high jinks. Ben arm-danced to *Orinoco Flow,* waving even his weak right arm high. We looked and sounded almost the way we had except for Ben, stuck silent in a beanbag.

Sail away? Oh, Enya, how badly I wanted to. Crash upon a shore? How I longed for the shore. This lonely, sickening treading of water, head barely held above choppy seas, buffeted by grief-strength gales, exhausted. And I couldn't even see shore. I agreed wholeheartedly with Jane Austen's Lydia, "If one could but go to Brighton!"

No seaside vacation on the near horizon, we thought resuming our previous lifestyle would be our best attempt at recovery. We gradually began attending church. I found it both uplifting and draining, as folks poured attention upon us. Often appropriate, a nod, a welcoming smile, a brief word, a light touch on the hand, but sometimes not. Unhelpfully, people offered trite, perky, yet heartfelt, Christian lingo, and once, worse.

Smashed into the wall, squeezed tightly in a stranglehold of love, I could barely breathe. A woman's breath, sibilant in my ear, spoke soft, urgent words, imploring God on my behalf. Sucking my remaining energy. She meant well, comforting me in her own way, but for naught as it was not my way. Touch my fragility at that point in time, and I disintegrated. She could not read the invisible sign "Do Not Touch, I Am a Shattered Woman." She did not see, or feel, my life force ebb. Or, if she did, I suppose she interpreted it as melting into her soothing arms, when I only surrendered to her strength. I had nothing with which to fight her off. When she released her grip on my body and left, I slid down the church wall to recover from her mission to strengthen and encourage me.

For five weeks, my mother returned daily to care for Sam and Sarah, while I took Ben to day therapy. He slept at home, but worked at the hospital Monday-Friday rehabbing with Psych, OT, PT, and Speech all day long.

Starting in Comaland, and for years after with rehab, I became so accustomed to driving the four miles to the hospital that on the rare occasions I wouldn't take the exit, it felt wrong. Awash with freedom, I'd feel a little naughty, driving furtively like an escaped convict, one eye keeping the hospital in my rearview mirror. But I wasn't the only one in 1996 having dreams of hospital freedom.

Ben articulates now, "When I was in the wheelchair, and couldn't talk, whenever I went to the hospital, I would gaze into the big silo barn painting when we went past it in the hallway on the way to rehab. It reminded me instead I could be out at the farm, watching my grandfather and grandmother making a prairie."

But Ben's therapies paid off quickly, and his leg muscle strength improvement allowed orthotics to fashion his first AFO. He evolved from using a walker, to touching his PT's finger, to nothing but spotting, and soon learned to climb stairs, useful in our tri-level home.

OT worked with his weak right arm and hand. He practiced picking up beanbags and plastic bowling pins, and dropping them. He tried batting a plastic soccer ball, throwing balls, arm-wrestling, and holding on to the ropes of the therapy swing, all grueling work for a non-working wrist, hand, and fingers. OT also fashioned an arm/hand/fingers-stretching splint for him to sleep in at night.

Ben found babyhood, round two, coupled with craniotomy recovery, brutally tiring. Unfortunately, he yawned a great deal through Speech. Particularly susceptible, one of his therapists frequently did too.

Holding a mirror for feedback, Ben relentlessly practiced vowel sounds, consonants, then putting the two together. Hit or miss, a lot of miss. Hours and hours of index cards with pictures on them and verbal prompts from the therapist might result in "ah-mmm." Or "mmm-oh." No matter what, he earned a "Good, Ben!" It broke my heart to watch, but I never averted my eyes. (I attended every PT, OT, Speech, and Psych rehab session, leery of leaving my vulnerable boy's side.)

Speech therapists thought perhaps unconnected phonetics bored Ben, so using flash cards and mimicry they tried to prompt natural phrases, like "I love you," or "Your turn," while playing a game. To elicit spontaneous words they tried, "This is Mr. Potato Head's...?" and "When Mom gives you a treat, you say...?"

Who would learn first to speak intelligible sentences, Ben or Sarah? While Sarah babbled incessantly, outside of Speech Ben remained almost perpetually silent. Sometimes he answered "no," a word Dan taught him. Once, he spontaneously spoke "tie," after playing checkers with Grandpa Syrup.

Then, mid-spring while driving him home from the hospital, sitting at a stoplight, Ben attempted another word without any prompting, "ssssop." When the light turned to green, he said, "gggo!" Talk about distracted driving, I about ejected out of my seat. For each light he told me what to do, "sop" or "go," then grinned from ear to ear. I have never been so thankful for hitting reds in my life, in fact, I hoped for them. Ben kept up his habit from that point forward.

Late in the spring, he vocalized "sssssomm-sssssing." We froze. Ben wanted to say something! It became his attention-getter, and we hung on that lone, drawn-out word. Ben's face would screw up, and his mouth would work, emitting unintelligible sound. Or else, not surprising, knowing his previous life's constant flow of communication, trying so hard for more than one word at a time came out as nothing. We tried to access his thoughts via yes/no questions, intuition, and charades, but most often Ben resigned himself to incomprehensibility. Frustrated, he would sigh, but wouldn't cry, become angry, or sulk. We apologized for not knowing what he wanted to say, and then told him to tell God. Ben wasn't alone. We celebrated the few times Ben came up with a word, or we understood.

A resident thought that since Ben's leg muscle strength recovery occurred in quick fits and starts, perhaps regaining speech would happen the same way. It did not. (We found out years later that Ben's speech remained nonexistent for so long even the therapists doubted he would fully regain it. Thankfully, they hadn't told us.)

Residents, doctors-in-training, occasionally spoke of what they knew not.

"Hmm. He's going to need knee surgery," announced one resident confidently that spring. My heart dove to my stomach, somewhere near the bottom of the North Atlantic. Only a couple months off from the craniotomy, now Ben required knee surgery? When? Before or after brain radiation in sunny California? The resident decided we'd better trip on down the hall to the orthopedic surgeon and get things moving.

The veteran surgeon wiggled Ben's kneecap this way and that. Shockingly mobile, it caused my stomach to flip.

“Perfectly good example of a child’s patella,” came his curt diagnosis. (To be completely fair, Ben did require a complete knee overhaul, titanium nuts, bolts, screws, and chainsaws, albeit nine years later.)

But from that moment on, I decided to never let a Latin-speaking Doogie Howser Wannabe rattle my world with firm residential pronouncements.

In preparation for Ben’s re-entry into academia, a mega-meeting between Ben’s hospital rehab team and school district personnel occurred in March. Super Principal arrived with the largest entourage of personnel the hospital team had ever seen. (We do live in the “Good Neighbor City,” after all.) RehabDoc, RehabPsych, and all therapists gave reports to their counterparts in the school system. School occupational, physical, and speech therapists, the school psychologist and nurses, as well as a social worker and special and regular teachers, all helped craft Ben’s first Individualized Education Plan (IEP).

Just before spring break in late March, I visited Ben’s second grade class to prepare them for his return. I asked the kids to communicate with each other without speech or writing, and to use their non-dominant hand to perform a task, all challenges Ben faced. A therapist had filmed Ben practicing speech, and I played the video. Kids could see the new and improved Ben, gruesome scars and all, and hear him struggle to speak even one word, his name. Prompted by the therapist, “My name is...” he failed time and again, rolling his eyes, shaking his head in frustration, grimly smirking in disgust. I explained although Ben seemed so different, rode in a wheelchair, and had an AFO on his leg for standing and minimal walking, he still loved to laugh.

Ben returned to class in early April, and the kids did not disappoint. In particular, one David, Two Tims, and The Twins took Ben under their wings. He'd met them first in kindergarten. Ben remembers, "In kindergarten, I thought if I didn't do anything, step up and say 'Hi, my name is Ben,' then I would lose friends, just like I lost them when we left Japan."

Japanese kindergarten, yochien, begins at age three and lasts three years. Ben experienced one year of yochien in Nagasaki. One day, while driving him to school on a rainy day, he observed, "Mama, the windshield wipers are saying, 'Nureru pantsu, nureru pantsu, nureru pantsu.'" I asked him to translate. "Wet pants."

Ah, so. His yochien teachers said the same things I did to a boy who never met a puddle, faucet, sprinkler, hose, or body of water he didn't embrace as he did humanity.

Despite the language barrier, Ben had made friends in yochien. His outgoing personality in US kindergarten brought him friends for life, handy at the end of second grade when he couldn't speak at all.

Soon, school staff tweaked Ben's IEP, as the initial plan for half days in hospital rehab, and the other half at school in class with an aide, did not work. It tuckered him out. Super Principal helped us navigate, allowing Ben to receive academic therapies in lieu of all classes.

On April 21, my mother moved back in for two weeks to care again for our healthy two. Only three months out from Comaland, Dan, Ben, and I flew to California for attempted glue embolization. Docs hoped to completely close off the AVM, or at least reduce it for better radiation results. Leaving the cold, rainy Wisconsin spring behind, we landed in California with hopeful, yet chilled, hearts.

We met first with Stanford's kind, and funny, BlueEyesNurse. Ben remembers her as the "nurse with the bluest eyes." I remember her like I do Favorite Nurse: nurses who cared for me. (A few years later, I met another wise nurse at a party. She knew some of Ben's story.

After we briefly spoke, she tenderly embraced me, "Deal gently with your self." I wept in relief, although I didn't understand her words. Not then.)

The brain glue made it across the Canadian/US border, but not into Ben's head. Another angiography, using dye, revealed glue would block arteries taking blood to good parts of Ben's brain, causing more damage. This really disappointed CA Doc. But, since February, the AVM had already shrunk. Now, two smaller sections remained, improving chances for a successful radiation.

Over the course of eleven days, the preparation for radiation required experts in Stanford to perform Frankenstein-like science right up *Bill Nye the Science Guy*'s alley. We played up that aspect. "Ben, you get to participate in a science experiment, like Bill!"

A dentist, part of the prep team, took a mold of Ben's mouth to manufacture an unwieldy bite-block. It would be attached weeks later to an apparatus in LLUMC, to keep Ben perfectly targeted. But first, anesthetized Ben wore the bite-block through a CT scan. Stanford docs also implanted four titanium screws into his skull, as markers for radiation accuracy. (These screws came in handy during Ben's sassy teen years, when I accused him of having not one, but four, loose screws.)

While we waited for the screw placement to finish late one night, only two others remained in the pediatric surgical waiting room. A man, killing time, struck up a conversation with me, while his chagrined wife looked elsewhere. For the first time, I played the game Which Is Worse?

"What are you here for?" "Where are you from?" "How long are you staying?" he pumped. They were in hour seven of their son's eleven-hour surgery, one of many repercussions from spina bifida.

"It's worse, I think, in your case," the man commiserated. "You started with a perfectly healthy child, and boom! In our case, we knew from even before birth what we were up against. We had time to prepare. You didn't."

I failed to see how our situation ranked worse, and said so. Ben had 7.5 years of normal childhood before "boom!" We bantered a while, then called it a draw. His wife didn't contribute anything throughout the entire bizarre exchange. Guess she didn't feel like playing.

But the game doesn't have to be played with a partner; I often played it afterward like Solitaire. Mulling it over, I based my final conclusion upon the wisdom of our ancestors, those women and men who suffered commonplace illness and death of children. Their meager silver lining, a communal, pervasive understanding of suffering, shared experience often labeling them "never the same again."

For me, the odd-man-out feeling of not really being understood by peers and family, and thus not fully belonging, partly ended in 2009. "You're their rock, you're the matriarch, now. They're looking to you," a friend counseled, the summer both my sisters' worlds blew apart, one a widow at age forty-six, the other pregnant with a special needs child, viability iffy.

"You'll be able to show them how to walk the path of pain," Psychotherapist encouraged.

Rock? Not really. Matriarch? As eldest sibling, I saw the title fit. As for the path of pain, I considered myself a well-seasoned veteran with vast expertise. Yet I secretly labeled myself Twisted Sister. Hurting for them, never wishing pain upon them, yet so relieved my sisters had joined me in the sacred hush of suffering. They understood me in a way they never had, a beautiful gift that could not have been wrought any other way.

Perhaps my generation of suffering women is better off than our ancestors, my imagined communal camaraderie only an illusion. We of the 21st century are allowed to seek help, speak of our anguish, and admit and exhibit our emotions. Most women I know from 3Rs class were raised to stuff theirs, expression of feelings taboo. Some of them, now in their twilight years, are finally finding their voices, speaking the pain of their childhood and young adulthood hearts. What a privilege to hear.

As for playing Which is Worse? family lore recounts Eliza Wildman McDermott once observed, "Never ask a prairie woman how many children she had. Ask her how many she saved."

Had I lived during her era, neither of my boys would've been saved.

I patched our Northern California accommodations together between my extended family (whose car we borrowed) and Dan's, and the welcoming home of friends of Pastor M's. They lived twenty minutes from Stanford, and we came and went as hospital brain procedures dictated. The family owned a dog, and Ben played therapeutic fetch, standing for fairly long stretches.

Between appointments we had a four-day break, so drove north to Santa Rosa, to sightsee and stay with Dan's aunt, uncle, and cousins. Dragging a hospital wheelchair with us, from there we took brief day trips with Ben to see the sequoias, Sonoma vineyards, and Calistoga, where we viewed a geyser and petrified redwoods. At Bodega Bay, site of Hitchcock's *The Birds*, we ate at the restaurant where Tippi Hedren once sought refuge. Outside, a smirking Ben stood next to a whale head bone wearing his cap to protect his tender post-titanium-screw-embedded head from the sun. I asked him to remove it, revealing the bandage and mesh covering on his shaven head. The sign next to both bony heads reads, "Notice the blow hole." (Yeah, Mom's humour noir.)

At the beach near Bodega Bay, a park ranger gave us a temporary disability-parking sticker. He suggested getting a permanent card. Impossible to push the wheelchair through sand, Dan carried Ben to the beach. We watched sadly. What would our boy, no longer able to run through waves, do? We brought no beach toys, but seeing Ben's obvious plight, a woman offered to share her child's. Ben didn't need them. He dug lefty. And dug. One-handed, our seven-year-old dug a hole to Japan. It would become his favorite pastime on future family vacations.

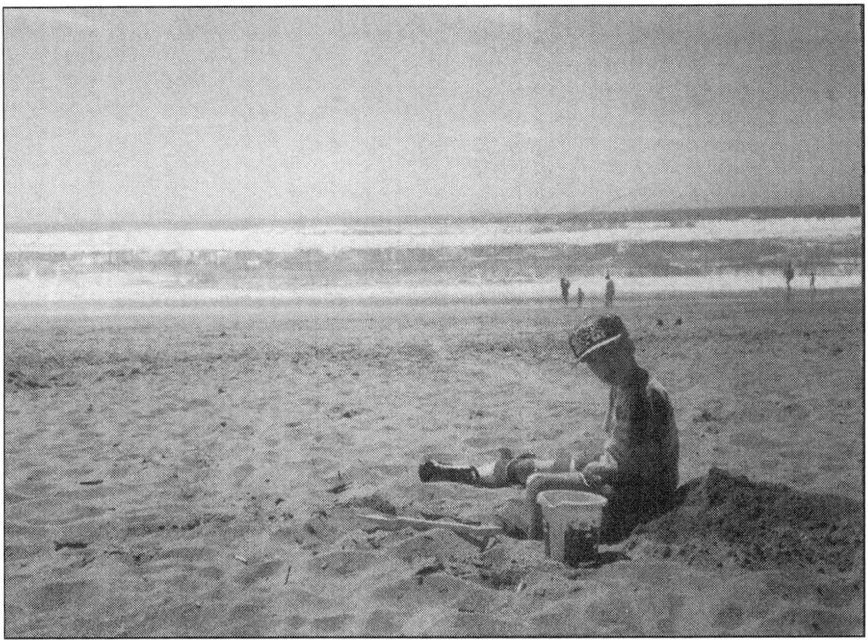

After the beach ranger's temporary card, I thought rehab docs, nurses, social workers, somebody should have a practical checklist for caregivers, number one, applying for disability parking. The idea shouldn't fall to a ranger 2000 miles from our home. Next item on the caregiver list, have you considered psychotherapy? And what about respite? In fact, I believe hospital staff may have broached some caregiver support topics with me early on, but at that time I couldn't hear them and didn't understand the road I walked.

California radiation prep finally concluded, without mishap we flew our newly titanium-laden boy back to Wisconsin. Titanium does not set off security beepers at airports.

While we were gone, according to stickers on Sarah's calendar, she had cut two bottom molars. Grandma Jo ensured I wouldn't entirely miss my baby girl's milestones, unable to focus on anything but Ben. Besides bonding deeply with her grandmother, Sarah had also become attached to rubbing soft cloth against her nostrils, preferring Grandma Jo's scarf. But the corner of any cloth would do. When I rocked Sarah's soft, malleable body, she often shared her comfort. Looking into my pained, distant eyes, she would raise the corner of her baby blanket to my nose, rubbing gently.

Sam, too old for Grandma Jo to keep a calendar, had coped in his own quiet way, with Legos and protecting and playing with his sister. To this day, Sam is Sarah's protector extraordinaire.

In May, between April's Northern California prep and June's So Cal radiation, Ben played a little at school. All the second-graders put on a major event, The Second Grade Circus. With aid, Ben slowly headed the circus parade, dressed as a clown, carrying a large sign with his left hand, "Our Circus Is Here." Through sweet and sour tears, I watched sixty children perform; thrilled with Ben's participation, yet disappointed. I figured the boy he'd been would've made a great second grade ringmaster.

Ben, The Twins, and Two Tims

In mid-June, we returned to sunny California, flying into Orange County. The trip started off goofy. While we were airborne, a cockroach climbed my leg. A violent storm, first stranding us at O'Hare, caused a midnight So Cal arrival, then late rental car drive. For the four of us, it felt like 2:00 a.m. Sam came too, Disneyland bound.

LLUMC's PhysicistDoc, a kind man who directed much of the radiation, proclaimed himself a perfectionist. We believed the German scientist-doctor. "I vill make it pahfect," he stated, relieving more of my fear. (We have used this phrase often in our family, in deeply affectionate remembrance.)

Dan signed the radiation permission sheet; we understood the risks. It made me sick. Radiation had to be perfect, or disaster would strike. Even so, disaster might strike.

Under anesthesia, Ben received half doses on consecutive days, several proton beams focused on the AVM. The radiation odds offered 80% chance of success with a 6-7% chance for undesirable complications. The negatives could begin as early as six months post-radiation or even twenty years hence. More loss of speech (not yet even regained), and increased right-side weakness seemed the most likely. But the long list of awful possible outcomes included loss of vision. We did not take lightly subjecting Ben to this dangerous hoped-for cure.

Doctors declared the radiation "medically successful," accomplishing the procedure as planned. Two or three years would pass before we'd know if the malformed blood vessels in Ben's brain had thickened, shutting down the main portions of the AVM. A domino effect, docs hoped, would close all the tiny feeders leading out of the main AVM. MRIs every six months would monitor Ben's brain.

Just before the trip, for Ben's home rehab, we'd received our first computer from a local charitable trust. I discovered email, launching my more-than-decade-long habit of sending updates to our global support network. When we returned, I debriefed everyone on the So Cal radiation and our day at Disneyland.

Doctors orders limited Ben to shade and mild rides, but Disneyland's generous policies for those with disabilities allowed us to wheel Ben to the head of lines. Once, Dan took a break with the boys, allowing me to wait in line for an hour. When the magic of Splash Mountain ended, I didn't want to get off or return to reality. *Everybody Has a Laughing Place* and *Zip-a-Dee-Doo-Dah* looped bittersweet in my brain, all summer long.

Chapter 14

One Damn Thing After Another

June Birthday Week, both boys' cakes offered ambivalence. The last time I custom-designed a birthday cake, the night ended in emergency craniotomy disaster. But I kept to my tradition. Every year, I created the cake each kid requested, painting with frosting on a simple sheet cake. As she grew, Sarah chose things like an orange truck, another rainbow, girl with an umbrella stomping in a rain puddle, and a collie. The boys first ran through the gamut of every ball imaginable, then branched out into orca, waterfall, and motorcycle racer (Sam), and Gila monster, boy in field with butterfly net, and bird-eating spider (obvious). That summer, June's Disneyland trip fresh on their minds, I had only enough energy to frost Sam a Goofy and Ben a pirate. A few weeks later, I let the boys have their friends over for a belated celebratory squirt gun fight. To level the playing field, because Ben couldn't yet run, we gave him the spray hose to douse his friends. From that year forward, the boys' parties featured water balloon and squirt gun fights, Ben granted special dispensation to use the hose and buckets.

Ben's summer rehab schedule at the hospital dropped to Monday, Wednesday, and Friday afternoons. On the other days, Dan and I helped him with his home PT and OT exercise programs. We'd do so for years.

Ben and I slowly walked through hospital halls to and from his nine hours of therapy each week. UW Hospital City's population numbered well into the thousands, and we always met people Ben knew. His face lit up as he greeted each with a hug and an enthusiastic "Hi!" – one of his few words. The network of hospital supporters included spectator docs, not Ben's own. Much later, after Ben's speech finally returned, one such doctor yelled down a hall, pointing back at Ben, "Sales, Ben, sales!" Years later, Ben took the doctor at his word. On his own, Ben won a middle school prize for selling the most fundraiser coupons. Most were to medical personnel.

By late summer, Ben practice "ran" in hospital halls for PT. Fifteen yards winded him easily. He tried running a bit in our uneven backyard, and then on the sidewalk. Beautiful. Until he fell on his face, requiring an x-ray of his arm. Not broken. But even walking caused falls, from imbalance and an easily tripped, weak foot. Over the years, Sam occasionally burst through the door after school announcing a fall. Once, I shocked Sam, bolting barefoot to scraped-up Ben sprawled on the sidewalk. Falls still accompany Ben in adulthood. One winter, he fell off the steps of a city bus as it pulled away. Lying in the snow, crying, unable to get up, he says it took ten minutes before someone from his college noticed and helped. He relies daily upon the good will of strangers.

The last month of summer 1996, Ben partly regained childhood. OT gave him a Joe Cool Thumb Splint, made by the Joe Cool Company, named after Snoopy and Joe, a boy with Traumatic Brain Injury. (When Sarah's vocabulary increased, she referred to it as Ben's bracelet.) Ben wore it during the day to hold his thumb out, opening his closed-fisted fingers. He couldn't wiggle his fingers, but Joe Cool allowed him to better grasp the chain of a swing, swing a Whiffle bat, and hit a tennis ball the length of our yard. Best of all, Ben could wrap his hand around his bicycle handlebars. Boosting Ben's self-esteem, Dan taught him how to ride again. He learned to put his right foot, which often fell off the pedal, back on while still riding. His AFO, stiff from the knee through the toes, did not allow his ankle to hinge. PT expressed surprise at how well Ben learned to bike and run without flexing. By early autumn, Ben's muscle tone allowed orthotics to fashion a hinged AFO, allowing more freedom.

In August, Sarah put her first two words together, "hot tea." But Ben beat her with four words, all in proper order, and shortened pauses between each. I didn't record the sentence, only that he spoke it barely better than a toddler.

Ben still required help getting in and out of the bathtub, and bathing; imbalance still prevented his showering. After rinsing the bubbles off, I handed him the hanging showerhead to monitor his speech improvement. How quickly and smoothly could he yell his life-long, end-of-bath custom, "Who shut the water off?"

For months, only sad, dead silence. Then slow, mixed-up attempts, but by late fall he hit almost normal speed. Would the UW grant me a Speech Ph.D. if I submitted my incredibly scientific method as a dissertation? Recovery Life With Ben should result in some sort of degree, I felt, even if only honorary.

Dan deserved another diploma as well. Using an old ESL trick called "backward chaining" he helped Ben pronounce multisyllabic words. To this day, Ben employs the method to better ingrain pronunciation in English, as well as other languages. Breaking down the word in reverse: tic-tis-sta, then statistic. Tadh-us, then ustadh, "teacher" in Arabic.

Dan and I celebrated Ben's gains true to form. The return of his sports buddy revived Dan, and Ben's increased ability to express his thoughts resuscitated me. However, Ben's attitude dwarfed ours much of the time. Uncomplaining, he worked hard at his new lot in life, taking his disabilities in stride, our happy, smiley Ben.

Boo, my sister ten years my junior, the first baby for whom I changed diapers, flew back for her wedding in August. I wanted it to be the first day in seven months I wouldn't cry. Wedding? Boo's? I didn't stand a chance.

The rehearsal filled me with laughter, but on our way into the rehearsal dinner, her imported pastor pulled me aside to recount how they'd all been praying for Ben. Thanking him through tears, I quickly shut him down. No focus on Ben's trials, not on this weekend! He apologized that his intended encouragement caused me pain. But mostly the weekend brought a smile to my lined and exhausted face.

At the wedding dance, my father sang Irving Berlin's *Always*, a love song he'd secretly practiced for months. Driving forty minutes to and from work, at the top of his lungs he had diligently prepared to serenade his wife and three daughters. At his insistence, we stood at the head table while he crooned beautifully. None of us knew he could sing. We choked. He didn't. But those were happy tears. Then a Packer-jersey-wearing dude on a bet crashed the reception at UW's Memorial Union for one dance with the Bride. Even better, Ben led the conga line and we danced the night away.

The brightest twenty-four hours since BC. Before Coma.

Third grade began at the end of August, and with it I glimpsed a mirage. Because of the new schedule, I thought I'd catch a big break from Recovery Life With Ben.

During the summer, Ben's hair grew back, no scar visible. He walked slowly, and could speak short, simple sentences, so we hoped his third grade classmates would adjust easily. Yet, he sounded like a baby and I was concerned he might be teased, discouraging him from further attempts to speak. On orientation day, his teacher allowed me to give a short account of Ben to his classmates and their parents, buying good will.

Right away, school staff implemented a new IEP. Among other things, it granted Ben Monday noon dismissal, allowing him to rehab at the hospital for three hours. We went after school on Wednesdays, as well, but had to quit in November; too taxing.

IEPs, federally mandated by the Individuals with Disabilities Education Act (IDEA), are conducted at least annually with school personnel and legal guardians. IEPs set goals and provide variously disabled students with extra school support. For example, Ben's lengthy IEP required school personnel to pull him from class for Special Education in reading, writing, and 'rithmatic, as well as PT, OT, and Speech, as related to academics. An IEP-provided aide accompanied Ben at all times. Someone even watched him at recess, as he stood while his classmates ran. In addition, Ben did not take Wisconsin's standardized tests, did not participate in gym (attending PT instead), and was allowed longer time for homework completion and tests. Tweaking throughout the year, requiring another convening of parents and personnel, sometimes occurred.

Expensive? Absolutely. Time consuming? Definitely. Crucial? Yes, for those children requiring extra assistance to learn. Taxing? Unbelievably. Ben's anxiety producing and depressing IEP meetings mostly kicked off the school year for the next decade. Thankful for the school support, still I found the meetings brutal as we focused intensely on how Ben struggled, differed from his peers, lagged behind, and how the gap continued widening in some subjects. (Ben never heard; he didn't attend IEP meetings.) Each August, my heart melted with the heat of a new IEP, new teachers and/or an aide to train, and new sets of problems for Ben.

Fall of third grade, staff conducted extensive multidisciplinary-team (M-Team) testing, to determine Ben's cognitive and academic abilities. He achieved a first grade reading level, but sixth grade science! We owed it to Bill, Bill, Bill...Bill Nye, that kid-friendly scientist. We counted ourselves lucky. Ben had barely received academic instruction since mid-January, and suffered cognitive damage when the AVM burst.

Ben wasn't the only first grade reader in our home. Supposedly, I mothered two other children. Late summer, I decided to home school Sam for first grade, as I had Ben, ostensibly for the same reason – a strong phonics foundation for reading. Ben and twenty-month-old Sarah demanded my attention. Contently quiet six-year-old Sam fell through the cracks, inducing a heavy dose of motherhood guilt. Sam and I slogged through phonics, but primarily we became reacquainted. I've never regretted it.

Ben's next surgery ambushed me. An oral surgeon waltzed into our lives because of a late summer, routine teeth cleaning. At age eight, Ben still sported his top two baby teeth, the central incisors. I wondered why. An x-ray revealed two honking molar-like mesiodens: extra teeth blocking the adult incisors.

"Nooo!" I wailed loudly, my head in my hands, when our dentist told me. He knew me well – another high school homeroom chum of mine. The mesiodens, he explained, required surgical removal. More doctors? And because of Ben's unusual head, for safety everyone insisted surgery must take place at the hospital, under anesthesia.

The oral surgeon seemed excited by the prospect of removing the mesiodens on an AVM patient. I asked if he'd prefer to pay us for the privilege. Naw. I didn't. I just wanted to.

The news felled me. In the entire population, 1-4% had hyperdontia (extra teeth). Neurologic AVMs affect about 300,000 Americans, only 36,000 of whom will have any symptoms, and only a fraction of those will have debilitating or life-threatening symptoms. Ben's yet-undiagnosed ADHyperactivityD, another issue. Mesiodens, AVM, ADHD – all unrelated conditions.

Who had put this kid's head together, anyhow? I had a few ripe suggestions. Especially when it took three more years before Ben's adult teeth even began to drop. His annual song, *All I Want For Christmas Is My Two Front Teeth*, lasted through four Christmases.

Would nothing come easily for my firstborn?

Honestly, nothing seemed to be coming easily for either of us. Rehab isn't sexy. The on-the-seat-of-your-chair thriller of January 1996 morphed into drudgery, turning the summer of '96's deep sorrow to fury. It stayed with me for well over a decade, waxing and waning according to how dire the damn straits.

Attempting to stop the anger and previous eight months' details from rattling around inside my head, I wrote nearly every weekend that fall. A heartbreaker of minutiae I called Purge I and Purge II. They acted as cathartic kryptonite. (Thirteen years passed before I again could read my words, and even then they sapped me.)

Sue, mother of The Twins, began checking on me regularly, partly as sounding board and dumping ground, and partly to encourage me spiritually. She supported my writing out the angst. We kept up our habit for years. She held my hand through some awfully dark days and did her utmost to be the friend I needed.

But no one woman could be that friend other than the one trapped inside me. Until my late forties, I didn't even know she existed. Instead, I remained defined by Ben's trauma, hating life as Ben'sMom-cum-CaseManager, unable to find my way out. A woman, forgetting to whom she spoke, once thoughtlessly remarked of suffering women like me, "Mothers of special needs children, they just don't get any better!"

She might not have known why, but I did.

It's the routine that's a killer, I wrote in Purge I, fall of '96. *Keep going, going, going....We have hardly had one week since Sept. 1 that hasn't had an additional medical appointment as well as the usual 2X/week rehab. Neurosurgeon, dentist, oral surgeon, AFO casting, AFO fitting, AFO fitting II, and pre-surgery exam. Next will be the October teeth removal and nearly a whole blown week of school because of it. In November the EEG, and in December the MRI. Of course there are labs, phone calls, etc. for all this stuff too. And follow-up appointments.*

In addition to the medical interruptions, there are the scholastic interruptions. M-team meetings, testing, and homework that takes so long because, well because it does.

And of course there's the usual rehab. PT keeps on "Now, every day I want you to do this exercise ten times," in addition to the ones Ben's already doing. And OT says, "I want you to do it this way now, not that way." And everyone says, "You could do this at home. It just takes a few minutes."

We've been maxed out of "just a few minutes" for months now. We can't add any more. I need to say so, but I haven't. So, the stress to fit it all in is constant, and it's impossible to do. I am angry for Ben. When does he get to be a kid who can do what he wants? All day long someone is telling him what to do. He needs time for himself.

At school and at the hospital, meetings concerning Ben focused on what was wrong. Ben's life brimmed with specialists, each expertly in charge of their square inch, trying their best to improve him. Good, helpful people earned their livings this way, with noble, if impossible, multiple goals. Even perfectionist me could see rehabbing Ben could become a crazy-making killer, but for Ben's future life, he had to do it all, and I had to help him, head down, plowing.

I "had" to help others too: elderly neighbors, other kids, various groups of women, and four other members of my family. My inability to say "no" to people, perhaps especially to myself, spread me waiflike thin. Would I ever ask of a friend what I asked of myself? I found myself a hard taskmaster, with unrealistic and misplaced expectations, born of perfectionism, fueled by my chosen faith tradition, and rewarded by feeling useful. People asked me to lead/join various groups at church and I agreed every time but one. Church and hospital staff asked me to visit other patients from time to time, since I was "already there." Eager to redeem good out of Ben's bad, and to remove myself from always being the needy one, I agreed to check on sick kids and families I did not know. Yet in hindsight, "doing my rounds" at the hospital added to my frustration.

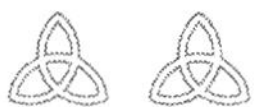

Simultaneously, my mother's ovarian cancer screamed, "I'm baaack!" Her diagnosis, surgery, and chemo, first arrived within six months of our return from Japan in 1993. In recession when Ben's head blew, she continued to be my go-to person for babysitting while I took Ben to all the appointments a professional patient required. The fall of 1996, more surgery and another round of chemo put her on babysitting sabbatical. Just before it, she sent me a card.

Under two small boys, playing with a toy boat and string on a lake pier, the outside of the note card reads, *"Thinking of You,"* inside, *"A beautiful day to you!"* In between are my mother's words, written in her lovely script:

Dearest,

When we talked – and cried – I couldn't think of what I always want you to know. That is, I'm always thinking of you and wishing there was someway to help ease your burdens. I guess my vases of flowers for you are meant to bring a spot of comfort and beauty.

It has always been my pleasure and delight to stay with the children whenever you wished. Sometimes I can't and unfortunately that will happen more now – much to my sadness and displeasure.

The day we stood in the driveway and you told me how much you need me I couldn't bear to tell you about my tumors. You know I am going to do my very best to be here for you for a long time.

So Much Love, Mom

Several times a year, I pull this note, a bit bent and stained, from its hidey-hole in my oak roll-top desk. Whenever I miss her because I have great news to share, or more burdens I wish she could help me carry. Seeking warmth, I rub my thumb across her words, so fortunate she wrote them before the age of computers, with their sterile, uniform typescript. Her script floats her face before me, "Kathykins, I love you!"

But that fall Mom had her own battle to fight. My angry Purge II diatribe continues:

So, there's the stress of finding someone for Mondays (and the other appointments that crop up continually) to watch the kids. Not to mention it's my mom we're talking about, and I don't feel I even have the energy to be sad for her at the moment. I can only focus on what her absence means to me, and my family. Anything beyond that is unendurable. We just found out Ben's teeth are coming out via general anesthesia in one week. I didn't freak. My mother has cancer again. I didn't freak. What I feel is sort of a calm (grim?) resignation. So this is real life and welcome to it. I'm with whoever said, "Life is one damn thing after another." The stress level continues to rise, like floodwater. Sometimes I want to put my head under and drown. But I don't know how. The storm doesn't look like it's going to let up yet. I need an umbrella. Sometimes I burst and a lot of anger and cursing comes out. Usually I'm marching along grimly to the beat of the drum that's being banged out for my life right now.

At the start of the '96 NFL season, I snail-mailed a letter to Green Bay Packers HQ requesting gifts for a sick boy and his brother. (They sent a team printed-autograph football for Ben, and a pennant for Sam.) I mentioned that Ben chose yellow Velcro for his new AFO strap so I could write "Go Pack" on it in green, and told them we expected Brett Favre to throw a boatload of touchdowns. Fortunately, he did not disappoint any of us, including Ben's OT.

Part of Ben's rehab included signaling "touchdown." Sundays, Sarah learned with her brother how to say, "Tuh Duh!" her arms raised in goalpost formation. She even extrapolated. Whenever she saw a football, or a Packer in uniform in *Sports Illustrated*, or even a Green Bay Packers logo, she signaled loudly, "Baw-baw tuh duh!" Arms up! Practicing just like big brother Ben.

The Pack went undefeated at home, finishing with a 13-3 record, boasting the highest-scoring offense and fewest points allowed on defense. (A feat accomplished once in a blue moon in the Super Bowl era – as in twice.) Then the beautiful thing happened. In the playoffs, they first knocked off the San Francisco 49ers. I sent Niners' fan, Stanford's BlueEyesNurse, appropriate ear-ware, converting her, at least for the Super Bowl. How could she resist wearing dangling cheddar wedges? Those bright spots, culminating in the Super Bowl win almost exactly one year after Ben survived the emergency craniotomy, allowed us to weekly expend some pent-up emotion.

But mostly, 1996 sucked. Counting a medical calendar year from October '95 to October '96, Ben underwent anesthesia ten times. Much more than most kids annually even receive antibiotics. After day therapy discharge in March, Ben attended over 100 medically related appointments in nine months. And that's counting OT, PT, and Speech as one three-hour appointment. Not just Ben needed the docs in 1996. Even excluding him, our family endured a ridiculous amount of bizarre. The medical appointments, for Sarah, Sam, and me piled on, Sarah, a case in point. First, she damaged a tooth from chewing on a Disneyland souvenir light saber the day after our return from radiation. The pediatric dentist said she wouldn't lose the tooth, "that's for sure." Gone the next morning, we never found it. Next, impetigo on her toes, and for a grand finale, she broke out in hives in December while we attempted to vacation at Koo's house, and then on the Florida panhandle. On that same trip, the rest of the family, self excluded, simultaneously succumbed to a nasty GI infection. Ben started it, explosively, in a hotel room. We tried to clean it up, and left a big tip. I spent Christmas day mopping up and flushing toilets.

Still, ever publicly upbeat, the last line I wrote in my 1996 Christmas letter elicits violent Elsa Snorts now. "The grieving process has pretty much run its course, we think, and we're living with a new and futuristic perspective on life."

(Oh honey.)

In her thank you for the earrings, and response to my much-expanded Christmas missive, BlueEyesNurse wrote, "Reading your schedule makes my head spin! I hope you have a boring 1997."

I did too.

Chapter 15

Thank You, Domo Arrigato, Gracias, And Cheers

In my behind-the-scenes administrative role at WESLI, I work closely with a group of women at various times throughout the year. I fondly refer to them as The Team, never more so than when I run English proficiency testing six days a year. Those days, I start and stop multiple-choice tests for up to eighty new students, running two stories of stairs for hours on end. Dividing the higher scoring students into groups for an additional writing test, I am privileged to slaughter the names of people from everywhere around the globe. Especially those from China. Not a chance, until I learned "xi" is pronounced "she." Or Thailand, where national law must decree birth certificates display first and last names with a minimum of fourteen letters each. The testing day job is a perfect match for a highly efficient, fair-minded, detail-oriented, good-humored, take-the-stairs control freak. (I like creating order out of chaos, but you wouldn't know this by opening my kitchen cabinets.) At the end of the day, I check to make sure students have not written in the test booklets. They sometimes don't understand my slow, clear directions, shaking head, and frown "Do Not Write In This." It's the worst part of my job, and not just because of the erasing. I especially hate Test Q, with its fill in the blank questions, "Why is Katherine's house always_______?" (Dirty.) And, "Why won't Katherine help Paul_______the windows?" (Hint: it's not open or close.)

In mid-October 2011, with my hubby-boss's permission, I corralled The Team for a brief meeting having nothing whatsoever to do with work. They all knew Ben well.

"The Boss down the hall has just given you clearance to take thirty minutes off work on the twenty-fifth, and walk over to the museum for this!" Hitting the mega-spots on the invitation the museum had sent to me, I read "press conference," "national significance," "VIP speakers," and "introduction of a valuable community friend."

"But what's it for?" "Who are the speakers?" "How are you involved?"

"I can't tell you! Gotta wait." A good-natured groan went up.

"I'm so excited," burbled one, "that I won't be able to focus on my work!"

"Yeah, I've had to sit on this since the early part of September. It's making me crazy. It might be crowded though, so you'll have to herd together."

"Gaggle? Can we be a gaggle instead?" asked one.

You gotta love working at an ESL school.

The MCM invitation allowed me to share only tantalizing information, but for my sanity I had to relay the full story to someone. Of course I had told Ren.

(As Ben so aptly put it, "Telling people gets rid of some of the pop fizz.")

Three weeks before the press conference, Ren called. We rarely managed to connect first try. "It's a beautiful day here," she said. "I thought you might be on one of your walks with your cell, so I tried. I've got ten minutes before I coach swimming."

"It's a beautiful day here, too, and I want to be on one of my walks, but I can't right now," I sighed. (So easy to slip into self-delusion and non-choice thinking.) "My life has been rearranged again."

"How so?"

"I'm not having the fall I thought I'd have. I'm helping Ben a lot, to cope with the news, and going with him to appointments. I helped him edit his bio, and I'm writing how this whole deal unfolds, and I'm leaking what I can to my friends here –"

"Ah," she interjected.

"So, I invited two friends this morning, one on the phone, one in person. Leslie I scared badly, emailing to see if I could pop by to tell her something. You know her, the actress, my friend from middle school? She looked awful when she answered her door, expecting I had bad news. After I told her she said, 'But you don't get good news.' She's so happy for me and she can come to the press conference! But I'm not inviting very many of my friends, a bunch are working, and some of you are a flight away, and I'm not expecting anyone to –"

"But I'm coming."

"You're –?"

"I got my plane tickets already!"

I screeched "*What??*" eight times, hitting C sharp octave by octave. "Ohmygosh! And I was already car dancing today! What am I gonna do the rest of the day? It's a good thing I have a massage scheduled after Ben's psychotherapist appointment."

"I wanted to surprise you, I wasn't going to tell you, but it just seemed right."

"Oh yeah, it's right." Thank heavens the woman told me in advance. Ren materializing out of thin air would've caused emotional circuit board overload.

I shuddered to think of it. It had precedence.

The previous fall, on her fiftieth birthday, her husband planned a surprise party for her, and I flew in as secret guest – double surprise!

Hiding in a quiet lair, I watched from the darkness as guests arrived. I didn't want my presence to detract from her friends' greetings, and they didn't know about me. I intended to sneak out after things settled down, and mingle unobtrusively in the crowd of thirty or so. Sooner or later she'd stumble upon me. No rush.

I heard the initial cheers upon her arrival, and a quiet speech, followed by happy buzzing. I held my ground. Someone tapped on the bedroom door, cracking it open.

"Kath, I want you to carry the cake to her," Ren's husband whispered.

"Cake? I don't have a cake," I glanced uncertainly around the dark bedroom.

"No, I've got the cake. I'll come get you soon, and then you can carry the cake."

Seemed simple enough. But me? Carry her cake? Didn't he know my propensity for klutziness? I'm the only woman I know who's taken out a hallway thermostat with her shoulder while racing upstairs. Some days, it's safest for humanity if I just sit still, removing the danger to self and others. Cake-carrying theatrics I hadn't counted on, but should've expected, dramatic guy that he is. Breathing deeply, I gave myself a pep talk and at the opportune moment, after another tap on the door, I slipped into the empty entryway undetected. I figured I'd have to walk about ten feet with the cake.

Wrong. He handed me the enormous, towering chocolate cake on a pedestal, topped with fifty, anorexic, flaming candles. Ren's eleven-year-old daughter grabbed the glass base, while I held the top, starting to sweat. As we walked, the candles flickered and one extinguished. We slowed. From the other room the crowd sang as we shuffled, my eyes glued to the spluttering flames, gauging our speed. Ten feet through the hallway, turn, and then I saw the gauntlet of strangers, like the cheerleaders' entrance for a football team. It looked the length of a field too. I snuck a furtive peek, where was my friend?

The singing ended, and we continued our funereal procession pace in what seemed like mournful silence. Except for my pounding chest and dripping armpits.

But where was my friend?

As we approached the end of the crowd, I spied her, off to one side. We made eye contact briefly, and then she glanced away, a frozen smile on her face. Some women noticed and started laughing. She hadn't recognized me. Puzzling over the shaking confection deliverer, Ren was flipping her mental Rolodex, "Who is carrying the cake? Which of my friends suffers from MS?"

No, at the press conference, I did not want a repeat of last October's uncontrollable trembling. What a party this October would be! Glitter and streamers from heaven! And some of my posse of women would be there with me, for me, drowning in the colors, the light, the confetti, the cameras...the cameras.

Oh. My. Gosh. The. Cameras. What if, as Mother of Ben, they stuck a mic in my face?

I needed a tune-up from Psychotherapist.

Since 1999, off and on, mostly on, psychotherapists have played a leading role in my life, teaching me new ways to see through life's prism. Accordingly, I went to discuss the bits and bobs raked up again, things I thought I had put to rest, topics I had not planned to revisit the fall of 2011 – the whole roiling mish-mash of triggered feelings.

And I had an ulterior motive too. Goose bumps, chill bumps, making arm hairs stand on end, that's how people reacted to Code Cheese. Ben's basic story from 1996 also had often induced involuntary physical reactions in others. Second only to inspiring laughter, I guess I loved raising bumps on folks' arms. Friends, family, acquaintances, anyone would do. But psychotherapists especially.

After mentioning her oath of professional confidentiality (just as a friendly reminder dontchaknow), I began telling her Ben's news, intentionally leaving the words "First Lady" and "White House" for the end. Watching her, just as intently as she had watched me for five years, I saw her eyelids flutter while her pen hovered.

"Hah! Your eyelids flickered!"

What fun messing with Psychotherapist! Fun wasn't always part of our time together, but enlightenment and relief were. Over the years, practicing the word "and" was one of the best things she taught. I thought some of my life problems had concerned my vision: seeing life as black and white. Thinking it over, I decided that wasn't so. I naturally saw black or white. "Or" excludes, divides, and overlooks paradoxes, uncertainties, and the blurring of life. "And" allows for ample mixing – this and that can be true at the same time. Psychotherapist taught me I could be a good mom *and* not attend Ben's next medical debriefing. My years with her enabled me to navigate the gray of life, empowered me to see choice, and encouraged me to resist victimhood. When I first met her in 2006, we worked on managing Posttraumatic Stress Disorder (PTSD). Among other things, she said, "You forgot to breathe," and, "Maybe God wants more for you than a trauma-based relationship." She taught me that trauma fragments and remains thus without processing. But processed trauma is narrative.

On this day, again by asking questions, she dislodged me from faulty thinking, helped me sort, decipher, and plan. She did not tell me what to do. Equally important, she did not tell me what God wanted me to do.

"Thing is, what if the media asks me questions? After Dan, family, and friends," I continued impishly, "I would want to thank my Hired Help."

Psychotherapist knew my term of endearment for my string of therapists, psychiatrists, yoga and tai chi instructors, massage therapists, and a chiropractic kinesiologist. These professionals had taught me over the course of a decade how to listen to, and care for, myself. Not selfishness, but self-awareness, strengthening me to function well in caring for others. I'd paid a pretty penny for their priceless assistance in processing, helping to put this Dumpty together again.

"Thank you" is quite safe, always safe, right? But whom else would I publicly thank? Obviously, Yahara House and Madison Children's Museum, but don't forget personnel from four schools, one college, and the significant chunk of humanity who'd invested medically in my son. I held a love-hate relationship with the latter. Loving they were there when we needed them, liking them as people, but hating we needed them so much. I found my ambivalent emotional attachment to medical professionals disconcerting, yet knew I owed them the most heartfelt thanks of all.

As with those first-time Oscar-winners who never want to leave anyone unacknowledged, the exit violins would play long before I ever reached the end of Ben's cast of thousands. Why this stressing? I'd be lucky to even squeak one "thank you" out of a choked larynx. If the media wanted a tremulous mother's response to Ben's upcoming DC trip, and I still had my voice, I'd say, "Thank you, family, friends, well-wishers, and professionals, very much, all of you. Present, past, and undoubtedly, future. You know who you are."

If no one asked my opinion, well, I'd just have to insert a chapter in a book, including a tip of my hat to the long list of county, state, and federal taxpayers, as well as the United States government.

Much of our family life boiled down to, "What is best for Ben?" (And secondarily, "Can Mom handle this?") Too often we lived hard pressed to choose between the proverbial rock or hard place, fire or frying pan, mortality or morbidity.

We always chose the brutal ground, sizzling metal, and damage.

Ben's rough life came with a thin silver lining, a gift from the federal government. Bless the inclusive Americans with Disabilities Act of 1990, defining disability as "a physical or mental impairment that substantially limits a major life activity."

Major life activities include work and play, and I tossed the ADA card whenever it suited, enabling our family to safely participate in fun events together. We'd paid dearly for this benefit. Disneyland. Coldplay concert. Brewers baseball.

NFL football tickets could be another. Packer policy fall of 2011 allowed me to purchase only four ADA tickets, wheelchair-only seating. The Pack was on a winning streak and Packer nation envisioned its continuation. The Christmas night or New Year's Day games I knew we wouldn't be at *The Freakin' White…!* One day I talked it over with Dan while he was at work.

"Well, so what should I do? Which game?" Both had advantages and disadvantages: timing, weather, watching archrival Bears, or the until-this-year immaterial Lions. (Tigers didn't feature.)

Dan analyzed, "January first, we may have the season wrapped up, so starters might not play at all. Or, we could be playing for all the marbles."

(Marbles? Puries, cat-eyes, or jumbos?) Really, I preferred beating the nemesis Bears on Christmas night – what a present for the kids and me. On the other hand, a noon game, possibly accompanied by weak sun to kick off the New Year? Either way, we didn't call it the Frozen Tundra for nothing. Our butts would certainly freeze to the bleach– bingo.

"What's best for Ben?" I rhetorically asked. No choice whatsoever, New Year's Day meant warmish (heavy on the ish), no messing with Ben's sleep regimen, and less chance in the light of his getting hurt by tipplers in the crowd.

"Do you think he's gonna be okay with being in his wheelchair if he doesn't need it?" Dan asked thoughtfully.

"We'll just explain he has to bring his own seat. There isn't any other way. The ticket-seller said Ben had to arrive in his wheelchair for ADA. It's not like the concert or ballgame where there were no disability strings attached in order to get the extra space he needs."

Ben had gone to Lambeau once, as a kid with his cousins and Sam. Rows then had been all right. Now, row seating at sporting or other events with frequent traffic posed trouble. Even if only model-thin, alert, sober people shuffled by him all day long on their way to pee, purchase, and pee, it endangered his weak AFO leg. And I'd been to enough Wisconsin events to know better. He also couldn't sit smashed in rows with excited folks jumping up and down, leaning backward into his leg, or dumping their stadium seats on his foot. Surgeons had hinted more surgery was in Ben's future. We didn't need it hastened, certainly not with a trip looming to meet the First Lady.

We/he – the pronouns became interchangeable. What happened to Ben deeply affected us all. Yet, in our search for familial inclusivity, because of ADA we could enjoy extraordinary experiences with the most extraordinary member of the family.

After I purchased the four tickets, Dan emailed, "Well Done, Mom!"

I replied, "After we get into the stadium, Ben can stand and cheer with the rest of us and just use his wheelchair as a seat. And if anybody decides he isn't 'disabled enough' they're gonna have a fight on their hands."

Dan sent a quite large picture of a quite large mama Grizzly and her cub, "They'll think better of it."

Lions, and Packers, and Lambeau, Oh My! Were the kids and I gonna have a great 1/1/12, or what, dontchaknow!

Chapter 16

A Woman Is A Woman

Finished with WESLI just after noon on another gorgeous October day, venturing out from my paper dungeon, into bright, white light, I blinked furiously. Ben and I would meet on the Capitol Square later. Plenty of time to stroll and people watch before sitting on the grounds to work on my laptop.

The tourists of downtown Madison are like tourists everywhere: gawking, camera laden, slow moving. If they've hit any of the local establishments during bar time, possibly slightly tipsy as well. Unless it's our state's schoolchildren on Capitol field trips: oblivious, loudly marching buddy system, on natural out-of-school highs.

A line of adult Caucasians sauntered, cameras ready, pausing to snap the impressive edifice of the State Capitol. Out-of-towners. Wisconsin Rapids? Wauwatosa? Hayward? Maybe even from south of the border, Illinois. Alton? Sterling? Savanna? Suddenly, a small phalanx detached itself, stealthily stalking en masse one of Wisconsin's prevalent residents. The common gray squirrel, referred to by one of my older friends as a "glorified rat," skittered about in the leaves, just ahead of the whispering and bent paparazzi. These folks then, presumably not even from North America. One look at their incredible shoes confirmed.

"Where are you from?"

"Italy. Milan."

"Ah. Milano." (So easy to add that vowel and speak Italian. And now I understood their shoes.)

"You speak-ah Italiano?" one woman asked in surprise.

"Ciao, arrivaderla, tanti baci, molto bene...." I ticked off my best six words, with proper inflection and a smile. "Hi," "bye," "many kisses," "very good."

"Bella Italiano! Bella Madison!" she returned with glee.

"Grazie!" I spoke the seventh, and last, Italian word still lingering in my head from college. For good measure adding in English, "Welcome to Madison."

Walking past the delighted Italians, I heard speechifying coming from pink-clad, pink-beribboned folks on one Capitol corner, surrounded by pinkified law enforcement, elected officials, and fire fighters. Pink cops in October meant only one thing, breast cancer awareness. My nose twitched. Could there be any freelance hometown story here, for Instant Media/Reporter At Large?

Reaching the corner just in time for the break-up of a very large group photo op, I spoke to the local Susan G. Komen for the Cure executive. After giving me twenty seconds of lovely quotes, she handed me a copy of her speech encouraging women to take ownership of their own breast health by making healthy life choices. Then she quickly pointed me toward a lone Middleton cop waiting in her squad car for the Parade of Survivors to begin. One female from my town, just enough of a feature angle for my editor to approve.

The officer hastily scribbled her name as the fire trucks, motorcycles, bicycles, horses, and cancer survivors moved forward. We'd connect later for the story.

As I turned, I spied Joe Parisi, our new Dane County Executive. I'd been meaning to drop by his office, to congratulate and offer him copies of the speeches Ben and I had given the fall of 2010. Joe hailed from my hometown, but I hadn't seen him since high school. I approached impeccably gray-clad, distinguished Joe, much as the Italians had earlier stalked the gray squirrel, and caught his eye. (But I didn't implore him in Italian to sit still on his haunches so I could take his picture.)

"Hi, Joe. Do I look at all fami-"

"You look *really* familiar."

"Oh, good. I hoped so." I spoke my k-12 name, and my big girl name.

"I thought you looked like someone I went to high school with," he said.

"Right. I just wanted to say how glad I am you're our county executive. I have a son with multiple disabilities, he recently got connected with Yahara House."

"Ah."

"I was going to stop by and give you copies of the speeches we gave at last year's county budget meeting. We didn't have to testify for them this year, thank goodness, but maybe you'd like copies? For your files? It was really nice to see you."

"Thanks for introducing yourself," he finished graciously, shaking my hand.

Then, spur of a nanosecond, as I often decide and articulate my most memorable ideas, I gabbled, "My son and I are going to be part of a press conference soon. I don't know the who's-who list, but maybe we'll see you there!" Capping off my cryptic pronouncement, I grinned enigmatically, or leered, displaying some strange visage to bolster Joe's new impression of his old classmate. To my credit, I did not rip off my seven bits of Italian, although Joe, being a Parisi, probably would've understood. Leave 'em clueless and wondering – that's my motto.

Soaking up the sunshine on the Capitol lawn, fingers flying across the keyboard for my latest feature, sipping my soy chai tea latte, extra hot, no foam, Ben arrived as planned. We had more government paperwork to fill out. This time for the Code Cheese direct deposit per diems. And more press conference to discuss as well.

"You know those doctors you wanted to tell? I didn't email them yet. You wanna call now?"

Suddenly bolting upright, he dug in his pants pocket for his phone. "What? Where is it?"

Oh. No. He had called me earlier, so he mentally retraced his afternoon path. After checking WESLI's lobby, no luck, he returned thinking hard.

"I sat over there, in the leaves."

"I'll call it." I punched buttons as he ambled over to a leaf pile, kicked around with his shoe, bending over to rustle with his hand. Dejected, he walked back hunched, suddenly holding up his phone, beaming at me mischievously. Drama king.

The next thirty minutes I spent Elsa Snorting, listening to Ben leave one message after another, on one specialist after another's voicemail: RehabPsych, Speech Therapist, OT, Slim Jim in the Gym (PT), then RehabDoc. I'd never had so much fun with Ben and the medical world.

"I've got really great news," Ben exulted. "The children's museum hired me and that's not all. But I can't tell you! Watch the news on October twenty-fifth. I'm going to be in a press conference!"

For Chief Neurosurgeon's assistant Ben added, "Tell him, 'Thanks for operating on me!'"

I hoped she wrote that down verbatim.

In a little, black dress a woman could never be over- or under-dressed, or so I once read. But I didn't own one, and at age fifty, it was about time, eh? I felt my mother would approve. She grew up relationship rich, yet materially poor, during the Depression. It hadn't helped that her dad died from strep throat when she was seven. (That explained her high anxiety any time we three girls complained of a sore throat.) Mom saved everything and penny-pinched her way through life, except when buying experiences and classy ensembles.

Generally speaking, heck, even specifically speaking, I hate shopping. With. A. Passion. I am a destination-only shopper. Need a red top? Goodwill, clothes organized within size by roy-g-biv, rainbow order. Need a vintage sweater? Agrace HospiceCare Thrift store. Local resale shops abound, so many brands all in one spot. Thank you for doing the spadework, ladies! But, unbelievably, I'd been "skunked," as my father would say, looking for appropriate White House-wear on earlier resale shopping excursions. Where next?

Requiring my mother's touch, on a Saturday morning I took my daughter to State Street. The charming, pedestrian-friendly street offers outdoor cultural education, brief forays into eclectic money laying-out, big time people watching, and punctuation by indie coffee shops. I don't categorize this as shopping.

Another 80-degree October day (how odd!), Sarah and I meandered through the isthmus' Farmers' Market to get to State Street. Is there anything better than spur-of-the-moment purchases of a robust rosemary plant, and $5 faux gold, tiny, coin earrings inscribed, "Queen Elizabeth The Second," atop Cleopatra's bust?

As a woman now seriously on a mission, I dove into a new women's clothing store. Perhaps it contained the dress of my dreams. It did not, but I looked around anyway. It was...umm...the clothes were... umm...I tried on...umm. I'm not really sure. Attracted by the oddities, my picks kept getting nixed.

"*No*, Mom, you can't wear that skirt with that jacket." "*No*, Mom, you can't wear that jacket with that top." "*No*, Mom, you can't wear that top with that skirt."

The clerk agreed, quizzically shaking her head, "No, no, no." What, then? Wrong store? After Sarah repeatedly trampled my fashion sense, ever so helpfully she held out a top. No sides. Plenty of bangles down the front, though.

No luck anywhere, we tried one more store, Citrine. If only to touch the long, pretty dresses. A yard across the threshold, turning my head to the left I spied it. Elegant, throwback, sweetheart bodice, slit-pencil-bottom. Little. And black!

"Fit me, fit me, fit me," I ordered. It did not. A medium; how could it not? (Perhaps it was runway medium?)

"Let me try our other store," the clerk offered. Success! However, upon arrival, I found State Street mistakenly asked Hilldale to put aside another medium. No larges available. Rats. Foiled again.

"What about this swing skirt bottom," the clerk offered, "with the identical bodice?" I put it on. And bought it. And bought black, way-shiny shoes.

"*Mom!* Those heels are really high," Sarah pointed out the obvious.

"They're the lowest they've got, and they look so cool with this dress," I countered.

"*Mom!* How are you going to walk in those?"

(Umm, carefully? Mincing steps? Holding onto walls and plants and things?) "I'll figure it out," I retorted stubbornly.

"*Mom!* What about your knees and your sports PT?"

(Shut. Up.)

Back home, I fashionshowfashionshowed as my mother had taught me.

Dan commented, "Cute."

"Cute?"

"Uhh, wrong word?"

"Elegant was what I had in mind."

"Nice. You look nice."

Good gravy McDavey. I needed women. Should I take a pic and zip it via the airwaves to my cousin, the one who'd threatened to sign me up for *What Not To Wear*?

Sure, my closet no longer contained voluminous denim jumpers, which I'd worn ubiquitously during what my sisters labeled my Prairie Woman Phase (long, stringy hair complementary). No Mom Jeans hung in my closet either (got rid of those after watching the *Saturday Night Live* sketch with a snickering husband). Not many sweatshirts were left, deep purple or otherwise. And no bright, white tennies with laces (if you don't count the ones I use for rapid walking). But I still required serious fashion help.

Happy Psychologist then.

With four others, Happy Psychologist and I composed a Group of Authors. Or rather, as author wannabe, I tagged along in their bona fide Group of Authors. We met once a month to discuss our latest submissions, editing for one another. Including Chris Hollenback, up and coming thriller/mystery writer of the Casey Thread series, currently in press. Editing his first book enabled me to add another item to my Reverse Bucket List – I have written one word of a mystery.

The first time Group of Authors met, they'd hauled out their published works, and I shrank. But that evening, after Happy Psychologist had explained her memoir, she and I exchanged furtive eye contact, and I'd blurted, "Maybe we can be traumatized writers together?"

After reading her astonishing words, *Notes From Nethers,* which explains growing up on a sixties commune, approximately forty-seven billion detailed questions jostled, two pressing to the fore. "Do you regret writing all this personal stuff so it's out there forever?" And, "Do you ever get harassed by your readers?" (No and no, please?)

In addition to her words, I also admired her ensembles. Accordingly, we met at The Great Dane, both close to her office and Citrine, so I could first return the shoes. The return policy gave me a week's grace period to think, but after having paraded around at home for, oh, say thirty-seven seconds, I knew the shoes flunked. My knees, my PT, my propensity for tripping even barefoot – all added up to a disappointed heart, but a safer existence. Assuming whatever shoes I wore wouldn't trip me up the stairs, skinning my knees in *The Freakin' White...!*

As Citrine's clerk refunded my money, a different group of dresses caught my eye, prompting a rash, three-minute-try-on, second-dress purchase. Two options!

Happy Psychologist's twelve-year old daughter joined us for a mid-afternoon snack. The girl shook my hand firmly, looked me square in the eyes, and, since she planned to purchase an electric guitar the next day, announced with great poise and authority, "There's no way you can acoustically play *Back In The U.S.S.R.*"

She had a point. In fact, because of her myriad points I forgot she was twelve, and asked if she played any Jimi.

"Who?"

"Okay then, Foster the People?"

"Who?"

"They were on *SNL* the other night." (Not that I actually stayed up to watch *SNL*; we taped, yeah, you read that right – as in VHS.)

"*SNL*?" the girl blurted in confusion.

As a rule, I never attempt to chat up the tweenie set, especially not invoking Jimi, *Saturday Night Live,* or the cleverly disturbing lyricism of *Pumped Up Kicks*. It just makes me feel old and tired. Let it be a lesson to me.

Happy Psychologist volunteered that Electric Guitar Girl had an eye for fashion, so we all toodled to my car, checking out Little Black Dresses Plan A and Plan B.

They loved LBD Plan A, but holding it up, I had grave doubts. Hanging in a plastic bag all day in my car, not bunched up, but not perfectly flat either, the flare bottom had wrinkled. A lot. I switched to LBD Plan B.

"Definitely this one," stated the Hendrix-deficient girl. "I'll tell you why."

And she did. She was all over the neckline, saying it would be so flattering, making me look as if I have a long neck. Which I actually already have, so I wondered, "Will I look too giraffe-like?" She assured not.

Then I enumerated its wonders. 1) It was bumpy. All over. So when I spill it won't be so obvious. 2) This dress had bumps. Everywhere. So when I run into walls and such the smudges won't show. 3) The multitudinous bumps embellished my scrawny, boyish figure. 4) The bumps, tessellated across the dress, would easily hide wrinkles. Including my fifty-year-old knobby, crunching knees!

The three of us glowed at little black Bumpy Dress.

Back home, fashionshowfashionshow, I wowed Sarah and Dan. Unanimous, Bumpy Dress wins!

Now for my glass slippers.

I bought four pair of shoes, fashionshowed them, and settled for mulling over two, pondering a question of grave import. With Bumpy Dress, should I wear the low-heeled, sensible, yet lovely, classy shoes? Or the minimally vampy, cut-away, higher-heeled shoes, with what Dan referred to as "I-don't-like-those-flowers" on the peep-toes?

Happy Psychologist and I met again, this time sans daughter. She made an emergency house call, and I modeled classy shoes first.

"Oh! Perfect. They look great with that dress."

"I've got one more pair to show you. They've been rejected by my family, but I said, 'Well, we'll just see about that.'"

While I was changing shoes upstairs, she read the museum's official press conference invitation on my laptop. I wanted her there. Would I, at any other time in my life, invite a woman I'd gone to lunch with only once? But a memoir counted for years' worth of lunches. We should all have memoirs to hand out to potential friends. It would save a lot of time. (Or not.) Besides, she had picked Bumpy Dress.

Reading bits and pieces of the invite loudly, "Announcement of national significance! Valuable community friend! Media questions at 9:15!" she finished with, "This is so strange. What a funny invitation!"

"Yeah!" I hollered. "It's so cloak and dagger. I'll be glad when this part's over."

"But," she argued, "you're pretty cloak and dagger yourself. Serves you right!"

"You know I'm just going to quote you?" I teased, clomping knock-kneed in the vamps down the seven wooden stairs, holding onto the banister for dear life.

"Oooh! I *love* those shoes! I'd wear those shoes." (Of course she would.) "Is it for evening?" she inquired. "For evening, they'd be perfect."

"Umm, daytime," I considered. "I think. I dunno yet."

"But is it an event? Like a reception? Will there be food?" she persisted. She really loved the vamps.

"I don't know about food, but it is an event and the venue, is ah..." I replied with a twinkle in my eye, leaving my words hanging. I really loved the vamps.

What would the First Lady like? Classy or slightly vampy? Did the women of the East Coast even think a Wisconsin woman could fancy it up? Not counting Milwaukee, home of *Laverne & Shirley*, our closest metropolis is Chicago. The women there had dressed to kill since the days of Al Capone, getting off trains, and out of big cars, all dolled up in Wisconsin's then mobster-infested North Woods: big hats, big shoes, incredible outfits, putting the duds of the Up North women to shame. (I know this because my ancient neighbor lived there just after John Dillinger's hey-day and heard the stories.) Now, our North Woods remained mobster free, except when *Public Enemies* filmed at Little Bohemia Lodge in Manitowish Waters.

Our hunting women toted rifles just fine, but dress up? Some Wisconsin women feel most comfy in shapeless hunter camo, neon orange, and/or Packer jerseys. Self almost included. I never mix blaze orange with the green and the gold. (I don't hunt.) I wanted to knock 'em dead in DC, nicely, of course. Or, more accurately, blend in.

The First Lady hailed from Chicago, not too far south of Milwaukee, right across the border. Her full name is Michelle *LaVaughn* Robinson Obama. (Did she have a friend named Shirl? I have two.) Now First Lady Michelle had a fashion team behind her. A newsfeed recently reported the fact. Under a photo of the fit and strong transplanted First Lady, the caption read, "stunning," and "fashion team behind her." (Not literally, of course. It would detract from the stunningness.)

My possible two pairs of shoes left only one burning question. Just how many banister-clutching steps in the White House would I have to navigate? Naw. Classy Shoes win!

(Mom? How'd I do? D'ya think First Lady Michelle will like my Sparkling- Bling-Bumpy-Dress-Classy-Shoes ensemble?)

The Middleton police officer and I met in the parking lot of our new police station for the breast cancer feature interview and photo op. She explained she'd participated in the Justice for the Cure event at the Capitol to honor her beloved aunt who had succumbed to the disease.

Asking her to position the squad car sideways for optimum lighting, I attended to the colors just in case my editor didn't go with a black and white: cream brick background with red ivy, pink plastic ribbon on car's antenna, pink ribbon decal on door panel, pink beribboned officer next to door.

"Is the squad dirty?" she asked nervously, grabbing a cloth, wiping down the doors. "Can't have a dirty squad! Of course, I had a cleaner squad for the parade. Can you see this dirt?"

“Uhh, it’s probably gonna be a black and white picture in the paper, so I don’t think anybody will notice.” I didn’t notice the dirt in living color. (That’s not saying much.)

“How’s my hair? I’m having a bad hair day,” she voiced her next concern. Blonde hair up in a ponytail, I failed to see how a ponytail could possibly have a bad hair day. (But I didn’t say so. She had a gun.)

“You look fine!” I complimented.

I took several pictures and then she interjected, “Was that a fake smile? Are any of them fakes? I don’t want to have a fake smile!”

“Umm, this one here looks good,” I guessed, but I couldn’t completely tell on the small digital screen, even with my reading glasses. It looked like an honestly smiling woman with a blonde ponytail, pink medallion around her neck, wearing black shades to complement her badge-enhanced, navy-blue, polyester uniform, and black, regulation-issue footgear. Packing heat.

(I saw no dirt anywhere.)

Backing up in my car to leave, clobbering on my window startled me.

“Can I have copies of the pictures? To give my mom?”

Thank goodness the shots turned out beautifully.

A woman is a woman is a woman.

Chapter 17

Death Is Not My Friend

I am in a quandary at this point in my treatise of triumphant woe. How much do you, Dear Reader, wish to get bogged down in the miserable mire of Ben's life? I mean, I am so sick of it. And from it. And exhausted. Mon pauvre petit garcon, Ben! Thus, I offer you a prescription: Rx ad lib prn. (Rx: recipe, "take," ad lib: ad libitum, "as much as one desires," prn: pro re nata, "as circumstances require.") To make Life With Ben easier to swallow, I promise to regale you with happy-happy and humor.

Dog or cat?

To reward Ben for maintaining an incredibly upbeat attitude in his year of ridiculously hard work, subjection to numerous rounds of torture, all after miraculously surviving an emergency craniotomy, we offered to buy him a pet. Thus far our pets had numbered gold and beta fish. He asked for a dog. Knowing full well who would be responsible for walking, feeding, vetting, grooming, and toileting a dog, we counter offered cat. (My comfort level was much higher with willfully independent cats that didn't require my energy. Besides, "cat" had not been the species chasing me down as a four-year-old in Oklahoma, nipping my butt.) Ben accepted. Golden Brown Pancakes, Goldy, became our already spayed, ex-feral, fractious pet for the next twelve years. She'd languished, caged, for two months at the Humane Society before we took her, figuring her feisty nature suited our family. Picked up on a country road by someone whose house already brimmed with animals, Goldy's rescuer had recorded pertinent information, "This cat doesn't get along with anyone."

Goldy found home with us just in time to watch the Super Bowl – a great Packers trounce Patriots omen! Unfortunately inaccurate, as death began and ended 1997: Dan's grandfather, great aunt, and father, Lou.

I missed seeing my father-in-law for the last time as the family gathered in Illinois for deceased Great Aunt Mary's funeral. The night before, I waited for three hours to be seen in an After Hours Urgent Clinic. The alarmed doc almost sent me by ambulance to the hospital, instead hooking me up to IV antibiotics for forty-five minutes. I agreed to forgo the out-of-state funeral, returning instead for day two of high-powered drugs, opting for timesaving injections. Nurses counted to three as they timed double cheek stabs. Making it ten yards to the waiting room, I suddenly seized up, butt refusing to let my legs work until my muscles gradually thawed. Stuck home alone, grounded with a strange infection, I mourned with the rest of the world the day "we" buried Princess Diana, and the family buried Aunt Mary.

Lou's light went with him two months later, but residual, radiant beams live on. I see them in Dan's wit and eyes, but especially in Ben, whose character mirrors salesman Lou's. The day he died, in post-surgical recovery, one lung removed, the other sickly remaining, Lou hallucinated nine-year-old Ben perched on the end of his bed. Lou and Ben, a pair of the shining people.

With perpetually twinkling, bluer-than-the-waters-of-the-Minnetonka eyes, Lou emitted the brightest aura in any Perreth family gathering. Drawn to his light, we sought to be pleasantly zapped. He expertly exercised Irish raconteur, holding the conversational reins.

A joke waited upon his lips, a song queued in his lungs, and a quip hovered at the ready. Lou involved his whole body in the pursuit of making us laugh.

When we lived in Nagasaki, Lou made a point to write weekly. His long letters on yellow legal paper acted like rays of sunshine.

My father-in-law, Lou, and my own father, the jolly pair of them never met a hand they didn't want to shake. They descended full-bodied in Ben, a double portion, sparkling eyes and all. The kid had no genetic choice but to talk again.

Every year, Ben's speech slowly improved in fluency, vocabulary, idioms, and expressions, and at age twelve, courtesy of braces hauling down his front two teeth, pronunciation.

Throughout elementary school, Ben steadily achieved academic and other gains. Staff pulled him for Special Ed and therapies according to his IEPs. But slogging with Ben through homework after school (and his range-of-motion exercise programs after dinner), weighed heavily, sucking a fair chunk of time, energy, and emotion.

Ben's internal drive and bonhomie carried him. He insisted on running the mile with the rest of his class, even though he practiced PT in lieu of gym. Unable to run that far, annually he finished gimpy, blistered, but victorious. Fiercely independent, nine-year-old Ben taught himself how to tie his own shoes, so his mommy didn't have to. I watched in awe the day he waved me off, his right hand assisting his left.

OT gave up on Ben's right hand becoming anything more than a helping appendage. In addition to shoelace tying, his right arm/hand helps these days by flipping light switches, closing cabinet doors, bolstering carrying things, and giving great hugs.

In addition to the splint he slept in to keep his fingers, hand, and wrist stretched, Ben's rehab team soon fitted him with a thigh-to-toe night cast. The two halves fastened by Velcro, positioning his leg and foot to grow correctly, hopefully preventing future surgery. Rrriiippp! Rrriiippp! Rrriiippp! On a nightly basis Ben removed the cast, and often the arm splint. Whether 11:00 p.m. or 2:00 a.m., we awakened to the telltale sound of a child seeking freedom. Rarely did Ben make it through the night, and our guts clenched in anticipation of failure, especially his perfectionist mother.

As a quickly growing boy, every three months he required a new night cast. Between that, casting for new AFOs, fashioning new arm splints, continued therapies, and other doctoring, the hospital remained our home away from home. Setbacks, like postural scoliosis caused by his uneven gait, added further therapy. Aiding his weak leg via different experiments, like zapping his leg muscles at home with electrical stimulation, added more contraptions to Ben's boyhood, taking up more time. My heart soared every occasional gain, no matter how irrelevant to ordinary life. After 2 ½ years of rehab, Ben stood on his tippy-toes one day. My reaction prompted him to warn me prior to attempting anything else new, "Mom, don't cry!"

(Ah, but I still did. On nearly a daily basis.)

One gain deserved a kazoo band. After almost three years, doctors weaned Ben off anti-seizure medication. It took five weeks. Christmas morning we paraded noisily as he received the blessed present of no pills. It would be short lived.

Stealthily, in the background of Ben's hectic rehab life, lurked the AVM. Chief Neurosurgeon debriefed us after each of Ben's follow-up MRIs, sending the films to So Cal. After reviewing, PhysicistDoc regularly emailed his opinion. The first MRI report, June 1997, concluded, "Benjamin's AVM is progressively obliterating. We are optimistic it will fully obliterate within the next two years."

Thrilling, because if it's in writing it's gotta be true! Naw, but it gave victory of sorts; a silently melting away AVM required no more decisions from me.

Ben loved the forty-five-minute MRIs every June and December. He counted upon them, just as he did getting presents every twenty-fifth day of those months. (He had exquisitely timed his birth date.) Using MRI machines as his personal beatbox, he created songs in his head to the various noises. I sat at the foot of the machine and a mirror allowed our eyes to meet. Those reflected baby blues – I'll never forget them.

Another man's biannual MRIs oddly coincided with Ben's, and Ben looked forward to seeing him too. The man befriended Ben in 1996 when they both mutely rehabbed. Back then, whenever he saw Ben in OT or PT, he meekly burst into tears. Emptying his pocket of any coins, he pressed them into Ben's good hand. Through the years, expecting to see Ben at MRIs, he and his wife came loaded with quarters. Then they sent letters and packages. The man's daughter once said, "He used to drive truck. Now, he blubbers like a baby when he sees Ben hard at work. All sixty-five-year-old men should get a knock on the head."

Ben's less-frequent angiographies fully monitored the AVM, providing more information than the comparatively easy MRIs. Each angiography required general anesthesia, a catheter from Ben's groin, through his heart, and into his brain. Radiologists filmed pumping dye, watching it flow into Ben's brain on a monitor. Ben called the dye "food coloring." One year, he requested blue, the color of the Obi-Wan Kenobi light saber he carried on Halloween, a boom box strapped on his chest playing the Star Wars theme song. Angiographies were risky and rough on Ben. Ten hours after one, Ben still couldn't keep water down, but we received the best news in years. The AVM had shrunk so much that docs recommended one more year of monitoring. Perhaps the last 20% would disappear, preventing any further decision-making regarding Ben's incredible brain.

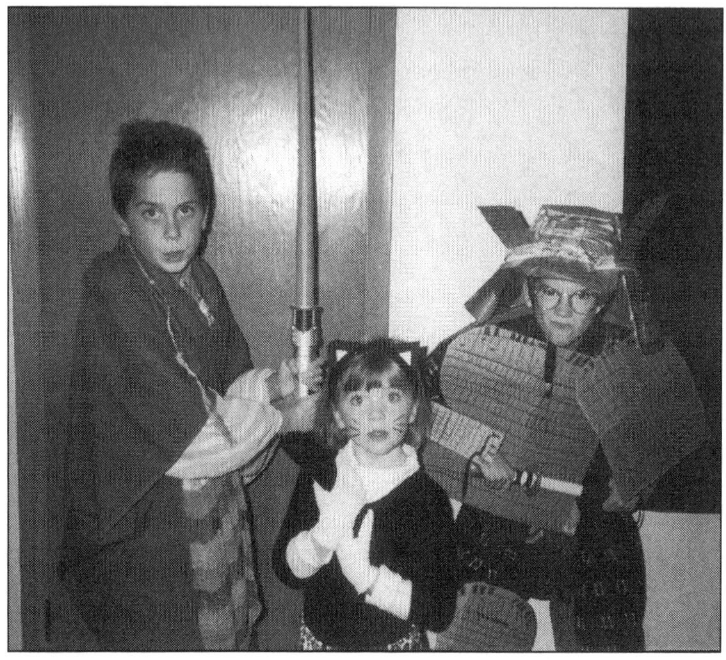

Obi-Wan Ben, Kitty Cat Sarah, Samurai Sam

As Sam and Sarah grew, their strong limbs easily eclipsed Ben's athletic abilities in many respects. Unable to play as before, they made adjustments and compromises, whether shooting hoops or playing cards, board games, foosball, or darts. Grandpa Syrup carved a wooden cardholder for Ben, enabling him to more easily play Uno, Go Fish, and later, Hearts and Poker. Sarah kept up with her boys, running conversational circles around both, but she especially latched onto Sam. He reciprocated. The two became inseparable as Ben went to specialist doctors and therapists, and rehabbed at home.

Often, Sam and Sarah had to come with me to Ben's myriad medical appointments.

Ben successfully channeled his innate athleticism with one endeavor his siblings did not. Bored one day at school, he picked up two beanbags and tossed them about, left-handed. From this humble start, he taught himself to juggle. Over the years he honed his craft, and will pick up about anything to juggle. Neighbors, no doubt, can attest to my frequent yelling during his teens, "No, Ben! No juggling of the food! Put down the fruit!"

Gregarious out and about, at home Ben often contented himself with searching for insects, reading about insects, and playing with insects, while Sam and Sarah cavorted. Multiple summers, Ben kept the quarter-sized arachnid, in its web at the edge of the driveway, well fed. (Yes, Ben, I know. A spider is not an insect.)

In the winters, I taught Sarah and Sam to ice skate, while Ben slid around the frozen rink and pond in his boots. Then I taught them downhill skiing. Ben tried it once with us, on semi-adaptive skis, tethered to a guide. The guide let go of the ropes at the end of the day, to give Ben a taste of freedom, but Ben's right leg wasn't strong enough to turn. The day finished wildly, with my swooping in to prevent Ben "skiing" into the trees, scaring all of us. But Ben could sled with the best of them, although it was harder for him to walk up steep hills wearing an AFO stuffed in an oversize boot.

In the summers, Dan threw up "moon balls" for the kids to catch, they played HORSE in our driveway, and Dan tried to teach the boys to golf. Holding and swinging the club didn't work for Ben, though. For years, Sam, Ben, and later, Sarah, played baseball and basketball on rec teams (Dan often helped coach). But Ben, unable to run well in his AFO while ball-handling one handed, had a difficult time. The same applied for batting and fielding. Sam traded both sports for soccer, and Ben upgraded to drama.

On a whim, the summer Ben turned ten I signed him up for drama through Middleton's recreation department. Ben's lengthy acting career debuted with *The Pied Piper*. On cue, he shouted his one line with gusto, "Amazing!" I wonder if his director gave him that line on purpose?

Summers still meant rehab and summer school, but mostly family vacation and drama. Drama proved to be the most highly motivating speech therapy Ben ever received, challenging memory, attention, enunciation, pronunciation, and offering reward. Oh, the heady reward of applause and laughter! Since laughter is the air I breathe, I could imagine what it meant to Ben. Those eight years of summer drama were our halcyon days. I say our, because I played too, creating props and applying make-up for the cast. Make-believe life in the theatre was *good.* Ben worked his way up in roles, culminating as a teenager with fifty-four lines as Grandpa Joe in *Charlie and the Chocolate Factory*.

One year, for a vignette musical, his directors correctly cast Ben in multiple roles as the ham. Lurching across stage as Christopher Columbus encased in a large cardboard Mayflower, his limp sent the boat crazily swaying. Yanking the microphone from a showcased singer to mimic a few high notes, Ben stole the show.

Generally, after Ben's summer shows in late July we loaded the car, driving west 1,000 miles, or Up North, a few hundred. In terms of sacred family events, vacations only rivaled nightly dinner together. In their late teens, the kids still insisted vacation begins in the dark, an early morning leave-taking, plastic cups with straws holding juice, donuts handed round. No one ever asked, "Are we there yet?" often trapped a minimum of ten hours in the car the first day, reading, playing games (no electronics), coloring, sleeping, or looking out the window. They understood long car days meant novelty at the end. Oddly, for short trips, to Thanksgiving for instance, they predictably whined, and without exception, fought with five minutes to go. But never on our marathon vacation days.

Tents, sleeping bags, coolers, camp stove, old clothes, toiletries, groceries, Ben's RX, night cast, electrical unit, night arm splint, AFO, and Joe Cool thumb splint...my camping lists flexed depending on Ben's accoutrements.

We visited Yellowstone and the Tetons, "The Faces" (Mt. Rushmore), bodysurfed in Lake Superior's 65-degree water, hiked to waterfalls, up hills, and across mountain meadows. Dan and I often carried Ben on our backs. No matter where we went, we sought water, to drink and to play in. Rushin' rivers, burbling streams, or placid lakes, water kept the five of us happily occupied. And I would go off alone, allegedly searching for moose or other wildlife, but mostly seeking healing solitude amongst the green, the blue, and splashes of wildflowers. My most nurturing minutes, spent lying on a rock in the middle of a stream (the wilder the better), allowed dancing waters to flow around me. A portion of my perpetual heartache leaked, carried downstream with the force.

Although a family tradition and love, camping included work. After Lou died, Dan's mother, Barb, snow birded in Arizona. She aided us more than once, generously providing warm air during cold winters, and true respite for me: no camp set up, no cooking, no dishes, no work, nearly responsibility free.

The closing years of the '90s brought an end to my mother's dance of death with cancer. The fall of 1998, her last, we took long walks in the UW Arboretum, holding warm hands, the leaves drifting at our feet. I thought, "This might be it. Remember this."

Under her supervision that fall, I learned ripping out plants, and digging in the dirt with my hands, helped. After Mom's death, I branched out from the back and side yards, attacking the front yard, replacing non-native Kentucky blue sod with throw rug prairies, iris, lavender, oregano, thyme, and more. Therapeutic throttling of the ground with a vengeance paid off. Dan's sister, Mary, sent a sign reading, "My Garden Kicks Ass," only true if one is fond of unkempt, botanic chaos. (This same sis-in-law, ever since my 4:00 a.m. movie-star hug in 2008, sends annual Captain Jack Sparrow birthday cards in increasing size. By the time I'm fifty-five I expect the pirate to arrive bodily on my porch. Savvy, Mare?) Later, mourning my mother's death with me, neighbor Carol commented contentedly, "I knew you'd turn out to be a gardener like your mom. When I see you in your front yard, crawling in the dirt, I see her."

Ben's 1999 Memorial Day baptism in Lake Mendota gave opportunity for the last extended-family celebration before the death of Grandma Jo. Senior Pastor, knowing my mother would not remain long on the planet, did us a family favor. He performed Ben's ceremony at the same secluded beach Dan and I had sat at, freezing in the car, during the darkness of Comaland. Seventy-six people watched Ben get dunked, and then licked creamy Babcock ice cream made from the UW's cows. My mother wore her embedded painkiller system, the pack slung over her shoulder.

All through the summer, she lay dying in the country living room, a gigantic Hospice bed taking up a third of the space.

"She can't always be dying in the living room," I thought. "If we can only help mom do this, die well, everything'll be okay."

Under our mother's instruction, Koo, Boo, and I delved into her saved wardrobe, 1950s and on, and fashionshowfashionshowed. We modeled dresses, gloves, hats, shoes, purses, and jewelry, complete ensembles. And my mother divvied it up, bequeathing this or that on each daughter and granddaughter. We played dress-ups while our dying mother applauded. Rather, her eyes applauded, her hands were too weak.

Mom's body bloated as if she were a beached beluga and her face narrowed and wizened like an Auschwitz victim. She sprang watery leaks in her legs.

"Yes, that's normal. That's called weeping," Hospice Nurse answered my shocked inquiry.

What a concept. The whole body can weep. Good to know there's more to squeezing out Life's Tears than just through the eyes. Why hadn't I known this before?

Morphine supplied Mom's nutrition. The heavy diet muddled her mind.

"Look at that – the cows got into the graveyard, again!" she would say of the cemetery down the hill and across the road. We saw only headstones, flowers, tiny flags, and a space waiting for her. The farmer's Holsteins stood safely in their pasture.

After an especially thorough ears-to-toes washing from Hospice Nurse, Mom exclaimed, "She really did a good job cleaning my lobelia!"

Mom, such a great one for gardening.

Gullible, good-natured Grandma Jo, loads of fun to tease, modeled how to laugh at one's self. And also, by taking up downhill skiing and backpacking, at ages thirty-six and forty-two respectively, taught me guts, and how to cry through hard, even fun hard.

She died without me. On our end-of-summer family vacation, camping in the Rockies, I took respite from caring for her, as my sisters had taken their turns before me. My father took his respite on August eighteenth, permanently. A National Forest Ranger approached our campsite five days after we'd left Mom. My smile vanished from my face. My legs buckled under me. He didn't need to say a thing.

Mom allowed us to get there, get settled, have a few days of fun, and then return for her funeral. Nearly unconscious when I left her, she could not have planned her deathbed better. Unless she never had to lie in it at all.

I cried through packing up camp, loading the car, and driving out of the mountains. I cried through the foothills and sage of Wyoming, through the endless sunflowers and prairies of South Dakota. If you've ever done that stretch you know how many tears evaporated in the dry, summer air, leaving streaks of salt behind. I cried through the farmland and flats of Minnesota, and down through the rolling, lush hills of my cherished Wisconsin, all the way home. And then, unpacked with wet, swollen eyes, and drove to the farm, grabbing the blanket that had covered my mother all summer, wandering around the farm, to The Rock, through the prairie, near the hammock, through the wildflowers, tears marking my trail.

And the living room was empty.

Boo told me some things happened at the end that I didn't need to see. I should consider it a gift I wasn't there, not a guilt-inducer. Wise baby sister.

Hospice Nurse told me, "She wasn't going to die while you were here. She knew how much you needed her."

Indeed, her slow demise baffled the Hospice experts. How could she possibly hang on for eight weeks? Doctors and nurses called her death imminent in mid-June.

My little ones, four, nine, and eleven, and my big one, thirty-nine, grieved the loss of their second mother with pictures and words, as I gathered flowers for her funeral with my sisters and father.

Mom died during gladiolas.

"Honey, I'm slowing down," she'd told me during daffodils, tulips, and bluebells, as I'd sat on the floor at her feet, my head resting on her knees, softly weeping while she stroked my hair.

She fought through severe pain, self-administering push-button relief, determined to drive herself in from the country to her grandkids' end-of-year school events during iris, bleeding hearts, poppies, and daisies.

Spiderwort, columbine, peonies, and lupine bloomed on her way to the hospital, for what she knew would be the last time. I watched her take a last, brief stroll through my garden, hers before it was mine.

She suffered intensely during lilies, bergamot, purple coneflower, and ox eye. Born and married during gladiolas, it was only fitting she should leave then too.

We decorated the church with glads and prairie flowers, and I read the eulogy I wrote with help from Koo and Boo. But our mother had been the first to hear it that summer. After I read her what I planned to tell the world, she said, "Oh dear. Don't you think people will think I'm conceited?"

"Mom, it's okay, these are our words, not yours."

I remember only a few things from her funeral. Poking fun in the eulogy at some of Mom's handicrafts' creations. A handful of unexpected faces from my childhood, which meant the world to me. And I remember the faces of Mom's sisters and brother. Nancy, who once told me my sense of humor had served me well (I didn't understand what she meant), Von, who wrote me multiple letters every year of my adulthood, Butch, who taught me as a child how to fly free on skis by laying down sweet ribbons in pristine snow, and Jeannie's caring touch on that day, "You look tired."

"I am," I replied. Sorrow saturating the marrow in my bones.

After her service, Mom's cortege confusedly stretched behind on the curvy, wooded back route, on the western edge of Dane county. We followed the car bearing her coffined body, decked out finally in her Plum Suit. Twenty miles out to the rural cemetery, my father rode shotgun in the hearse, choosing the long and winding road that led to her grave, the cemetery she'd watched all summer from her deathbed. Where the cows weren't. Her last drive with my father was to be deliberate, thorough, and lingering. He took the long way home.

And then we planted Mom. After the graveside prayer, I stayed behind to give her a proper covering. I wanted to grab the spade and do all the shoveling myself, but with self-restraint tossed only one spade-full of dirt onto her coffin, as if sheltering daffodil bulbs, waiting for spring.

We didn't have the custom, but I didn't care. I mumbled the right last words to myself, "Ashes to ashes, dust to dust," last rites for a gardener of faith.

That summer, as my mother had steadily declined, Ben underwent extensive neuropsychology testing. It began with an oral interview, details from me about Ben's conception forward, and then two days of rigorous testing for Ben. Neuropsychologist concluded that the massive hemorrhage might have exacerbated Ben's previously undiagnosed ADHD.

"If he were my child, I'd medicate him 24/7," he advised. But, because of the unique qualities of Ben's radiated-AVM brain, Neuropsychologist wasn't sure what effect, if any, medication would have.

I took Ben in late August to his first psychiatrist. After spending a short amount of time watching Ben happily draw and play, he explained that Ben's demeanor displayed anxiety. In children, that meant depression.

"He's depressed?" I blurted. "*I* just buried my mom five days ago."

Child Psychiatrist and his resident looked taken aback. And undoubtedly further displeased as we decided to medicate Ben for ADHD only. They wanted Ben medicated for depression and his "non-contingent good mood." We didn't. Ben's non-contingent good mood seemed a major asset. (Six years later, Ben obviously needed more than one kind of psychotropic drug. My imagination heard Child Psychiatrist then, "I told you so.")

Three weeks after burying Mom, I pulled up in the car in front of our home. Dan came out the front door, yelling, "Mom called!"

A tsunami of relief washed over me, "Great!" Quickly followed by a rush of annoyance, "Well, it's about time." Crashed by a chaser of grief. His mom, not mine. All took less time than the flash of an eyelash, as my friend used to say.

"So, everything'll be okay if we only helped her die well? We did that, and what've we got? A dead mom!" I complained, as I sat angrily crying on the curb.

Then, "She'd call, if she could, but she can't," the sadness enveloped again. Last, "She's safe now, can never be hurt again, and is healthier, happier than I ever saw her on earth." Finally, I found some comfort and peace.

I took my mother's sage advice, "Honey, if it gets too bad, go see someone."

That fall and winter, a counselor led me through grief work, encouraging me to explore and write out my grief, even if just a list of what I missed about her. My grief was not depression. I learned to let grief bite me in the butt, whenever it wanted. I learned not to hate trios of grandmas, daughters, and granddaughters. Driving Ben to his medical appointments, I learned to sob and steer at the same time, but I don't recommend it. I learned to never underestimate the power of a good mother. From beyond the grave, her exceptional mothering still screams for attention.

During Mom's early days of morphine, she had given express instructions for the types of flowers to surround her grave, paying careful attention to blooming order, texture, color, and height of the plants, "No peonies."

"Okay, Mom." (Although I still don't know what she held against peonies.)

"The tall ones go in back, Kathykins."

"Yes, Mom." She knew my gardening capabilities didn't match hers.

Prairie flowers etch her headstone, and around her grave every spring, up come the daffodils, tulips, shooting stars, trillium, and bleeding hearts. Throughout the growing season, the parade of flowers continues. We did our best to follow her directives, but if we had planted all her desired selections she would've decorated other plots as well. Was that what she had in mind?

Chapter 18

Radiation, The Sequel

To remember the turn of the century/millennium (in case nothing came of Y2K), we constructed decorative New Year's hats, and spent over six hours downtown. Bopping from venue to venue, we took in dancing, a magic show, and a horse-drawn wagon ride. Taking a kiddie movie break at WESLI, resting up for the midnight fireworks, I snapped a picture of my kids under a clock at the stroke of midnight. Wearing his festive hat, my widower father accompanied his grandkids.

As Dorothy Parker was prone to ponder, what fresh hell would the future hold? Or would we be granted reprieve?

The summer of 2000, before Ben's seventh grade, I met with a middle school principal about Ben's education. Only two years left before high school spiked my anxiety. I'd found a tiny, first through eighth grade, private school with thirty pupils, two miles from our home. Walbridge School specialized in teaching kids with different learning styles and abilities. Besides methodology and flexibility in determining how to best teach my boy, the small student-teacher ratio excited me. No more pulling Ben from class with his peers. No aide ever required. Although he loved his public school aides and excellent Special Ed teachers (the more the merrier), over four years Ben learned to despise the word "special." To him it still means "abnormal, weird, not belonging."

Walbridge's philosophy completely banned me from helping with homework. Walbridge staff gauged each child's capabilities, making adjustments so the child could succeed on his own in every class. Walbridge spelled respite for me, and empowerment for Ben.

"I'm not interested in politics," I told the public school principal. "Or rules or protocol. I just want what's best for my boy. If you'll allow him to take Communication Skills here first hour, I'll pick him up and drive him to Walbridge." Ben adored his middle school speech therapist and continued to make gains with him.

The principal agreed, and my dead mother made it possible. Grandma Jo, posthumously, kept on giving. For two years, we spent a chunk of my inheritance buying hope from Walbridge School. Had I known she planned to leave me money, I would've held onto my saint's ankles, wetting her feet with my tears in thanks.

Ben spent two glorious years at Walbridge, including month-long summer school, improving academically by leaps and bounds, learning how he best learned.

The fall of 2000, seventh-grader Ben readied for another angiography. Just before the procedure, he joked to the radiologist and anesthesiologist, "I hope you aren't quacks!"

Results: a hypothalamic AVM, 20% still dangerously remaining two millimeters from the optic chiasm. Our UW and So Cal docs encouraged us to return to LLUMC for more radiation, even though it would be more risky and less effective the second time. Ben's situation remained sketchy whether we radiated again or not. If we chose retreatment, docs cautioned the possibilities of affecting his speech, blinding him, or further hindering his motor abilities. They doubted we'd kill him.

I sent a Ben Urgent Update to our supporters, detailing the above, and Super Principal read it to Ben's former elementary school staff. I heard from one teacher, Lori, that some teachers cried, so sad we must wrestle again with a life-altering decision.

By the end of Sarah's elementary school years, Lori had taught all three of my kids. She called our family a career highlight. We simply called her the best. Volunteering often, I watched her impressive work. Teaching without raising her voice, she engaged her class, endearing herself to them all. Ben still remembers her "wonderful teaching." Habitually, Lori insisted the kids give her a daily H: handshake, high five, or hug. Just before the year she taught Ben, someone cautioned her about touching students. Reluctant any longer to offer hugging, she didn't stand a chance with Ben. She credits him with restoring her third H. True to form, Sam high-fived ("the least possible human contact"), and Sarah combined high-fives and hugs. Lori's class celebrated every Packers win with a mini party.

But we threw no parties at our house, as we thought about Ben's brain in late 2000. Dan focused on the probability we wouldn't harm him. Not me. After all the gains Ben had made by working so hard? Risk wiping them out? Furious, I issued a challenge to God, not exactly a pink slip (that came a decade later). "Where are you? Do you see this? What are you going to do about it? What are we supposed to do about it? Are you going to send me any encouragement, or not?"

Three minutes later, my friend Sonja knocked unexpectedly on my door. Seeking an infant car seat of all things, getting an earful first. Then, finishing a Bible study, not because I wanted to, I read Joshua 1:9, "Have I not commanded you? Be strong and courageous. Do not be afraid; do not be discouraged, for the LORD your God will be with you wherever you go."

At home with preschooler Sarah until she started full-day kindergarten the fall of 2000, I spent my free time volunteering, either in classrooms or with church. In my home, I led weekly Bible studies for a revolving door of Japanese women. They came, usually for no more than two years, generally for their husband's research at the University of Wisconsin. Over the span of seventeen years, through late 2009, more than seventy Japanese women visited my home. Every week we laughed hard as I tried to answer their perplexities concerning English, American customs, products, culture, and the Bible. Everything from, "Why are American vacuum cleaners so loud?" to, "Hallowed? Isn't that the light above angels' heads in paintings?"

They taught me so much as we poured over our mainstay, St. Mark's account of the life of Jesus. Word by word, in slow motion, we broke down the English communicating Jesus' teachings and actions. We analyzed meanings and motives. I don't know about most of them, but I fell in love with his tender, caring ways, his interest in the whole person, spiritual, mental, emotional, and physical.

Besides the Bible, I read everything from *Green Eggs and Ham* to *Pride and Prejudice*, but mostly British and Irish mysteries. Some cope with the pain of life by consuming massive quantities of alcohol or food. I went on reading binges. Of an evening, and often during traumatic recovery days, the family knew I planted myself firmly in England, Wales, Scotland, or the Emerald Isle where somebody tidily, sensibly, always solved a bloody mess. If I chose, I could either calmly discuss or argue passionately with any and all imaginary characters. These friends waited to keep me company, and didn't take my energy, unless I offered. I owe their authors great thanks for engaging my mind and lifting my load. They provided laughs, history lessons, and inspiration to create an herb garden, visit new places, and learn smatterings of languages, including English. Best of all, they introduced me to other writers. "Katherine, meet Henry James. I think you'll like him."

But I wanted more than the life I had, something just for me, about me. And I wanted to be paid.

We always thought I would head back into the workforce full-time when Sarah went to school in 2000. Impossible. My free time each week differed, and even when I thought myself free, Life With Ben often dictated otherwise. Dan thought subbing might work – a morning-by-morning decision. Fifth-grader Sam, looking sick to his stomach at my intentions-to-sub pronouncement during one dinner, gave permission for "anywhere but my class."

Ben gave advice. "Just be nice, Mom. They will talk about you if you're mean. Well, either way, they're gonna talk about you, so just be nice."

November 2000, on a very part-time basis, I started subbing as a teacher and an educational assistant for our district. Little by little, I whittled down what I felt I could do best, gym and Special Ed. People rarely wanted to sub for those, and I felt comfortable. I learned every school has a flavor all its own, and that if district administrators wanted to know how a school fared all they had to do was check with substitute teachers for tales from the front. Impartial, objective eyes and ears open in the teachers' break rooms, quite revealing. I also learned why break rooms often contained pick-me-up, comfort food. One day, one of my emotionally disturbed pupils threatened to cut off his fingers. After persuading him to drop the scissors, and escorting him to the principal's office for backup, I dodged into the break room for five seconds. With my bare hands, I abused the cheesecake, stuffing it into my shocked face.

I kept my subbing certificate for several years, until Ben's health and my own entangled and welded, stopping me in my tracks, unable to commit to anything.

Awaking on March 6, 2001, at 4:00 a.m., with a tight feeling in my head and chest, in vain I sought to regain the oblivion of sleep. Fear, impatiently waiting all night, roused me. What were we thinking? Mulling over radiating Ben's head *again*? It seemed too big a decision for a forty-year-old girl from Wisconsin, one who nearly hyperventilated over countless choices in the yogurt aisles. I ran through my biblical arsenal, gaining strength and courage, setting my face like flint against the time bomb ticking in Ben's head.

Dan and I considered the AVM annoyingly illogical. Despite its substantially shrunken size, the risk of re-bleeding remained the same, 2-4% annually, the consequences of a bleed, also the same. Compared with 1996, the stats for radiation outcomes diminished for cure rate (70%), and rose for risk (6-7%). Still, pretty decent odds for one with his life ahead of him. We thought Ben, almost thirteen, should be part of the thinking equation. One evening we sat on the couch, explaining doctors recommended re-zapping.

"I just want to thank you and everyone who prays for me," Ben cried. "I know God is with me, and this may sound silly, but I know he's with me right now. And he's telling me something."

"What?" (Any, and all, billboards welcome.)

"You're going to be safe, you're going to be safe."

Unanimously, we decided to ganbatte (go for it). The next day, I set the wheels in motion for spring double trips to California. (As Shakespeare wrote in The Scottish Play, "If it were done when 'tis done, then 'twere well it were done quickly.")

The timing and logistics required our kitchen phone surgically implanted in my ear, and a spreadsheet the size of my kitchen table. Working backward from the radiation dates in So Cal, I plotted the rigmarole of appointments. First, remove the braces on Ben's teeth, no metal allowed in the California machines. Even after just one year, the braces had fixed Ben's front teeth debacle. We would forgo year two. Second, create a dental mold in Madison to be shipped to California for the bite-block prep. Tasks three through 100, to follow.

I hauled out my trusty notebook, filled with all the sticky notes and details from Ben's first radiation in 1996: itineraries, housing, flights, car rentals and borrowed car arrangements, packing lists, prep lists, phone numbers of medical facilities and insurance company personnel, questions to ask, directions, etc.

Just as in '96, we procured airline tickets to San Francisco and LA by a combination of purchased tickets, free tickets from friends and family with frequent flier miles, and free tickets for children with medical needs donated directly by airlines (obtained by letters of proof and request, from a doctor and from me). Again, the outpouring of community support overwhelmed.

While Dan stayed home with Sam and Sarah, Ben and I flew to San Francisco on spring break to prep for Radiation, The Sequel. The strange trip kicked off with two planes struck by lightning as they landed in Madison – our airline's last two incoming planes for the day, grounded. Although no one got hurt, burn marks showed on both. Explaining Ben's tight schedule, the ton of medical appointments lined up, I said I'd be happy to wait. However, the next day tornadoes, high winds, and hail were predicted for Madison. The sympathetic agent quickly transferred us to another airline, on standby.

As we waited, a two-year-old boy took a liking to Ben's shoes. For the next twenty minutes he begged for "Ben's big boy shoes!" Joshy's mom appreciated Ben's humor-filled reasoning on why Joshy could not have Ben's shoes. But his public meltdown escalated, his mom leading him away as he screamed, "I want Ben's shoes!"

Complimenting Ben on how well he handled the child, I reminded him a decade before I'd been that mother, in her shoes.

Grateful, we squeezed on a full, twenty-seat regional jet to Dallas. I sat in a jump seat. Ben now claims he's been to Texas; tarmac, anyway. Fourteen hours after leaving Madison, we arrived in San Francisco, wrecking one sightseeing day, yet preserving all appointments.

But Tour Guide Katherine is not easily dissuaded. For five free hours before hospital world, we packed in Muir Woods National Monument, Muir Beach, a drive down the squiggles of Lombard Street, lunch near Fisherman's Wharf at Ghirardelli Square, and a drive through Golden Gate Park, where we pit stopped for fifteen minutes worth of seahorses at the museum/aquarium.

One of Ben's all-time favorite memories with me comes from those five hours. Cars whizzing by at sixty miles an hour, my acrophobic wits urging otherwise, Ben coaxed me to the first, tall, orange tower of the Golden Gate Bridge, "Ganbatte, Mom!"

At age twelve, Ben didn't require general anesthesia for the bite-block CT and angiography, thrilling him. He hated anesthesia most of all, the smell, taste, and sickness after. Given anesthesia "flavor" choices in the past, he'd been permanently put off mint.

Although the CT took only fifteen minutes, bite-block placement in Ben's mouth proved tedious, time-consuming, and atrocious without sedation. Ben felt he couldn't breathe, and I wondered if even I could do it. Cheering him on with many "Ganbatte, Ben-kuns!" I also spoke reminders from his dad.

Before we left, Dan wrote us each the verse of encouragement and strength from the book of Joshua. As if he were Eric Liddell crossing the Olympic finish line in *Chariots of Fire*, Ben kept the piece of paper clenched in his hand. He asked me to read from it often during our two hospital days, even though he had memorized it. Comforting both of us, we heard his father's voice and Our Father's voice in those words.

After the bite-block CT ordeal, we met our friend from '96, BlueEyesNurse. Hanging out in the cafeteria for treats, we ended day one on a high.

Day two we spent thirteen hours at the hospital. After a tricky IV placement, Ben endured last minute, surprise pokes by phlebotomist One Vein Vic. She said he ruined her record. She tried drawing blood from both Ben's arms to no avail, finally hitting a vein in his foot to fill multiple vials. Mid-draw, Radiology Fellow suddenly appeared, ordering, "Forget the blood! The room's ready."

After One Vein Vic stopped her unfinished work and left us, Radiology Fellow called to report the room was not ready. Ben waited anxiously, expecting OVV to return for more bloodletting. But soon, staff switched him to a different procedure room, for the very happy reason Ben suddenly did not need to wear the bite-block through the angiography.

The difficult IV placement and blood draw pokes, and the thought of wearing the unwieldy bite-block during the angiography, this time awake, combined to scare Ben silly. Radiology Fellow did not help: "The hurting part is over. No more blood draw. Nothing else will hurt as much; the angiography will just feel like your head is on fire."

I stuck by my boy's side, determined to stay until staff kicked me out. When prep began I'd have to leave. Head Nurse, with a lovely across-the-pond accent, observed as I calmed my boy, "You look like a sensible mom who isn't going to faint on us."

"We've been through anesthesia twelve times in five years," I explained.

Head Nurse kept one eye on me as I stroked Ben's head, soothing him. Suddenly she announced, "Mom is staying. Get her a gown."

I'll never forget the look on the radiologists' faces when they entered and saw me stationed at Ben's head, wearing my blue gown and lead apron.

After the doctor made the incision at Ben's groin, snaking the catheter up, I took my eyes from the monitor to sneak a peek at real time. Only for Dan. I knew he'd be insanely jealous and want a full report. My split-second viewing proved enough. And I was not going to get woozy on Head Nurse, disappointing her.

As I focused on my scared boy, they performed their tasks without concern. Fascinated, my eyes darted to the monitor revealing the wiry thing flinging around inside Ben's rib cage. The radiologist was searching for the vessel he wanted to send the catheter into, to pump the dye.

"Mom, my head feels hot!" Ben complained, starting to panic as the dye flowed into his brain.

"That's right. Can't you just feel the California sun beating down on us at the beach? Listen to the waves. Feel the warm sand, you can dig a big hole."

For protection, all of us nurses stepped behind the window partition when they actually filmed Ben's head. Procedure over, Head Nurse exclaimed, "You were excellent!"

"Thanks! Can I have a letter of recommendation? For other facilities?"

One radiologist chimed in, shocked, "She never lets anyone in here!"

Another nurse sympathized, "I don't know how you could do that without bursting into tears. I know I would've."

"I've seen a lot," I muttered. Only thinking, when you've seen your seven-year-old in a two-week coma with life support and fifty staples in his head, this is nothing.

Fully aware, because the sedation had not put him to sleep, Ben complimented, "You guys did great! You're the best doctors and nurses. This was a piece of cake!"

In the recovery room, lying flat on his back for six hours, Ben sucked on Popsicles as we watched *Star Wars Episode I.* While there, a nurse approached me. She'd only been with us for a short time.

"That boy of yours. There's something about him. It's like he's... he's...bright. No, no! I don't mean bright. I mean, I'm sure he's smart and everything, but it's just that...it's...it's...there's something about his spirit!" She broke into a relieved smile.

"You're right," I choked, after watching her search for words.

Our Santa Rosa cousins came down to visit, hoping to take us out for California-style pizza. Although I was unsure we'd be able to after the three grueling days, Ben perked right up when they entered his hospital room. At 7:30 p.m. we discharged from Stanford Hospital for the last time. At 10:00 p.m. I dragged Ben away from his cousins, and pizza topped with tandoori chicken, shrimp, and Peking duck.

Back home from Stanford radiation prep, after hearing my stories, my father shook his head with pride, "Girl, you're tough as nails."

I sincerely thanked him for beginning my boot camp training early. First, by tents-only vacations from age six months forward, then at age thirteen, Rocky Mountain backpacking-only vacations. In middle and high school, we were the only family I knew who not only backpacked, we experimented. (Scientists dontchaknow.) While Mom made lists, accumulated supplies, and sewed water resistant nylon around foam for five sleeping pads, and the bags to carry them in, with Dad, Koo and I learned how to best roll individual servings of instant coffee, sugar, and dry milk into plastic wrap, taping them shut. Ditto for Tang. We counted out per day cracker rations, and packed tubes of peanut butter and jelly. We filled Baggies with oatmeal and brown sugar, and hard candy and lollipops. We made up our own gorp (trail mix). To our neighborhood's amusement, for days each year we tromped the train tracks single-file, our family of five breaking in our boots and backs with increasing weight. Dad color-code graphed our progression in a research notebook. (I'm only half joking.)

Dad and Mom taught me how to train for hard fun, then do it for real. The knowledge has come in mighty handy. As a kid, I bought Rocky Mountain highs with blisters, heavy packs, hailstorms, and cold. As an adult, I bought perseverance. Yet even "tough as nails" has her breaking point.

A week before traveling to So Cal for Radiation, The Sequel, our insurance company informed us they would "decide in the next twenty-four hours whether radiation for AVMs is experimental, or not common, in the medical field."

They might not cover the cost of the treatment! Customer service explained that "conflicting opinion in the current medical articles" required the Insurance Company Powers That Be to make a decision. "Generally, they side with the patient," she confided.

Pre-authorized for the Stanford prep segment, I had understood that pre-authorization for the LLUMC radiation three weeks later depended simply upon "we're ready" information from Stanford. (Why would we bother to fly to California to prep for an upcoming unauthorized portion of treatment?) I had assumed that a successful Stanford prep meant our insurance would be satisfied. (Yes, Dad, I know. Assuming leads to "Ass-u-me.") But I felt it a fair assumption. We'd done it five years before. However, we did not have the same insurance company.

Cleared two days after the disconcerting phone call, I hadn't become too flustered, by now so accustomed to mysterious insurance snafus. Our excellent health insurance didn't pre-authorize protecting me from insurance fights, proofs, and threats. For a year I did battle with one hospital's screwy records. They kept telling me on the phone we owed nothing, even sending a letter to that effect, and yet?

"This notice is to advise you that unless satisfactory arrangements or full settlement is (sic) received by or (sic) client within 15 days. (sic) Your account will be transferred to our Collection Department."

If I offered to edit pro bono, would they finally quit pestering me?

But we rarely received any medical bills. Those I saw turned me to jellyfish. Even Dan and I, with our extreme ability to squeeze pennies out of a buck, would've been sunk by our million dollar boy's medical bills.

("An AVM? Oohhh, those are expensive!" one family member had exclaimed when he first learned of Ben's condition in '96. He headed an HMO. He knew his stuff.)

Before leaving for LLUMC in So Cal, I emailed another update to our supporters. For the first time, Ben dictated,

I want to thank everyone for all the praying they have already done and God bless you for it. I can't repay everyone for this, so I say, 'Bless you!' Please pray for me that nothing bad would happen to me – nothing wrong with my eyes, talking, or that I won't be alive.

Three weeks after he and I returned from Stanford prep, all five of us flew to So Cal. Sarah, five, Sam, ten, and Ben twelve, bound for Disneyland. I planned a hope-filled hero sandwich: two days of fun, two of hospital, and, if possible, two more of fun.

At San Clemente beach, the day before Disneyland, the late April sun so badly burned the backs and legs of our two youngest I thought I'd wrecked our theme park plans. Sam tried jumping out of his burnt skin. Close to midnight, Dan left our cheap hotel to forage for relief. We unintentionally stayed across the street from a prison nine miles from the hospital, instead of at The Ronald McDonald House, as their fire code prevented five in a room. Wandering the dodgy neighborhood, Dan found an open store and bought a fifty-two-ounce container of aloe that lasted for years. After liberally applying gel to Sam and Sarah, I stewed all night, kicking myself for forgetting that spring So Cal sun is fierce. Late April in Wisconsin, we'd barely thawed.

Awaking in pain the next morning, Sarah declared, "This is the worst day of my life." But Mickey and Co. waved a magic wand, changing her opinion to, "It's the best day of my life!" Undoubtedly because she and I looped four consecutive times the catchy-tuned small world extravaganza.

This time, unlike '96, we visited Disneyland before the radiation. Ben, restriction-free! We got our money's worth, courtesy of Ben's multiple disabilities. Ushered to the front of lines, Ben, Sam, and I rode Splash Mountain numerous times. And Ben turned dizzy after back-to-back wild rides with Dan, finally declaring, "That's enough!"

How I wished that applied to the next trip segment.

The first day in LLUMC, staff requested our written permission for radiation round two, stating we understood known risks and the possibility of unknown risks. Radiation would be administered in half-doses, over two days, just like before.

We knew the small, hypothalamic AVM still tenaciously clung to Ben's optic chiasm. As well as mood, the hypothalamus controls basic life-or-death activities, like body temperature and blood pressure. The optic chiasm controls sight. Ben already had subtle peripheral vision loss, detected by the most recent four-hour neuro-ophthalmology testing in Stanford. Doctors didn't know if the AVM or the 1996 radiation had caused it. It didn't hinder Ben, but I feared further radiation might damage his sight.

Determined to be the parent to sign this time, I grimly read the list of potential negative consequences, divided into categories.

"Early Reactions: skin and scalp reaction with or without hair loss, nausea, vomiting, headaches, fatigue, drowsiness, altered sense of taste or smell, inflammation of ear canal, increased risk of infection and/or bleeding resulting from depression of blood count, seizures."

But anti-seizure meds were administered for a short time after the procedure, to reduce the possibility.

"Late Reactions: permanent hair loss of variable degrees, altered texture and/or color of hair, persistent drowsiness and fatigue, changes from former thinking ability, memory, and/or personality changes, loss of strength, feeling or coordination in any part of the body, vision changes possibly causing loss of vision, ear irritation and possible hearing loss, pituitary gland changes requiring long-term hormone replacement therapy."

The sign-off sheet continued, "Radiation may cause injury that could range from mild and temporary to severe and permanently disabling. There is also a possibility of injury to critical areas of the brain within several months to years following treatment. There is a small chance of bleeding into the brain, and if bleeding or necrosis (cell destruction) occurs, the results could be very serious, including the possibility of brain damage or death. Risks may be higher for children than adults, because of the effect of radiation on the developing central nervous system. Intellectual development may be interfered with."

The sheet did not list two additional risks communicated to me verbally in '96 by one of the doctors, future brain swelling and tumors.

Paralyzed, I stared at the paper before me, running through my options. Sign or bail. Here we went again. Fear of consequences from Radiation, The Sequel hit hard. I knew proton beams, carrying a smaller dose of radiation than in '96, would slightly overlap the area radiated before. Radiating an area twice increased risks, so doctors targeted a tiny edge of the AVM, programming radiation to fan out, impacting the area by degrees. As if ripples emanated from a stone thrown into water.

Verses from chapter 38 in the book of Job, when God argues with Job (I love that), popped into my head, "Who shut up the sea behind doors...when I fixed limits for it...when I said, 'This far you may come and no farther; here is where your proud waves halt'?"

Most of the targeted AVM from '96 had successfully shut down, but the AVM feeder area had not. This is where those proud proton beam waves needed to go, then *halt!* Heartened by the fact that Ben came through the first radiation without complications, and that an army of well-wishers on five continents pulled and prayed again for us, with knots in my stomach, I signed. My signature preemptively combated any thoughts of blame I might have in the future; I would have no one to accuse but Ben's mother, God help me. Writing my name on that line, one of the hardest things I have ever done.

Day one, the first hospital day we ever slogged through with all our kids, lasted twelve hours. Ben's IV placement did not go well, as usual, taking forty-five minutes and three attempts. The line would administer light anesthesia, rather than the heavy gas from a mask.

Staff kept offering, "Wouldn't you rather have the gas? It's fast and doesn't hurt."

"No! I don't want the gas!" Ben adamantly insisted he never wanted gassy anesthesia again. Every time someone brought the mask near him, he looked absolutely petrified. Gassing him would make the job so much easier for them. Everyone stresses when IV placements take a long time. But we backed Ben up. Within reason, patient's wishes and comfort first.

During IV placement, the other two kids stayed outside the room, just around the corner. (I wonder now the effect of hearing their brother fighting off the gas?) Ben's IV line finally worked. As the anesthesiologist administered the drugs, he asked Ben if he'd seen the picture of himself descending Splash Mountain. (Disneyland takes pictures of all people on that ride.)

"Yes! And five out of four times closed...." We watched his eyes flicker and shut.

After we joined Sam and Sarah outside the treatment room, doctors placed the bite-block in Ben's mouth, and radiated his brain. Dan and I wrung our hands in the waiting room, wondering if we'd done right by our boy.

A hospital social worker delivered presents to Sarah and Sam, apologetic for the paucity of "boy" choices. Sarah's favorite, a fancy-dress doll, and Sam's favorite, a pile of yellow legal pads. Between the gifts, their own toys, books, and imaginations, and frequenting the cafeteria, they stayed fairly entertained.

Radiation finished late, at 6:30 p.m., after the Pediatric Recovery room closed. Instead, staff wheeled out-of-it Ben to General OR Recovery: No Parents Allowed, Ever. But the advocating nurse by my side told me to hang out by the recovery doors while other nurses settled Ben inside. She'd tell them to come and get me soon.

While I made myself as inconspicuous as possible, in a corner of the floor near the stairwell, staff whooshed in and out the double doors, giving me strange looks. After thirty minutes, another nurse came out, asking if I was Ben's mom. She went back to let them know I still waited outside to see my boy.

Then I played my Lolita card. Lolita worked as an LLUMC OR nurse. While immigrating to the US in the 1970s, Dan's grandmother had befriended her in an airport. They remained friends for twenty years, until Grandma K's death. We also had met Lolita, in '96, courtesy of Grandpa's letter to Lolita explaining his great-grandson, Ben.

"Excuse me, is Lolita on duty tonight?" I asked a passing nurse.

"No, I don't think –" she answered, as Lolita burst through the double doors looking for me.

Coming in on her day off, working on an evening project, Lolita had just read Ben's name on the recovery chart. Escorting me to Ben's side, she left to check on Dan, Sam, and Sarah. Angelic Lolita stayed with my family the rest of the night, taking us on as her new evening project, alternating between Ben and me, and Dan and the kids. Besides helping me obtain anti-seizure meds from the hospital pharmacy, a surprisingly difficult task, she vouched for me. OR Recovery staff let me stay in No Parents Allowed, Ever.

Later, one nurse complimented, "It's been a godsend having a parent like you in here caring for Ben tonight." She said I lightened their extremely busy load, and explained the policy, "We've had so much trouble with other parents, upsetting their kids, looking at every patient but theirs, pointing at and asking about the other patients, 'What's wrong with him?'"

Serious? I always kept the curtains drawn around Ben's bed any time we were in a medical facility. Ben's trauma and wellbeing were more than enough for me to handle.

Ben ended recovery with a soy cheeseburger and fries in the cafeteria at 9:00 p.m. (The Seventh-day Adventist-affiliated hospital has dietary regulations.) Eating for the first time all day Ben declared, "This is the best burger I've ever had!"

Lolita helped us load Sarah, Sam, and wheelchair-bound Ben into the car late that night, making sure the IV remaining in Ben's hand still looked okay. To prevent torture for everyone the next day, anesthesiology staff let the IV remain overnight.

We arrived at the hotel at 11:00 p.m., parents and kids equally trashed.

Smooth day two lasted only five hours. We told Ben the loopy thing he said the day before, as the drugs sent him off to La-la-land. This time he insisted on singing. Dan often "sang" at the top of his lungs, "I Am Opera Maaan!" with long held vibrato on the final note, hand gestures to boot. Ben always answered, "I Am Opera Booyy!" The pair habitually engaged in a delightfully weird, testosterone-laden, musical chest thumping.

Lying on a gurney by the proton machine, waiting for anesthesia to take over, Ben got cut-off mid-note, "I Am Opera Booyy! Ooohh, saayy caann yoouu s –"

We stood cracking up at our son's antics as he went under. Atypical for parents to be allowed to watch, we weren't typical parents. Fifteen knockouts in five years, many by his side, had earned us our stripes.

Post-radiation, helping wheel Ben's gurney to the Pediatric Recovery room, I didn't need to play my Lolita card, parents definitely allowed in peds recovery. No sooner had we parked anesthetized Ben in the bay than one of his mega-baby blues cracked open and he croaked, "Need cheeseburger." My firstborn, two months shy of his teens.

Ben thought his best-ever recovery should qualify for a Guinness record. But his usual great spirits turned to dismay and confusion when he heard that the AVM remained. He thought Radiation, The Sequel meant instant cure, no more risk of a bleed. Again, I wondered, had I done right by my son? Dan, as always, helped both of us emotionally process.

Docs deemed the radiation technically and medically successful. Once again, we would have to wait several years for final results.

After the LLUMC all clear, we drove to San Diego to attempt two more days of fun. One day, we pushed Ben in a rented wheelchair through the world-class zoo, keeping to the shade to protect his newly-re-radiated head. The second day came as a surprise to the kids. The LLUMC social worker had secretly handed me five free tickets to Sea World. Again avoiding the sun, we made a brief exception to get splashed.

In the hotel the last night, watching cable, a treat for us as we've never had it or wanted it (and still don't), two commercials raised my hackles.

One purported two Wisconsin guys showed up at the California border requesting cheese. As if. Another portrayed a sunny, lush, cow-studded field, two calves sweetly asking Grandma cow about her youth. She flashback-shudders, lonely, sad, in a blizzard. So traumatized she could not make happy milk in such a wintry place.

Hah. We learn to hang tough in The Dairy State, not hang ten. Cows, parents, and kids. Just sayin'.

At the end of the trip, I overheard my three happily in a round-table discussion about all the fun they'd been able to have because of Ben's hemorrhage. I eavesdropped in awe. True, we laughed hard along the way, but at what a cost.

During the summer of 2001, Middleton's rec department committed to a major undertaking, putting on musical smash *Joseph and the Amazing Technicolor Dream Coat*. Ben wore purple in the Children's Rainbow Choir as he correctly sang all twenty-nine colors in one song, including ochre, mauve and azure. Even Sam and Sarah had memorized the song by the conclusion of the show.

After the musical, we camped Up North near Lake Superior for ten days, canoeing down the Bois Brule. Hint: don't take a lightweight canoe down the rapids, loaded with three kids, one with disabilities, unless you're crazy. We did it twice.

Sam clenched his teeth, Sarah screamed, and Ben insisted we perpetually almost tumped in the froth. But Dan in the back steering, with me up front navigating, kept that boat afloat.

Chapter 19

Santa, Ben's Buddy

The voicemail from Ben, two weeks before the press conference, sounded typically unusual, yet outlandishly cryptic. "Mom! My phone's dying! There's fifty dollars in my account, is that from cheese? Check it out, Mom! My phone's dy –"

Still, I knew exactly what he meant. Checking online, fifty bucks had indeed been deposited in his credit union account, but my suspicions did not point to Code Cheese. Some time we expected the federal government to dump money in our accounts for the DC trip, but not quite yet, and substantially more than fifty. Nope, the mysterious sum added up to Ben's first paycheck. Ever. Unaccustomed to any deposits except his government Supplemental Security Income (SSI) checks, the $50 depositor's acronym could also have been government code for "Quiet! Top Secret Information." No wonder confusion reigned in Ben's head. I called him to report mystery solved. After laughing heartily, unable to believe his good fortune, Ben thoughtfully paused. Receiving money for doing much the same as his volunteer work, he wondered, "Is that fair, Mom?"

Later that day, another message alarmed me. "Mom, I'm okay. I fell and the nurse at Yahara House bandaged my arm. But you should see it! The nurse even winced."

For as long as she could stand it, a few days, Nurse Mom put off checking on Ben's arm. I brought him home for an early dinner, but he couldn't stay long; filming for another movie with his theatre friends started at six. However, first things first: the four-inch long, one-inch across, oozing, scabrous wound on his arm.

"I knew I was falling so I twisted my body to land on my good arm, so the strongest part would get hit," he explained.

"Wow, Ben, that was really athletic and smart," I commended. Ben frequently doubted his intelligence, playing a lethal comparison game against his peers. And despite one-handed foosball, juggling, and Frisbee-tossing prowess, he questioned his athleticism.

"I can't even run, how can I be athletic?" he mumbled dejectedly.

I argued athletes come in all shapes, sizes, and abilities. Familiar with Paralympics, I had also just finished writing a feature on a Special Olympics fundraiser. Organizers thought Ben might qualify, and suggested bowling.

"What about badminton, Mom? Do they have that? When I played Wii bowling with the blind guy at the Senior Center, he always beat me. But I beat him in tennis!" Ben had volunteered there for two years, organizing the Wii Club for older folks.

Further inspecting Ben's forearm, I determined it looked swollen, maybe needed x-rays.

"It's his muscle," Dan correctly observed. Ben's muscular left arm had developed naturally, by working overtime. People mistakenly think he pumps iron. It fooled Nurse Mom too.

While cooking dinner, I dictated three questions for Ben to ask museum staff. With the press conference only ten days away, I wanted a heads-up, even if he didn't. Ben's wardrobe chiefly concerned me, should he wear the suit, or something less dressy?

During Ben's favorite dinner, chicken curry, I implored him to stop shoveling food as if competing with Takeru Kobayashi, the 2006 world record bratwurst-eating champion.

"I got in trouble at the museum," he confessed suddenly.

(Uh. Oh.)

"I'm not supposed to be in the building if I'm not working. It's a breach of confidence. I can't volunteer there if I'm working there. I didn't know that."

(I didn't either.)

Then Ben segued nicely. "Grandpa called, after not calling for two weeks, and he had a snake and said he'd be there in fifteen minutes."

(This ought to be good.) "At the museum?" I asked.

"Yeah."

"And you were there to meet him?"

"No. I was eating lunch at The Old Fashioned." This popular Wisconsin-fare eatery is next to WESLI, a stone's throw from the museum.

"Eating with friends?"

"No. Alone. You know Grandpa, he's on his way, so I ate my food really fast."

(Aha. The food shoveling light bulb, revealed.) "So Grandpa called while you were eating lunch, and you hurried to get a snake from Grandpa?"

"Yes."

"Why was Grandpa bringing you a snake?" Oops. Why ask why? One of my main coping strategies for a long time. I forgot.

"I asked for one."

"Okay, you asked for one."

"Yeah, like if Grandpa saw one in the wild he should get it for the museum rooftop."

(Grandpa lived in the country. Earl the Eastern Milk Snake lived alone on the museum's rooftop, ergo he needed a friend. Seemed logical.)

"Grandpa met me in the parking lot and gave me a jar with a snake in it. I took it to Santa and we looked for a terrarium."

(Santa. A mystery novel red herring if ever there was one. I did not take the bait.)

"But while we were looking," Ben continued, "and we found one! I got into trouble. I wasn't supposed to be there. And I wasn't supposed to bring a snake. But I knew someone brought a tree frog once, so –"

"Who?" Dan interjected, jumping into the ping-pong conversation.

"Shh!" I waved him off, one red herring enough. "So, you found something for the snake to live in, but staff said you weren't supposed to?"

"Yeah. Because I didn't know she wasn't my boss! It was really confusing."

(I can imagine. Wisely, Dan and I ignored the She-herring.) "Did you know there were rules about bringing things into the museum?" I queried.

"Yeah, but I didn't want to do it that way. Someone brought a tree frog once," Ben said again, plaintively. (Dan let it alone.)

"So you're up on the rooftop with the snake, and staff have busted you?"

"Yeah, lots of supervisors. But they were smiling. I asked if I was in trouble and they said 'no.'"

Thinking I understood the gist, gearing up for a teaching moment, I drew breath, "You know about getting written up? For breaking rules? That's not what you want in your files." I further pontificated, finishing up with, "The kind of writing up you want, is what you did last Friday. You saw gourds hanging over the top of the building, swinging in the wind, and you went in and told them about it so no one would get a gourd on the head from four stories high. That's the kind of thing you want in your files, being a good employee who takes initiative." (Obtaining a free snake also showed initiative. I didn't say so.) "So, did they say they were going to write this up?" I nervously persisted.

"No, they said they wouldn't even have to tell the executive director."

"Okay, that's their call, they're your bosses. So you understand now, if you get a great idea you need to ask someone before you go ahead and do it?"

"But I did! I asked my rooftop boss and she said, 'Yeah, maybe' and I thought that was 'yes.' And I told Grandpa, and he called two weeks later, and was coming in fifteen minutes! And then my other supervisor tells me the rooftop woman isn't my boss anymore. She is! She was when I volunteered, but not anymore! It was so confusing."

Elementary, my dear MCM staff, elementary. This case of circumlocution involved education and communication, not flagrant flouting. A ninety-minute verbal employee orientation, complete with handbook, simply wouldn't cut mustard. Ben's language processing issues came significantly into play. In order to succeed, Ben is a hands-on learner, requiring repeated, clear guidance until a strong routine is established. Then he's absolutely brilliant, as his years in dramatic productions proved. Doubtless MCM staff would continue to experience incredibly wonderful, richly frustrating, mysterious, and glorious interactions with Ben as they grew in understanding the unique brain working on and under their rooftop.

Welcome, welcome, to my world! I have been waiting for this, with trepidation, for a long time. Unleashing my amazing son upon an unsuspecting world. Would it learn? Could it learn? Persistence, patience, and taking time with Ben will be amply rewarded. The world will find, as I have, a gigantic golden heart at the end of the rainbow.

I walked Ben through a few scenarios, choices he could have made. "First, you can always tell someone, like Grandpa for instance, now is not a good time. 'No, I'm sorry, I can't do that right now,' is all you have to say." ("No" coming late to me in life, I wanted my kids to have the tools to use it respectfully.) "So what happened with the snake?" I needed reptilian closure.

"His name is Jake the Snake, and he's on the rooftop by Earl," Ben exulted. Excellent. The real snake's predecessor, and namesake, had been Ben's treasured comforter. Purchased in 1994, in a Connecticut museum gift shop, Ben christened the stuffed green and gold boa (Packers bonus!) with a rhyming name. Jake the Snake, about a yard long, sported green plastic eyes and a red felt tongue. How a jungle snake came to reside in a maritime museum on the Eastern seaboard I never understood. Possibly it had escaped from its non-native habitat in the Everglades and moved north. My son and his snake remained inseparable into adulthood. Just seventeen months after his purchase, Jake the Snake kept 24/7 bedspread vigil with my fully wired comatose son, the PICU's life-keeping gadgetry guarded by a fierce predator. And for the next ten years, that snake saw more insides of medical facilities than most snakes ever will. He sustained damage in his rough Life With Ben, the loss of one of his eyes. But in some recovery bay, in some facility, in some city, staff once wheeled my son's gurney to me, Ben still under the influence of ether. Jake the Snake kept one-eyed watch on the gurney, his other eye socket covered with a bandaged eye-patch. Bless the unknown, tenderhearted nurse. I wept.

So the Madison Children's Museum now owned a live Jake the Snake, still keeping vigil over my son? Good. Almost better, for this particular snake drop, my father had donated directly. The last time Ben requested a snake, in a by-the-way manner Grandpa Syrup placed the contained critter in my car at night, during one of Ben's summer plays. After the show, in the pitch black, I found the container empty. I love snakes, yet I drove the mile home with my left foot up on the car seat, the big toe of my right foot pressing gingerly on the gas and brake pedals.

Dropping Ben at the Humanities building on campus for his movie shoot, I told him to break a leg. Better that than his arm.

And next time you see him, Ben, be sure to give my love to Santa.

Ben explains his communication style thus, "I must say what's in my head, so it's out there, so that I can understand what my sentence is all about. Even though people are bewildered, I explain. It takes a few seconds for me to understand it, by saying it out loud, and it may make a mysterious maze for you, but if you keep on letting me have five minutes, or three minutes, or ninety minutes, those frustrating few moments will be regarded as nothing."

From the mute days in 1996, his deep love of interaction with all people motivated him to regain speech. Nothing could stop this kid from communicating with humanity. And Ben's talkative ways, if allowed, always included touch. He is a Freelance Hugging Feel-gooder At Large, FHFAL. (Pronounced fuffle.)

When President Obama campaigned on the UW campus in 2010, Ben attended a rally of 26,000, wearing a "Free Hugs" sign. Sarah, at the age when the existence of other family members merits mortification by association, nearly died when another teen posted on Facebook a shot of the weird guy offering hugs.

But most people love Ben's outgoing ways. "He's the sweetest/nicest/greatest guy!" "He just makes you feel better." "The world needs more people like him." "He gives the greatest hugs!" "When I'm having a bad day, I look for Ben." All were sentiments spoken repeatedly to me over Ben's lifetime, the last from a public middle school teacher, not even his own. The general public usually wanted him cloned, bottled, and available. When people ask if I know Ben, the wind blows favorable. However, I never assume all humanity adores Ben's outgoing antics, and that nagging thought makes me hesitant. The day I first met my hairdresser, Lisette, a case in point.

On the day Ben's academic life hit a brick wall, leaving him bewildered and broken, and me an emotional wreck, I drove through campus. After spying "Walk-ins Welcome" in the window, impulsively I barged into Lisette's salon.

“Can you help me?” I mumbled, eyes downcast. “I want my hair different, but I don’t know how, and I’m scared.” (I wanted change just like President Obama. But drastically and instantly.) “Also, my sister says I need my eyebrows fixed.”

In 1976, my mother had sweetly called my eyebrows my “best feature.” She meant it with the utmost kindness. A gentle soul, to this day whenever a family member sticks it to another in Monopoly, Uno, or Hearts, standard procedure requires exclaiming, “Grandma Jo never would’ve done that!” Thus, I ignored my eyebrows until December 2009, when Koo carefully brought them to my attention, pointing out the obvious.

When camping as kids, I had done the same for my sister by helping her through numerous bouts of flailing, pitch-black claustrophobia. Awaking in a tent, she believed herself in a deathtrap, suffocating inside malevolent nylon. I would grab her head, shove it against the mesh window, and loudly command, “Breathe!”

Decades later, Koo simply returned the favor, albeit with the big, black, bushy things on my forehead.

“So, what brings you downtown?” friendly stylist Lisette inquired.

“Too hard a question.”

“Ah. So, do you have kids?”

Heavy sigh. “Three.”

“Are they around? Must be nice, if they’re around.”

(Umm, next?)

“How’re you?” she asked with concern.

“Bumpy,” fat tears rolling down my cheeks.

“Yeah, it’s always something,” she commiserated.

“But sometimes it comes so fast, and furious, and thick....” I whined.

“A screaming shit storm?” Lisette nailed it, as she ripped my eyebrows from their follicles.

"Oh! Thank you. I wondered where I was," then adding shyly, "I like my new eyebrows and what you're doing to my hair."

"I will make it perfect."

(She sounded like Ben's So Cal PhysicistDoc.) "Good. Something will be, then. Thank you, Lisette."

"Your last name," Lisette mused aloud. "I met a guy named Ben a few months ago. Do you know him?"

(Oh. No. Fuffle or kerfuffle? I couldn't take more bad news. And this woman, she held scissors.)

"I ran into him on State Street on my birthday last fall," she said brightly. "He gave me a great hug and sang *Happy Birthday*. It made my day!"

Hugging then singing to a perfect stranger on State Street? Lustily belting out the song with flourishes? (I am well acquainted with Ben's version.) Who did that?

Buddy from *Elf*, that's who. Yes, Santa, Ben is Buddy.

The night Dan and I had rented *Elf*, when Ben was sixteen, multiple scenes cattle prodded me from my chair. Mailroom, breakfast, dinner, and gum, not to mention the fervent public singing. As soon as I got comfy, Hollywood launched me again. Had they been creepin' me and mine? I almost gave up. I lived with Buddy then, after all. Not an easy existence sometimes, for example, in elevators. Or on the street, in our home, or anywhere else one found people or opportunities to impulsively push buttons. Not everyone loved a Freelance Hugging Feel-gooder At Large, no matter how sincere or naive.

But MCM had figured out a way to work with exuberant, Fuffle Ben. He still proudly carries with him, and often reviews, "Ben's Guidelines For Success," the cheat sheet of simple "do's and don'ts" he created with his supervisor after the Jake the Snake contretemps.

"My personality is extremely extroverted," Ben explains, "but I cannot hug even one person, kid or adult, when I'm working. At first it made me sad, but now it gives me great joy that I am being responsible and trustworthy. When people see me juggle, or my smiley-face AFO, and then talk to me about life, sometimes they want to hug me. But I tell them the policy says, 'I cannot hug you, but you can hug me if you want.' Sometimes they laugh and respect me by not hugging. But mostly they laugh, and still respecting that I can't hug, they hug me while I bow with my hands clasped behind my back."

I know she can take it, look at her pipes. But I hope Mr. President doesn't mind the free bionic bear hug my Fuffle son may lay on the First Lady some day soon.

Free hugs, anybody?

Chapter 20

Pixie Dust

Two days before the press conference, T minus two and counting, we brought Ben home to watch the Sunday Packers game and prepare. As if he were a hobo, he carried a paper sack of clothes with him. Unintentionally distressed cords, faded, dark brown, and holey –"Yeah, can you fix that Mom?" – and a severely wrinkled, black and blue plaid, flannel, button-down shirt.

"It's clean," he opined of the shirt. "Just needs ironing."

(What? Was he auditioning for *The Red Green Show* or something?) "Absolutely not! You cannot wear this stuff to the press conference," I blustered. "How about like staff said, khakis? And a button down shirt, but one that goes with a tie? If you wear the purple dress shirt and Jerry Garcia tie, you'll match the museum's colors, you know."

A wee factoid only occurring to me the second after I uttered it. Sometimes my subconscious scares me; it's way smarter than me. According to junior-class-AP Psychologist-Sarah, my brain is chock-full of crystallized intelligence, and I'm guessing much of it's subliminal. Earlier that Sunday, Sarah had explained.

"Mom, I'm done with my homework. Finally."

"Good." My monosyllabic answer should've given her pause. As well as knowing to discount any answer I gave while feverishly typing, she knew better than to approach the Writing Throne unless The Writer had extended her scepter. My head remained bowed, glassy-eyed, my fingers whizzing.

"Mom! Wait!"

I glanced up, eyebrows slightly raised, fingers hovering. She trod dangerous ground and she knew it.

"Didja know –"

(My eyebrows raised another few millimeters. Not another psych-related bit of breaking news. Nowadays, she constantly analyzed the family.)

" – the reason you became a writer is because you're old?"

(My eyebrows reached their full yoga height.)

"I mean, like, you became a writer because you wanted to, but also because you need crystallized intelligence."

(Getting better.)

"If you wanted to be a scientist now it wouldn't work, but a writer needs all the information from past experience, crystallized intelligence. So that's why you became a writer, I mean besides the reason that you wanted to. In case you were ever wondering," she smirked.

(This from the girl who once insisted I was too old to say, "Dude"?)

My fingers had resumed typing while she spoke, (fresh quotes!), but I rewarded her with an impressed, sardonic smirk of my own. Sometimes she scares me.

Instead of watching the Packers game, I utilized my crystallized intelligence. The taped game I saved for later, no commercials. And with writing done for the day, I would be able to focus solely on the green and the gold. Hopefully. As I once elucidated, football is a thinking woman's game. Other than on the long passes and runs, my mind can be just about anywhere.

The writing over, but never finished, I whipped up chicken fajitas, corn, salad, black beans, and rice. At 6:06 p.m. complete silence emanated from the basement, indicating a game on the line. Starving (writing burns crystallized brain calories), I ate alone.

"Game over!" Dan suddenly roared. At that point only figuratively, but within ten minutes they all stomped up to the kitchen in excitement.

"Thank you!" Dan exclaimed. Grizzled and scruffy, he had spent most of the day outside. "You are a good woman." And he did that "we are not worthy" thing with his arms.

"Make y'all come eat when I could tell the game's not sewn up? C'mon. And you're a good man." He had left me alone to write, all day. He went to get Ben, which I'd said I'd do, took out the compost, winterized the rain barrels, and swung a maul, stacking his woodpiles, moving a bunch to the deck, priming us for winter. We use a wood burning fireplace insert to help with heating, the perfect marriage of our frugality and Dan's hobby. Whenever he heard chainsaws in the neighborhood, Dan displayed salivating Pavlovian conditioning. Some neighbors even kept Dan informed about "wood futures." That afternoon, Dan started his 2013 stash, for proper aging dontchaknow. Not exactly *Little House on the Prairie*, residing in the city, but we tried.

As they ate, I sat with them. Usually intent on my food, this dinner I watched my three. Dan kept raising his gaze to the pictorial collages I'd made of our June 2011 trip to England and France, the trip Tour Guide Katherine outdid herself. The three in the kitchen were my favorite, except for two others in our bedroom and living room. Which pub now caught Dan's eye? The Inklings' Bird and Baby in Oxford? Or was he taking tea, and where? In London's Fortnum and Mason's? Did he linger upon the yellow door Jane Austen walked through near Covent Garden, or Lewis Carroll's little green door? Was he punting on the Isis? Did he pay homage again on the infamous beaches of Normandy? Was he reliving our surreal, five-course, fine French meal in a restaurant tucked away quietly at one end of blood-bathed Omaha Beach? Or did he wander again through a museum? A garden? Down a footpath? I couldn't tell, but grinned all the same. Refuge in the kitchen.

I watched Ben, silently tapping my lip to signal food stuck yet again to the part of his face he hadn't felt since 1996. It happened at least once every time we ate together. Who cued him when he ate out and about? Anyone?

Then Dan's eyes roamed to the fridge. The bag, drying for reuse? The family pictures? Magnets with pithy sayings? No, there, the Packers schedule.

"I already did it!" Sarah read Dan's mind. They kept track on the fridge scorecard.

"Seven and Oh!" Dan crowed, ripping off the rest of the season schedule.

Some seemed like a cakewalk, but I knew better. Every game a battle, twists and turns, expect the unexpected, up and at 'em again. Like life.

"Can I have the car at 4:00 tomorrow?" suddenly interjected Sarah.

"You can have it for jazz at 7:00."

"Why can't I have it at 4:00?"

"What do you need it for?

"Milo Zylo's toe is coming off."

Huh? Who was this kid? I swore every dinner she revealed heretofore unheard of teenagers, "Oh, I've known (him/her) for years, we're good friends."

"Who is he, and why is his toe coming off?" Never mind what it had to do with the car. She probably wanted to visit him in the hospital.

Her turn to look gobsmacked. "*Noo,* it's not a he! It's the new Coldplay CD, it's coming out, and I gotta wait six hours for it! I want to hold it in my hands!"

"*Milo Zylo's Toe* is the name of the new album?"

"*Noo! Mylo Xyloto*. It looks weird when you see it."

"It sounds weird when you hear it," I countered, especially when teens either mumble or machine-gun. (It couldn't possibly be my hearing at fault.)

"So can I have the car at 4:00?"

I surreptitiously gave Dan a wink, agreeing. If possible, Milo Zylo's Toe would be waiting for her after she walked home from school. Not on my T-1 and counting do-list, but I owed Sarah a make-up for my overly stressed motherly outburst a few days before.

Turning my attention to Mom's Agenda, I inspected Ben's hair. It actually looked good. For decades, I sufficed as the family's beautician, first replacing penny-pinching Dan's college self-barbering. Poor guinea pig Dan. First cut I made on the back of his head had left a horizontal hole. Lucky for him, and later the kids, I quickly learned. Years later, I taught our kids another lesson on Real Life, Real Math, the time value of money: $10 x three guys x six annual cuts x eighteen years = $3,240 = six summer camping vacations.

"I don't think we need to do anything to your hair, Ben," I commented.

"Good. I really don't want it cut, I've got a few more takes."

"Ah, yes. How did your shoot go?"

"Shoot?"

"The filming?"

"We've done about twelve hours and have a few more to go."

"How long is this movie?"

"Fifteen or twenty minutes."

"Twelve hours for twenty minutes?" I couldn't believe it, not of amateurs.

"You know the scene in the *Lord of the Rings* when they're all just sitting in a circle having a discussion?" Ben asked. "It took Peter Jackson five days to film."

"Oh, Poohbeedooz!" (My word, "stuff 'n nonsense," spelling disputable.)

At the mention of LOTR, Dan pounded Orc-like on the table, grinning evilly, while over the din Sarah yelled her confirmation of Peter Jackson's filming expertise.

"It did! It took five days!"

"How would you know?" She wasn't an LOTR aficionado.

"I'm friends with Evan."

Who's Evan? I should know, but the kids understand my memory's statute of limitations expires at thirty days. Usually. Suddenly remembering the ridiculous amount of time it took Michael Mann to shoot the death of Red, a fifteen second blip in *Public Enemies*, I believed them.

"I'm tired," Ben suddenly sighed. Filming for five hours that day compounded the half-Ben's-body-carries-the-whole/doubly-radiated-AVM-brain fatigue. (I'm not even going to try to concoct an acronym for that one.) In Ben's teens, a teacher once suggested Ben wouldn't have blood-shot eyes if he slept more. Nope. Ben sleeps a ton, exhaustion part and parcel of his existence. Excusing himself, he rose to leave.

"Hey, go put your pants on!" I barked, before he got too comfy elsewhere.

"Mom, that just sounds wrong," snickered Sarah, as Ben got up to get the khakis.

"And I've got a belt, Mom," he offered. "It's helping me a lot."

"Mmm, hmm, let's see this belt."

"Mom, it's a good belt."

"Show me...nope."

"What? Why?"

"We can do better than that. Look, it's scuffed. We're going to look put-together on Tuesday. For the cameras, you know." Belying our insides.

"No one's going to be looking at his belt," Dan moaned in his "all right-all ready" voice.

"People have those high-def TVs, you know. You can see anything." We didn't own one, I just guessed. (Dan and I enjoy our 13-inch screen DVD player; nothing looms larger than life.) Suddenly-fashionista Mom refused to back down. Sighs all around.

"Okay, I'll give him one of my belts," Dan surrendered.

"I've got a question for you, Ben," I queried to thin air. Now where'd he gone? Our cozily modest home still allowed for up or down. Must have gone up, the laundry still hung intact in the kitchen doorway. I still hang clothes on Japanese laundry clips outside in fine weather, and in the laundry room and doorways in wet weather. More Laura Ingalls Wilder. Planet and money saving.

Ben clomped downstairs, his AFO shoe on, his other barefoot. At least half free. He sat on the stairs putting on his other sock and shoe, readying to return downtown.

"I've got a question for you, Ben," I repeated.

Concentrating on tying his shoe one-handed, he spoke haltingly, "I go in the...kid door...of the...museum."

"The what?" My question could wait.

"Didn't you know there's two ways...to get in? One for adults...one for kids. I go through the...Hobbit door. It signifies...I'm an adult, but then when I'm...on the other side...I'm a big brother...caring for the kids, cherry...and helpful...and all. Making everyone... happy." He finished his shoe and stood up.

"Cherry?"

"Yeah, you know, cherrily, happy."

"*Cheery*, cheerily."

He rolled his eyes, sorry for his benign language faux pas. As far as they went, this one sounded mild. "Cherry, cheery," he mocked. (Must be hard to take basic-English correction as a twenty-three-year old male from a word nut perfectionist mother.)

"Ben, I've got a question for you," I really needed an answer. "Did you show museum staff the last paragraph of your bio? Did they say it was okay for you to read it?"

"Yes."

"All of the last paragraph?"

"The whole thing!" Then he commenced recitation. "I'm memorizing it."

"You don't have to, you know. You'll have a sheet in your hand."

"But I want to."

Of course he did. Just like a dramatic script.

Then suddenly, rushing me, "I love you! Thanks Mom! It's my dream job! I love you!"

"It really is, isn't it? I'm so happy for you and I love you too." Pulling away from his embrace, I turned away momentarily and when I looked back, my cherry son wore a new monkey hat with braided ties hanging down. I bust out laughing.

"It's Curious George!" he explained, as if he needed to. As a child, besides Mr. See-Do, we had nicknamed him Curious George. With good reason. Recently, he had asked me to dig out a certain picture of him at age seven, the summer before his brain hemorrhage. While visiting our college friends in Chicagoland, the total of seven children got on like a house afire. Ben found their dress-ups bin, donned a monkey suit, climbed a tree, and requested a banana. Even then he exuded a flair for realistic drama. No surprise he would choose a monkey hat now.

"Where'd you get that? On State Street?"

"Yep! At the same place I got you the rubber peanut," he said enigmatically.

Of course, the mysterious gift for my fiftieth birthday, signifying who knows what. But there's always a reason. I've learned if I wait long enough, often it is revealed.

After dropping Ben at his apartment, that evening, Dan and I watched the Packers game on tape. The Words mostly took a backseat, so I saw nearly every play. Snuggling on our newlywed couch from 1985, in the darkened basement where the ancient VCR resides, I asked during a huddle, "Why were you staring at the collages during dinner?"

It took him a few seconds to recall, "I was noticing paddrens." (We'd pronounced "patterns" that way ever since Ben first did.) "I see the pubs, the tea...and the flowers are obvious, but the other one is doors and arches, bricks and pathways."

Doors and arches, bricks and pathways...going through, curving around, leading where? Hobbit doors? Yellow brick roads? Ladders to the stars?

If I could sing a lullaby for my cherrily-cheery-man-child, I couldn't do any better than the troubadour from Hibbing, Minnesota, Bobby Z's prayerful *Forever Young.*

The spring of 2008, *Public Enemies* spent a great deal of time filming in Wisconsin. The day I first stumbled upon them on the Capitol Square, I declared myself a freelance writer in search of a story. I hadn't done that since age nineteen.

Twenty-eight years earlier, for the final project in my one semester of journalism (Agricultural Journalism), I hadn't wanted to write about cows or soybeans. As a UW frosh, I begged my instructor's permission to explore the newly arrived punk rock scene in Madison. A young woman in one of my classes, with the most gorgeous hair I had ever seen, had chopped her hair off and dyed the remaining spikes purple. I wanted to understand her motivation. In June 1980, *The Capital Times* published my article as the lead-story in the *P.M.* section. You'd think I'd've caught a clue. On my first teenage try, people bought my words? Not only that, reporting legitimized my insatiable curiosity. But it took nearly three decades for me to try again; finally proving that mother knows best.

My first reporting gig had occurred at age eight, in third grade. Papers and pencil in hand, I skipped next door to the decrepit, yellow, two-story building adjacent to Elm Lawn Elementary. It housed the Superintendent, Mr. Stofflet. The wooden stairs creaked on my way up, increasing the tantalizing fear. But I was prepared. Dressed for success in my hand-me-down plaid, polyester jumper, the yarn in my hair matched my knee sox, but clashed with my corrective shoes, annual choice between ugly and uglier. (I wore parentally enforced jumpers and dresses until my hissy fit the summer before seventh grade won me the right to wear pants – not denim, mind you, not yet.) Ready to pepper the Super, I clutched a bodacious hodge-podge of thirty-eight questions, starting with, "What kind of tests do you give the principals?" segueing into, "How many suplis do you oder evry year?" "Have you ever fierd anyone?" "Do you ever run out of food?" and, "How do you hire Janiters?" I ended with, "What do you think of us having a news paper?"

He thought it a "very good Idia."

So did my mother. She already knew poetry came out my childhood fingertips, spilling over from a heart so easily filled. She read, she believed, and she gently coaxed with compliments.

My love of writing continued throughout my public schooling. I wrote creatively through high school in Ms. Maribeth Mohan's classes. My most treasured possession of high school, my portfolio. On the last day of senior year, in my excitement, I put it down somewhere, losing it forever. We never made copies back then.

I wrote research paper after paper for my UW-Madison classes, and wrote more poetry for myself. The Bachelor of Arts perfectly suited my love of organizing words.

Then The Words stopped. I first worked as an office manager, one of three founding employees at The Greater Minneapolis Food Bank. Then marriage, Ben, stay-at-home mom, move to Japan, Sam, return from Japan, Sarah, and Ben's head explodes. The Words made spotty appearances, trying to decompress their mistress, but I had no time or energy for them, and no thought but one, survive. But The Words would not give up on me as easily as I gave up on them. Their niggling presence caused an internal churning, resulting in a wail to friend Sue in 2006, "I'm a writer who doesn't write!"

One day, the fall of 2007, as I rode my bike past the library on my errands, The Words urged me inside, and propelled me downstairs to the computer lab. I wrote two paragraphs, but they may as well have been *War and Peace*. Two whole graphs! In one sitting! Could there be more Words? God, it felt *good*!

"Serve from your sweet spot," I once heard a baccalaureate pastor charge the graduates. Could The Words be my sweet spot?

But I wrote no more until spring of 2008. In March, the house brimmed with eye opening experiences courtesy of living with three teenagers, thirteen, seventeen, and nineteen. While Dan traveled to Asia, an epiphany possessed me. Dormant, latent, The Words poured out. Sparks flew between my fingertips and the keyboard like the Wicked Witch of the West and those ruby red slippers. The kids noticed. We owned one computer, located in the freezing basement. They could hardly miss their wild-eyed mother atypically arising at 5:00 a.m., typing feverishly all day in the soon-to-be Johnny Depp Touched These rainbow mittens with the cut-out fingers.

On writing day four Sarah asked, "Are you writing a book?"

Ben returned from spring break on day five, immediately asking, "Are you writing a book? Is it about me?"

I knew I must've hit Sam's radar as well, he couldn't get on Facebook after school, but he held his tongue until day eleven. "Are you writing a book? You've been typing for four hours straight."

After his thirteen days in Asia, quizmaster Dan rcturned and served as prosecution, jury, and judge delving into The Case of The Suddenly Manic Writer.

Bang! Bang! The gavel sounded, court in session. One by one, I answered Dan's probing questions, "What is the purpose of all this writing?" (Publish), "Who is your audience?" (Hurting Women), "Genre?" (Heartache). Besides the presumptuous publishing part, Judge Dan got hung up on the writing part, skeptically asking, "Whaddaya mean you have too written a book, it's just in your head?"

(Read my stubbornly glaring eyes. Your Honor.)

The prosecution continued for what seemed a humorless hour, rare in our household. At one point Counsel for the Defense even had to request no sarcastic, rapid-fire questioning of the witness.

The prosecution rested, and the defense began, "Why can you not be cheering for me? Why this pouring of water on the flame of my life's passion?"

"It's not my intent to stifle your writing, I'm happy you're writing, and I think you should continue, I'm just concerned about this expectation of publication."

"Is it because you don't want me to get my hopes up and be hurt?"

"Yes, and more. Remember, I've got to live with you and your friends don't. My role as your husband has always been to be a kind of anchor in your life."

"Yeah, well, sometimes anchors crush."

"Correct. I can see that. Also, an anchor is heavy and it takes me time to lift; sometimes I'm a bit slow when you start flying."

By general consensus, the judge and defense tabled the trial, witness remanded. Court would reconvene at a future unspecified date and time for further review, and only by mutual consent. Bang!

That was April 2008. In May, the *Middleton Times Tribune* (MTT) published the Johnny Depp stab-in-the-dark I entitled "Making Friends At Public Enemies." My newfound success bred confidence, and I decided to try again. This time, writing a mega-word feature on people in Middleton planting large gardens in their front yards. As if

I were a Jehovah's Witness, only on my bike, I rode around the city knocking cold turkey upon the doors of Middletonites.

Molly opened her door white aproned, rolling pin in hand, and deceptively dithery, just like Miss Marple, Agatha Christie's ancient, sharp-as-a-tack spinster. Pins, trying in vain to control Molly's flyaway hair, poked out from her dazzling white and gray bun. A smudge of flour covered the tip of her nose. I melted, love at first sight. We took tea in her Victorian living room, and at the close of my interview, she impulsively switched roles.

"Would you say any of the personal writing you do is reminiscent in nature?"

"It's all reminiscent," I rolled my eyes, finishing with an Elsa Snort.

"Do you have any teaching experience?"

"Uh, I subbed for the district for a few years, but –"

"Oh!" She leapt off her sofa, zipped out of the room, and returned post haste with an 8x10 of about twenty older folks, exclaiming, "We need a writing teacher!"

"But I'm not a writing teacher. I'm a freelance writer, published only one ti –"

"Well, we don't need a teacher, we know how to write. We need a facilitator!"

Exhilarated, I pedaled home as fast as I could (even taking the hill on South Avenue, the one I roared down in sandals one summer as a girl, then panicked, using my big toe as a bike brake). Reaching home, spying Dan in the front yard, I casually dismounted, sauntering nonchalantly toward him, priming myself for another episode of court drama with Perreth Mason.

"Perfect," he said with a grin, after I explained. Prosecution, jury, and judge declined to throw on the brakes? What gave? "It's perfect for you. Your love of older people's stories, your leadership of small groups, your writing skills. It's perfect."

Renegade Reminiscence Writers, 3Rs – such an easy birth! We fit together so well, the class decided it had the mark of Higher Power about it. I agreed.

That summer, Molly's yard featured in MTT's two-part garden novelette. The editor, Matt, was taken by surprise. Neither of us had expected me to freelance pitch again. But it worked and I was hooked, turning next to people profiles, singing the songs of my people in my little town. That sweet chariot swung low, carrying me home.

Matt inquired incredulously, "All these people you write about live on your street?"

Umm, more accurately, on the block on my street.

Matt endeared himself to me by describing me as a writing natural, a woman who wrote best when it came from the heart. I lapped up his compliments, and those of the women of 3Rs as well, printing, cutting, and pasting them to my computer. Having failed to read *Journalism For Dummies*, having spent so many years alone in my home grading my own self-worth (falling far below an A, never acceptable), I significantly required any and all confidence boosters. Sure, Dan always gave me props for home/kid/Life With Ben management, and occasionally someone in Ben's medical world remarked, "We've got to get your mother on staff," but the words of praise from Matt, a heady liqueur, gave me true belief in my abilities. As if I were Mary Richards on *The Mary Tyler Moore Show*, this man became my Lou Grant, holding my hand as he improved my reporting. He also taught me shorthand. Matt often replied to my emails with "LOL," prompting me to finally reciprocate (not wishing to seem off-standish toward his newsroom affection), "Dude, lots of love to you too."

I also adored him because of his office décor and fashion sense. We communicated mainly via email, but sometimes, like the fall of 2011, I stopped by the office a few blocks from my home.

The lair of my editor never failed to make me laugh, and I never felt bad about my dining room table or desk when there. The higgledy-piggledy leaning Towers of Pisa Paper stacked feet high, slid under all surfaces, and nearly wallpapered the joint. His office always looked like a Dickens' newspaperman's hidey-hole. But he was in there somewhere; Matt's beard, amongst the sheaves, a dead giveaway. To complete the picture, he just needed a cigar and a Scotch by his side, but he usually had coffee, not even his beloved beer. And he doesn't smoke. (It would be a fire hazard.) As Mary Richards used to say of her boss, "I think he's *terrific*!"

"Hey! C'mon in. I'm sorry, I didn't mean to pile things on the chairs," Matt apologized as he removed his laptop case so I could sit down. Obviously. It didn't look as if he meant to pile things anywhere. Pitch things about randomly, most likely. (Accuracy in words dontchaknow.)

"You look like Red Green," I complimented. He loved Red Green. "I like your curling handle-bar mustache and bushy beard." The plaid, flannel shirt and the flannel hat on his head reminded me of a North Woods lumberjack, sans saw. The computer served to disarm; no sharp implements in this room. Sharp words only, implemented on the screen.

After discussing a few of my current feature ideas, including covering Ben's press conference and DC trip, we reminisced the olden days. My coup de foudre, my thunderbolt, had remained the *Public Enemies* story. I worked so hard on it in 2008 that I made $1.00 per hour (not including the out-of-pocket I spent on gas and the hotel). Afterward, my freelance writer friend sent congratulations informing me my remuneration qualified me for official induction into the Freelancer Secret Society. But I waited in vain for my decoder ring to arrive in the mail.

"I got a lot of comments for the Johnny Depp story for a long time," Matt mused. "Mostly from other journalists in other small cities. They liked it."

I smiled. "What did they like about it, besides Johnny Depp? Was it the part you made me put in, about Ben?" My submission purposefully hadn't included a word about Ben. Must everything revolve around, or stem from, my life with him? Circs outside my control had planted me out of my league, but I thrived in some respects. Life With Ben certainly wasn't ever boring, and it honed my critical thinking skills, but also decimated my identity and wellbeing. Nope, I hadn't wanted a whiff of Ben in my inaugural launch of something finally and truly just about, and just for, me. But Matt insisted I put in the Captain Jack factor and Ben's piratey *Peter Pan* scars. Then he put the story on the front page.

"Yeah, it was uplifting, it was real," he said. "We broke all the rules, writing in the first person, including your personal story, but it had such a strong Middleton connection, and also was of such broad interest that anybody could read it."

I smiled, again.

"The other journalists wanted to know, 'How come Middleton always gets the interesting stories?' And I said, 'Hey, this had nothing to do with me! This one just landed on my desk.'"

That's right, my smile said, it came from outta nowhere. Somewhere Else.

Cinco de Mayo 2008, I joined the throng of bystanders watching *Public Enemies* filming taking place just outside the Capitol.

One young woman screamed, "*OMG*! It's totally Christian Bale!" Registering my blank stare, she enthusiastically added for my benefit, "Batman!"

Her friend, noticing I took copious notes with pen and paper, chimed in helpfully, "That's Christian with an 'h'. B-A-L-E."

"Right. Thanks," I replied, suddenly feeling old and decrepit. Mumbling to no one in particular, "Isn't Adam West 'Batman'?"

Two sisters my age heard me, laughed, and then inquired, Why so many notes? Freelance writer. Oh! Their two small-town Wisconsin boys were cast extras. Relatives of Johnny Depp or something? Nope, the boys just fit the bill.

"All moms of crew and cast should be allowed on the set," I opined. My comment must have impressed them, for The Sisters adopted me, inviting me to tag along as they searched for better views.

Up in the Capitol Assembly chambers, the handful of people gathered in the room took well-ordered turns peering out of the windows onto the award scene below. Fifteen sweltering, pubescent boys stood behind Billy Crudup, playing J. Edgar Hoover, and Christian Bale's FBI Agent Purvis. Between each take (well over ten), Make-Up and Hair dashed in, shading the baking boys with umbrellas while re-touching.

"Let her up front to see, she's a writer!" Brunette Sister admonished. The small crowd parted like the Red Sea. Yoiks! They were taking me so seriously.

"Freelance, only," I muttered in embarrassment, hoping I would not disappoint these two women displaying such faith in me.

Blonde Sister lived in Columbus, where *Public Enemies* soon would shoot. She gave me the insider scoop on when and where to go, providing invaluable viewing tips.

So I did. Spending twelve hours in rapt attention one day, from afar, I took my first newspaper photo. Johnny Depp, as John Dillinger carrying a rifle, or machine gun, or some weapon of mass destruction. Not too shabby a subject for my first newspaper photo methinks.

A man on the crew befriended me, as I watched him in utter fascination. While Vinnie worked all day, chatting with me on his breaks, I told him about Ben and my plan to bring him the following evening.

The next night, after checking in at a Columbus hotel with Ben, I introduced him to Vinnie by the set barricades. Then we staked out our Johnny Depp Meet 'n Greet site.

Pitch black had descended by the time the crew filmed the scene of Red's demise. We sat on camping chairs a few hundred yards away, unable to see the set, waiting with a hundred others. Ben left to stretch his legs, but did not return. Apprehensive, I went in search, but was stopped by Security from going further. I mimicked Ben's gait for descriptive purposes, and Security realized he had seen Ben go by along the edge, long ago. Ben finally reappeared, spinning the exciting tale that Vinnie had allowed him on the set. He had watched set-up of light, shadows, and positioning before the famous actors arrived.

Misty-May, bone-chilling rain began to fall, so I moved us away from the crowd. As Ben dozed, partially under a building overhang, I covered him with umbrellas and my trench coat. At 2:00 a.m., after miserably sitting in drizzle for three hours, Ben awoke with a jerk, loudly groaning, "Mom, I can't do this anymore! I gotta lie down."

I'd been ready for bed for hours, but with disappointed resignation we left. Ah, well, courtesy of kind Vinnie, Ben could always say he'd walked a bona fide movie set. As we passed Security, I asked how long he thought the shoot would take.

"They're done now. Should be wrapped up and out here to greet people within the hour."

(Attention Dear Reader: Johnny Depp Spoiler Alert!)

"Ben! One more hour?"

An energized Ben entertained the crowd in the light rain for the next two hours. Around 3:00 a.m. a local coffee shop owner-cum-angel handed round proper corpse revivers: scones and hot chocolate spiked with cinnamon.

"I just want everyone to have a good time in our little town," she remarked.

As if on cue, the robins sang in the pre-dawn darkness, and He emerged from a trailer. Pale, presumably exhausted, Johnny Depp played his last character for the night, Johnny Depp Most Courteously And Sincerely Greets His Fans. Walking slowly the length of his adoring people, he softly spoke his thanks, posed for photos, shook hands, and sometimes hugged. The guy hails from Kentucky and, last I heard, Kentucks don't typically employ the Queen's English. But his gentle, lovely British accent just kicked the night up into uber surreal.

When Johnny reached us, Ben tried to be funny and shook his hand, lefty. Afraid he'd move on without shaking mine, yet unable to rip my eyes away from the diminutive actor, I wearily moaned, "Ben, bud...Mom needs a hug."

"Aww," Johnny breathed, as he opened his arms to give me one.

Then Ben asked, "Can I have one too?" and the actor kindly complied.

I didn't care what character the man played, 1930s gangsta' or celebrity meet 'n greet. To me he would always be freedom-loving Captain Jack Sparrow, and young-at-heart Sir J. M. Barrie, creator of *Peter Pan, or The Boy Who Wouldn't Grow Up*. Mr. Barrie also informed us, "All the world is made of faith, and trust, and pixie dust."

Johnny would be the man who helped redeem 4:00 a.m. for me, as I pulled yet another all-nighter with my son, this one beautiful. After Johnny sweetly hugged me, I turned away to cry. Sarah's roy-g-biv woolen mittens on my hands first embraced the actor then covered my face.

"*Mom!* No one can ever wear these rainbow mittens again," thirteen-year-old Sarah commanded solemnly the next day, as she carefully placed them in a Baggie, writing, "Johnny Depp Touched These," on the outside in Sharpie.

Of course we've worn them again, both of us. Just as Molly, Matt, and The Sisters from small-town Wisconsin believed in me, the roy-g-biv mittens are part of my life's forever-young faith, trust, and magical pixie dust.

Chapter 21

Mothers, And Little Boys, Must Grow Up

When the calendar flipped to 2002, mid-way into Sarah's first grade, Sam's sixth grade, and Ben's eighth grade, six years of tumultuous waters subsided. Not quite placid, as on a daily basis Ben still presented physical, mental, spiritual, and/or emotional crises when I picked him up from Walbridge School. But a counselor helped me with a game plan for that. She counseled acceptance of the daily trouble, "it was what it was," the way it "should" be. I would learn to deal with that appropriately, calmly, and graciously. (All better, now?) If your working definition of "should," is "all that needed to happen for x to happen did happen," you're fine. But my fierce sense of fair play, justice, and misplaced high expectations always blockaded. My brain translated and distilled her injunction to anticipate and accept daily crises as Expect Trouble. Doing so, I didn't feel so blindsided and the rare days without trouble felt like gifts. But this thinking also trained my brain, as if it needed more help in the arena, to keep a negative outlook.

Ben's relatively peaceful existence bought me some space. This, understandably, yet to me at the time completely inexplicably, gave my body and mind permission to crash. I cooperated fully, falling disastrously headlong into my first debilitating depression. But the trigger was not Life With Ben. (Not yet.)

Instead of reserving the spacious gift as a time to breathe, to recover from what I'd asked of myself for six years, I began making grandiose plans to fly all five of us to Japan to visit many of our friends. Tour Guide Katherine's body emphatically put both feet down in refusal. The night we purchased our children's passports, I didn't sleep a wink. Severe insomnia settled in, linked so obviously to my plans that even I figured it out. Still, I couldn't understand it. Every year, I spoke at several schools as "The Japan Lady," walking the kids through a day in the life of a typical Japanese child. And, every week, I hosted Japanese women in my home. I enjoyed immensely these connections to Japan and my friendships with Japanese women. I also missed my good friends in Japan. Why were plans to visit them shutting me down? Throwing all in reverse, I halted and cancelled the trip, thinking it would be enough to flip the sleep switch. Too late.

Lead weights hung from my cheeks, the facial muscles in charge of smiling turned to concrete, my brain clogged with tar, and my sleep continued the game of Hide and Seek, refusing to be found. Doctors prescribed pill after pill, resulting in all sorts of effects but the one desired. One suggested a book on recovering sleep that about killed me as I tried to follow its recommendations. The vast majority of the population successfully follows the prescription: after fifteen minutes get up and do something. Every night I paced, freezing, from bed to couch, couch to bed, sleeping nowhere.

No conventional method or drug could locate my elusive sleep and knock me out. They only touched the symptoms, unable to reach the deep emotional trauma causing the sleepless depression. And sleep hygiene was not my problem. I had always cherished sleep, experiencing way too much life during my waking hours. A champion sleeper for decades, my timeworn routine oddly had quit working.

My three daily jobs for the first few months of 2002 – do not kill myself, cook dinner, do laundry. (Numbers two and three negotiable.) When possible, the fearful tasks took all day to accomplish, via shaky rote muscle memory and Neanderthal command form. "Cut onion." Rest. "Pour detergent." Rest. "Push button." Rest. "Choose life. Choose life. Choose life." Rest.

"Rest" meant rocking myself in the living room recliner. I hid in fear, draping a blanket over my head, despite being the only one home during the day. Fearing Dan's death, the silence, and any sound, I hid in my soul with the Lover of My Soul. And I rocked. Not easily, as if a woman planted her feet firmly on the ground and leisurely pushed the entire rocker back and forth. A whimpering fetal woman in a stupor, riddled with anxiety and few thoughts, arms clutching her knees, rapidly mini-rocking her folded torso, traumatized self-soothing. No words, no humor, shut down, shut off. My mind churned to Swiss cheese. Or, since I also live in hockey territory, a sieve. Even now, I feel the effects of those holes, life I lost.

When the kids would come home from school, I hid in my bedroom, my only whispered explanation, "Sadness sickness."

I asked Dan to hit me, to render me unconscious. He refused, rocking me gently instead. If he could've traded bodies with me, he would have. I became so desperate, if I'd known a doctor who made propofol house calls I would've availed myself of the service like poor Michael Jackson. As adults, the King of Pop and I shared severe insomnia and a love of his eminently danceable music.

First glimpsing the young heartthrob on black and white TV in 1972, I could tell we did not have the same shade of skin. He was the prize on a game show – a date with pubescent, afro-sporting, black Michael. But it didn't seem fair. All three bachelorette contestants also had dark skin. What about a white eleven-year-old from Wisconsin?

Following the train of hypothetical posers, as kids are prone to do (when still at the age when a mother is the receptacle of all wisdom), my set of 'ifs' ended with, "If I won, would you let me go on a date with Michael?"

Neither his color nor mine concerned my mother, only the fact that I'd recently left fifth grade. She gave tentative permission, as long as she chaperoned. I knew that wouldn't be a problem; both the winning bachelorette's mother and a game show chaperone would accompany. Theoretically allowed to date Michael Jackson, I found my first lesson in race relations immensely satisfying. From then on, I understood people are people.

Unfortunately, I did not also learn from my mother the bodies and minds of humans have limitations. Be self-aware in loving care, or beware. Fortunately my counselor knew it and thought for me, asking one day, "Are you open to alternative medicine?"

Dr. Puckette, chiropractic kinesiologist extraordinaire, provided relief. He first listened carefully to me, asking about the onset of the symptoms. As I briefly explained the Japan connection conundrum he homed in, "Tell me about actually living in Japan." Speechless, sobs wracked my body. Emotional trauma pinpointed, we began to deal with it. His work brought out the stored toxicity from nooks and crannies, and my counselor and I worked through exploring and grieving that period of my life. As I was unable yet to write coherent thoughts, she encouraged me to create a collage depicting what had been my daily reality in Nagasaki. Cutting and pasting words, letters, phrases, and pictures from magazines and newspapers, helped remove the poison from my system.

While I was waiting in Dr. Puckette's office one day, an elderly woman hobbled in, observing to all, "We'll see if The Good Doctor can work some of his magic."

As with string theory, or even evaporation or electricity, I will never fully understand his non-invasive, scientifically based "magic." I don't really care how it works – only that it does. Even as I write, he continues to enhance my life, and Ben's too, unpacking our emotions from our bodies so we can deal appropriately with them. Life has a knack for shutting down the mind-body connections in our amazingly wired bodies. Simply put, Dr. Puckette unsticks my pathways so my body can do what my brain asks it to – function, in other words.

Dan attended some counseling and kinesiology appointments with me, and hung gentle and tough through all – my silence, cradled shaking, slack face, panic, and anxiety-fueled pronouncements on economy. Slowly returning from the abyss, regaining intellect (even if not fully functional at first), earnest, complete sentences finally formed, such as "I need to die," and "If we used less bar soap, we could save a lot of money."

When "I" was gone, who or what, in what passed for my mind, egged me on with thoughts of self-destruction and clever housekeeping? Money-saving schemes featured prominently. Dan made money, I didn't, and my role had always been to stretch that dollar like taffy. But our insurance didn't cover either my out-of-plan counselor or any chiropractic kinesiology, invaluable recovery choices for me.

After I'd been relatively put back together, someone recommended *The Highly Sensitive Person*, by Elaine Aron. Dismissively reading quickly through the checklist at the beginning, I decided to continue even though I clearly was not an HSP. Then I hit chapter two, slowly reread the checklist in shock, and went over it with Dan. He laughed at an HSP not immediately recognizing herself. Among many other things, we both finally understood my shutting down with a book in my hand at 7:30 each evening, and my need for more sleep than anyone else we knew. I simply could not take any more stimulation. In college, people laughed incredulously at my nine or more hours of shut-eye, but in my forties I finally came to guilt-free terms with what my body required. And I learned people like me manage insomnia best by remaining supine, belly breathing with eyes closed, shutting out all.

Perhaps most important, through counseling, Dr. Puckette, and reading I began to learn to not resent not being Dan. He seemed able to roll with the punches much easier than I, and I had grown jealous of that. We both had erroneously assumed we'd taken the same life hits. Differently wired, we hadn't.

After the first depression, what I asked of myself without caring enough for myself in my Life With Ben triggered more of The Depressions. Off and on throughout my forties they spoke, but I did not understand, did not heed. "Your way of life is unsustainable," the mantra of my body 2002. Repeat 2003, "Your way of life is unsustainable." Still not listening in 2005? "Your way of life is unsustainable." Can you hear me in 2006? "Your way of life is unsustainable."

The Depressions nearly took my unsustainable life from me for good. Feeling unable to cope any longer with any number of things is what I consider the suicidal common denominator. With pain, guilt, shame, sorrow, fear, anxious urges, a burden carried, or the burden one has become, or the voices in one's head. Not telling anyone, and/or self-medicating, only compounds. In caps the red EXIT entices, slow seduction pulling, worthlessness pushing. One whispers, the other shouts, making it hard to fight off the deadly duo. Not fully grasped in the mistaken final solution is that one cannot simply call a do-over; sudden death remains sudden death. Those who can speak freely of their mental health challenges, and seek and find support, usually fare better than those who keep their mental darkness a secret.

Buried in a tiny newspaper column entitled "Briefly," government stats on our nation's suicidal state once presented these tidbits: over eight million seriously considered suicide in 2009, nearly 37,000 followed through successfully. Just over half used a gun (www.cdc.gov/nchs/fastats/suicide.htm). I felt those facts misplaced in the newspaper. The deaths of those 37,000, impacting personal and professional relationships, causing innumerable ripple effects, cannot be labeled "brief." It seems safe to say that every one of us has something at stake in the nation's collective psyche. By contrast, but no less tragic, more stats from Centers for Disease Control (CDC) reveal close to 17,000 people died from homicide in America in 2009, two-thirds by gunshot (www.cdc.gov/nchs/fastats/homicide.htm). Both suicide and homicide make up such small percentages of our nation's population, but leave such destructive wakes. Annually, these violent deaths equal the size of a small city.

In 2006, Psychotherapist taught me healthy families and individuals know when to seek help. If we can vocalize, "I am struggling, I need help," we begin to walk the path of working through our illness with support. If society embraces, funds, and implements easier access to effective Clubhouse services like Yahara House, we're on the road to uplifting our citizens. Long-term mental health treatment and support systems that actually work should be available regardless of individual ability to pay. Society always pays, either writing the preventative check up front, or multiplying it for clean-up crew.

Whether debilitating or not, mental illness embattles equally, no respecter of race, age, gender, religion, education, status, nationality, or any other boundary recognized by humans. Doctors, lawyers, homemakers, teachers, students, clergy, actors, writers, business people, skilled, and unskilled workers, mental illness is an equal opportunity employer. It abounds in our families, neighborhoods, circles of friends, and around the globe. As an integral part of the human experience affecting us all, how shall we best address it?

From years of self-introspection with support, I have learned what works best for me. My kindergarten teacher described my brain as "flighty," my sixteen-year-old girl said it contained "crystallized intelligence," a psychiatrist, Dr. Sparkle, suggested "hypomanic-depressive" (never having experienced full-blown mania), and I just say, "It's me."

Realization that I possessed a certain kind of brain slowly dawned. Not everyone owns a popcorn brain. Or maybe they do, but the heat isn't high enough so the kernels remain inert. Wildly unfettered access to what seems like everything I've ever read, experienced, and learned helps fuel my sense of humor, the strangely juxtaposed flotsam and jetsam in the popper. Life is really funny, and the longer I live the funnier it gets, if only just for me. Until my first depression, I had not realized how I delightfully entertained myself daily. As my own constant companion, I am the person who makes me laugh most. When I left me, I watched comedians Lucy and Gilda. Their antics lightened my heart, even if they couldn't reach my face. (For sheer stick-to-it inspiration I watched *The Biggest Loser*. I could answer the theme song's question with, "I feel proud of myself today because I didn't kill myself!")

Quirky humor, coupled with brutal honesty and the Highly Sensitive Person trip-up trap, rashly crossing boundaries to one's own detriment, sometimes results in trouble. I don't take psychotropic drugs for that very reason. (Oh, right. I do.) I don't take *psychedelic* drugs for that very reason. I don't need extra help with zippiness, flashbulb ideas and actions, or miscommunication. But I now love my mind, double-edged swords and all. That's life, right? We all live as best we can, juggling our multiple double-edged swords and personal paradoxes, bandages at the ready. Scrapes, cuts, and mortal gashes, resulting from the mismanagement of our minds, can be read about every day in the newspapers.

Although my mental illness is not a choice, I have learned I can exacerbate or reduce its impact by the daily choices I make. I love that by practicing new ways of thinking and acting, instituting new habits, I can even change my brain. I am learning its value, how to work within its parameters, and how to strengthen connections. We're hardwired to rewire.

During my brief period of clinical introspection with Dr. Sparkle, his exceedingly practical help included homework to read *The Bipolar Workbook: Tools for Controlling Your Mood Swings* by Dr. Monica Ramirez Basco. From it I learned how to better monitor and manage my moods. From Dr. Daniel Siegel's book *Mindsight: The New Science of Personal Transformation,* I learned the science of our brains and how life experiences and mindfulness impact brain chemistry. We have a powerful say in how we live our lives, by becoming aware of ourselves, and the choices we make. Often, the very best thing we can do is to decide to do some thing(s) differently. This is beautifully borne out in Jill Muehrcke's empowering book, *Waking Up Happy*, full of inspiring memoirs of regular folks who chose differently, and did just that.

I did too. In 2008, finally hearing myself, I began to rearrange my life accordingly. When I finally grasp the obvious, I can change. Precedence had been set when, as a three-year-old laundry helper, Sarah had proudly complimented, "Mama, you have the biggest undies in the whole family!"

I switched from briefs to bikinis. Not such an easy fix in 2008.

Ren prompted my March 2008 epiphany, gently asking, "Kath, what do you want?"

What I wanted hadn't seemed part of the equation since January 1996, when Chief Neurosurgeon had asked, "*What do you want to do?*"

Ren's simple question sat me hard on my keister, leaving me without words but with space and air to breathe. What did I want? Somewhere Else. What did I need? What I needed had been there all along, yet I couldn't see it clearly, and wouldn't grant myself permission to accept it. Just like Scarecrow, Tin Man, and Cowardly Lion. Ren steered me toward the yellow brick road, helped lead me home.

My new lifetime goal? Functional survival. First and foremost, I am human, close on its heels, I am woman, last but never least, I am myself.

Ben turned fourteen the summer of 2002, just before his freshman year. Liberally add hormones to a twice-radiated AVM, stir vigorously. As firstborn, Ben naturally functioned as our guinea pig through his teen years. We didn't know if his upwardly ratcheted behavior, and mental states, indicated normal teen, typical Ben, AVM and/or radiation brain, or a combo. We settled upon Teen Ben.

But Ben's teen brain was not our only concern. At a summer RehabDoc appointment, we discovered Ben's right foot required a complete remodel. The night cast had failed to keep his foot growing correctly. Orthopedic Surgeon instructed, "Go on vacation, start high school, make friends, surgery in October."

Seeking freedom, we drove like banshees, two twelve-hour days plus another three hours, to the Canadian Rockies in British Columbia. Border Patrol let our demented carload into Canada despite, one presumes, hearing four people yell, "Shut up, Ben!"

He'd volunteered loudly, "It's not like we have a nuclear bomb on board."

Ben's foot allowed little hiking, as we could only carry our teen short distances after he tired. Purportedly for Ben's sake, we stayed in eco-friendly cabins instead of tents, complete with wood-fired hot tub, composting toilets, and solar-powered electricity in the communal lodge.

Freed from my previous winter's depression, the August respite revived and strengthened me for Ben's fall surgery and new high school career.

After the three-stitched-together trailers and thirty pupils (a total of two girls) in marvelous Walbridge School, the public high school bowled Ben over. Halls everywhere overflowed with 1,700 teenagers, half of them "cute girls." His freshman choir boasted seventy-five girls, eight boys. Good odds. Ben died and went to heaven, and the seventh celestial sphere of heaven contained one thing, Drama Club.

I joined him in heaven. Ben's IEP successfully patched together a mix of class levels, and I no longer ferried him between schools.

Late October's foot overhaul occurred during the fall school break. For efficiency's sake, we kicked it off with a routine AVM follow-up MRI, and the next day proceeded to the OR. Surgery included five incisions, placement of four long screws, a lengthened heel cord, bone fusion, and rearrangement of a ligament, anchoring it to a bone to use it as an internal strap.

Knowing he'd be wheelchair-bound for about two months before learning to walk again, we moved Ben out of the boys' room upstairs, setting him up in what had been the TV room. On the lower level, with a bathroom, a door led to the garage. No steps for either. Both boys separately approached me, requesting the new arrangement last longer. We extended the wall and added a door to Ben's permanent new digs.

For nine days Ben suffered in bed or a recliner, crying out in pain. On addictive painkillers, he soon declared action movies just as good for relief. I weaned him off drugs, and overdosed with him on James Bond.

But the gods smiled upon us that fall when UW Hospital's Rehabilitation Department moved to its own freestanding clinic. Years before, along with others on a patient-feedback panel, the idea to remove rehab from the hospital had heartily been mine. I never dreamed they'd set up shop at the end of our street. It now took ninety-five seconds to get from our house to Ben's innumerable AFO casting, fix-it, RehabDoc, and therapy appointments.

On Ben's first wheelchair-bound day back to school, Chief Neurosurgeon called me with the MRI results. "We were very pleased with Ben's most recent MRI. We don't see any AVM, but that doesn't mean it might not show up on angiography."

Such fantastic news in the middle of another rough patch! Two hours later, just after I composed an Update of Jubilation, literally seconds after pushing "send," the high school called. Ben complained of strong chest pains. Middleton's ambulance transported him to UW

ER, and I followed behind. Docs ruled out heart attack and blood clot, finding no cause. Ben experienced more chest pain that night. The grind to euphoria to terror roller-coaster ride would not let up.

He wore a cast for three months, unable to even stand for nearly two months. The high school did an excellent job coping. So did Ben. It seemed not many of the teens and staff didn't know him. Constant high fives, hugs, "How's it goin's?" and help from "pretty girls" pushing his wheelchair kept him upbeat.

Ben grieved at home. Wailing, "Why, why, why is my life so hard?" from behind his closed door.

Finally out of the wheelchair, aided by a bamboo cane from Japan, the snowy sidewalks still made life difficult. Some physically and mentally capable people, even in the Good Neighbor City, choose not to shovel their wintry walks.

But Ben recovered enough to participate in a variety of Drama Club events, notably March's premiere performance in the high school's new, flashy Performing Arts Center. He played a juggler in *Romeo and Juliet*, as well as Capulet's Cousin.

"Mom, did you see me on stage, crying? We were supposed to cry for that scene, and I had real tears!"

Our So Cal docs confirmed the no-AVM-in-sight MRI report. UW docs scheduled a final angiography, the last hurdle to clear, for August 2003. Ben wrote his own update just before his sophomore year.

Dear family and friends,

I have another angiography tomorrow at 11:30 a.m. I have to thank you, each of you, that without your prayers, I would not have come this far in my life. You have been with me all the way, and I can't thank you enough. Now this is the final step, to see if the AVM is gone completely. I ask if you will join me in prayer to God that the AVM is gone. I will have to stay flat for six hours in bed after the angiography is done. I'm having a great summer. I was just Head Monkey in The Wizard of Oz*!*

The wizard's chief monkey did not get the news he desired. The tiny, lower tip of the perfidiously stubborn AVM still doggedly remained in his brain, threatening his life.

Our dear, So Cal, perfectionist PhysicistDoc commiserated with Ben,

I was afraid that a report like the one you described was the outcome of the study. I think you have grown a lot spiritually over the years, Ben, and maybe this is what is the good behind everything. I am glad that you feel protected from harm, and that may well be true.

AVMs sometimes still grow during childhood but this should stop soon. So it may feel like we are chasing it with our protons, but God willing we will eventually get it. So don't lose hope, and I am sure you don't.

Maybe Ben wouldn't, but ah, too late, I already had. Rocking in a chair in Ben's angiography recovery room, I had listened as the radiologist explained the film to Dan.

"And these, and these, and these, and these," he'd said, referring to all the remaining AVM feeders. Each "these," as if a sledgehammer, pounded me into the abyss. After praying for so long, after experts in two states agreed no AVM was visible in the last MRI, our angiography confirmation hopes had been Mt. Everest high.

"Hope deferred makes the heart sick...." reads one biblical Proverb. Yes. It does. And where was my God? Had he not heard my heartfelt requests? A strange fact I noticed years later, the notion that "answered prayer" is when you get what you want. What do we call it when we don't receive what we've asked for? Sorrow.

Ben still lives with an annual 2-4% chance of an AVM rupture, potentially destroying his life. This means he lives annually with a pretty decent chance of making it through the next year in one piece.

Really, when you think about it, that's about what many of us have in this fragile life, right? But we don't focus on our destructibility, not unless it's somehow borne home.

While once purchasing a ceramic plate from my local potter, she asked, “Would you like a bag for this?”

Usually eschewing bags of all kinds, this time I agreed, a nod to my klutziness. After a pause, I teased, “Like that paper sack’s really gonna help when I drop this.”

But I know the merest veneer of protection adds a huge psychological buffer. This is how we live with Ben’s dicey brain, embracing the illusion of safety, just like everyone else. People demonstrate this daily, hurtling down highways in aluminum foil.

Ben grieved his remaining AVM in spurts at home. Dan did the same. It took me longer to recover from another round of severe depression, using medication and my self-work tools, psychotherapy and Dr. Puckette. He and I found one word specifically troubled my mind-body. Bizarre, but to me completely understandable because of the tip-of-the-intense-iceberg it represented, the word “these.”

The word repetitively spoken as I learned Ben’s AVM still remained. And would always remain. Queen Boudicca of the Celtic Iceni, Warrior Mother, defeated. I had to accept I could never fix my boy.

Eight months later, the spring of Ben’s sophomore year, he put on a Fine Arts Week, one-man, multi-character, personalized show. Five hundred teens howled when Ben embellished comedian “Weird Al” Yankovic’s search-for-donuts-attacking-weasels script. Leaning in to the audience conspiratorially, Ben pointed at his AFO with the large smiley-face on the back, adlibbing, “They did this to me!”

Chapter 22

Savvy?

Sixteen-year-old Ben began in earnest to dree his weird Thanksgiving weekend of 2004, his junior year. Dree = endure, suffer, submit. Weird = destiny, fate. Scot for face the music. Those strange changes Mr. Bowie sang about, Ben's life so not hunky dory.

At first, Ben's pediatrician thought the symptoms viral: severe fatigue, dizziness, weakness, and bobble headedness. Hardly able to get out of bed, Ben complained, "My head has no place to go."

All tests returned negative. No virus. No thyroid issue. We thought maybe a rest cure over winter break would improve Ben. Besides the routine MRI in December, and his usual plethora of medical appointments, Ben's four wisdom teeth had been extracted that fall. In addition, his extra-curricular drama and choir life had tired him. He seemed better at the end of winter break, but at a January drama practice, Ben fell asleep backstage. Ridiculously uncharacteristic behavior – the kid lived for the stage.

While I put on "The Japan Lady" show for third-graders, and subbed a few hours, Ben, unable to function at school, stayed home most of mid-January's finals week. When he complained he couldn't draw breath, in alarm I watched my boy's chest rise and fall, forgetting to breathe myself. I drove him to UW ER, but they found nada.

The symptoms intensified and grew: trouble concentrating, blurry and sparkly vision, itchy attacks, ringing ears, a hot head inside and out, shivers and jolts, but not feverish or cold, and intensely bloodshot eyes.

Immediately, I notified our UW and So Cal AVM docs. Foremost in my mind, could the nasty, radiation-risk sign-off sheet of 2001 be messing with Ben's abilities? Or was the dastardly AVM causing trouble? Ben's symptoms seemed eerily connected to hypothalamic regulation and sight, the AVM's location. Or could it be psychological? The odd symptoms waxed and waned bizarrely.

We met with Chief Neurosurgeon to discuss Ben's strange condition and the recent MRI results. He suggested pursuing various specialists, as well as another angiography. As for the AVM, "upon conferring with half the world's doctors," they decided further treatment posed too much risk. Perhaps more shrinkage would occur from the second radiation, but until technology came up with something new, doing nothing remained our only option. Chief Neurosurgeon would monitor Ben's AVM every two years via MRIs. I felt relieved, no more decisions about Ben's brain, his wacky life already more than enough for me. But Dan grieved, his hope finally snuffed out.

The AVM meeting's bright spot immensely pleased teenage Ben. Miss Wisconsin 2003, Chief Neurosurgeon's resident. We shook the hand of Dairy State royalty, Dr. Tina Sauerhammer. I joked meeting her may have supplanted my 1995 best claim to fame, cutting butter pats for a Japanese Princess's breakfast at the International Crane Foundation in Baraboo.

At that time, standing in line with other early-morning volunteers, including my friend Kyoko who'd recruited me, I'd bowed as the Princess greeted us. But I'd refrained from asking then-Princess Sayako if she'd appreciated my most excellent, uniform squares. I made very sure to tell my mother, however, as she had rarely allowed me to cut the Brownie pan – too many sizes resulted.

Driving home after our appointment with Dr.-Miss-Wis, I realized I'd forgotten to tell the docs about a newly materialized symptom. When I woke Ben up that morning he'd been scared, "I heard voices near my ear in the night. Tiny voices."

In the car, he suddenly shouted, "I hear them again!" I didn't. After shutting the car off, I did. His bedtime CD headphones now lay on the car seat, leaking elfin voices.

At the end of January, I fetched a used wheelchair from Madison's Wheelchair Recycling Program. Ben couldn't manage school without one on the rare days he went, and I pushed Ben to most of his medical appointments.

While awaiting various testing, I took Ben to New Psychiatrist. (Ben's child psychiatrist of five years sadly had just left the state. I'd found him after my dismal meeting with the first child psychiatrist, the week I'd buried my mom. He'd become a trusted practical helper for Ben, and the first medical practitioner to really validate my teetering balance beam Life With Ben. As Ben's doctor, he'd medicated me with affirmation, and I had eagerly looked forward to Ben's appointments. But, just when we really needed him, he had moved elsewhere to help fill the nation's shortage of pediatric psychiatrists.)

Ben exhibited some symptoms in New Psychiatrist's office, eyes at half-mast, crying, lying down, too weak to sit up. Purposefully, I mentioned juggling and he rallied. Within twenty minutes Ben stood and juggled, but not with his usual gusto. New Psychiatrist explained the symptoms possibly were psychologically exacerbated, but not straight up his field. They indicated a physical basis, he concluded. Possibly seizures.

The barrage of testing commenced: angiography, EEG, video EEG, endocrinology, neurology, and neuro-ophthalmology. The EEG showed abnormality, but not serious. Probably. Ben's EEGs since the 1996 bleed always did so.

We slogged through the hospital video EEG, a seven-hour ordeal, checking for seizure activity. Staff said I must stay with Ben at all times; for lunch, we could order out pizza and they'd bring it to us. They attached electrodes to Ben's bad-hair-day head. While they filmed his brain activity, I administered my own tests, scrutinizing Ben like a mother hawk, taking detailed notes. The EEG video would pick up any blips in seizure activity, and I thought perhaps my notes could corroborate and/or elucidate. Making the grueling day harder than it had to be, on purpose I raised topics to gauge various emotional reactions. I wondered if any emotional connection triggered, or worsened, Ben's symptoms, and catching up on homework served a dual purpose. I tried to get him to focus on US Government homework (boredom), watched him play games on PlayStation (happiness), and brought up a home life problem sure to elicit anger. Testing attention, I read chemistry to him. He lay back with his eyes closed, but interacted with me verbally, attending. He violently twitched all day except when playing the games.

Directly after the EEG video, I drove Ben to his first paid juggling gig, at our elementary school's Fun Night. He had so looked forward to earning his first money as a sixteen-year-old. They gave him $15 for juggling while standing next to his wheelchair. Marshaling my reserves (hah!), I face painted for over two hours, because long ago I'd signed up to be in charge, and I didn't want to disappoint anyone. Besides, I reasoned, painting children's faces is creatively therapeutic. ("The lady doth protest too much, methinks.")

Afterward, Dan took me to the local pub for debriefing, only a stone's throw from Middleton's Capital Brewery. I sobbed into my pint of Wisconsin Amber, barely able to communicate the distress of the day. Ben, all over the map emotionally and physically, resembled a yo-yo in demeanor and behavior, except a yo-yo is fairly predictable.

Super Bowl Sunday, in his wheelchair at my insistence, Ben participated in his choir's fundraiser show. He wanted to stand on the risers with the others, but I wouldn't let him. (The symptoms had started two months before as he'd performed on choir risers, dizzily trying not to fall.) The choir sang from *Les Mis,* heartbreaking lyrics about a young life when dreams could still be dreamt, and hopes could still be high. Ben said, "It brought me to tears inside," although that day he wore his out-and-about happy face.

Lugging the chair in my car twice each day, I remained at Ben's beck and call, taking him to school late, picking him up early, and staying at home with him otherwise.

One day he called from the nurse's office to be picked up, but when I arrived the aggravating symptom had subsided. He wanted to return to class.

"Can I wheel you to chemistry?" I asked, knowing the science wing's distance from the nurse's office.

"Mom, you're my *mom*!"

"Well, Ben, I could wear my shades and be Secret Service. No one would know I'm your mom."

I should've known better. I wore my sunglasses through the halls during passing time, getting stared at more than if I hadn't. But Ben didn't want me to take them off, thinking no one would know me. My goofball back, at least for a moment.

Later, I discovered the reason for his chemistry-class high motivation. His instructor blew things up that day.

Over the span of two months Ben attended school only seven full days. My life stopped as I watched in fright, day in, day out, at home, and at the hospital. Ben leaned on me mentally, emotionally, spiritually, and physically.

Loving care is tangible. Folks dropped off dinners and gift cards as they'd done nearly annually since 1996. And I tried to help myself.

To help combat the horrible hours, I filled sachets with my garden's lavender, attaching them to wildly gorgeous labors-of-love my friend, Terri, knitted for me. (Women still stop me on the street, boldly requesting scarf removal to better inspect Terri's creativity: Dr. Seuss-ish, feathery, and beribboned.) Her precious support around my neck dangled lavender aromatherapy. Twenty-first century smelling salts, calm revival.

That winter, attending UW basketball games with my father, getting a massage, and dressing up in my mother's 1950s prom dress for a Valentine's Day dance brought additional relief and smiles. Dan spun me into non-alcoholic intoxicated oblivion; I determined I dance the hardest when I hurt the most. Then, at a perfectly timed pamper morning at church, I painted, had a pedicure, and did yoga. But I freaked some women out by unintentionally sobbing on the massage therapist's table. It didn't bother the therapist. She knew her loving art released improperly stored emotions from the body. And if there's one thing I have plenty of....

But I needed more, completely off-the-grid respite for more than a two or three hour stretch. So, Sam, fourteen, and I took an overnight ski trip one snowy afternoon, after Ben and I returned from the hospital. Dan made it possible, coming home early from work and accompanying Ben to the following day's hospital appointments.

After a day of skiing in fresh snow, Sam and I drove home in a blizzard. Alternately praying and singing '70s rock at the top of my lungs convinced Sam never to take another winter road trip with Mom again. (Years later, he changed his mind.)

My self-care enabled me to hold it together as Ben's reports trickled in: endocrinology – negative, CT angiography – negative, EEG video – negative. Hormonal glands – okay. No bleed, no seizures. Neuro-ophthalmology – okay. Well...one eye had slightly worsened, Ben's peripheral may also have declined, but docs called his sight stable, all internal mechanisms in working order.

It became increasingly apparent New Psychiatrist's pronouncement ("not straight up my field") had not been correct. All other specialists decided Ben experienced psychosomatic symptoms, truly physical and involuntary, but with an emotional/mental basis. (What I think of as the mind-body connection in its obvious form.) The list of twenty strange symptoms never abated, all tests returned negative, the AVM/radiation did not appear to be the cause, and the last doc on the testing list, a neurologist, pronounced, "Not us!" He recommended medication, anti-depressants to be specific.

"Hasn't anyone told you to expect this?" a friend later asked.

Years of cumulative physical and mental stress, in conjunction with pubescent chemical changes in the brain, had shut Ben down. How obvious! How could anyone remain unscathed by the previous nine years? Live with the uncertainty of an AVM? Grieve new losses at every age? Diminished in athletic, speech, and cognitive skills (requiring Special Ed), sporting a withered right arm and AFO-leg, his body image issues surfaced during middle and high school, the years when looks reign supreme. And the losses had not immunized him from normal teenage angst brought on by peer rejection. When more than one person spoke at a time, Ben found it impossible to follow. Simultaneous rapid fire, teenage chatter, quick-witted joking, and mumbling commentary excluded him – exactly what the high school offered.

At home, we tried to include him in our dinner conversation, but not always. We were exhausted. He was exhausted. Over the years, it became easier to just let things be, let him hear what he heard, think what he thought, sit quietly in his own world rather than try to keep up with ours. We weren't proud of that. Ben's language processing issues complicated conversation. A case in point, Mrs. Sperling. We occasionally conversed about her longevity, 108 years, but never more so than after Ben randomly exclaimed out-of-nowhere at the dinner table, "Mrs. Sperling is dead?"

No, she wasn't, not yet. The rest of us sat stunned, then burst into laughter. "Mrs. Sperling" became family shorthand for "Ben's not following."

To educate ourselves as a family, we watched the video *How Difficult Can This Be?: The F.A.T. City Workshop – Understanding Learning Disabilities.* Facilitator Richard Lavoie leads adults without disabilities through exercises simulating various learning disabilities. In a very short period of time, he turns them into sweating, confused, anxious classroom quitters as they experience a differently wired brain.

Popcorn conversation was only one of the normal teen activities remaining out of Ben's reach. While his peers had learned to drive the year before, now they discussed colleges. Ben's post-high school plans? A great, flashing question mark.

Of course the kid was depressed. But Ben's depression had presented differently than mine, and I hadn't recognized it. Neither had the docs, not even New Psychiatrist. Not until extensive testing came up with zilch.

Having exhausted the UW Hospital and its satellites, I took Ben to see Dr. Puckette. (For myself as well; by March vertigo and headaches plagued me.) Until anti-depressants reached a therapeutic level, until chiropractic kinesiology reintegrated Ben, and while Ben talked to a psychotherapist all spring, I watched my boy continue to live in pain.

That spring, I began to resent what life asked of me. All winter and early spring, I'd unhappily employed my junkyard dog skills, sometimes with the medical community but mostly with school personnel.

Because of Ben's varied and capricious symptoms, some staff viewed them as a ruse. I sensed a growing frustration and suspicion, directed toward Ben and me. I knew he loved both the social and learning aspects of school, and would never make up ailments to miss it.

First semester, I had re-taught Ben chemistry nearly every evening. Second semester, I could only help by typing his drama class stories, dictated off the top of his head. The missed homework had amassed.

Before third quarter's spring break, I wrote a letter to his high school case manager, requesting an emergency IEP meeting of nurse, teaching, and specialist staff – whomever necessary to hammer out details of a plan. Could Ben take class pass/fail? Would a medical extension, which some gracious teachers had already approved, work for an entire quarter, or even semester? We came up with a combination of things to salvage Ben's junior year, but I felt pushy.

Compounding troubling school life, on nearly a daily basis I fought with women I didn't know.

"Those mothers!" I spluttered in tears, storming into the high school one day.

The receptionist's electrified eyebrows zipped into her hairline. "*Mu*thers...?" (She worked with teens after all.)

"Mothers! The ones in the parking lot picking up their kids after school," I whined. "Parked in the handicapped spots, even though they don't have disabilities."

I grimly removed women from where they had no business parking, so I could push my teenage boy through the snow, haul him from wheelchair to car, fold up the chair, and outraged, heave it into the back. An unfair fight crystallizing the unfair life we led. High school staff instructed the parking lot monitor to come to my aid, at least solving that problem.

Ben's uneasily fixed troubles, however, were compounded by more loss. His winter and spring disappointments mounted, too sick to participate in Drama Club, or go on the spring break choir trip to NYC. But our families came to our assistance again.

My father, and his new wife, Alice, took the kids for a weekend in March, and for spring break, sis-in-law travel agent wiz, Sandi, found the kids and me cheap tickets to Arizona. Anne got us on the O'Hare plane, and Grandma Barb put us up in a nearby hotel. I pushed Ben onto the airplane in his wheelchair, but often in Arizona Ben walked around on his own, well enough to tour a cave and, unbelievably, ride a horse. Judging by the pictures, the kids and I hysterically laughed our way through Arizona.

Not so their dad. By one measurement, he was 12,500 miles away, only 6,500 miles as the crow flies. For Dan, spring meant two weeks of student recruitment in Asia. For me, early April always meant Happy New Year, the celebration of Dan's safe return from the Orient. In 2005, besides Ben's worrying condition, North Korea smarmily flexed its claim to nuclear weapons. Other years, my disabling depression, Dan's severely sprained ankle (knee-to-toe rainbow), SARS, and our government's bombing of Baghdad had added to the exciting stress of Dan's cross-global travel.

As Dan flew home from Asia, and the kids and I flew back from spring break, Ben's symptoms returned. It should not have surprised me. I had always experienced sensations myself when my sisters, Koo and Boo, and I rendezvoused at one or other of their homes for sisters' weekends. During those four-day bursts of my-kids-free, responsibility-free chunks of time, I would realize the enormity of the daily weight I carried. Upon take-off, I would become weightless, flying free, and remain so until return landing. Then a physical presence would push hard on my heart, and lungs, making it hard to breathe, until I adjusted again to my life. Kind of the reverse of altitude sickness, but with the same dangerous outcomes.

After spring break, Ben still leaned on me physically to walk from car to door, or upstairs and downstairs. He weighed more than I did.

Thanksgiving and Christmas 2004, New Year's Day, Valentines Day, St. Paddy's Day and Easter 2005, all came and went. Even in mid-April, Ben rode in his wheelchair some days, and sometimes couldn't make it through an entire day.

Spontaneously, Dan and I ran late April's Crazylegs Classic, an 8K event winding through university landmarks. Neither of us trained. My track days had ended in 1977, and I never ran long-distance, anyway. In my defense, I plead a sane desire to run as fast as possible from my life. We finished Crazylegs For Dummies in less than an hour, happily hurting.

In early May, Ben's extreme fatigue, twinkly vision, twitching, trouble breathing, ringing ears, etc., finally lifted. He made it through the last month on his own two feet, field trip and all.

With Ben back in school full-time, a frenzied, defiant creativity possessed me. Desiring a large canvas, I painted a flower mural on the garage door, adding a Ralph Waldo Emerson quote, "Earth laughs in flowers." Attacking the ground, I dug up another chunk of the front yard and planted. Fury-fueled energy still to spare, I dragged home a discarded outdoor table, and with about 100 pounds of lavender-hued grout, turned it into a mosaic. Of sorts. I'd never before worked with grout or made a mosaic. By the time I finished, I hated it. Yet, it still provides a backyard refuge with Dan, and I now love the cracked, leaf-stained, and disintegrating table. It's a functional mess, just like me.

Ben wore a tux to May's Junior Prom, accompanied by a luminescent young woman, a senior. They went to dinner with a large group of friends, including The Twins and Tim One, and finished with dancing at the Monona Terrace. I snuck downtown with a carload of moms to spy on my joyfully healing son, and to watch the Grand March. But mostly to buy my heart cheer.

Ben's junior year ended on a high. Ah, but for how long?

Chapter 23

CE-LE-BRA-TION!

The day before October's press conference, Sarah plodded up our front steps after walking the mile home from school. I met her at the door, something I hadn't done for years. As she crossed the threshold she groaned, "Dad took his car, not the bus."

As a junior, Sarah refused to drive my vanity-plated car. A point I'd happily considered before ordering a word to amuse myself, an inside joke between a favorite author and me. (Or rather, myself and me. The author doesn't know.)

"Is that a problem?" I asked, holding the *Mylo Xyloto* CD in front of me.

Her gigantor baby blues mushroomed, and I kissed my sweet-sixteen girl on the forehead, "Happy day!" (Luckily, her delirium allowed me to get away with that kiss. She'd recently reached the phase where I mentally hauled out my self-designed t-shirt. Front: "My kid is ____ teen." Back: "I am The Hated Mom." The shirt would come with reusable Velcro appliqué, thir through nine, affix as needed.)

"*Thanks Mom!* Now I have time to listen to it before meeting Abby at the park!"

But first, like an automatic weapon, she spluttered an all-italics thirty-second rundown of the day, topics coalescing, "I had a group presentation in APES, and I can tell my public speaking class has already helped; I'll tell Mrs. Finnegan! We're watching that horrible movie about the food industry again. It's gross! We have this tech guy; he's from England. Everybody just calls him the 'guy with the accent.' Whenever he comes in a class everyone is totally silent, and the teachers are like, 'Say something, the kids just want to hear you speak' and he says, 'I know,' and rolls his eyes. So he's in my study hall today? And I positioned myself sort of next to him so I could hear him, but not creepily, and he called his cell phone a '*personal mobile*,' and I'm like, '*Yes!*' Who's Gaddafi?"

Mr. M. Gaddafi, formerly of Libya, had splashed over the news, suddenly mortified as he was. As I opened my mouth to answer, Sarah earnestly required total silence to hear the reverential picking off of the plastic wrap from the Coldplay CD. The crinkling beginning of bliss, followed by careful inspection of the booklet inside.

"*This is why I love these guys!* Look at this!"

A bright medley of color creatively presented the lyrics. Exactly what my Sarah would adore, the girl who rainbowed everything, roy-g-biv mittens, clothes closet, every picture she'd drawn as a child, and my life. And Ben seemed responsible for his sister's rainbow connection. Making her rainbow birthday cake, the last thing Ben, Sam, and I had done together before that day of joy, her first taste of frosting, turned bitter. Had Sarah absorbed rainbows on her first birthday? But how, and when, had she transformed from my baby girl to Rainbow Girl?

Knocked out of my misty-eyed reminiscence, "*Mom!* Are you going to be on your laptop?"

"Definitely." It didn't have a disc slot, and she should've known better than to ask, anyway. My intense typing all fall had once prompted Sarah to mock, "Ooooh Mom, look! It's another conversation. Better write that down!"

She flew downstairs to Ben's old room, loaded the CD, and vaulted back upstairs, "Aaarrrgh! They need to let you listen to music *while* it downloads! One song's down and I can't hear it yet!"

Shoving a fistful of frozen peas in her mouth, she propelled downstairs one last time, shouting, *"Five, four, three, two, ONE!"* Musical liftoff. Ecstasy. *Paradise*, as the boys in the band sang. What a good use I'd made of thirty minutes and ten bucks. The next forty-two minutes contained only far away melody wafting up the stairs and the tap tapping of my keyboard. When the music stopped, Sarah bounded upstairs, roughly aiming for the door, "I'm gonna go to the park now. *I'm wearing my Coldplay jacket!!"*

Go, Rainbow Girl, go!

Reluctantly, I suspended the day's writing to attend to my family's nutrition. Ben would come home with Dan for dinner, and sleep over before our big day. I didn't want any confusion, say, a missed wake-up alarm, on press conference morning.

Nearly without exception, dinner begins with an onion. Chopping veggies for the Ben-requested curry, stir-frying them with chicken, mixing in the spices, suddenly something slammed my solar plexus. Inhaling, I couldn't breathe. Mental flashes accompanied, video and audio. My seven-year-old monkey boy perched in a tree. Senior Pastor materializing, Auntie Em-like in the Little Blue Room, sadly intoning, "Little boys should be outside making snow angels."

"What do you want to do?"

Rooted, the wooden spoon in my hand remained stationary mid-air, as tears rolled down my cheeks, dripping off my nose, naught to do with onions. Stolen from him, and the museum was giving it back.

My boy was working in Neverland!

As usual, a conversational three-ring circus occurred during dinner, only more so, "Wanna see all the juice that came out of my blister?" queried Sarah.

Not to be upstaged, Ben showed off his badly scabbed and scarring arm. Off and on, Dan and I held shining eyes. Dinner over, I turned the conversation to logistics, time for Mom's morning game plan. Putting Ben's speech in a folder, in case of a museum snafu, I sprang info on him.

"So, the speech you're reading tomorrow has changed a bit. They want you to read the last *two* paragraphs of your bio now."

"What!? That's news to me!"

"Yes, I know it is. They told me today. But you don't need it memorized. No one else will; they'll have speeches at the podium. Here, look. This is what everyone is going to say." Executive Director Ruth had sent me the day's script.

Ben laughed his way through in amazement. Would all these people really speak these words? His bio came at the end, about the last item on the press conference agenda.

"When the speeches are done, Ruth wants you and some kids to untie a banner."

"A banner? What is it?"

"I dunno. Probably something about the award. She wants you to help and she'll show you tomorrow."

He practiced his speech, mumbling disinterestedly.

"Don't say it that way! We can't even understand you."

Then he kicked it up a notch, or ten.

"No! Not Opera Boy!" we remonstrated. "Something in between, please."

But he couldn't concentrate at the kitchen table, songs blaring from Sarah's personal Coldplay concert. "If she doesn't turn that music down I'm gonna kill her," Ben growled. (More proof he'd grown up?) Sarah lowered the decibels, and Ben read aloud one more time. Perfect. Putting down his speech he mused, "Mom, why is this happening, why did they choose me?" The question, by now, should have been rhetorical. I didn't answer.

"Things that are so simple are complex to me, Mom." He thought some more. "It lifted me up and I'm lifting it up?"

"Yes, I think so, Ben. I think that's right."

"What goes around comes down?" He seemed content with his conclusion. I know I was. He made the complex simple for both of us.

Yes, Ben, it comes down.

Throwing it into post-dinner high gear, I ironed Ben's shirt. As I worked, my belly inflated; I looked pregnant and felt like a blimp. It happens every month.

"I'm wearing a tie tomorrow," Dan announced proudly just after I'd taken down the ironing board. As an ESL school director, he wore sweaters or golf shirts.

"You are? Wow! That's coo – waitasecond! What shirt are you wearing?"

"The blue."

"Go get it."

"It's fine, it doesn't need ironing. It was just washed three weeks ago."

"Go get it. Just because it's clean doesn't mean it isn't wrinkly."

"It's fine. I looked."

I believed that he looked, but not that it would pass muster. Wrinkled, not badly, but still. Humph. I made a racket setting up the ironing board again, plugging in the iron again, muttering under my breath about guys, and shirts, and belts, and pants...Pants! I needed to iron both guys' pants too!

Afterward, wearing my best grumpy Gladys Ormphby face, I took my ballooned nether regions downstairs to watch a movie. By. My. Self.

You remember Gladys, Ruth Buzzi's character on *Laugh-In*? The middle-aged spinster with the downturned mouth, frumpy clothes, brown hair yanked back tight in a bun, and winged bangs plastered to her head by a hairnet. As a kid, I thought something always looked drastically wrong with the middle of her forehead, as if a large black spider had taken up residence. Or as if a deeply furrowed brow, smack between her eyes, rendered her permanently angry. I've got Gladys Ormphby's forehead lines. Too bad they can't be removed by taking off a hairnet. Or ironing. (Maybe skin-colored duct tape?)

I left the ironing board sitting in the middle of the kitchen, taking up all of the space between the sink and the table. So. There. Who acted like a child that evening, eh? *Forever Young,* Kate, not forever immature. Even with PMS.

Awake with the robins! (Had there been any in my backyard to chirp the *Hallelujah Chorus* on the late October morn.) Quite a few days, the four o'clock hour had found me bolt upright. Ten years previous, the months leading up to Radiation, The Sequel, my old friend, Fear, woke me. Starting the next year, The Depressions repeatedly took their turns, four-o'clock such a lonely hour. This day, October 25, 2011, wouldn't be another day of terror or statuette sorrow. Contrariwise! A day of joy greater than Johnny Depp's 4:00 a.m. hug!

Silently, I let The Words write. I knew Dan lay awake too, but we didn't speak or get up until six. I rarely get up that early. And, whenever I do arise, I don't talk. He also is a quiet morning person, so our discussion was completely out of character. I started it.

"Were you awake before 4:30?"

"I got up to pee. Did I wake you up?"

"I usually don't hear you so I think I wasn't all the way asleep then."

"I had a bad dream about you," he offered. "I was running around the house, chasing you, screaming at you, dropping f-bombs."

"Was it about the blue shirt?"

“It was about Easter. You changed the whole house in October for Easter.”

“Ah, so it was about the shirt.” A deep-throated chuckle escaped, scaring me. I certainly never laugh at 6:10 a.m.

“Yeah, I’m thinking DefCon 3 last night,” he smirked.

“I’m sorry –” I began.

“That’s okay, it’s a big day.”

“No, I’m not apologizing. If you bring me a shirt –”

“I didn’t bring you a shirt.”

“If you say –”

“I said it was fine.”

“Yeah! And it wasn’t, it was wrinkly!”

“I woulda worn it,” he lobbed belligerently.

“And I woulda been horrified! You don’t go to a wedding in a wrinkly shirt, and you aren’t even wearing a jacket today!” No jacket, no wrinkles. Not even minimal. Someone would have to break the cycle, but not me. Not at 6:15, no strong Irish tea yet in my system, with a 4:30 Word-induced reveille, and an 8:30 p.m.(S) prickly resentment hangover.

“Thank you for ironing my shirt last night,” whispered Dan softly, looking deeply into my eyes. “Really...thank you.” Not waiting, he made kissy face at me from a few feet away, quietly adding, “Enjoy your day.” He meant it, and I thawed.

“You’re welcome. And thanks.” I meant it too.

“Mom, is it really happening?” Ben asked in the car. I supposed so, but couldn’t talk, too focused on traffic. Accustomed to driving downtown an hour earlier or later, I had forgotten about sharing the road with a few extra others.

In a traffic lull, I went over the main idea of the morning. Keep it simple. No tangents, no burying yourself in a morass of “illuminating” analogies, no trying to be funny with serious stuff. I meant it for us both. Some might say I micromanaged. For example, the owner and wearer of a certain non-wrinkled, blue shirt?

Born and bred a control freak (firstborn of two scientists, dontchaknow; I didn't stand a chance), the sixteen-year-long medical black hole had launched me close to uber-control-freakedness, the territory of Marie Barone, *Everybody Loves Raymond*'s mother. Generally I hovered somewhere below her symptom line, but occasionally briefly raided her stratosphere. On a daily basis I fought against my tendency to try to fix, control, and manage. Sometimes I actually won. (But not on this day.)

"How do you feel about this?" I prompted Ben.

"Happy?"

"Yes, and?"

"Adjectives, right?"

"Yep."

"Grateful, proud, honored, really thankful, and really happy," Ben concluded.

"Terrific, Ben." But out of the corner of my eye, I noticed the purple Jerry Garcia tie, tied the night before, twisting goofily. Dan would have to fix it.

I dropped Sarah and her celeb brother off at the museum and parked the car. Breathe. Standing at the locked front door of the museum, through the windows I could see greeters on their way to let me in. Ben and Sarah stood with their grandparents.

"I cleaned him up," Dan answered my anxious, "Didja fix his tie?" Attention to detail dies hard and slow. But after 8:30 that morning, I would not care a fig for, nay even be aware of, Dan's pants, Ben's pants, Dan's shirt, Ben's shirt, Dan's shoes, Ben's shoes, either of their belts, their ties, my hair, face, or ensemble.

As the crowd grew and milled, Ruth directed me to save three chairs near the front, then cloistered with Ben, giving him instructions. I disjointedly attempted to mingle, butterflies playing a wicked

Duck, Duck, Goose. Introvert Dan schmoozed smoothly, while Sarah hung out with the pastries. After a while she found us.

"Who's Jerry Frookie?" she asked innocently.

"Jer-?"

"This guy comes up and says can he share this table with me, and I said 'yes', and then he starts asking me questions and stuff."

"Jerry *Frautschi,* and his wife, Pleasant Rowland, have given the city about a quarter of a billion dollars," explained Dan. "They're behind this museum and a bunch of other community projects in Madison."

"Oh! I just thought he was some old guy."

(Oh. Help.)

My phone chirped, urgent text messages queuing up one after another, all from Ren. Due to fly in the night before and meet me at the museum now, she'd been stranded overnight in Detroit. Still, she hoped to make the tail end of the press conference.

My disappointment disappeared as the doors opened and another family member appeared. Anne. Her pragmatically tender love from our college days, through the zero hour in '96, through The Depressions, to the present (funny birthday cards still came eight months after my fiftieth), meant I highly desired, but did not demand, my sister-in-law's presence. I Elsa Snorted when she divulged her family's final press conference guess. Only knowing it to be of national significance, they had settled upon *Extreme Makeover: Home Edition.* What's with my female relatives? Cuz had threatened *What Not To Wear*, now Anne? Didn't they know, other than my kitchen cabinets, I am a materially content woman?

T minus ten minutes, more people poured through the door, middle school friend Leslie, new friend Happy Psychologist, twenty-year-friend Mitzy, Super Principal, Pavilion, the gaggle of women from WESLI, Molly, Edith, and Shirley from 3Rs class, Terri, and Hiroko, my Japanese friend, and others from our circle of life. Our lives represented, past, present, and future. It seemed like an army, even without a number of my key women.

Ben, Dan, and I took our front row seats, while Sarah held up the back wall. Catching my eye several times from afar, with perfect timing she pulled her teenage, twisted-lip, sassy "er" face, symbolizing I'm never sure what. I took it to mean "Chill, Mom." I reciprocated. Our cadre of comrades sprinkled liberally about. No matter in which direction I gazed, someone I knew radiated. Holding my eyes, hands, and heart.

"Mom, it *is* happening," Ben whispered and we squeezed hands.

Speechifying commenced, and the VIP *was* Dane County Executive Joe Parisi, my high school classmate. So my blathering introduction at the breast cancer awareness parade had not been amiss! The crowd oohed and aahed when Joe explained the First Lady awards the nation's highest honor for museums and libraries, The National Medal.

Then Ruth took the podium, explaining staff chose "one single person who exemplified the difference the museum can make in someone's life." She finished, "one person's compelling story floated to the top," and asked Ben to come stand next to her, following the script verbatim. Until, suddenly, she didn't. Gesturing toward us she said, "Behind every great child is a great set of parents. Katherine and Dan Perreth."

The applause sounded distant, muffled, as if it were the whooshing of the ocean in a conch shell. Ruth smiled brilliantly, while I mouthed, "Thank you" to her, my family's MVP VIP Ruth. Turning my head, through blurred vision I saw Dan swivel in his chair toward me, while his hands rose in slow motion. What were they doing? Back and forth, back and forth, palms tapping against each other. What was he whispering, his eyes glistening? "This is for you, you did this."

Shaking my head in disbelief, my Gladys Ormphby brow furrowed, and I mouthed, "No, no." Placing my shaking hands on his, I pushed them down. I knew better than anyone that safe liftoff requires caring ground control.

Then time, finishing its funky-warp-thing, returned. But Ben's voice filled the void, so the fairy tale spell remained unbroken.

That morning, I correctly expected at least one cheer. When County Exec Joe announced MCM won the prestigious award, a hurrah went up and I woo-hooed loudly along with the rest. But when Ben spoke, I remained intentionally still, waiting for the point when he boomed, with great feeling, "Madison Children's Museum hired me!"

The lionhearted Aslan roar came from behind, led by standing-room only, exploded sideways through the seated crowd, and swirled around my heart, lifting me up, up, up. As if it were a sponge, the holes in my heart absorbed the drenching reverberation of joy.

Ben finished his speech Ben-style, uncontainable and impromptu. "Thank *you* (pause) for letting *me* (pause) be part of this *National* (pause) *Medal* (pause) *CE-LE-BRA-TION*!"

On the last four syllables Ben shimmied. In his voice, his torso, and shoulders, in his shining eyes, and actor facials, the kid shimmied. Bringing the house down.

"The VIP speeches made it official," Dan whispered. "Ben just made it real."

I brought my camera that morning, but forgot about it. The moments etched forever, nevertheless. Perhaps in the darkroom of my mind joy can filter and develop, superimposing other forever engraven images? Press conference day supplied promising phrases, feelings, snapshots, and a few conversations.

After the confetti and glittering streamers had fallen, and Ben, Ruth, and the children unfurled the banner, I found myself tumbling into the double-embrace of two women I did not know, MCM board members. They approached me, timely mothers mothering. I dissolved. They upheld.

"I'm just a mom!" I blubbered.

"I want to tell you," one spoke through tears, "how glad I am, and how courageous of you and Ben, to include the mental health piece."

"It's something Ben feels very strongly about," I expounded, regaining some composure. "I asked him if he was sure he wanted that mentioned, because of the stigma. It's very important to Ben that it's included, because he wouldn't be here without Yahara House. One couldn't happen without the other." I suddenly clarified. YH could definitely happen without MCM, and had.

She leaned close to me, "We don't whisper, 'My uncle has heart disease,' we say it! Mental illness has got to be the same. We've got to say it!"

I totally agreed. The list of things that can go wrong with the mind nearly equals that of the body. I've seen the pages of diagnostics, back and front, minuscule type. But The Thing dividing mental illness from physical illness, and partly why I believe we still whisper about it in frightening tones, is with the latter you can remain mostly intact, possibly unrecognizable in feature, but still you. With debilitating mental illness, you're gone. Think Alzheimer's. No one wants to ponder for a millisecond where sweetheart Grandma went when her ravaged mind turned her feral.

Although both the CDC and the American Psychiatric Association's Diagnostic and Statistical Manual of Mental Disorders (DSM) categorize Alzheimer's as a mental illness/disorder, some rail against that because of the stigma.

In the 21st century, isn't it past time we dispensed with stigma and fully embraced compassion?

But I didn't say all this to the women embracing me. I only managed, "Ben is the perfect person to help de-stigmatize mental illness. He's so cheerful and friendly. His mental illness doesn't define him, like his disabilities do not define him. He's bigger than both. I have told him so, many times."

On our way out, Sarah asked, "Mom, who were all those people? Did you even know them?" She especially wondered about my warm, lingering handshake with Dane County Executive Joe. And to Dan she joked, "Nice shout out, Dad." Such refreshing beauty in the presence of a snarky teenager well equipped with words.

But taking the cake for crazy statements, the last sentence Ruth spoke to me, "I'll be in touch with you about the next phase, when IMLS lets us know about DC and the White House."

I floated out of the museum to go party with my posse of women, including Ren, who had made it at the conclusion.

Effervescent Ben bubbled off to his paid shift in Neverland.

Chapter 24

Cry Out, Write!

Fall arrived tardy in 2011, providing sapphire skies and a few sun kissed, lemony leaves still tenaciously clinging to branches well beyond nature's usual dictum. Dan and I took advantage on a midweek day (a first for Dan). Buying mental health, we employed a coping strategy I call Going To Mississippi. Doing so partly answered his anxious question, "When am I going to get my wife back?"

He meant from The Words writing incessantly in my mind. His first tip, that they had commandeered my life again, my personal hygiene. Hair in a ponytail three days running did too count for showers, I argued. (Besides, I wore fresh undies.) Other hints included my lack of coherent conversation with family members, or even noticing them, putting in the bare minimum at WESLI, and not even attempting rudimentary domestic demigoddess stature. Dan feared for my balance. Distracted, I cooked dinners at half-strength and heard dinner chat at quarter-strength. I treated the family randomly, as if they were www.perrethfamilylore.com. When Dan walked through the door at the end of his workday, I resembled a Southern Rockhopper Penguin. (You know the one, looks like an electrocuted Einstein.) But the dazed, glazed, and crazed look in my eyes really concerned him. Drained from writing, my two visible eyes blurred, strained, and reddened, while my intensely focused third eye proton-beamed through my heavy forehead. How could my head still be heavy when so many words had emptied? But just because The Words flew out of hidden orifices, attaching themselves to paper, virtual or real, did not mean I was finished with them. I knew it myself and I'd once seen a professional in action.

A playwright, at a rehearsal of his play, paced the theatre aisle, yanking at his short, salt 'n' pepper hair, barely resisting the urge to bound onstage and rip the script from the actors. The problem? "Slice of pie, *slice* of pie, not piece!"

I so felt his pain that day. My family now felt mine on the days referred to as Writing Days, more mot juste if they actually ended at sundown. Dan felt troubled by my scribbling in the dark on a night-stand tissue, and my purposeful sighs as I tossed and turned for the first forty-five minutes in bed.

Better than illegible hieroglyphics, mnemonic techniques aided shutting off the flow, allowing sleep to take over from The Words illuminating the darkness. "Blue, ballpoint, blue, ballpoint, double b," my little gray cells rehearsed one night, hoping The Words accepted the sacrificial but minimal attention. Usually this appeased, but the next morning I rose with double b on the brain and nothing more. No matter. I knew if I didn't force it, The Words would emerge at some point. And yet? Hearing one's spouse mutter over her morning tea, "double b, double b," has got to be disconcerting.

Thus, to buy some mental space, and marital wa (roughly "harmony," in Japanese), Dan and I took an overdue mental health day, invoking Going To Mississippi. Daily, we practice two perennial standbys, Divide and Conquer (ex: when the kids were little), and Can't Beat 'Em Join 'Em (ex: gum stuck stubbornly on black velvet now colored with Sharpie marker). Going to Mississippi, born of my having threatened multiple times to jump in the car and drive alone to the Gulf Coast where no one knew me, we now reserved for less drastic days. Theoretically, we could have driven the ninety minutes to the Mississippi River on the state's western edge. But parking ourselves on a Wisconsin River sandbar for a picnic took only half the time.

"I'm concerned about your writing," Dan offered his opening salvo kindly, as we settled on our blanket.

"What about it?" I queried warily.

"Well, you know, sometimes when you write it stirs things up and it's not so good for you."

(Rats. Should not have told him about the 50,000 words chronicling the fall.)

"I'm very supportive of your writing," he continued. "I know you say the words are in your head already and you've got to let them out. I get that. I also know that this fall is the framework that had been missing. So, I'm happy you're doing all this writing –"

(Super! Stop right there!)

"– and I don't mind your taking chunks of time on the weekends and other days to do it, but I am wondering if it's contributing to your stress? All this DC stuff you've gotta do, and the stories for the newspaper, plus 3Rs, Group of Authors, WESLI, stuff with the kids, your aunt's health, and on top of it you're writing a book?"

(Not to mention your enumerated list just spiked my heart rate.)

"Plus you do weird things, like forgetting to eat and holding your pee, you're so engrossed in your writing. That can't be good for you."

"I have a very large and strong bladder." (Always parry with the last spoken lawyerese.)

"So when we have extra stress, I'm just thinking, 'Frack the book.'"

"Frack The Book?" I screeched.

Fire and ice Dan calls us. Nowhere in our relationship is this more obvious than when we spar. I want to enter into the conflict, hash it out sparks flying, and emerge from it with growth. He wants to morph into a North Sea iceberg and sink forever. (But after allowing appropriate space, gentle and persistent warmth always melts ice.) Would Frack The Book turn into one of those tiffs?

"Okay, I hear ya," I lied. "Let me just say if you think I'm a stressed out woman now, if I wasn't writing this book the way I am, you'd have a furiously stressed out woman stomping all over the house. It would be just one more thing in my life that I've had to sacrifice. Besides, a bunch of this extra stuff is going to calm down soon." (Subliminal, crystallized intelligence pleased me again, not having thought of this before.)

"Okay, okay, just wondered." He capitulated rather easily. Preferring that to a messy decapitation meltdown? I only slightly exaggerated. The internal pressure to write the story as it unfolded overwhelmed. I believe Willa Cather once remarked upon that.

"I read some of what you wrote," he blurted.

"What? I thought you said you weren't going to yet, that you had plenty to read?" When I'd seen him after his morning run, he'd held the newspaper in his hands.

"I did, but I wanted to read your writing. I started and it was enjoyable. More fun than reading the Business Section."

(High praise indeed! What about the Sports Section, though?)

"I really like reading your stuff when you write about things that happened to us, your perspective," he said in a sudden burst of conciliatory words. "What you're thinking about when they're happening. It helps me understand you. And I like to see me in your writing. It's interesting, the way you put it, even though I was there."

"Really? Was it accurate?"

"Yes, it was. But it was also, umm...I found it emotional."

"Overly so? Did it detract from the writing?"

"Not so much detract, just it was a lot of emotions."

(A lot of emotions in my writing? Who knew?) This segued nicely into the emotional differences between us, like the fact that I actually exhibit some. Naw. Our marriage had been fraught with my many quick and strong emotions.

"She," Dan recently had replied to an inquisitive woman at a wedding reception, "is an Artist. It's been a Thing in our marriage." Indeedy, it had been.

While we mulled over our varying emotional intelligence, the late afternoon suddenly clouded, the wind kicked up, and an autumn chill rose off the river, encouraging us to walk the sandbar for warmth.

"You know," observed Dan, "I'm basically the same person I was thirty years ago. I haven't changed."

"Me, too."

"What? You've changed a lot!"

Shoot. I thought we'd settled that already. Just because in the past few years I had dropped a number of thirty-year-old habits, taken up a host of new ones, become a freelance writer, cut my hair, started wearing mascara, and rearranged a bunch of weekly activities so that the time I spent, the money I spent, and some of the people I hung out with looked a little different from the past? My outside now matched my inside. But I didn't rehash any of this historically old news.

"What I mean," I half teased, "is that I always was an emotionally unstable, fun-loving girl, with a certain je ne sais quoi. C'mon, you had some big clues in college." My bumpy mental landscape had not escaped Dan's notice early on. "Besides, I've gone through a lot of life-changing events."

"But I have too," he said plaintively, "and I'm still the same!" Meaning, an even-keeled, family-centered, reliable, and calmly listening man, a woman whisperer with a long history of using his rumbling, soothing voice to persuade people to abandon the ledge. I've been saying for years, the man needs to be sainted and cloned. Recently I rectified that. Cloned, then sainted; I guess you have to die to be saintified.

We strolled a few paces in companionable silence, until he turned and lifted me off my feet in a bear hug, shouting, "I'm so glad I married you!" And then he soliloquized rhapsodically over my growth, spawned in part by my writing, which he now supported 110%.

He proved it Christmas 2010, when he bought me a laptop. Since our gifts for each other are always well under $100, with impunity he could've claimed he was done shopping for the next 25 years. But he didn't.

Loose ends never make me feel good. This could explain my love affair with laundry. Just as there is nothing worse for a fixer than being presented a problem for which there is no cure, there is no greater way for a fixer to gain a sense of control and accomplishment than by washing mountainous piles of dirty clothes. (I always found the first day after returning from a ten-day camping trip especially gratifying.) Laundry means messes on the floor, in the chute, and in the basket. As I pick up, combine, and sort the three into color-coded, containable, and finite hills, I already feel vastly satisfied. But then washing, fluffing in the dryer for a few minutes, and hanging the clothes out to dry rockets my wellbeing. I eagerly watch the forecast for the holy grail of this Wisconsin laundress, perfect laundry days: gentle breezes, sunny, and warm. I reach therapeutic level when folding the laundry into neat, organized piles for others to put away. Done. Slap, slap. Lovely. The very best part? It never ends!

The enjoyable routine changed after both boys moved out in 2008, knocking me a bit off kilter. So much sudden space, provided by more than lack of laundry.

Although my fledgling writing career had flapped out of the nest, feet first, eyes shut, and I held the reigns of another five projects in my hands, by mid-2009 not one appeared manageable. Especially what I dubbed the *Magnum Opus*, MO, vignettes about Life With Ben. I questioned everything I wrote, determining it all a redundant, useless, mangled mess. One night I burst into tears for no apparent reason.

"Why are you crying?" Dan asked in concern.

"I don't know," I wailed. "I'm just generating piles of writing. I have piles everywhere," I said, flinging my arm wide for proof. "On the dining room table, on the floor, in the box, on the computer...(hiccup)...there are just too many piles and it's all I'm maaa-kkk-ing."

The dining room table served as my "office," covered in overlapping two-inch deep typescript, newspaper clippings, notebooks, loose notes, reference books, and wee cryptic notes scribbled in pen, pencil, charcoal, and purple crayon, on tissues, wrappers, and cardboard. The receipts for the occasional soy chai tea latte, extra hot, no foam, and chocolate wrappers, completed the ambience. Fourteen-year-old Sarah once proudly tidied the table, presenting it to me as a surprise. My hands clawed at my hair, and a bewildered Sarah, expecting praise, heard only a primeval cry escalating into a charge to, "Never touch my writing again! It's *organized!*"

Dan had expressed himself impressed with my ability to focus on The Words, encouraging me to do so, even in lieu of seeking consistent paid work. My lack of income didn't grate me any more than usual. The kind of job where I invested hundreds of hours without pay, and kept up my own morale while forgoing society, just reminded me of stay-at-home motherhood and Life With Ben. And yet, I felt dissatisfied with my apparent lack of progress, and was afraid I wasted my time.

"It's early days yet," encouraged my high school chum Fish Sister. "You've only just emerged, you've just found your voice."

But why couldn't the MO be like the easy birth of 3Rs, or even the laundry? Easily sorted, cleaned, and folded, then put away by others? Although giving great joy and release, if I didn't watch carefully and back away slowly from the kryptonite, the MO tended to bite me in the butt, plummeting my heart. But The Words demanded I write cathartically, building alphabetic towers. And I refused to give up on trying to organize them, deeming the serious pursuit my calling, my life's great work. This double-edged sword could sink me, but if handled correctly, could also redeem and set me free. I had plenty of proof The Words linked directly to my health, mental and physical.

One year, I took a lone two-day mini-retreat to the local monastery in hopes of self-detoxification, to rid myself of my own label, Unfit For Human Consumption. Often, my anger had sprouted from feeling victimized, without choice, without voice. Feeling shaken and stirred, sometimes when Dan would ask me what was eating me alive, I couldn't even coherently name it. Let me count the ways I hated my life? Thousands of words jostled in my head; I couldn't speak them, they presented themselves such an unruly army. (I wonder if Ben initially felt this way, all those months he couldn't put sound to the words in his head. Tongue-tied.) Writing let my words out, grammatically or not. And I knew just how many could tumble out of me in one sitting. Yet, such angst possessed me over them, over what to do with them. What should I do?

Desiring something to read, I ambled to the monastery library, crossed the threshold, turned my head, and received a smack between the eyes. *Cry Out and Write: A Feminine Poetics of Revelation.* The academic exegesis I couldn't understand. But the ancient accounts of female, mystic, Christian martyrs from the earliest centuries after Christ, reached out to hold me. I knew what to do. Cries of the voice, write!

My cathartic vignettes accumulated.

My father used to say, "If it's worth doing, it's worth doing well." I think he got that, or something like it, from his father. Fortunately, I only half listened.

I lived by two mottos, "If you want it done the way you want it done, DIY," and "If it's worth doing, it's worth doing half-ass. Just try."

Thus, on a whim, fall of 2010 I contacted a local newspaper columnist. He kindly offered to meet me at a coffee shop, and asked me to bring some of my stuff. Picking at the napkin, my eyes darted nervously as he read the Johnny Depp piece. He chuckled at times and my heart soared. Then he said I had talent. Juiced, I briefly explained the MO, finishing with, "Right now, I can't take rejection or even success. I don't have the emotional wherewithal to cope with either."

"Do what makes you happy," he advised, and then put me in touch with the newly re-emerging Madison Writers Network (MWN).

In early 2011, an email from our fearless MWN extrovert-leader-of-introverts, asked if anyone out there writing a book would be interested in meeting with others of similar pursuit. I jumped at the chance.

On a cold February evening, Dan and I ate together at Pasqual's on Monroe Street, for him dinner, for me fortitude. I was supposed to walk two doors down, sit with five people I'd never met before, and discuss organizing a book writers group. "What ifs...?" plagued me, self-doubt reigned. I only purported to write a book, and knew one thing for sure. I had absolutely no idea how to do so.

That night, Group of Authors was born.

The way they democratically set themselves up left me at loose ends. No, that's not fair. My ends would always be loose. They wanted submissions, after all. Organized, orderly, double-spaced, with chapter headers, page numbers, font Times New Roman, size 12, ten pages at a time, with plot, character development, climactic arc, and something they referred to as "negative space." (And an end in sight. And a title.)

Sheesh. My scattery, streamofconsciousness prolific stacks did not present themselves like that. They appeared Dickinsonesque, only in that they frequently lacked titles, and also that I suspected posthumous publication my best bet. From Emily, I took comfort. In her last years, I understood she entirely gave up editing and organizing, but never composing. Her last years would be mine now, should I die at fifty-five. Yet, she'd had a jumpstart on me – writing, editing, and organizing for decades. I'd only been at it a few years. Perhaps Group of Authors could help me catch up with prosaic recombobulation? Submission to submissions?

Our first Group of Authors therapy started at 6:30 in the evening, on the Ides of March, 2011. I wasn't quite prepared. It had been one of those days, the writing kind.

Over dinner, Dan inquired, "So, are you planning on changing, or will you be wearing that purple bathrobe to your group?"

(It's lavender. Good grief. Guys and colors.) "No, I won't be wearing my jammies tonight. I've still got time." Thirty minutes to be exact.

Staring at me, his smirk deepened into a crevacious grin. (Yeah, Dear Reader, I know "crevacious" is not in the dictionary.)

"What?"

"Well, I just had a flashback to a few years ago when I came home after work and you looked like this. I thought, 'uh oh' and asked, 'And how was *your* day?'"

"Another time, after two days in a row," I said, choking on my laughter, "you just asked, 'Has any personal hygiene occurred today?'"

"When you were depressed?" He looked shocked he could've been so callous.

"No, of course not! Just on a mental health day," I reassured.

The man had come home numberless times in the 2000s to find me the same way he left me, except usually out from under the sheets. Since I wore the same uniform on mental health days, taken to prevent depression, depressed days, taken to rob me of life, and writing days, it kept him guessing.

Pitching on my yoga pants and a sweatshirt, I splashed water on my face, didn't change the Holstein-patterned sox I'd worn to bed the night before, and grabbed my notebook, pen, and calendar, dashing out the door. My hair was on my head and makeup was not. Our first real writing meeting, our second time together, honeymoon over. Group of Authors might as well see with whom they were really dealing.

On the way over, as usual, I rehearsed. I didn't know how they would receive me, since I hadn't done my homework. Weighing my bright and amusing one-liners, I finally chose an honest, self-deprecating remark as I parked the car.

A total of six, we sank cozily into our positions on soft, creamy chairs, with soft, creamy lighting. Happy Psychologist, for it was her office, offered a wide variety of herbal teas. The room oozed mellow comfort and relaxation, and whispered there was nothing, shh, absolutely nothing, to fear. It scared me in a soothing leather sort of way.

When it came time for my introduction, "Hi! I'm Katherine Perreth. I brushed my teeth today, got out of my jammies thirty minutes ago, and I'm here. But I've got trust issues. I didn't send you anything and I haven't read anything you sent." I did not mention they would be carefully scrutinized and put on trial.

As we wrapped up the evening, I sought to gather a little more information from the man who had missed our first meeting. He spoke so eloquently, so professionally, so intelligently throughout the night. Upon being pressed, he allowed that he'd published five books. (Five? *Five?*) He seemed reluctant to expound, but I persisted like a reporter with a scoop, "What kind of books? What genre?"

Numerous: a novel, a collection of short stories, and some nonfiction, as well, "technical/historic." Wow – we had a versatile writer among us. His most popular book, in its fifth printing, had sold in the tens of thousands.

"What book was that?" I kept at him.

He looked slightly uncomfortable, hesitated, and then said, "*Traditional Voyeurs of America*. It's basically the history, and technical detail of, yada, yada, yada..."

He lost me back at "voyeurs" and I wasn't the only one shot by the stun gun.

Tradition? History? Technical detail? As in, "How To Climb A Ladder With Binoculars In One Hand?"

Several sentences later, he dropped the word "archery."

Voyeurs with lethal weapons? But he looked so mild mannered swallowed up in his chair. I decided to take a stab, "Umm, so this book is about archery?"

"Yes, about bow hunting and bow making, *Traditional Bowyers of America*. What did you think?"

Nevermind. Naw, I told them, got a great laugh, and that was it for me. I decided to trust them. A few weeks later, I rashly sent three of my humorous vignettes over the airwaves. Friends and family as critics had been one thing. (I make the Thanksgiving pumpkin pies, after all.) This would be my first time involving innocent bystanders.

For four months, as I slowly revealed my vignettes, The Bowyer, Quiet Helper, Happy Psychologist, The Vet (author of *Hitchhiking From Vietnam*), and Token Young Man showered me with praise. They also wanted to know from whence came that sense of frantic desperation in my writing.

(The holy trinity? Motherhood, morbidity, and maelstrom?)

The Bowyer said I exhibited what writers call "hitting a vein."

(The mother load?)

Since 2008, the *Magnum Opus* title had changed as I'd changed, from *Tunnel*, to *Out of the Tunnel*, and the summer of 2011, to *I Got No Idea About This Shelved Book*.

"I cannot do this," I thought, supposedly only to myself, yet aware of Father Goodness' habit of eavesdropping on my mind. "If this thing is ever gonna happen, it's gonna havta come to me."

I listened to and learned from Group of Authors. Having no energy to even attempt finding an agent, editor, publisher, sending out query letters, receiving silence, after silence, after silence, until one tenuous bit of acceptance, I gave up before even trying. Group of Authors mentioned a book typically required ten to twelve rewrites, and I knew I simply could not do it. Not the conventional way. Not now, anyway. Maybe not ever. In July 2011, I quit Group of Authors, letting go of my dream. Particularly upsetting, as I'd never had one before.

Six weeks later, the strange phone call from the Madison Children's Museum changed everything, providing the sweet backdrop required for all the toxicity.

Like I said. Father Goodness listens at keyholes.

Unaccustomed to having the unspoken desires of my heart met when it came to Life With Ben, everything happening after that phone call, flabbergasted. Ben and I had discussed collaborating on a book "some day." Apparently, it had arrived.

As I wrote like a madwoman the fall of 2011, I puzzled over the title. A greater mind than mine would have to give this some attention, the farthest I got, *Bit in the Butt by Ben.* Naw. (Although it was a sweet piece of alliteration.) My subliminal, crystallized intelligence popcorn brain thought better of it, and came up with other ideas.

Candy, Cotton Candy, Caramel, and Corn Syrup: My Trapped Life With Ben. (A twisted trivia movie tome? Playing loosely upon *Elf* and *Notes on a Scandal*?)

Candy, Cotton Candy, Caramel, and Corn Syrup. (Just plain? No hints whatsoever? *That* would blindside 'em. Cookbook? Sweet story? Heh, heh, heh.)

But Life With Ben required tart too. Lemonade? Making Lemonade? *Making Lemonade With Ben*? Yes! Hey! What if I –

Candy, Cotton Candy, Caramel, and Corn Syrup: Making Lemonade With Ben. (A book on childhood obesity?)

Nope. Just plain, *Making Lemonade With Ben.*

"I may as well get it over, dagger to my heart," I thought, surfing the web for my title. I wanted an original. Recipes abounded on the first page, including a bit on Ben Stiller's kids making lemonade, but there were no direct hits. *Making Lemonade With Ben* it is!

Energizing walks are good for more than the knees, heart, and temper, they joggle The Words around like a game of pinball, allowing them to fall where they may, making conversational pronouncements like,

You forgot part of the book's title.

(I did?)

Yeah, 'member when you laughed out loud today when you tweaked that stuff you wrote yesterday?

(Yeah, I remember, I changed "audacity" to "audacity to cope.")

Yep. Get it?

(*Making Lemonade With Ben: The Audacity to Cope*?)

Yep.

(Cool!)

Yep.

(Thanks!)

De nada.

Only one other person had to agree on the book's title.

"Mom, the people at Yahara House said 'audacity' usually means negative. What's the difference between 'austerity' and 'audacity'?" asked Ben.

"'Austerity' can mean harshness, strict, but also a kind of simplicity. Like the 56 degrees we keep the house at in the winter, at night. 'Audacity' can have negative connotations too. But you see how I switched it up? Piggybacking on the President's book title, *The Audacity of Hope*? And you know the idiom, 'If life hands you lemons, make lemonade'?"

"I was only born in 1988, Mom."

"C'mon, this is an idiom even now. What do you think it means?"

"When the hardship comes, go through it, don't give up?"

"And add sugar."

"Sugar?"

"Yes, to make lemonade. Take the bad and change it for good, as much as you can. That's the second part of the title, too."

"Audacity?"

"Yes. Audacity is boldness, gutsiness, cojones –"

"Mom, don't ever say that again!"

"Okay, well it's courage –"

"To cope?"

"Yes, to survive. Have the guts to plow through, sprinkled with sugar."

"So, it's *Lemons to Lemonade, Audacity to Cope*?"

"No, it's *Making Lemonade With Ben: The Audacity to Cope."*

"I'm on the cover?"

"Who else?"

He grinned his approval. "That's good, Mom."

Chapter 25

500 Miles, 500 More

Nearly a decade post-Comaland, describing my existence with Ben, I settled upon, "If you have a kid, picture your child's worst health scare. How did you feel? What did you think? How did you function? Now, imagine it doesn't go away."

One woman exclaimed, "But that would make me crazy!"

B. I. N. G. O.

In addition to perpetual educational adjustments, and insurance issues, Ben's physical, occupational, and speech therapies, blood draws, medication changes, MRIs, angiographies, AFO castings, fittings and tweaking, arm splint creating, electrical stimulation, full-length leg night cast and Botox injections for loosening his leg (before they were de rigueur for women's faces), surgeries, radiations, and perplexing mental health challenges kept me unhappily occupied through Ben's elementary, middle, and high school years, consuming vast amounts of time.

Time at home, but especially in Hospital World. There, time stretched and compressed as if it were an accordion, as we recited the code, Hurry Up and Wait. Complications, other patients' and ours, caused O'Hare-like stack-ups. Waiting on the tarmac, even for fairly straightforward appointments, became a way of life. Depending on which specialist's waiting room, I either read or focused on Ben. If not too nerve-wracked, I read a book. If fazed, I kept up with Hollywood via magazines.

Over the years, we waited in small waiting rooms and large, pre- and post-procedural rooms, OR recovery bays, inpatient rooms, lobbies, stairwells, and hallways. We once logged some time parked in a large linen closet, diverted at 10:00 p.m. en route to a late night brain procedure. The wheelchair barely fit, yet surrounded by soft, white, fluffy towels I felt crazily comforted.

Hospital Time proved an excellent trainer in the art of waiting, something our culture does not teach, value, or understand. The enforced slowness, as one is stuck, out of control, can be very frustrating until surrender comes. And come it must. It is either that, or madness. As a professional patient, one learns to be professionally patient.

There was only one guaranteed quick in and out. The dentist. Cavity-free Ben.

In attempts to relate, people sometimes offered that they'd read/seen/heard something about AVMs or hospital life, thinking I'd be interested. Nope. Those shows/articles were for the uninitiated. I lived the hazing. And if I may presume to be perfectly candid, I gritted my teeth, bit my tongue, and hardened my heart when women complained of their busy lives spent chauffeuring scheduled children to sports practices and games, and various lessons. As a medical mom, not a soccer mom, my kid played on OR, ER, hospital, and clinic fields, where refs dressed either in blue scrubs or white coats. My sideline cheers were for Ben to endure suffering in order to survive. Another setback meant heartache. And the playing time took years of real life. My life often seemed relegated to rifling through my deck of business cards, playing Fifty-Two-Pickup in frustration, searching for the name I wanted. Or rather needed. I didn't want any of them. Which of these medically related numbers did I wish I didn't have to call today?

As well as stooping to pick up the stray comments people may have left behind, I sometimes took whatever umbrage was offered, even unintended. As the years wore on and folks routinely asked only, "How's Ben?" my resentment grew. The answer they hoped for seemed to imply if Ben is well then Mom is well. When was Ben ever "well"? Reversing the theory of transitivity, if Ben was never "okay," neither was I. Even when we enjoyed a lull, it often meant time for mom to crash and burn. But sometimes lulls meant Tour Guide Katherine kicked into high gear, a desperate run for fun.

By natural inclination, and of necessity, on a daily basis Dan and I were frugal homebodies. Other than the mortgage we didn't do debt. Not even on an ESL single-income. (People go into the ESL profession because of fascination with other cultures and love of spreading the Mother Tongue. Not accumulating cash.) After giving, we saved money and hoarded Dan's frequent flier miles. We rarely spent money on ourselves. In hindsight, I would have lived differently, the way I do now. Still debt-free, but with permission granted from Deity, and self, to purchase more frequent pick-me-ups and regular respite.

Dan's annual trips to Asia helped us defiantly purchase lavish Rainbow Days. Storm-filled rainy days, they never seemed to let up, so every five years we laid the money down. Instead of replacing kitchen cabinets (whose age still equals mine), or buying new cars (we buy used every ten to fifteen years), or new furniture (for most of our marriage I decorated in the time period historians call Early Garage Sale), we took overseas trips to Ireland and England, B and B'ing our way to true R and R.

In 2000, we dumped our three youngsters with Grandpa Syrup and Auntie Anne. Touring western Ireland, we tracked down the castle ruins where Dan's great-great-grandmother served in the 1800s before her emigration to Nebraska. Visited the gravesites of another branch of his family, and stumbled upon living relatives whom we didn't know existed. They insisted we return, stay with them, and meet more folks in front of a peat fire. One aged relative, Paddy, engaged Danny in conversation, first inquiring after the strength of American whiskey. Danny didn't know. He only drinks beer. Paddy looked mildly scandalized.

Although German genes comprise most of my DNA, Dan's relatives guessed Ireland coursed through my veins as well. I spoke my one known ancestral name.

"Ah! County Mayo," they lilted.

Thus, Mayo is mine. It's Joyce Clan country, after all, and completely coincidentally, my middle name too.

One woman had asked of our stay in Ireland, "How long will you be home?"

I wept. Home. How lovely. Home. Ireland. Home. Somewhere Else.

Dan and I planned to spend more overseas Rainbow Days in October of 2005, the fall of Ben's senior year. Our hopes were high, after Ben's five months of myriad depressive symptoms had finally lifted in May.

To love up my teenage boys, on the first day of June's summer vacation, I took them, and Tim Two, to an outdoor water park at the Wisconsin Dells. We first dropped Sarah at an indoor water park in the Dells for her friend's birthday party. It was a sleepover, but Sarah had refused to go the night before. Still, at age ten and for years to come, she suffered intense separation anxiety. (I continue to believe it to be triggered by what stemmed from the night she had turned one: her mother suddenly gone, fallen with her eldest brother into life-sucking quicksand. And I have often wondered, during my desperate clutching days of '96, had I instilled fear and anxiety in my daughter via sick cellular osmosis?)

Sarah would get a ride home with the birthday girl's family, so the boys and I had all day together. I rode the slides with them for a while, and then retreated to my book, touching down on the terra firma of virtual England, Shakespeare's "blessed plot," my beloved, pastoral, mystery-laden refuge. After cutting my teeth on Agatha Christie as a child, I blew repetitively through adulthood favorites Ngaio Marsh, Dorothy Sayers, Margery Allingham, P. D. James, and Martha Grimes. The womenfolk's detectives solved bloody messes, straightened out conundrums, attempted to fix the unfixable, and even made me laugh.

The three boys pit-stopped occasionally. Late in the afternoon, Tim Two found me deep in the English countryside, "Uh, Mrs. Perreth, Ben got hurt. He needs you."

With a jolt I landed in Wisconsin, my insides turned to cement.

A large crowd, held back by personnel, surrounded the base of one of the waterslides. Tim escorted me through, but I knew the way. I followed the screams. My boy wailed in agony, cradled by two lifeguards in the water, his weak knee severely dislocated. Staff discussed what to do, how to lift Ben out of the water.

"*Oh, my poor boy! My poor boy*!" I lifted my face heavenward, shaking violently.

A woman put her arms around me, another brought me water, while I heard one of the gawkers mutter, "It's only a dislocated knee. He's fine." Dismissive, sure, but disappointed too?

Fourteen-year-old Sam surged out of the blurred faces, held me up, and piloted me away from the scene. I wept uncontrollably, burying myself on Sam, while he rubbed my back, mumbling soothing words. His brother still shrieking, my voice melded in harmony. The crowd thought I cried for a "normal" child, one who would recover quickly from adversity. Indeed, punching-clown-like Ben always bounced back, but this on top of the previous freaky five months? I knew we'd just taken first steps on yet another road few traveled, one with plenty of thorns, no roses. Sirens, again, came for Ben. Scalpels would too.

For the first time in all those years, in all those facilities, I couldn't go to my hurting boy's side. Ben's piercing cries disabled me. But the quick glance at his knee completely wiped out my coping mechanisms, giving me paroxysms of horror. I asked Sam later what he'd thought when he'd seen his brother's knee.

"I didn't think it should look like that," Sam calmly replied.

Sam didn't have his license, and I was in no shape to drive, so Tim Two drove my car. I rode shotgun in the ambulance on the bumpy road, listening to Ben in back. We took the winding roads to Baraboo, slowly, no lights or siren. The EMTs thought slower meant smoother. They were right, but the drive seemed endless. They also thought the dislocated knee wouldn't be a big deal. They were wrong.

While Sam and Tim Two waited in the hospital lobby, I tried to stay with Ben in the ER bay. Staff supported his knee, still badly out of whack, reducing his pain. But then a doc came in and pushed it, Ben screamed, and I fled, nearly taking out the plate glass door in my frenzy. Running through hospital hallways, to get as far away from the sound as possible, I flew past the boys in the lobby and out the front door.

After pacing the parking lot, I asked Sam to check on Ben. Was his knee still crooked? Did he still scream? Was it safe yet for me?

We loaded Ben sideways into Grandma Jo's old Subaru wagon, his relocated, immobilized leg straight. His brother sat smashed with him in the back seat, and Tim Two rode up front. I shakily drove the forty-five minutes home, one eye on the highway bumps for Ben's sake, the other eye on a droopy-looking Tim Two. Could trauma exacerbate his diabetes?

Murphy's Law dictated I arrive home to a mysteriously dead kitchen phone, so I borrowed the new neighbors' to call Dan and the UW hospital.

Ben waited a week to see Orthopedic Surgeon, the same doc who'd performed the foot remodel three years before. Then he had to wait another two weeks for surgery.

"Mom, it just won't stop," Ben justifiably complained, grieving alone. "It hasn't stopped since 1996." He mourned the loss of his summer plans: cancelling his repeat summer gig as a volunteer juggler for children at the Rehab Clinic (four blocks from our home), withdrawing from a weeklong service project with church, and giving up hopes of finding paid work. All erased. In the past, most of Ben's traumatic life had occurred October-May, safely away from sacred summer, family vacation, a break, and rec drama.

Previously cast as Prince Charming in *Snow White,* Ben made it to play practice a few times before surgery. In two scenes, with fifteen lines, he couldn't envision Prince Charming as a wheelchair-bound liberator. I told him plenty of real life heroes required wheelchairs, *Superman,* Christopher Reeve, for one. But summer's drama crown seemed iffy; the show was scheduled only one month out from surgery. An upper thigh-to-toes cast would remain on for six weeks.

Ben's physical condition was not the only thing worrying me. With summer sabotaged, would the strange depressive symptoms return en masse? To fight the possibility, I lined up fun with people, a wide array of weaponry. Limping in the leg immobilizer, Ben celebrated his seventeenth birthday with a squirt gun/badminton party, six friends, pizza, and bottles of root beer. Next, we hosted our annual BBQ party for our Japanese friends. (We tried at least one get-together each year, if not a summer party, then for New Year's Day we threw a bonenkai, "forget-the-year," party. Except for Ben, our home is shoes-off, just like in Japan. One bonenkai, Sarah had counted seventy-four neatly arranged shoes in our tiny entryway.)

The June parties partially took our minds off what would come. Round seventeen of anesthesia? Honestly, we had lost count. Ben chose a cast to honor our nation's birthday, blue stars with red and white stripes. He joked he'd charge people $5 to see it. I countered I'd stick sparklers in his toes.

The total knee reconstruction, more screws and moved ligaments, took place on Sam's birthday. But Sam was gone, backpacking in the Colorado Rockies. Secretly, I'd sent balloons, a candle, and confetti in a Baggie with Sam's guide. Secretly, I wished I were there too. (But alone, in the middle of a rushin' mountain river.) While Sam hung out in the mountains, his brother had another eleven inches of scar carved into his body, adding to the ten on his head and eight on his foot.

Post-surgery, I slept with Ben in the hospital overnight, just like for his foot reconstruction. With his friend oxycodone coursing through his system, further reducing his inhibitions, Ben always put on a marvelous show. Once, in the middle of the night, he needed to pee. Unable to, in great distress he loudly demanded a catheter.

"I bet you don't get many guys requesting a catheter," I said to Night Nurse.

"Hah!" But she complied.

When she inserted it, Ben accused with a yelp, "Were you raised hard or something?"

He kept the nurses laughing day and night, with what one called "a superhuman sense of humor." At 2:00 a.m. vitals checks, he asked nurses if they were nocturnal, and offered to shake hands, "Thank you for staying up all night to help me."

Back home, stuck in his bedroom convalescing, even a millimeter of movement sent Ben reeling. Cautiously, I adjusted his leg on the large foam cushion they sent home with us.

For weeks, when not racing back and forth, waiting hand, foot, and knee on Ben for food, drink, toileting, and position adjustments, I lounged in the backyard corner of refuge, shell-shocked. Staring at the molten summer sky through leafy branches, crying dry tears and wet, and complaining internally.

"Where are You?" I accused. "And who will take care of me?" I whimpered. I couldn't take caretaking any more. I couldn't maintain the lifestyle; my electrical connection to every facet of Ben's suffering was slowly killing me. In my mind's eye, I held the cord of freedom in my hand, but it remained firmly plugged into the socket, and I had no strength or knowledge to pull it out.

The Whisper returned, "I will. And I will show you how to care for yourself. You will learn to deal gently with yourself."

These would be true statements about the future. For right then, I flipped between Ben's necessary reality and an alternative. Unable to handle Wisconsin, I fled again to England. Voraciously consuming Daphne du Maurier and any other literature pertaining to Cornwall's regions, fantasizing my upcoming October trip with Dan, all acted as a finger in the leaking dike. I read Blackmore's *Lorna Doone*, not set in Cornwall, but we would drive through Devon on our way, passing just south of Exmoor. In one of my favorite chapters, hero and lover John Ridd single-handedly rescues sixty-six lost and stranded sheep after a heavy snowfall. Other men stop, complaining of the freezing wind. Head down, fighting, strong John Ridd plows through deep windswept drifts, carrying the sheep two at a time, "one beneath my right arm, the other beneath my left."

I vowed nothing would prevent my taking refuge in October's Rainbow Days, celebrating a twentieth anniversary with my Dan Ridd.

As I cried and read for weeks that summer, Ben's friends and siblings played Mario Kart until our ears rang with the jingle. We had borrowed friends' Nintendo and games. (Again.) And had stocked up on videos and books from the library. (Of course.) His prom date brought a two-foot wide singing balloon activated by touch, "Don't worry; be happy." Ben smacked the pick-me-up all summer, declaring it worked. Again, Team Ben stepped up tangible love, in the form of cards, food, emails, care packages, and visits.

I emailed an update of thanks. "Ben, would you like me to relay any message from you to your supporters?"

"Tell them, 'I'm getting better and I kind of like the cast.'"

"You're weird, son."

"It brings him games and people," quipped Tim One.

"Yeah, say that too!"

I should've known better than to interrupt the middle of game #3,267 with Tim One, Tim Two, and one of The Twins.

Ben rarely left his room all summer. On July fourth, we parked at the top of a hill for the fireworks.

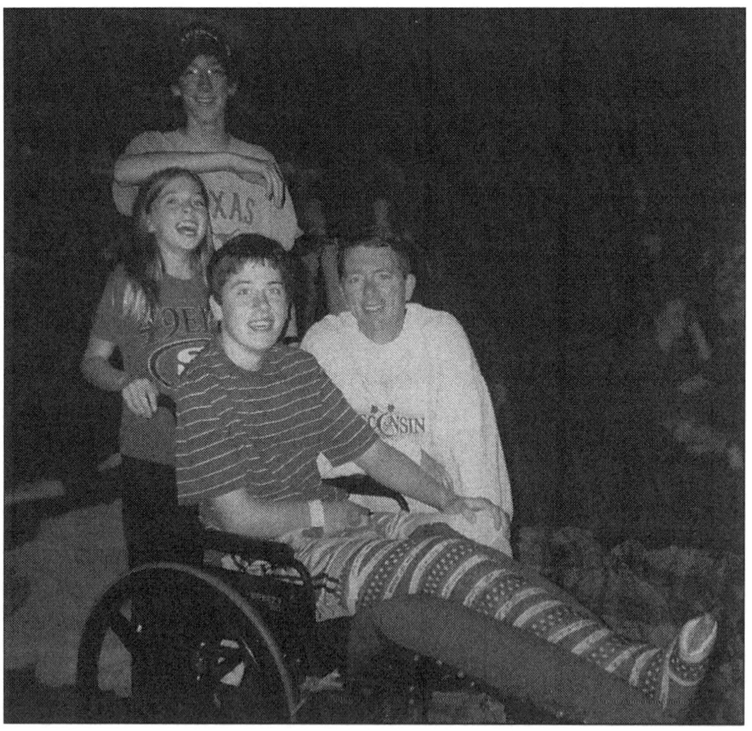

July 4th, 2005

Our other fun outing that July, for the first time ever I took the kids to a movie on opening day, *Charlie and the Chocolate Factory*.

We risked the crowd, protecting Ben's outstretched leg with our bodies, so Johnny Depp's Willy Wonka could make us laugh. It worked. In late July, I positioned Ben in the backyard for his senior portrait. On my non-digital camera, fortunately two developed shots, of many, captured Janus-faced Ben. Sweet and imp.

Ben also left the house for weekly weight-bearing appointments, and a mid-way re-casting. The waterproof material finally allowed him to shower, but best of all, his hard work meant he could wear his crown for an audience.

During the show's last scene, casted Prince Charming hobbled up two steps to the throne of Snow White. Then, without looking, he slowly backed down. I missed some of the Prince's lines and facials, desperately biting my tongue from adlibbing my own, "Look out, Ben! Stop!"

But I wasn't the only surprised person in the audience. Slim Jim in the Gym, Ben's PT through the foot and knee reconfigurations, expressed his pleasure at Ben's mobility and ability. The show must go on!

And it did. The day after the final cast removal on August third, ahead of schedule to accommodate our family, we five piled into the car for another gluttons-for-punishment round of driving. Knowing we'd find adventurizing and paradise 1,600 miles away, just like three years before, at Cross River Cabins in British Columbia. We had planned the trip in the early stages of Ben's angst-filled junior year.

Orthopedic Surgeon gave his vacation blessing, "Bring plenty of ice for swelling, stop often and let him move around. He can take off the hinge to get in a pool or hot tub." I left the hospital pushing Ben in a wheelchair, his list of rehabbing exercises and pain meds clenched in one hand, free at last, free at last, thank God....

On the twenty-eight hour trip, Ben rested his post-op leg on the cooler. Knowing he would have few mountain adventures, we helped him limp to a landing pad for a touring helicopter ride. He took his birds-eye view. Then we took ours.

Cabin owners drove the four of us to the base of a nearby mountainside, with instructions to climb uphill. No switchbacks, unless we made them. Puffing our way about as straight up as one can go without rappelling equipment, when nearing the top I broke into a frantic scramble, as if the hound of hell snapped at my boots. Hurling myself, I fell panting onto a field of wildflowers, surrounded 360 by majestic Canadian peaks. Rattled to my core, but not from the altitude. My tightly wound frame lay inert, a rock for a pillow, and I sobbed Thanksgiving 2004 – August 2005.

Too, too, too much torque.

The possibility of Ben tumbling into another declined mental state had me worried all summer, but it was I who succumbed. Gunning for the magic number in August, the start of vacation. Respite. Freedom. Then? Ben learns to walk, Take Four! The tailspin began on the drive home, suddenly sleepless in North Dakota.

This time, I left the family for ten days, unable to function at home. I holed up alone in my father's country home, while Dan settled the kids in fifth grade, sophomore, and senior years, taking Ben to appointments. Fighting for my life, I could not watch as short-lived, yet violent, Katrina pummeled the Gulf Coast. I could not watch any one hurt any more.

Yet I had to. And this time, I had to watch myself. Nearly a decade had passed before I began to fully address my own internal trauma stemming from January 1996. Fall of 2005, I submerged myself in the healing waters described in the last chapter of the biblical book of Revelation, and camped out with Moses in Deuteronomy 33, "There is no one like the God of Jeshurun, who rides across the heavens to help you and on the clouds in his majesty. The eternal God is your refuge, and underneath are the everlasting arms."

I determined to sit in my own vulnerable pain, for as long as it took to locate and begin walking the road of healing. From I Am, I asked for help to yank the electrical cord out of the socket. I got it.

Through a painted red heart, I stabbed my own red and black Edvard Munch silent scream, slashing jagged, raw, black shards. Streaking across, I painted words, speaking them aloud: craniotomy, proton beam radiation, MRIs, CTs, OT, PT, Speech, blood draws, depression, EEGs, anesthesia x seventeen, cranial, foot, and knee scars and screws, and on and on, the days, weeks, months, years, and hours of Ben's life. And mine. The list of medical words barely fit on the paper.

Suddenly roaring up from the depths, I superimposed everywhere thick, large, and black, *"NO! NO! NO!"* This was the word missing from my vocabulary ever since 10:10 p.m. January 19, 1996. This was what I had wanted to say that night, even if futile. And this was what I couldn't do then. Ejecting from my electric chair of torment, I raced to my bedroom calling an audible, the real screams of motherhood.

For six weeks, Dr. Puckette, psychotherapy, my own intense grief work, and medication put me together enough to travel to Cornwall. I discarded my ambitious Cornish sightseeing plans. Content enough to be held in Dan's arms watching the Atlantic tide come in and go out. To take tea in a B and B garden, nibbling scones with lashings of strawberry jam and clotted cream. To meander the shoreline path to gorgeous Mousehole and back, pausing at bushes dripping fuchsia, marveling at palm trees on England's mild, southern coastline. To take one teeny, scorching sip from Dan's pint of mild ale while we sat on picnic benches at the Lamorna Wink, deafened by the rooky wood. To hear R.E.M.'s *Everybody Hurts* on BBC Radio 1, as we both cried. To be alive, thankful, and quiet with my man. And on our way back to the airport, to stop and view the home of Thomas Hardy's birth, the window whence he had sat writing *Far from the Madding Crowd.*

In early March 2006, the high school put on *Peter Pan,* complete with flying apparatus for Wendy, Peter, and Tinkerbelle. Inspired by Captain Jack Sparrow, Ben's piratey-self sported a gold tooth and one braided and beaded strand of hair. There the resemblance ended. Together we created. Half Ben's shaved head revealed the battlefield of scars, blood red paint on all. His withered arm and curled hand swung visibly in the air, no sleeve on that side of his purple, silken shirt. He limped sea legs, using his normal gait. And he put on a fierce face.

Katherine And Her Pirate

For March's spring break, while Ben toured DC with his choir, the rest of us flew to Arizona – Dan first via Asia. Sam, Sarah, jet-lagged Dan, and I climbed Picacho Peak, scrabbling five miles to the thirty-mile an hour wind-buffeted summit, where holding wiry guidelines prevents falling. There, matching my heart, I rubbed dirt on my face, declaring myself a victorious Celtic Queen Boudicca, Warrior Mother, my wild-tossed hair backing me up.

Sure, if I could have healed Ben by watching and willing, he would've been well long ago. That victory would never be mine. But I claimed another. My boy would again limp across a high school stage, this time to receive his diploma.

End-of-senior-year celebrations included Ben's induction into Thespian Troupe 2960, testament to how far his speaking capabilities had improved in a decade. Cue credit and applause for Ben's hard work, the drama directors of Middleton's excellent summer rec and high school programs, as well as public school, and hospital speech therapists.

That spring, in numerous grocery store checkout lines, my cart filled to overflowing. The general public was simply dying to know, "What is all that (fill-in-the-blank) for?"

When I explained, they beamed and wished me well. My favorite question, "How much wine are you making with all those grapes?"

For Ben's graduation bash, I mailed, emailed, and hand-delivered flyers to family, friends, and our faith, medical, and educational communities. The invitation read:

> Benjamin Perreth, when he was seven
> Well, he nearly made it to heaven.
> But all the King's women and all the King's men
> Helped put Ben back together again!

People sent letters of congratulation, and I put a binder together, representing all seven continents (the penguins of Antarctica even sent their greetings). Since Comaland 1996, our mailbox had never held so many cards. Including a printed congratulatory card from the Green Bay Packers, with a sweet, handwritten note commending Ben for his perseverance, signed "from all of us."

But the best were gushing congrats from people who knew Ben well. Super Principal wrote, *I have never met anyone with a stronger soul than Ben.*

School staff wrote, *No other student I have ever known has met each and every day with so much joy. When Ben asks how you are, he sincerely means it.*

RehabPsych wrote, *Ben is the benchmark for teaching us all about keeping perspective, about being positive, about enjoying each other and working so incredibly hard to overcome obstacles. I will always remember Ben for his humor and smile, and for his ability to roll so incredibly smoothly with the punches.*

PhysicistDoc wrote, *What a great accomplishment to graduate, considering the things you had to go through during high school. You can be very proud of yourself.*

And Chief Neurosurgeon wrote, *You have put such a tremendous effort into every aspect of your life, and yet managed to live it with infectious joy that you should never lose sight of. We are all very proud of you.*

On a sun-splashed June day, at our high school's stadium, my alma mater, we sat with relatives who flew in from coast to coast. When Ben crossed the stage we erupted, then drove to the park shelter for the mother of all graduation parties. For almost a decade I had entertained the notion of such a party, reserved for when Ben's AVM disappeared.

Instead, nearly four hundred people helped us celebrate Ben's ten years of perseverance through adversity. With a live band, balloons, the pictorial Wall of Ben's Life, four sheet cakes, and $1,000 worth of Subway sandwiches (the local franchise's penultimate order, first place belonged to a multi-millionaire), people Ben-overdosed that day. The presence of his supporters whirled Ben's head as well.

Standing by the nametag table for hours, he greeted every new arrival, and then joined in the dancing.

Dan and I, in a circle of people, jumped, kicked, and gloriously spun to *I'm Gonna Be (500 Miles),* the song about a man walking 1,000 miles for the love of his life.

Chapter 26

The Smell Of Hospitals In December

In 1996, a hospital social worker encouraged me to apply for medical assistance under a federal and state program called Katie Beckett (KB). So named for a little girl who'd had a world of trouble. I didn't think I should bother. Ben could breathe on his own, Katie, ten years older than Ben, couldn't.

"Trust me. Just do it," the social worker counseled.

I did, we qualified, and every May for eleven years either a caseworker came for a home visit and the filled-out thirteen-page form, or I just mailed the form. Forty-nine questions, some with a, b, c, d, some even b1-b8, delineated everything wrong with Ben. While Wisconsin flowers bloomed every May, my heart wilted. But the agonizing extreme detail meant KB picked up Ben's substantial insurance co-pays.

(In May 2012, at age 34, Katie died. In 1981, her namesake legislation changed Medicaid, as her parents successfully lobbied President Reagan. During her three decades of advocacy for those with disabilities, she impacted millions of Americans. Rest in peace, Katie. Bless you, Katie's mom, advocating fairy godmother for all of us with special needs kids.)

When Ben turned eighteen a few weeks after his high school graduation in 2006, his KB eligibility ended. But participation in the program made qualifying for federal and state SSI benefits, and Wisconsin Medicaid, easy.

Or so I was told. Still, the online application for SSI required filling out a ream of virtual paper, detailing Ben's disabilities. Our computer couldn't handle it, so I went to the Middleton library. The day I completed the all-consuming, gruesome task, I could barely drive the five blocks home for the dry heaves, violent shaking, and blurred vision. Those hours, buried in the synopsis of Ben's decade of trauma, made me wretched. The SSI application, plus the high emotion prep and mega-celebration of Ben's graduation, sunk me post-party, to the depths. My Dan Ridd plodded another 1,000 miles to keep me here on the planet with him.

As I suffered through another depression, Dan helped Ben with his post-high-school life. That summer, Ben took his first class in the Hospitality and Hotel Management program at our local technical college. An outgoing person deserved an outgoing occupation. Only six to nine credits counted as full-time for him. He would attend year round, taking fewer credits in the summers. I imagined our insurance company, supplied with proof of Ben's disability schooling status, sucked it up.

For two years, Ben lived at home, walking three blocks to the bus stop through snow and ice. He rode to the Capitol Square, transferred, and took another to the East Side. Dan taught him this life skill, and Ben proudly wore his independence.

A company with a heart became Ben's new BFF shoe fairy, allowing him to buy two-for-the-price-of-one incredibly grippy-on-Wisconsin's-snow-and-ice pairs of shoes. (Annually, they still supply "RAK" coupons, random act of kindness, dontchaknow. In turn, I pass on Ben's unused shoe mismatches to National Odd Shoe Exchange.)

After his complete knee overhaul in 2005, Ben never again rode a bike or ran. However, that didn't stop him from organizing summertime games of Ultimate (competitive Frisbee) at our local park. Ben quick-walked down the field through the whirlwind of his friends and siblings. Several neighbors complimented on the cheering and laughter whenever Ben and crew played. He still loves this sport.

In March 2008, like a typical college kid, Ben called one afternoon to inform me he'd be heading south the next day for spring break. Tim One, Bridget, and Joey would actually drive, while Ben rode shotgun – 1,600 miles to the Florida Keys. They'd camp at a state park upon arrival. (I'd forgotten how spontaneous age nineteen could be.)

Wringing my hands in our driveway, as they packed the little car to overflowing, I implored Bridget to watch out for the guys, brave young woman! She nodded her agreement, with wisdom in her young eyes. As they drove off into the setting sun, I stood nervously panting, but took a deep breath. Then lurched inside to have dinner for the first time with seventeen-year-old Sam's recent announcement, his first girlfriend.

(Ben on a college road trip? Sam, what? Which planet did I now inhabit?)

Ben's trip highlights included iguana sightings, feeding huge spiders, and sand. His friends buried him up to his neck on the beach and Ben startled passersby, talking with his soccer-ball head. He set a new personal record for largest hole to Japan. Lowlight? The hundred-mile detour through Chicago on their way to St. Louis the first night. (Could have been worse. On one of my college spring breaks, a carload of guys drove to Indiana equipped with the letter "I" encyclopedia. Helpfully, only IL lay between WI and IN.)

Later that spring, I party prepped again, this time for Sam's graduation from high school. Since he prided himself on his birthplace,

Nagasaki, I cooked a ton of Japanese food. We expected about sixty-five in our house. The day before, I spent thirteen hours slaving in the kitchen, ignoring storm sirens. Besides American BBQ beef, Hawaiian chicken, and salads, Japanese dishes of tamagoyaki (sweet eggs), onigiri (rice balls), nori (seaweed), tofu, and karaage (fried chicken), required my full concentration. Tornadoes-be-damned. About eighty-five showed on the rain-drenched day, packing the garage and house. Who were all these kids we'd never seen or heard of before?

In August 2008, two weeks before we moved Sam three hours away to college, we moved Ben to downtown Madison. As eldest, Ben successfully beat his brother out of the house. Tim One and Tim Two, moving into a rented house on campus near the Kohl Center, had invited Ben to join them. They called it the little, black shack. (I called it the scummy dump.) All could not have been more pleased.

I bought Ben adaptive cooking equipment, taught him a few basic kitchen-smarts, and showed him things he could prepare on his own. (Recipes, even simple ones, baffled him.) But I believe he survived that fall as most young bachelors do, on frozen pizza.

When the boys left home within such a short span of time, suddenly our home, but especially my brain, felt gloriously spacious. I put my finger on the reason, but couldn't do the math. My numbers man calculated 70% of the relationships had moved out, leaving a lone thirteen-year-old girl with two parental units. Yes!

The spaciousness did not last long.

For three years, Ben had remained medically and mentally stable, but the record-long lull ended a few months after moving out. The emotional load of a forty-year-old homeless man he'd befriended, Ben's mistaken understanding of a church challenge encouraging him to consume less in order to give more to others, and his newly independent home-fullness weighed heavily. Hauling laundry one-armed to another building, foraging for food, and managing life, while attending college, Ben fiercely clung to independence. Yet, his grip slipped.

His chosen degree proved increasingly problematic, the math and business courses too hard. "Hospitality" Ben breathed. "Management," not so much. Ben voiced second thoughts as well, "Mom, I don't want to be a hotel clerk or concierge. People will just want to get their room keys and leave, not talk."

The combined stressors sank Ben, requiring ER admittance to UW Hospital's psych unit in December. Outside the ER bay, one nurse brought me water, then gently laid his hand upon my shoulder, speaking sweet words of comfort.

Psych Ward, Take One! A nurse asked me cautiously, hopefully, "You will be coming on Christmas Day?"

Apparently, plenty of people do not visit those under lock and key, not ever. But we did, and so did a steady stream of men: friends, family, and non-psych UW medical personnel. Staff discharged Ben before the twenty-fifth. That year, we waited for Sam to come home, then Ben to come home, to get the Christmas tree.

We removed some pressure from Ben's life by purchasing a private dorm meal plan, and helped him switch associate degrees.

Until fall of the next year, it seemed to work.

Ben's love of drama meant Halloween served as his high holiday, 364 days of preparation for the Event of The Year. (Easter came a close second, followed by St. Paddy's Day, and Christmas, holidays allowing costumes, although pre-ordained. While living at home, for several years Ben had plunked down serious cash to rent a full springtime costume. I found out by crossing paths with someone who'd seen Ben's telltale gait: a large, yellow rabbit limping to the bus stop, wearing a backpack, and carrying a bucket of candy.)

Fall of 2009, Ben assembled artifacts to be V, the Guy Fawkes masquerading, cape cloaked villain in *V for Vendetta*. The all-black costume covered him from head to toe. Eye slits allowed him to see through his pallid, creepy mask, and from his wigged head flowed black, scraggly hair. Two sheathed wooden rapiers hung from his waist.

As always, Ben rehearsed his accent and gestures to complement his costume. Receiving accolades on State Street at Halloween Freakfest (when tens of thousands of costumed people revel), he decided to remain in character a few days longer. Wearing his ensemble to college, he badly scared a woman alone in her office. She called security. The officer explained to Ben that in this day and age people could not dress strangely and act so well without getting into trouble. Especially when it's after Halloween. No exceptions even for a Guy Fawkes costume on Guy Fawkes Day, November fifth. (Celebrated in England.) Mortified and remorseful, Ben apologized profusely.

A month later, college staff called me for a meeting. Although Ben had succeeded in the new degree's spring and summer courses, he had not in the fall. Staff thought he should take a break, perhaps seek employment rather than a degree. The only daily structure he'd known since kindergarten screeched to a halt. We consoled Ben somewhat with the knowledge that his college credits would never be taken from him. It wasn't like high school, as he thought. But Ben, yet again, suffered the consequences of his unique brain. In vain, I tried to prevent another ER psych unit admit. Two Decembers in a row Sam came home from college finals week to, "Your brother is in the hospital."

This time required a longer stay, but because of his supporters, Ben never remained alone for long. One evening, our family crammed into his room, bringing in Mexican food. Staff hushed us, too ebullient; our strong emotions erupted as raucous laughter.

Both years, induction into the unit seemed somewhat of a joke. The dozens of questions for psychiatric admit were impossible for Ben to answer, difficult when unable to think straight. I gave an accurate picture of my son so they wouldn't waste time on unhelpful things, causing Ben to suffer through more hospital crap than necessary.

Upon admission for Psych Ward, Take Two! I remained silent for the answers I knew he knew, translating for those he should know.

"What color is your bowel movement?" Intake Nurse asked.

"What?"

"Your bowel movement, your BM?"

Blank stare.

"She means your poop, Ben."

"Brown."

Good. Intake Nurse beamed gratitude for my work, saving her an s-load of time. But sometimes Ben's answers surprised all of us. Before staff even asked, he recited "truth," "blue ball," and "pink Cadillac." These had tested his short-term memory the previous year. He remembered them so well, he said later, because he had used them as his mantra in 2008, enabling him to focus on something besides his dismal mind. In 2009 I didn't know this and only thought three things. One, amazing. Two, they really should come up with new lists annually, for regulars, like, and three, Mary Kay and The Boss?

Ben remembers his sorrowful mental state both Decembers, "And I hated it. I don't like to remember those times, to think about it for too long, because I was hanging onto hope that I was going to get out of it, but I saw no end in sight. It was very hard. They were the lowest points of my whole life."

During Psych Ward, Take Two! I learned many things. Like, how staying in the psych unit long enough can make you crazy. In the lounge and halls, usually parentless adult inpatients wandered, breathing in despair, loneliness, confusion, and rejection. One mother strolled with her blank-faced, middle-aged daughter. Our eyes met briefly, in grim acceptance, sorrow, and support, speaking clearly. I have noticed this often, the visual connection to the soul, no words necessary between mothers of children with extra challenges. Solidarity and affirmation take less than a second.

Patients wear street clothes. I found out the hard way. One put-together woman requested I remove my Terri-created, lavender-sacheted scarf (typical), inspected it carefully (ditto), and then wrote her name, phone, and address on a piece of paper. With glowering eyes she repeatedly demanded I contact her in the future with scarf directions.

And during Take Two! I learned the chronic mental health support system itself is based on insanity. A hospital social worker, nearly pulling out her hair, muttered how she hated the system. Nervously picking at her papers, her eyes roamed around the room as if the answers revealing the location of True Help were hiding under the chair, standing behind the door, perching on the arm of the sofa.

Finally, she coherently said, "The three easiest ways into the mental health support system are, one, court order. You have to get the police involved and a judge gives orders. Two, homelessness, you have to abandon him. Or three, do you know anyone famous? Like the Governor?"

The silence after this pronouncement deafened. Not even my gasp was audible.

The previous year a male social worker had told me Ben was "too high functioning," there were "no services for him." Was that true? Would Ben forever fall through the cracks, until something got him on someone's radar screen? Because I sure didn't know the Governor, and I was not about to abandon my son; should I tell him to rob a bank? As Ben's mom, I long felt he, thus we, lived in Crackland, Ben, "too high functioning." How could this be for a guy on SSI, with diagnostic AVM/radiated-brain alphabet soup after his name, still requiring so many therapies?

My utter despair over Ben's situation, the dearth of true help, and my depleted ability to search any longer for rescue, induced me to quickly run through the pros/cons of murder-suicide. With just a couple of wild and crazy eyes, I logically reasoned thus: if I eliminated my son and myself, he'd be forever protected, and my family would be spared a homicide trial. (Win-win!) Ben and I wouldn't hurt anymore, but the rest of the family would be scathed beyond belief. (Win-Lose!) So I'd have to take out the rest of the family too. Which would cause great pain to Sam's girlfriend. (Lose! Lose!) So – naw, *that* won't work. Sorrow for hundreds. (Lose-Lose-Lose ad infinitum!) Either I killed the entire planet, or I killed no one.

Something is not right when a lucid, UW-Madison grad entertains thoughts this preposterous. (Double major dontchaknow, Sociology and *Social Work* for Pete's sake.)

But I didn't voice my thoughts, settling instead upon pleading, "Look, isn't there a saner way?"

The hospital social worker started explaining "the system" to me. I mentioned my degrees, omitting they hailed from 1983. Shouldn't have done that – she started speaking in acronyms. I took notes as best I could, with my mush brain trying to follow. "Look," I sniveled, "I don't have the energy to pursue dead ends or things that will bleed me dry without winding up helping my son. I can't do all this stuff, anymore. Where, which ball, should I start rolling?"

She named two possibilities for me to pursue, and another two for herself. She could fill out paperwork on Ben's behalf. I'd do the other two. Fine. Consider it done. Although I had to apologize to the trees, more forests were to be felled in aid of Ben.

With Ben still in bad shape, staff discharged him Christmas afternoon. Dan and I were already at the hospital by the time Sam and Sarah awoke Christmas morning – to no presents under the tree. No decorations on the tree. The only year the five of us had not cut down a tree together. With papers indicating that the medical system considered our son free, able to live alone and take care of himself (yeah, right), Dan and I wheeled Ben out the hospital doors.

I began, in earnest, to hate Christmas. What sort of presents were these back-to-back Decembers? Had I not already cried lakes Wingra, Waubesa, Monona, Mendota, and Kegonsa? Now, I must cry Michigan and Superior too? Crying, the family could handle. What I did on the darkened Christmas afternoon scared the hell out of them. As I hid with God in my bedroom, an unbidden sound emitted from my lips. Beyond words, beyond broken-heartedness, beyond hurt, too far beyond, a soul keening. A ranger had once taught me to wolf howl, a similar sound, but fake. Keening comes honestly, without pretense, or effort, and when it finishes, numbness sets in. It supersedes the bay of the wolf as the most mournful, eerie, and distinct sound on the planet, because it is human. Or almost so.

We "celebrated" the holiday little by little over the next few days, an hour here, an hour there.

Shortly after Ben's discharge, Dr. Sparkle, a sane psychiatrist with a twinkle in his eye and practical ideas for help on his tongue said, "Ben, we're going to strengthen the healthy part of your brain by choices you make. Most of your brain is healthy."

My breath caught in my throat. No one had ever said that. Didja hear that, son?

As Cheerleader-Case-Manager-PTSD-Recovering Mom, I desperately tried to buoy Ben's spirits. Yet on a daily basis, his bloodshot eyes lowered, registering sorrow incarnate and downtrodden exhaustion. I couldn't let it stop us; we had to find the future. I dragged my drugged adult son around town in a wheelchair, his head down on tables. "Sign your name here, Ben." Scribble. His doing so enabled me to fill out the rest of the paperwork, meant to help, not steamroll.

"Mama, I'm lost and I don't know where to go," my twenty-one-cum-seven-year-old whispered, decimated in voice and psyche.

"I know, kiddo. I'm sorry. You'll be with us. Your junkyard dog Mama is working so very hard for you. It will get better, I promise. All you gotta do is wait, help is coming." I've learned how to lie well, or at least to convincingly speak words I fervently wished were true. No GPS in life. Problem-solving skills required.

Three weeks later, a few days before Comaland anniversary, the day I annually struggle to focus on my daughter's birthday, I snapped. God on trial, found guilty of dereliction of duty, going AWOL, and forsaking me and mine. We had taken each and every hit dished out for fourteen years, but these latest Christmas rounds...? Couldn't anybody help, since God had clearly abandoned his post? The Deity Removal flatbed truck backed up, loaded The Director of the Universe, and hauled him away from my heart. Much like when I saw my city's dump truck disposing of park playground equipment now deemed dangerous. The slide, jungle gym, and merry-go-round that I'd played safely upon as a child.

Dan gave me space to grieve Ben's latest round of trauma differently than he. My stifled voice unleashed as I verbally threw the yellow flag on God. Foul! Unjust! Unfair! Go be God somewhere else! Leave me alone! You hate us! It pained Dan to hear me rant as I took Job's wife's advice, curse God and die. I cursed, oh, did I curse, flinging F G skyward, and it didn't stand for Father Goodness. But I did not die. And I did not live, not on the inside, unless fire-breathing rage counts as life.

I went to yoga, although unable to do anything more for ninety minutes than Child's Pose. Not even Happy Baby. Especially not Happy Baby. And when our yogini instructed us to hold our hands open, signifying we're ready for whatever is coming next, I kept mine clenched tightly. Not ready. At all.

A timely trip to Koo's, planned well in advance of December's disaster, provoked my thoughts. A friend Koo knew from church looked me deeply in the eyes, touched my arm like a whisper, and quietly said, "Keep the faith, sister."

Whose faith? Which brand? My us/them, I know/you don't, go-go, people pleasing, self-denying and not self-affirming, frenetically happy-happy do-list of a faith tradition had proven toxic. Insidious tendrils of wrong thinking had packaged God. My elitist pride had convinced me I was getting an "A" in Godology. No longer.

For the time being, I comforted myself with my own wisdom. When I had taught my kids to clean their rooms, I reminded them a truly messy room would only get worse before it got better. Taking apart, sorting, donating, recycling, discarding, shifting, and rearranging take time, perseverance, and contemplative breaks. A new order will be achieved; it just doesn't look like it at first. I sifted through the detritus of a three-decade long faith, finding much fault all around. Self included. The self- and Spirit- illuminating dark night of my soul turned out to last only a year.

As I fought through Life With Ben that late winter 2010, the hospital social worker sent notification that she had duly requested help for Ben by filling out paperwork on his behalf, but nothing ever came of her leads. After a few months, one of the ideas she'd given me dead-ended as well. However, I struck gold with the very last suggestion she'd offered, "Or maybe...Yahara House?"

After five minutes in YH the aroma of hope and life overpowered – so easy to distinguish after the stench of despair, stamped in triplicate. I told YH Director what I detected in her building and she said, "That's right."

"I want this for my son! I will do whatever to make this happen for my son!"

"I hear the desperation in your voice," she empathized. "I am going to help you."

I wept, and thought, "If you help me, I swear you will never regret it. I will tell the whole world you are my family's deus ex machina, our eleventh-hour deliverer."

Curiously, in order for Ben to receive YH services, we had to remove him from our insurance plan. YH Director explained that unfortunately HMOs in our area do not offer financial coverage of Clubhouse Model treatment and recovery services, despite evidence-based approval by the federal government body, SAMHSA. If our insurance declined to pay, so would Ben's government-run Medicaid, automatically. Taking Ben off private insurance meant Medicaid would be free to pick up the bill. In our area, it is often the only type of insurance available to people living with severe mental illness. I can only imagine the party our insurance company threw the day they no longer had Ben on the rolls.

Yahara House is partly funded by your tax dollars. I firmly believe, along with YH members and staff, that evidenced-based, accredited ICCD Clubhouse Model treatment for mental illness should be a civil right. This is a grand country we live in, caring for those who require extra help. We are forever grateful for Ben's government-provided Katie Beckett, SSI, Medicaid, and 2½ years after finding YH, federally subsidized housing. Yet access to long-term help in the mental health arena shouldn't have to be so hard.

Mid-spring 2010, Ben moved back to his shared apartment, resumed volunteering at Wii Club for the downtown Senior Center, and walked to YH, seven blocks away.

I walked downtown too, pondering Ben's future. My way into WESLI took me past the under-construction new digs of the Madison Children's Museum. I wondered if they'd like a volunteer juggler in their massive building, and called Ben one day to broach the idea. Called as I walked. Yep. The latest round of Life With Ben had convinced me to finally enter the twenty-first century.

At age forty-nine, I purchased my first mobile phone. Wireless technology had made me leery, just as James Thurber's early twentieth century grandmother had freaked out over the then-new-fangled thing in homes called "electricity." She swore plugs must be in the sockets at all times to prevent the dastardly stuff from leaking. Who knew what cell phones emitted? I also objected to the expense, and additionally reasoned, "If I have a cell, people can call me anywhere. Can't have that happening."

The cell phone's priceless value quickly became apparent one day late in April. Dan and I returned from a lovely walk; I hadn't taken the cell with me. (See third reason listed above.) Things were perfectly primed to take a turn for the worse. Things complied. Sometimes I think I have a hotline to Things.

SOS voice messages on the cell. Two phones pressed to my ears, I called Ben with the ancient kitchen phone, while listening to his distressed pleas, garbled mumbling, and tones of despair. He begged me to return his call. I did. No answer. My face reflected alarm.

"What's going on? Where are you going?" Dan asked.

"To get Ben! You go to Sarah's soccer!"

I gave him no time for argument, Tag, I'm It! Out the door in a flash, I drove while calling, breaking my own rule for safe driving, no cell while driving. Imagining overdose, breaking down the doors, calling 911."Not yet, not yet," I told myself. Breathe.

My phone chirped. "Mom?" a tiny voice enquired.

"Where are you?"

"At the hospital."

"UW?"

"Yes."

"ER?"

"Yes."

"I'm on my way. I'll be there in less than five minutes."

"I love you, Mom." Cell phones are good.

What lay ahead? Psych Ward, Take Three? Boundaries. Calm. Rational. Thinking. Breathe. I gave myself some talking points.

An ambulance had delivered Ben after he dialed 911. When I arrived at the hospital, Ben already lay on a gurney in the bowels of the behemoth, dressed in ER hospital garb and hooked up to a heart monitor with the O2 clip on his finger. What a relief. For once, I'd missed the admittance procedure.

My son and I had plenty of time for a heart-to-heart. His symptoms started to "ebb off," he said. I stayed ridiculously calm, throughout.

A resident doc entered and the three of us discussed a chest x-ray. I put the kibosh on that, believing Ben's breathing trouble another highly annoying medication-induced panic-attack. If medically concerning, his doctors would've checked it out in December, January, February, or March. They hadn't. The resident concurred. I thought docs should switch Ben's meds back to what had previously worked, but increase the dose. The ER docs had no authority to do it. (Later, Ben's psychiatrist agreed, and the meds have worked beautifully for him ever since.)

During another doctoral interlude, I imparted some wisdom learned in my forties. We practiced deep belly breathing.

"What are we doing, Mom?"

"We're taking control."

"We're taking *control!*" Ben shouted, laughing, fist pumping the air.

"Look," I said. "Here's what really helps me, besides breathing and yoga. Since yoga's not something you can really do, this is better. I've only done it twice, so I don't know much, but stand up."

He stood.

"Watch my hands. This one's called Wave Hands Like Clouds. See how they move slowly through space, and I turn and watch them, focusing on them with my eyes?"

He tried. "It's beautiful, Mom. It's calming."

"Yeah, if I thought yoga was slow, tai chi is like moving through Jell-O."

"Jell-O!" he said with a laugh, and then paused. "Hey! My side effects are gone."

We talked more about his life and mine. About The Depressions and things I've learned because of them, how we have choices and control over some things, even when we feel we don't. About learning how to take care of ourselves, something especially critical, since simply living is traumatic for him and, consequently, for me.

"You've had a lot of trauma, Mom."

"Yes. But not direct. You've had fourteen years of direct and repeated trauma."

Then, another knock at the door and a new doctor, the real Dr. McDreamy, appeared. I levitated, my brain floating right up and out of my skull, his features indelibly seared into my shocked retina.

"Hi! I'm Dr. –"

(Wha'? Greek God?)

"... so, I'd like..."

(Other than one female Colombian student at WESLI, I had never seen such beauty. And this guy, without any make-up whatsoever.)

"...feel a lot better if..."

(To whom could I compare this male perfection? A lapis lazuli-eyed Cassidy-Sundance Kid hybrid meets Pierce Brosnan meets Michelangelo's David's forearms?)

"...EKG..."

(How does he expect me to listen? It's not fair. Gasp! Can he tell what I'm thinking by this stupid look on my face?)

"...perhaps..."

(Get a grip, girl. Pay attention!)

"If that's all right with you?"

I formulated the best sentence I could, under the circs, "Yes."

While staff conducted an EKG, I stepped out into the hallway to chat with the nurse, a perky woman about my age. Out of earshot, I explained my thinking, using a titch bit of profanity to communicate Ben's life. Sparingly used, I find raw language helpful at times, cutting through euphemisms. I told her Ben's symptoms had abated when we talked, breathed deeply, and practiced tai chi.

"Good job, Mom. Do you feel good about that? You should!" she commended.

"I feel damn good about it. Thanks."

After the EKG results returned "normal," she gave Ben talking points. Let's just call it what it is.

"You may feel shitty, Ben," she instructed, "as if you can't breathe. But the numbers on the machine are excellent. The feeling is real, but what you're thinking about the feeling isn't true. You aren't going to stop breathing and die."

Ben decided to go back to his apartment that evening. I dropped him off, after running through the talking points again.

"I love you, Mom."

"I love you, too, Ben. Get yourself a treat tonight. You've been through a lot, again. Reward yourself for making the right choice, which has taught you much today."

Taking control, making choices, setting boundaries, in the way I knew how, I drove away. Tai chi in the ER. It was good. Dr. McDreamy, not too bad either, but he had nothing on Dan.

That evening, after another Ben-ER debriefing, Dan suggested, "That's your book's first chapter."

"What is?"

"What you just said, about being a mother, having a baby, about what motherhood does to you, the connection, about the anguish of your mother's heart." He continued, "You never expected it; a baby coming out surprised you. It's on the tape recording, you know." Dan thought it richly funny, my astonishment at Ben's birth.

Ben had arrived a week early, with a rush of blood, not breaking water. (Talk about foreshadowing.) His pitocin-induced birth, then epidural, left me so drugged nurses commented they'd never seen someone so "out of it" post-partum, prompting them to further monitor my pulse. Sarah diplomatically debuted smack in between two due dates. A midwife beautifully delivered my 9 lb. 3 oz. daughter, after what seemed like days of pushing through a sunny-side up logjam, but was really only one hour. The creative positioning the midwife offered, and my experience with Sam's birth in Japan, enabled me to forgo pain relief. In Japan, pain meds not even an option, I gave birth to a gallery. (Everyone wanted to watch the American deliver.) Staff there in 1993 urged me to practice push. I refused, and Dan backed me up, "She's a good pusher, she doesn't need practice."

He also first recognized my impending hyperventilation. If you force an L & D woman to lay flat on her back for hours, feet up in stirrups, because you've already sterilized the area, hyperventilation is what you'll get. Even so, Sam's Nagasaki birth was my favorite. Ever the easygoing child, Sam arrived on his due date. My body did its thing, its way, only four pushes needed. Utterly alert euphoria followed, despite having just left deep fingernail impressions on the hands of the two people flanking me, Dan and Tsuji-san. I'd met her soon after we'd arrived in Nagasaki. She loved helping pregnant American women, paying it forward fifteen years after Minnesotan women had treated her kindly when she'd lived in the States.

Japan's birthing customs dictated a mandatory seven-day stay in the hospital. What rapture to be taken care of for a week post-partum, to have women alleviate the discomfort of hard footballs suddenly appearing on my chest, to have nurses and midwives watching out for my welfare as I learned the ways of my new son. Staff and I suffered a few cultural clashes, notably when I refused to have my mid-section bound tightly in cloth (to help my figure return), and when the air conditioning turned off overnight. Intentionally. Sam's first day in Nagasaki was 85 degrees, 86% humidity. Tsuji-san took pity on a panicking post-partum American, brought in a fan from her home and set it up. Staff didn't want it blowing on me, but I did.

When my week was up, the young student-midwife, assigned to me because of her English ability, presented me with a beautiful (pink!) handmade booklet "Post-partum Life." On the cover she'd drawn a singing mama penguin pushing Jr. penguin in a stroller. Inside, illustrated instructions offered troubleshooting during my "6-8 weeks" recovery period. Lochia duration and coloration, when it was safe to bathe ("doctor's permission"), when I would be allowed to have a haircut ("after 2 weeks"), permanent wave ("after 1 month"), nutrition ("Don't forget! Necessary for you 'vegetables'"), household chores ("You don't force, start cares slowly, and had better relax a bit"), contraception ("You can't coitus until doctor give you a permission"), and what to bring to my "uterin" medical exam in one month. She even wrote the Japanese phrase I would need to say upon check-in at hospital reception. Besides the extremely useful information, and adorable artwork, my favorite part of the booklet explained how to care for my "bleast." It came in handy later, when my milk ducts plugged. Given her tender attention to detail, I imagine she's had an excellent midwifery career. (But I never did figure out the connection between post-partum recovery and my hair length.)

Nurses and midwives had commended Dan at all three kids' births, Minneapolis, Nagasaki, and Madison. They'd rarely seen such an attentive, wise birth coach-husband, or such a birth team. This surprised me, as I was part of the team and occasionally would bark rudely at him, "Out *loud!*" My focal point? Dan's voice.

He still uses it beautifully, as he did that April 2010 evening, talking me through another Life With Ben UW ER debriefing.

“Yeah, I remember,” I said to Dan, reminiscing our firstborn’s birth. “Mom rocked her first grandchild then, and whispered, ‘So much to learn, little one.’ At the time I thought she spoke only to baby Ben. Then a doc came in, one I never saw before or after, and he gave the best advice I’ve ever heard, ‘Babies are creatures of habit.’”

We had steered our babies toward habits we could live with, and they had reciprocated. (Sort of.)

“Ben’s fingers and toes astonished me,” I murmured, viewing again my mind’s snapshots of Ben’s first breaths. “His little personhood, fresh out of my body...how the heck had that happened?”

Surprise, followed immediately by motherhood’s Electrical Killer Instinct. In one breath, one heartbeat, pacifism traded for protectionism. I’ve never expected a lot of things.

Hard. Hard. Hard. Thank God I knew how to do it.

The summer of 1986 Dan and I backpacked together for the first time. I taught him how, just as my father had taught me. We packed up our gear, including fishing poles, hiked thirteen miles into the Wyoming Rockies wilderness, and set up camp. Neither of us fish, but it would save us from having to eat reconstituted freeze-dried cardboard. It took us about ten minutes to kill our catch by repeated weak attempts to bludgeon the flopping, slippery fish. We didn’t relish killing. Following my dad’s chicken-scratch notes, I barely made it through the cleaning process without throwing up.

Over twenty years passed before we next backpacked. This time, only I fished. Following my dad’s 1986 cleaning notes again, I quickly dispatched my catch with one major blow. Without compunction I slit the belly, ripping out the entrails. On the killing rock, I stared incredulously at my freezing, bloody hands. What had happened to me? Twenty-plus years, that’s what, 1996-2010 in particular.

My father called me "tough as nails" in 2001, after Ben and I returned from his second round of radiation-prep. If my father had thought that of me before The Depressions, before Ben's multiple reconstructive surgeries, before Ben's mental health challenges, what was I now? A hammer? But, out and about, a happy hammer with a smile on her face, and laughter on her lips. The hammer only hangs her head when alone, mouth down-turned, like two steel prongs.

Just like Ben.

Ben's 2011 Bio For DC

My name is Benjamin Perreth. I am 23 ½ years old. When I was seven, I was a healthy, active boy. But that same year, I had a brain hemorrhage that turned my life upside down. The neurosurgeons expected me to die during emergency brain surgery. I was in a deep coma. I still have an AVM in my brain, the thing that caused the hemorrhage. Because of it, I had to learn how to walk and talk again, had brain radiation twice, and several major surgeries. Then I had to learn how to walk two *more* times, and along with my physical disabilities, I started to have mental illness, too. But I'm still here!

After high school I tried to get a degree in hospitality in college. What I wanted in my life was a job that was 100% fun for me and one I could do. Because of the mental disabilities and illnesses, I failed. The classes were too hard for me and I had to quit. I had no hope.

The Madison Children's Museum has been a quintessential lifesaver. I had never been able to have a job because surviving and school had taken all my energy. At first, MCM gave me a chance to volunteer as a one-handed juggler. My first opportunity was juggling off-site for kids and their families; some kids were like me, with special needs. Then after over a year of volunteering, MCM hired me! It is a dream job come true, literally, and has made my life a lot more bearable.

I want to make the lives better for people with disabilities and mental illness, and those who are just stressed. Because everybody has stress. Working at MCM has fulfilled my dream job by letting me use my juggling and thespian skills. When I was a little kid, I always told my mom that I wanted to make everybody happy. The Madison Children's Museum lets me do that.

Chapter 27

Hold My Hands

Breaking News! National Medals For Museum and Library Service Washington DC, Celebration read a subject line on my email, Thursday evening, November 10, 2011.

Monday, December 5, 6:00 p.m., on Capitol Hill in the Cannon Caucus Room. We are hoping to get a photo op scheduled with Mrs. Obama at the White House sometime on Monday or Tuesday, but have no confirmation yet.

Less than a month away? Between Thanksgiving and New Year's? My breathing space sucked to outer space, imploding like dark matter. Too many emotionally charged events, chief among them Beloved Aunt's newly diagnosed cancer, same kind that took her sister, my mother. Soon, I would join my aunt at her first UW cancer appointment.

DC now? Dan held me long and tight that night, November 10, his overwhelmed woman of exactly thirty years.

It took twenty minutes to walk through the doors of the UW Hospital, not just because they signified trading normalcy for sorrow. Half the time I spent driving from home, the other half circling the monstrous parking ramp. On the fifth floor, I steeled myself to dash down the stairs and enter the building I hated to love. For once, Ben did not accompany me.

Clinic or Hospital entrance, which to take? As if it were a wishbone, the way splits, giving momentary pause, allowing one to wish one didn't have to choose, which is the lucky side? I should not have read the signs; I should have allowed my muscle memory to guide. My legs knew where to go better than my brain, even though this time I headed for an uncharted department. Despite my limbs urging right, I wrongly dodged left.

The mammoth, continually spinning revolving doors simultaneously accommodate wheelchair-bound folks and shuffling bipeds. Over the years, my children always cut it as close as possible without getting clipped by the glass panel door, which stops if touched. They became experts, rarely halting the merry-go-round. If others were present, I never let them play the game, but with so many visits to hone their skills they learned to accurately gauge those doors. A few yards in, one walks through what had been my children's next favorite childhood hospital game, the entrance's echoing chamber. Someone's architectural bright idea lifted the ceiling so that footfalls below resonate. This never failed to delight my three, as they stomped their way through ten little strides, making as much noise as possible.

Now, I did not find my unintentional, loud vibrations amusing. The sound only verified my location, my home-away-from-home sterilized living room. Funny how time and life make you forget certain details and remember others. The spinning door, the bracing footfalls, led me back to pain, making me vulnerable.

My addled brain overriding my legs again, I disastrously chose the next path. Bypassing the elevators to get down one floor, I cleverly took a stairwell. Shoulda known better, labyrinthine building. Spokes from each elevator pod lead to other pods, and stairwells don't always coincide. In incomplete alpha order, B, D, E, F, H and K, all pods are color-coded roy-g-biv. The yellow, a long line on the floor, does not lead to the Emerald City.

Nevertheless, when there, sometimes I think I'm in Oz. Diabolical, winged monkeys, agents of evil with cosmic GPS tracking systems, search me out. Their ability to drop down from the sky, snatching me unawares, seems much scarier than a witch circling high overhead on a broomstick, writing threats in the clouds. Or so it is with me, and the timing of PTSD triggers.

Among other things, the triggers over the years have included ambulances (many), a sermon using an OR clip with docs in blue scrubs (once), a speaker unexpectedly delving into brain mechanics (once), hospital Code Blue Stat alarms or school emergency personnel rushing by (many), others' loud conversations regarding medical trauma, held in restaurants, a spa, or in the yoga studio (numerous), research phone calls requesting Ben's AVM history (several), and books and movies whose plot lines and/or character names suddenly mirrored my own life (too many; e.g., pages 3 and 4 of Billy F's *The Sound and the Fury*, and page 327 of John Grisham's *The Appeal*. The latter sent me to bed at 4:30 one Saturday afternoon).

The common denominator, Surprise! With each unexpected reminiscent event, my heart rate spikes as adrenaline floods my system. And she's off!

Fleeing the church sanctuary, the tai chi and yoga studio, the high school cafeteria, the middle school hallway, or the hospital, running for the exit, sprinting for safety, shaking, crying, gasping. Or else, as with ambulances coming from behind, pulling over sharply and sitting paralyzed, waiting for the wave to subside, talking myself through, "That was then, this is now. Ben is safe. Breathe. Breathe. Breathe."

"Are you lost?" asked a woman wearing a UW lanyard.

Trapped like an animal, paws up to my face, not knowing which way to sanctuary, I stood rooted (but not grounded) and lost, as well. "Umm, yes," I gulped. "I'm just having a little PTSD moment too."

"Oh! Can I help?"

"Please! I'm trying to get to the cancer place and I got lost in the cafeteria maze and I don't wanna go *that* way, because suddenly I'm back saying good-bye to my dying son and –"

"Oh! I'm sorry! Is he going to make it?" The woman froze too.

"No, not now, I mean, yes, he did. It was almost sixteen years ago, but he wasn't expected to and I'm tryin' to find where my aunt is, and suddenly I come around the corner, and damn it, it's *E/3*!" Then I really dissolved.

"Oh, you poor woman!" she sympathized, enveloping me in her arms, completely comprehending emotional unintelligibility. "I am so sorry."

After a few moments, she deftly led me away from dreaded E/3.

"Thanks," I mumbled. "At least they got the rehab outta E. I helped do that. I was asked to be on a panel. I use'ta hav'ta come to E all the time for his rehab. It was hard."

For years, the rehab appointment check-in desk remained where I had sung *Benjamin's Song*, for presumably the last time. The receptionists' chairs, those that Dan and Senior Pastor had sat in while my tears stained the floor. The exact longitude and latitude where Chief Neurosurgeon had asked, "*What do you want to do?*"

The complete stranger, accompanying me in my PTSD moment, received the abridged story, garrulity another PTSD factor of mine. (Or maybe simply a regenerated character trait.) The initial trauma, then the subsequent traumas, fragmented my world and my language, held chaotic words inside, my own torturous iron mask. But with PTSD the words tumble out. Really, since March of 2008 The Words rushed out, scriven and spoken. People don't realize when I speak two sentences at once it is not a plot to confuse. My raconteur rolls are only making up for lost time, when frozen words entangled and I couldn't voice my overfull heart.

"You'd think after so long I'd know where I was going," I complained. "We've been on just about every floor."

"This is a crazy building," she agreed.

"Yeah, it is." Some floors crazier than others, I well knew.

As we neared safe familiarity, I slowed down. "Now, my son gets to go to DC to help the Madison Children's Museum collect their national award, and I getta go too, as mom of disabled mentally ill kid!" I smiled at her through my blurry rose-colored glasses, my language PC left behind somewhere between E and K. Ben is a young man *with* disabilities, suffering *from* mental illness. There is a difference, a small semantic difference indicating a serious identification difference.

"Well, now! You have a great time in DC!"

"Thanks, I will! Who are you?"

"I'm Audrey, and I work here."

"Thank you so much, Audrey."

She and I parted, Audrey Rescuer of Damsels in Distress. What was Audrey's real job title? She wore an ID, but at that moment I couldn't read it. Social worker? Admin? Psych? PT? OT? Speech? Food service? Housekeeping? No scrubs, no white coat, no known hospital creds other than compassion.

Well done, Audrey.

On a mid-November Saturday afternoon, I met my father at the UW men's basketball game.

"Where'd you come from?" I asked. You never knew with him.

"Country. I was hunting."

Of course. Mammal or bird?

Growing up, we had to watch our heads in our home; our walls sprouted a wide variety of the animal kingdom. Ringo, the ring-necked pheasant, flew above the fireplace for years until displaced by a large tumbleweed we snatched from the wind Out West. A yard in diameter, we stuffed it in the back of the station wagon on top of the camping gear. I counted myself lucky. My high school homecoming and prom dates would now only have a dead bush for a picture backdrop. But the living room wasn't our only showcase. In the tiny TV room, we learned to not round the corner quickly lest Rudy's rock hard nose pop us in the face and our hair snag on his antlers. Yet, the deer kept the fish company, Mom's 1967 contest-worthy, 8 ½ pound northern pike. Her catch, from a canoe with two frightened girls seated in the middle, had earned her a photo in *The Capital Times*. The fish, lure, and lake received their proper names, but the caption identified her as "Mrs. Dad's First and Last Name." The pike's sharp, toothy grin leered at us when we watched *The Brady Bunch*, *Love, American Style,* and apropos, *The Partridge Family*.

But before the trophies were relegated to the brown paneling in either room, we ate them. My parents were in cahoots, supplying food and décor in one shot. Which is also what Dad said every time we ate wild game, "Watch out for the shot!" We competed at dinner, collecting and counting little pellets. Throughout my school days, various other fauna regularly graced our table: squirrel, rabbit, grouse, woodcock, duck, and goose. Sometimes there were leftovers. In seventh grade, Leslie chose to be my friend despite my lunchtime fare: an apple, carrot sticks, Ho Hos, and a pickle, ketchup, and venison heart sandwich. (Is it any wonder I have loved Leslie for life?)

Ah, the reminiscences of sweet youth. Forty years later, Dad hunted still every fall with guns and arrows. At the UW game, I wondered which he'd used that morning, and if he'd had success.

"Dad, didja get anything besides that red gash on your forehead?"

He laughed, shaking his head. "Nope. Saw three squirrels, a few turkey, and a deer, too far away."

"So, what is that red mark?"

"I got a new crossbow –"

(Oh, this should be good.)

" – and it says not to get your eyes within 2½ inches but –"

(Like I said.)

" – it's got this great sighting and I had my eye down there, looking, and pulled back, wham! Bled like a stuck pig." He giggled. "It doesn't have kick like a shotgun, but it's got kick."

(Had the man forgotten *A Christmas Story*?) I knew about kicks. I fired a shotgun once as a teen, at a can. First gun, last gun I will ever fire. I'm not fond of guns. Too impetuously, irrevocably used to maim and kill.

"At least you didn't get an arrow through the head," I countered, relieved.

"Almost did, once. Did I ever tell you that story?"

(Here we go.)

"When I was a kid, we had this game, shoot the arrow up and see how close you can get it to land. To yourself, you know; I didn't flinch. I think it missed me by about an inch." He guffawed loudly, my seventy-five-year-old father.

"Dad, Dad, Dad, you should not tell me these things! You know you're just providing writing fodder."

Some day, no doubt, he will be found with a crazy grin plastered upon his deadened face, having broken his back falling from a deer tree stand, or with a bullet through his heart having shot himself unintentionally, or blown to smithereens from mixing things in the garage, erstwhile chemist that he is, or with an arrow through his head from reenacting his youth.

The not-quite-death-defying options from his younger years, spilling into his twilight years, are nearly limitless. He may be found crispy in a field from burning his prairies, the way he started that grass fire in a field once in Amarillo. As a six-year old, you know, just to see if it would burn. The firemen put it out. Or crashed off a cliff sledding down the hill from his farm, recreating the exhilaration he felt flying down the cobblestone street in Alton. As a ten-year old, you know, where you had to make the curve, or die. Or God knows what other story I have not yet heard.

But my best bet is he will simply have a heart attack in one of his prairies. After discovering the failure of his best efforts to eradicate the "wrong" kind of thistle and goldenrod, and the bane of his existence, the always wrong wild carrot, namely Queen Anne's lace. Yes, one of these days, Queen Anne is going to kill him, frills and all.

But I didn't say these things aloud to Dad; I only mulled them over during the UW men's basketball game held at the Kohl Center. And I people-watched.

Scanning the crowd, my father was not the only man there to interest me. In a metro area of a quarter of a million, I possessed an uncanny knack for crossing paths with the medical community outside their spheres: nurses, doctors, and therapists of all stripes. Run-ins included a man high on my shortlist of men to be thankful for. Although we rarely saw each other anymore, and when we did, we were cheering in the venue holding 17,000. Chief Neurosurgeon's basketball seats happen to be ten feet from my father's. But the brain surgeon is a busy man, on a very unpredictable schedule, and cannot make all the games. Neither can I. If we attended simultaneously, I always nipped over to offer a quick Ben update.

Just before tip off at this game, the distinguished gentleman caught my eye, broke into a gigantic smile, and eyes gleaming, rose to greet me, pushing politely past his male companion. *He's* coming over to me?

Grabbing my two hands with his, "Congratulations!" he exclaimed. Still holding my hands, my cheek grazed his as he spoke into my ear, trying to communicate through the deafening roar of rabid Badgers fans.

"Thank you!" I grinned back at him, switching cheek sides. (Were we French or something? And why was he not letting go? He hadn't held my hands since January 1996 when we'd prayed together before Ben's craniotomy.)

"Thank you so much for sending me the news!" He referred to the post-press- conference email I had sent out to Team Ben. It contained a TV news link showing Ben unfurling the banner with Ruth and kids.

"You're welcome. We just found out DC is December fifth!"

"December fifth!?" He squeezed my hands as he let go, and my son's neurosurgeon air keyboarded, "Send me an email!"

"I will!" Had I almost kissed the top doc's cheek as my lips brushed by his face? Yes, I had. Almost. It's the Irish in me.

According to an article in the *Wisconsin State Journal* (WSJ) just before Thanksgiving, the official 2011 White House Christmas Tree stood straight and tall, a Marquette County balsam fir hailing from central Wisconsin. The tree farm of Tom and Sue Schroeder, located just outside of Neshkoro, about halfway between Oshkosh and twin cities Friendship and Adams, to be exact. Tom and Sue displayed differing reactions the day they chopped the regal fir for transport. Sue couldn't watch. Tom called the tree, cut off at her ankles, "drop dead gorgeous." A dark green beauty, bound for the Blue Room of the White House.

As Sherlock Holmes often remarked, "You interest me strangely."

And this tree did. From Wisconsin, goin' to the White House in December, officially invited to shine for the holidays? Oh, yeah, baby! Well you are, for sure. And I *might* get in for a White House photo op with the First Lady.

All fall, I referred to Ben's employment as a double-decadence chocolate cake, the honor of the trip to DC as thick, dark chocolate, butter cream frosting, and meeting the First Lady as the vermillion, glistening cherry on top. But would my cake have its cherry? Led to believe the First Lady would be involved, I had not been promised. Could I still hope that "events" closing the White House for all tours on December fifth and sixth included a private IMLS National Medal winners photo op in the Blue Room? You betcha, ya dere hey! But if not...exactly how would I feel? First L. Michelle, you've wrecked The Book's grand finale? Or curses, foiled again? Or, the government flew my boy and me to DC, so he could help a life-saving museum collect its national award, and we dressed to kill doing our selves and Wisconsinites proud? A woman's prerogative, acknowledge and feel all. A woman's wisdom, choose door number three. I knew a great frosted chocolate cake when I saw one.

And now it was time to lick the mixing bowl, spatula, and frosting knife.

Hair cut? Check! Eyebrows? Check! Bumpy Dress? Check! Classy Shoes? Check! Sparkling Bling? Check! Mascara and blush? Check! Bitten fingernails? Check!

Uh oh. Nylons with holes? Uh oh. Deodorant leaving white marks on black? Uh oh. Black, long coat, one button re-sewn with green thread? Uh. Oh.

What else did I havta do in the two weeks before flying on December fourth? WESLI, 3Rs, Group of Authors, writing, groceries, pie making, cleaning, Thanksgiving in Chicagoland, cooking for five at home, Beloved Aunt's UW surgery, a few appointments, and Leslie's brilliant, charitable fundraiser, ca. 1940s *Home for the Holidays* show.

Breathe. And grow a pair of nails, but fast. Maybe I wouldn't help with potato peeling duty at Anne's for Thanksgiving this year? Unwieldy things that peelers are.

Thanksgiving 2011 –

Besides my whole-cranberry sauce, and two pumpkin pies (one regular, one my mother's chiffon), we brought Ben's Saudi Arabian soul mate, Ali, to the Perreth Clan Thanksgiving festivities. After rooming together for only three days Ben had exclaimed, "It's like I found another brother!"

Ali and Ben, one brown-eyed, one blue-eyed, one Muslim, one Christian, both laugh infectiously as storytellers and thinkers with huge hearts.

Piling into the car after the celebration, Ali tried expressing his heart in English, only managing, "Your family! Your family!" Arms held out rapturously.

I understood. Years ago at Thanksgiving, unable to get a word in edgewise, I'd grabbed a silver spoon, holding it like a microphone, "I've got The Spoon! It's *my* turn to say something!" (I know, right?)

The tradition stuck, The Spoon, my trusty mic. Always raucous affairs, this year the house had rocked in belated honor of my fiftieth. Our Thanksgiving antics usually do not include my sisters-in-law handing me a feathered tiara, tambourine, and The Spoon to sing into while the entire family serenades me with "Writing Queen," a re-worked *Dancing Queen*.

Black Friday –

The morning after Thanksgiving, the WSJ printed a large color photo, with a fat caption beneath. The First Lady, and her girls, stood outside the White House, welcoming the Neshkoro fir tree. A decades-old tradition, the tree arrived in a horse-drawn wagon.

Wait! What was the First Lady wearing? A skirt and a sweater – grayish, tasteful, subdued. Hair up tidily in a bun, crisp white shirt under a soft, gray, cashmere fitted cardy, print flare skirt. (Nothing like the skirt and sweater set Gilda Radner's Lisa Loopner always wore.) Dude, wouldja check out her suede, gray, high-heeled boots! No wonder she towered over the only other adults in the shot, a man and a woman.

Who were they, anyway? Tom and Sue from the Neshkoro tree farm. *Wait*! What was Sue wearing? Black pants with a royal blue sweater. Uh oh. (Bumpy Dress?) S'all right, calm down. The First Lady gets this dressed up to get a Christmas tree? You're gonna be just fine. At least there's no way you'll be taller.

November 28 – Monday

Due to fly in less than a week, I still didn't have flight, hotel, or First Lady photo op information. Uncle Sam keeping me on my toes.

An IMLS email arrived late in the day, outlining the following Monday's video interview schedule. It made complete Who Hash of my best-laid Tour Guide Katherine plans. I'd been emailing with Alyssa from Congresswoman Baldwin's office, setting up sightseeing tours for Ruth, Ben, and me, and would have to change them.

Late Monday night I checked our answering machine. "Hi, this is (sweet, young voice) calling from (sweet, young voice) about your upcoming (sweet, young voice) Eeee. So if you could call me back at 202-???-????"

Eee? Area code 202? D. Ceeee? Must be the Congresswoman's office.

November 29 – Tuesday

Bright and early I called, simultaneously workin' all the technology I knew, landline, cell phone, and email.

"Congresswoman Baldwin's office, how may I help you?"

"Alyssa?"

"No, I'm (sweet, young voice)."

"Oh! I'm Katherine Perreth? I'm returning a call?" (Since I knew my identity and that I was on the phone, what was the point of those question marks?)

"I'll see if she's free to take your call."

"Thanks!"

"Hi, Katherine, this is Alyssa. Congresswoman Baldwin would like to meet you in her office at 10:30 on Tuesday morning, the sixth. A tour of the Capitol to follow, if you'd like."

"Oh, that's so great because I was going to have to call you and tell you a bunch of the tours you arranged for us aren't going to work anymore! You see, I got this email yesterday telling us about the interview times with IMLS? And it's the *same* time as our Capitol tour. And then I got another email, from the Executive Director, Ruth, about her flights, and she isn't even going to be in the city when the money Engraving tour is. So, since she was the one who wanted to go on that, I'd like to cancel it."

"Cancel the –?"

"Engraving, because Ben has some disabilities and an eight a.m. tour on the day he's going to have a video interview, and then an evening celebration, is not in his best interest."

"Oh, I see. Okay."

"So if we could cancel that tour, and then we can see the Capitol on Tuesday instead of Monday, like you just said, because Ruth will still be there then, and she wanted to pop by the offices of the Senator and Congresswoman anyway – *Hey*! is she invited? I mean, when you say Congresswoman Baldwin wants to meet 'us,' does that mean all of us? Ruth, and me too?"

"Does she want to discuss legislation?"

"Uh, no, she just wants to, umm – ya know, I don't know. I'm just gonna shut up about that. I don't know what's in her head."

"Well, if she wants to discuss legislation that would have to be at another time. This would be a short photo op with Congresswoman Baldwin, with a tour to follow."

"I see. So I'll tell Ruth, and we'll plan on being at your office at 10:30 on Tuesday...geez, that's almost exactly a week away!"

"Yes, it is."

"Oh! One more thing, we're still waiting to hear if there is a photo op with the First Lady, and it might be on Tuesday sometime. I hope so. I mean, in the newspaper the other day there was a photo of her greeting the Christmas tree from Wisconsin, and I'm thinking, 'Oh! We're from Wisconsin, greet us too!'"

Something sounded like a muffled snicker.

"We don't have any pull with the White House," Alyssa concluded seriously. "Just let us know if your plans change."

"I will!"

Sheesh. Gabble anyone? Poor Alyssa – and so early in the morning too.

Immediately, I called Ruth, explained the sitch, and told her I'd take care of things for her with the Congresswoman's office. And that's when it hit me. The United States Congresswoman from Wisconsin wants to meet us? In DC? For a photo op? *She* requested our presence in her office?

Immediately, I sent Alyssa a brief, fairly non-gabbling thank you, and apology for not quite catching the enormity of the invitation.

Suddenly, like a timely "Beam me up Scotty," the first of the day's IMLS itinerary emails materialized on my screen:

> *7:15 a.m. flight from MSN, arriving DC at 10:10 a.m. Sunday.*
>
> *8:35 p.m. flight from DC, arriving MSN 9:52 p.m. Wednesday.*
>
> *Confirmation Number: GASLIT*

Crack O' Dawn Sunday flight to DC?

"I'm gonna puke!" I croaked to nobody in particular. Just needed to be said. GASLIT. Sounds about right.

November 30 – Wednesday

An email appeared in the morning, requesting an ASAP interview with a reporter from the WSJ. Ben and I met Samara Kalk Derby that afternoon at the museum, along with award-winning photographer John Hart. John delightedly snapped about 200 shots of Ben interacting with kids and juggling. Samara interviewed both of us, closely observing my emotional pendulum. She recorded when I choked up over watching Ben for the first time at work, but thankfully ignored my two audible Elsa Snorts. Her pen flew over her notebook when Ben greeted a group of teens from Shabazz High School, with a bold and bodacious, "Welcome to the Wildnernest, Dudes and Dudettes!"

That evening, at the UW hospital, I kept vigil with my aunts, uncles, and cousins for several hours. We awaited news of Beloved Aunt's cancer surgery.

December 1 – Thursday

Home alone, I tried to calm myself for Sunday's trip to DC, too wired to read, too upset over eighty-year-old Beloved Aunt's eleven-hour surgery. Quieting of this magnitude required the big guns, *Pride and Prejudice,* the 5½-hour, 1995 quintessential saga featuring Colin Firth and Jennifer Ehle. I watched the fusillade of Fitzwilliam and Elizabeth for an hour or so, then checked email. One subject line prodded unfairly for a woman already with too much First Lady on the brain: *Sometime soon, I want to meet you.*

I'm excited for the chance to meet you and whoever you decide to bring to dinner. I really hope you give this a shot. Give $3 or whatever you can to be automatically entered for you and a guest to have dinner with Barack and me.

Hope to see you soon, Michelle

Well, F. L. Michelle, how 'bout Monday or Tuesday next? I have a long list of greetings from the good folks of Wisconsin, including my eighty-year-old tai chi instructor. But right now, Michelle, I need Jane. Blessed Jane, come take me to England again.

Later, I checked emails just in ca –

We have good news to report. The White House has offered a special tour for recipients of the National Medal for Museum and Library Service. The tour is scheduled for 7:30 a.m. on Tuesday, December 6, 2011. The tour is offered to the directors, board chairs, community members, and community member caregivers. The White House is decorated for the holiday and the tour will be very special.

"We're *in!*" I bellowed to no one in particular, it just needed to be said. Jane. Need Jane. Must have Jane.

Miss Elizabeth Bennet traveled to Kent for a visit with Charlotte and Mr. Collins. One of my favorite scenes, the two women greet each other, tentatively at first, vocalizing nothing, but you can read the blaze orange tickertape across Miss Eliza's forehead as she cocks her head, questioningly, "Charlotte? You've been stuck here with this utterly stupid man for months, isolated, hidden away, are you still sane?"

Maybe Charlotte had maintained her sanity, but I struggled mightily with cerebral exclamation points, as I alternately contemplated DC, wrote, watched the movie, and grieved for Beloved Aunt clinging to life in the UW ICU. Pots of mint herbal tea, so calming to jumping jacks in the gastro-intestinal tract, about all my system could handle.

Then it hit me. The email called the White House tour "very special." Yeah, it's the White House for one. And there's that decorated Christmas tree from Tom and Sue's tree farm, for two. But could it possibly be? Would F. L. Michelle dodge around a corner offering a tray of scones and muffins, having arisen early to bake for us? Would Mr. President be close behind with choice of hot chocolate, or soy chai tea latte, extra hot, no foam? Would the glistening, vermillion cherry photo op occur?

All fall I had received mighty strange signs. Within days of writing something clever (or not), the subject would mysteriously show up in my real life. But three bizarre calls in as many days really piqued.

On Tuesday, I missed a cell call from Iowa. Iowa? When I returned the call, a woman answered, “Hello, this is Michelle.”

(Was F. L. Michelle on the campaign trail in Iowa?) “I'm Katherine? From Wisconsin? Returning your call?” (Again, as I knew perfectly well who I was, where I lived, and what I was doing, what was the purpose of those question marks?)

“I'm sorry! I must've dialed wrong,” Michelle apologized.

“So, you aren't Michelle Obama calling me from Iowa?”

Michelle from Iowa laughed as we hung up. The people of the Hawkeye state already know the people of the Frozen Tundra suffer Winter Brain Freeze (WBF), so I wasn't letting the Hodag out of the bag. Our men supremely demonstrate WBF (rhymes with WTF) phenomena when driving trucks and ATVs onto kinda, sorta frozen lakes for ice fishing, losing way more than the one that got away.

On Wednesday, I answered my ancient kitchen phone.

“Chocolate frosting and saltines” ordered a woman, imperiously.

“Hello?” I said. “*Hello?*” Nothin.' Was Lewis Carroll's Red Queen calling, or something? Since I don't have anything attached to my landline, except a stretched out twelve-foot cord, I had no way to tell. The chocolate frosting command I understood just fine. Confirmation it definitely featured in The Book, but saltines? Must I somehow work in crackers? Perhaps the week's hoopla would make me even more ill?

My Thursday 4:45 awakening, head, heart, guts in upheaval, prompted Dan to caution, “Beloved Aunt's surgery is enough for one week. DC prep is enough for one week. Writing a book is enough for one week. You've got all three. You love yourself today, you take care of yourself.”

But while watching *P and P* that afternoon, another odd cell call occurred. I missed it, but called back immediately.

"Gundersen Lutheran," answered a female.

"Uh, did you just call me? I got a call from this number."

"The calls don't go out from here, this is just the switchboard and I have no idea who just called you."

"Who are you?" (Really, who claimed responsibility for this rash of curious butt calls?)

"Gundersen Lutheran Medical Center in La Crosse, Wisconsin. It was probably just a wrong number."

"Yes, I think so." God, I hope so! Ben wasn't in La Crosse. Was he? Bad things in threes I completely understood. Peculiar things too? (Right. Shakespeare's Three Weird Sisters once messed about with "eye of newt and toe of frog.") What about good things? (Right. The Trinity.) And if "scones," "hot chocolate," and "Barack" cropped up soon....

"Your humor is still intact," a relieved Dan commented Thursday evening. He knew the true litmus test of my psychological wellbeing. Yes, still intact. But what should I wear to the White House? Little black Bumpy Dress would not do at 0700 hours. And would She be there or not?

Thursday's WSJ newspaper weather forecast had predicted Friday, December 2 "Sunny and Quiet." Quiet? I took it as a meteorological order from Father Goodness and cooperated.

December 3 - Saturday

At morning yoga I ran into Mitzy. We became friends as pen pals in 1991, when I lived in Nagasaki. She'd found my name and address at church, and wrote, *I met a Japanese woman at the grocery store, what can I do for her?*

Love her, I'd written back. *Show her around town, introduce her to your friends and family, explain food, transportation, and the weather. Attempt to answer why our country is bombing another – a hot topic here that I've been asked to explain, but since I don't have access to much English news, the Japanese know more than I do about the Gulf War. Explain US customs. Go with her to the doctor. And help her get a library card!*

"Is there anything I can do to help you?" Mitzy asked before yoga. "Any errands?" Mitzy, free agent helper at large. The world needs more Mitzies.

"Nope, thanks, bought clear deodorant and nylons at the drugstore yesterday, the most expensive ones they had."

"Two pair, in case one runs?"

"Yep! A time to lay the money down." (I'd toyed with purchasing two deodorants too. I only sweat when I'm nervous.)

We parted for class. During shavasana, the blessed last pose of yoga, flat on our backs, eyes closed, simply breathing, the whirlwind of joy filtered through my mind, and Jane Austen's Jane appeared, "How shall I bear so much happiness?"

Then, I imagined Ben shaking hands with the First Lady – would he use his bionic left hand or his withered right? Either way brought uncontrollable shaking as power point images accompanied, flashes from coma night, and radiation and surgical recovery bays. Overlaying the traumatic images, Ben running, six months before the hemorrhage. My little boy, wearing his Batman t-shirt, a butterfly net streaming above his head. The photo, taken by my mother, encapsulated boyhood Ben. And now? Ben dressed at age twenty-three in a suit, Jerry Garcia around his neck, brightly adorning who Ben was, who Ben had become, the struggles that had made him the indestructible person he is. Pinned underneath the twisted arms of darkness, Ben's spirit had broken free time and again even knowing his tussle with black holes is never over. And now, MCM and DC. How, indeed, shall I bear such happiness?

Yogini softly, gently, brought us back to reality. I'd missed most of her words, but heard these, loud and clear, "Take this with you this week, the creativity, the peace when we flow freely, and combine that with the strength, the courage, and the power of warrior. Namaste."

Someone bear-hugged me from behind, whispering, "Namaste."

"Oh, Mitzy! Maybe if I cry enough now I can hold it together on Monday and Tuesday?" I buried my face on her shoulder as we shared the give-and-take of love.

Back home, looking carefully into Dan's eyes I murmured, "I've been listening to Dave Matthews in the car, *You and Me*. It was just you and me thirty years ago playing football in the snow, me in Mom's coat. Now look where we are."

"Yeah, and Anne had looked out her dorm window and wondered who was reenacting that scene from *Love Story*, 'Oh! It's my brother and Ren!'"

"She did not think it was Ren! She knew it was me," I protested. She should have known, anyway. Family lore counts Anne as my first date in the Perreth Clan, replaced soon after by Dan. At their sister Mary's wedding, Dan and I were put in charge of entertaining Great Aunt Evie from Sshkkennekktadee. G. A. E. assumed us boyfriend and girlfriend, shamelessly dropping hints, sending out feelers. (Another wedding in the air?) We credit her perspicacity as three months later we started dating.

"At first Anne thought I was after your best friend, Ren," Dan continued to argue.

"Yep, she did," I conceded. "But she was wrong." Just like the sorry line from *Love Story*. Since 1981, Dan and I had discovered love means more than having to say you're sorry an infinite number of times. It means allowing enough space until the other is in a place to hear and accept an apology. Then love means honest forgiveness.

But we knew none of that in December 1981 when we frolicked in the snow. The long, gray coat I wore at that time was my mother's cast-off coat, ca. late 1950s. As a vintage freak, I absconded with it for the last two years of college. I fell in love with Dan while wearing it on our walks and talks. Then the rose-mauve lining tattered, hanging in shreds, and I had a fight on my hands. (Just as I had at age six, when my mother – wrongly – corrected, "You cannot wear red with purple.")

"You can't wear that now, you know," Mom had cautioned me about the gray coat in 1983. After numerous battles, I gave in and let her buy me a new long coat, a woolen, navy Mary Poppins-ish coat. In my heart it never replaced the ancient gray.

Now, I owned Mom's long, black wool coat, black lining, ca.1990s. After she died, I inherited it and purchased her car, the car so often previously parked in my driveway. I wrapped my heart in both through years of Wisconsin winters. (What's the purpose of buying something different if the old suffices?) The black coat had lasted longer than the car, but from time to time, I heard a telltale rrrriiippp. As is my way, I never paid attention. When I put the coat on, it still fit, kept me warm, looked black, and held my hand. Just fine for tooling around my little patch of the planet, where I usually didn't care what I looked like. But DC? Another galaxy altogether, the national seat of power, where I guessed influential women did not wear torn coats.

Saturday afternoon, as I held the coat up for inspection, the outside looked as it should. Laying it out revealed the lining. Its seams hung loose at the bottom, the middle seam had separated up the back, and there was a gash about a foot long. Ripping sound solved. Desperate times required desperate thought. Fortunately I knew what to do. I'll just bop down and get the duc –

"Kathykins! No! No duct tape."

"It's okay, Mom. It's not gray. I bought black duct tape in London last June, to fix the suitcase. It'll totally work."

"Kathykins, it's the *White House*! Needle and thread."

I knew better than to argue with a dead mother, even though in the past I had successfully repaired pants hems, a pillow, and car scratches with duct tape. (A gray car, although now duct tape helpfully comes in a rainbow of colors.)

Hanging the coat in the kitchen doorframe, it took only seventy minutes for me to hand sew, and step back to admire. Yoiks! Look at that dipping hem! Another fifteen minutes, good to go. Then I used my trusty pin, double-sided tape, and black Sharpie, more tools of my sewing trade, to fix a few other clothing contretemps. (Mom said nothing, but I thought I detected a sigh.)

After toiling with the coat, I played with my usual early December project, sachets. Every year since 2005, I harvest my lavender, hang it to dry, and when the post-Thanksgiving rat race hits, I fill small organza favor bags. Then I hand them out to deserving women, meaning any woman who happens to be in my life at that time. Lavender, a calming herb, is just what December orders, and most women enjoy the fragrance. The kitchen, redolent with relaxation, turned sachet factory. For a flash of color I added my dried rose petals to the twenty sachets I would take to DC. I expected to meet some powerful women in need of serenity. Then I packed. For me, for Ben, for the butterflies accompanying us.

And last, paid a quick visit to wrapped-in-white, unaware Beloved Aunt in the UW ICU.

Chapter 28

As One Lamp Lights Another

December 4 – Sunday Morning

The usual "Welcome to the Dane County Regional Airport" digital sign communicated something of greater import. Beaming neon in the inky pre-dawn, "Go Pack! NFL Champions!" in green, and "6:09 a.m." in yellow.

Properly sent off, I felt accompanied and propelled, as if well wishers from the previous weeks fit in my suitcase. Team Ben and the Packers would fly east with us. For us, the White House. For them, a battle with Giants.

Only a handful of pilots milled among the approximately fifteen TSA employees more than eager to have something to do so early in the morning. "It's not because you have any metal on or anything, it's just a random search," informed one as he removed my bags. I knew not to argue. I had jousted once over blackberry jelly.

"See? Jelly. That's a gel!" TSA Woman had snorted triumphantly.

"Okay, then, jam!" I had lost, but learned. It helped me keep my mouth shut the next time, when I got busted for too many words.

"These. Are. A. Lot. Of. Books," TSA Man had pompously stated, staring me down like Clint Eastwood. But he'd returned my tall stash from special x-ray. My one-word agreement had saved my mystery books and *The Complete Works and Letters of Charles Lamb* (all 1124 pages) from total confiscation.

No problems for me this time though, as I smiled at TSA searching my stuff.

Ben, as always, fared worse. Standard procedure for him includes completely removing his smiley-face AFO and standing through a swipe and total pat down. Or if he's in his wheelchair, a much lengthier rigmarole ensues. (I think TSA should be held to compassionate ADA allowances.) As always, Ben cheerfully submitted, improving his shtick, declaring TSA gave him a great massage by stroking his Packers t-shirt.

While we waited, I thought. The last time I took a trip alone with Ben, on that day of trepidation a decade ago, we flew via Dallas to California for Radiation Prep, The Sequel. Such a different day today, no fear, or electrical storm snafus, on December's horizon.

Ben perused the WSJ Sunday paper seeking to learn. "Mom, how do you say, 'm-a-n-s-i-o-n'?" and, "What's 'utopianism'?"

I had always served as his walking dictionary. Dan fielded the grammarian posers. (I do neither windows nor grammar. I just use 'em. Sometimes even properly.)

Upon boarding, Ben immediately befriended our flight attendant and insisted on calling him "Captain" for the duration of our acquaintance. He received Ben's full story, *Reader's Digest* version, 1996-2011, mesmerized and astonished.

"Wow. Just like that...I'm glad you made it. Would you like to move up if the Captain okays it?"

After the move, Ben and I sat across from each other, the aisle between us, reaching out to squeeze hands on take-off.

"You okay?" I inquired.

Ben did a cleansing breath, whether he knew it or not, a deep inhale through the nose, and slow exhale through the mouth. "Mom, the audacity of my life."

"Huh?"

"I'm trying to use your words."

"Don't, sweetie. Use your own."

"I am alive and happily content."

Perfect. Life changes. Sometimes you can almost see it coming, smell it from afar, like a long-awaited summer's rain, drenching parched hearts.

Sunday Afternoon -

In DC, the hotel concierge allowed us to check in four hours early. But before sightseeing, we had to wait for someone to fix the safe. I had brought my mother's Sparkling Bling and my laptop along, after all. We assumed the knock on the door meant maintenance.

"Here's your packet. This information is given to all IMLS groups," instructed a uniformed woman. Ben and I snickered. Just like getting secret documents from *Mission Impossible*.

We walked a fair distance from Capitol Hill on the blue-skied and warm December day, eating a very late lunch at the National Gallery of Art. Ben's hunger and fatigue added to his snarl when I'd said I wanted to see Samuel Morse's painting. Grumpy, he tagged along anyhow. While I stood gaping at the scene set in the Louvre, Ben chatted up the docent. The man did his job, flipping Ben's light switch. Ben then, unabashedly, evangelized, "Mom, these are real paintings!"

The docent, overjoyed at his convert, supplied more information, pointing out the painting of a woman in blue whose eyes watch the watchers. Ben playfully slunk past her several times, keeping his eyes on hers. It reminded me very much of three-year-old Ben, "Mama, I'm wookin' for stuff," his one eye made humungous by a magnifying glass.

"I wish I had his energy and happiness," sighed the docent, as we walked away.

"Mom, how do the artists go so deep? It's just paint!" asked Ben.

"I know, right? And anyone can come here for free," I added, stopping Ben in his tracks.

"Who did this? Who made the rules? Anyone can come here for *free*, any day?" For the next hour, he jaw-dropped everywhere, with ceaseless commentary. "This is so amazing! Thank you so much, Mom. It's a Christmas present!"

Since the Pack kicked off at 4:15, Ben and I trekked back toward our hotel, located just behind the Packers bar, or so the concierge had told me earlier. On our way, we stopped by the reflecting pool at the base of the Ulysses S. Grant Memorial, and traded picture-taking favors with Martin from Manchester. Ben launched into his version of Brit-speak. The two discussed Man U and Liverpool football, and Ben's Liverpudlian friend who'd loaned us a tiny video camera.

While we gazed upon the flanking Union cavalry and artillery, more tourists arrived, and Ben engaged with them all. "Where are you from?"

"He's from France," a woman replied.

"Ah, Frahhnce, bon jour," Ben greeted a suddenly perked up guy. "Comment ca va?"

"Ca va bien!"

Ben did not ask monsieur why French words sometimes have so many letters, for so few syllables. "I mean, Mom, the Marseillaise has three syllables and twelve letters. I counted!"

Tromping up Capitol Hill, suddenly Ben froze, "Mom! This is where I sang with my choir in high school. Right here!" Standing tall, he belted out *Shenandoah*. Tears running down my cheeks, I filmed.

We made it almost back to the hotel when I suspected the concierge's directions did not match the address given to me earlier by three Packers' fans in the airport. After the men had kindly checked their phones to tell us where Packer Nation convened in DC, Ben had led them in a huddle, "Hands in the middle! Count of three! Go, Pack, Go!"

Indeed, after walking an hour, Ben's foot afire at the end, we wound up back by the National Gallery. Still, Ben proudly declared he'd circled the nation's Capitol on foot.

The Packer bar flew the Packers G-Force flag, welcoming our people. Over the course of the next five hours, Ben juggled, entertained, led cheers, and drank massive amounts of milk with his dinner. I drank Guinness with mine. (Not massive amounts, though. I know my brew limits.)

The Pack over the Giants, 12 and 0! Looking good for our trip to Lambeau on January 1, 2012.

Sunday – Evening

After the game, we took our first cab since Ben's toddlerhood in Nagasaki. "Where are you from?" began Ben.

"If you guess, it's free!"

"Namaste?"

"No. What's that?"

"India. Merhaba?"

"You know 'merhaba'?" the cabbie sounded incredulous.

"Assalamu alaikum?" Ben tried the Arabic greeting.

"Wa alaikum assalaam!" replied the delighted cabbie. I didn't understand a word for the next few minutes. "What's your name?" he asked Ben, as he pulled up to the hotel.

"Benjamin."

"Netanyahu?" he asked sniggering.

"Huh?"

I couldn't stand it any longer, "Close!" I Elsa Snorted with great gusto, "Benjamin David!"

Our cabbie absolutely roared, palms smacking the steering wheel, rocking, and tipping his head back.

"What's so funny, Mom? What did you say? What did he say?"

But I couldn't answer. The cabbie and I were doubled-over, wiping our eyes. He was honest. He'd stopped the meter from running.

For our three days in DC, we treated ourselves to cab rides on the government per diem. While I sat back in silence, Ben worked his captive audience and added to his vast repertoire of global greetings, learning “hi” in Urdu, Amharic, and Tigrinya (languages in Pakistan, Ethiopia, and Eritrea).

Sooner, or later, Ben always mentioned the reason for our trip to DC, each time ending with what we’d punch lined all fall, “We’re your tax dollars at work!”

(One woman had returned the wisecrack, “Bomb Afghanistan or send Ben to DC?”)

Ben’s cabbie conversations were equally illuminating. One man from Ethiopia had worked long ago at the UW. “I’m still a Packer fan,” he insisted, as Ben led the mandatory cheer.

Another cabbie had just turned fifty-eight on December first, adding that he’d reached his native country’s life expectancy. Ben sang *Happy Birthday*, and then inquired if Pakistan was in India.

“No, next to it.” Then he mused sadly, “Here, we sit and eat with each other, we are friends, but back home we are enemies. I don’t know why. Fighting only creates problems, let’s do business instead!”

As I exited the cab, he leaned toward me, “Ben is so smart! He should work for the State Department.”

Or for the United Nations, as Global Good Will Ambassador: Mascot to the World.

December 5 – Monday Morning

Not due across town until 1:00 for the IMLS filmed interview, Ben slept in, while I ate a hearty breakfast and found the *Wisconsin State Journal* article online. Madison woke up to Ben splashed across the front-page. Enchanted, I read Samara’s corker of a story, and marveled at John’s color photos. They captured Ben’s heart perfectly. Gazing at Ben sleeping in DC, a warm whooshing of surreal washed over me.

"You're famous, Ben," I croaked, gently waking him up. He read in silence, while I busied myself applying Bing Cherry polish, another day for my bitten fingernails to shine with justice.

"Mom, it says you're here as my 'caregiver'?" He sounded offended.

"Well, I'm gonna iron your shirt, help you get ready, figure out when and where we have to go today, and how to get there, so isn't that giving you care?"

"Yeah, I guess so."

Ben's multiple issues require assistance for some things, but not all things, on some days, but not all days. His needs ebb and flow like the tide, just less predictable. On this trip, I was necessary, even for shoes. Under his supervision, I could barely shove his AFO foot into one of the dress shoes, let alone double-tie the short, slippery laces.

"Really tight, Mom."

Daily, Ben depended on the good will of others. On this day I would too.

Monday Afternoon –

Our cab dropped us at IMLS with plenty of time to spare. We rode the elevators to the ninth floor, entering a hushed reception area. Ben approached the desk, giving the receptionist his name, and then I asked, "Is there anyone here who can tie his tie? I can't do it for him."

As she thought aloud, a voice behind me languidly spoke. "He needs a tie tied? I can do it." A sharply dressed man sat on the sofa, his mind on his handheld electronic. He stood up, putting it away, and stepped toward Ben.

"Hey bro! I'm Ben!"

"Hey bro!" smiled the man, introducing himself as Chris. The first three attempts, Chris declared, "Too short," "too long," "too long."

"Do we tip you, or what?" Ben asked, laughing.

"I'm just tryin' to get you right," murmured Chris, holding coherent conversation while concentrating hard on the tie.

"We need you to follow us around the next two days," I half-joked. "You're clearly a tie perfectionist."

"If I was a tie perfectionist, I would've got it the first time."

"Where are you from?" asked Ben.

"Atlanta. I'm working with IMLS to get more folks to museums, and more money for libraries."

Ben explained our trip to DC. After Chris congratulated, he questioned, "All the way from Wisconsin, eh? Packers fan?"

"Go, Pack, Go!"

"I played for the Chicago Bears four years."

"*You* did?"

"Yeah, and then, if you're a Packers fan, you remember when the Falcons came up and beat them; I was on the team. For the first time the Packers lost a playoff home game," Chris teased with a smirk and twinkling eyes.

"Thank you for reminding us," I rolled my eyes.

"Packers fans are great, or I wouldn't have said it," he offered with a grin, back on tie duty. "That was when the Packers had Brett Favre, after he'd left Atlanta."

"We call him Butt Favre now," volunteered Ben, as our waiting escort and the receptionist burst into laughter.

"Hey!" I remonstrated. "You've got an autographed picture from him, 'To Ben, #4 Brett Favre.' He helped see us through some bad times. We owe Mr. Favre a great amount of joy."

"Yeah, we do," agreed Ben. Then, thinking about the interview, suddenly serious, he confessed to Chris, "I'm afraid."

"Afraid? *You*? Naw. You been talkin' junk to me this whole time, bro! Go shine, Ben, go shine for Wisconsin!"

According to the website, *The Chris Draft Family Foundation* encourages education, healthy lifestyle choices, character development, personal responsibility, self-discipline, and physical fitness. I knew none of this that day. Or that Chris had just wed, and his bride,

Keasha, battled lung cancer. She had never smoked, yet she died a month after her wedding, three weeks after her NFL groom tied Ben's tie. In his website tribute, Chris called her "a light, and a force that led the way with a beautiful, sweet smile, and bright, shining eyes, that both belied the pure steel of her strength and determination. She held onto life, and love, with a forcefulness that was absolutely awe-inspiring."

Oblivious of Chris Draft's full heart, only knowing it good, I again felt accompanied and propelled by unseen forces as our escort walked us down a long hallway to the video shoot. After just having flown in, MCM Executive Director Ruth waited for us with a copy of the morning's WSJ. The online was fine, but the hard copy, oh, the newsprint in my hand!

"Sorry we're a little late," I apologized. "We had trouble tying Ben's tie. I can't do it, so a man in the lobby helped us."

"We rarely entertain NFL players here," piped up our escort. "How incredibly perfect that he was waiting out there."

Like I said, Accompanied and Propelled.

Lights, camera, action! But, first, make-up. Off to one side, I sat in the darkness close to where Ruth and Ben sat in the limelight. Make-Up held her own while Ben juggled candy bars, and offered scintillating conversational turns.

A woman on the film crew a few feet away suddenly leaned toward me, "We were talking about your shoes." "We" meant her and the camera guy.

(My sparkly shoes?)

"Where'd you get them?"

"Goodwill, four bucks! They were never worn, but I know why. When I got them home and saw sunbeams falling on them in my closet, I could tell the fabric was put on backwards, so they don't really match. One sheen's silver, the other gold."

"You can't tell!"

"Thanks!"

"And your nylons, show us your ankle."

(My black nylons with designs?) I complied, sticking my foot out.

"We were talking about your whole ensemble," she concluded.

I sighed my thanks. (Really? My ensemble? My Princess shirt from Heathrow airport, the front held down with double-sided sticky tape? My $20 black pants with the burn mark from the fireplace, but you can't really tell? My $10 nylons and mismatched, $4 Sparkling Resale Shoes? Hear that, Cousin? Hear that, Stacy *What Not To Wear* London? I listened to both of you! Mom, hear that? A DC woman loves my ensemble.)

Another IMLS staff woman approached after the shoot, introducing herself. "I want to say how this is his story, but it's your story."

(Huh? I didn't expect anyone to pay attention to me as Ben's tag-along, caregiver mom.)

"You've done a great job of looking for opportunities," she complimented.

(How would she know that?)

Momentarily confused and nervous, doing what the circs required, I yammered. "I'm writing a book about Ben? *Making Lemonade With Ben: The Audacity to Cope*?" (Those pesky question marks again! Whatever for?) "One editor didn't think the title 'definitive,'" I muttered. "Probably didn't call *The Guernsey Literary and Potato Peel Pie Society* definitive either." (Punctuation, an Elsa Snort, this one tinged ever so slightly with derision. If only I carried duct tape with me....)

"The what?" she asked.

"Haven't you read *GLPPPS*? It's one of my all-time favs!"

"I wanna read *your* book. Please keep in touch." She didn't know it, but a string of encouraging women had preceded her. From the late

’90s, various women had proposed I write a book. Consumed only with survival, I’d thought them all crazy.

After doling out fragrant lavender sachets to all the complimenting and helpful IMLS women, Ben and I descended the elevators, decompressing in a café at its base. Between sips of chai tea latte, extra hot, no foam, I gushed. “Ben, you were brilliant! You spoke eloquently, profoundly –”

“What’s that mean, Mom?”

“Super deep. You could’nt’ve done it any better if you’d prepped for weeks. I am so proud of you! It’s like you were born to be in front of a video camera.”

“Maybe I was.”

Monday – Late Afternoon

On the way back to the hotel, we detoured to the White House Visitor Center, run by the National Park Service. A thirty-minute video walked us through our nation’s home. The narration offered marvelous bits and bobs of history on the small Blue, Red, and Green rooms, as well as the larger East Room. We learned The White House and grounds are a National Park, owned by the American people.

First Lady Michelle Obama introduced the film from her favorite state floor room, the oval Blue Room. (Tomorrow morning, would I shake the First Lady’s hand, perhaps just before a photo op next to Tom and Sue’s decked out Wisconsin tree?)

A portrait of George Washington hangs in the East Room, the only part of the White House collection to survive since 1800. During the War of 1812, when our Red Coat Cousins torched the White House, Dolly Madison refused to leave until George was safely spirited away. He’s watched over celebrations, weddings, performances, awards, treaty signings, and both Abraham Lincoln and JFK lying in state. (Maybe George watches photo ops with First Ladies too?)

Monday – Evening

Back at the hotel, Ben lay down in his suit, resting for an hour, while I donned Bumpy Dress, Sparkling Bling, expensive drugstore nylons, and Classy Shoes.

Ruth met us in the hotel lobby to walk the few blocks to Cannon House for the medal ceremony and reception.

"Katherine, you look wonderful!"

"Thank you, I tried."

"You succeeded."

"You look natty!" Ben complimented his executive director.

"No, Ben!" I corrected obnoxiously, laughing, "She looks lovely; *you* look natty."

With mincing feet, so careful not to get a heel stuck in a sidewalk crack, I walked ball-of-feet first, not realizing I was grinding the soles into hamburger.

We climbed the steps to stately Cannon House, part of the US House of Representatives, waltzed through security, and entered a huge room. The kind of room I've seen only in England and in Wisconsin's State Capitol.

The reception spread, supposedly just schnibbles, sufficed for dinner: croissants (real!), finger sandwiches (crab, not tuna fish!), fruit (strawberries!), cheeses (brie!), crackers, crudités, and desserts (raspberry mousse and chocolate truffly things!).

I took a picture.

No beer, but plenty of wine. I enquired. Do The Feds pay for alcohol at these shindigs? No, they do not. I was told on this night it was supplied by *History,* formerly known as the *History Channel.* (I like to know who is buying my drink.)

Loading up my plate, I grabbed a glass of white wine, and successfully became invisible. Other than Ruth and Ben, I didn't know anyone. I didn't want to talk anyway, just wanted to get super small, soak it all up, eat, and attempt to remain calm.

Breathe.

Ben wisely chose not to eat before the ceremony; afraid he'd spill on his suit. As is his way, he wandered with glee, working the room until the ceremony began. Groups of people poured through the doors. Some I recognized from the earlier video shoot.

Off to one side of the podium and screen, rows of chairs waited expectantly for the medal-winning museum and library participants to take their seats. I huddled in the back of the room with the rest of the observers, taking a chair against the wall. But IMLS staff upgraded me, placing me next to Ruth and Ben, right up front. Twenty-two inches in front of me sat award-winning journalist, author, and keynote speaker Cokie Roberts! Noticing my raised eyebrows, gaping mouth, and quickened breath, Ben's eyes danced as he offered, "Should I tap her on the shoulder for you, Mom?"

Federal support for our nation's 123,000 libraries and 17,500 museums comes primarily from IMLS. Each year, IMLS honors five museums and five libraries with the National Medal. (You should know this already if you've been paying attention. But so much has happened I'll cut you slack.)

Dave Isay, of StoryCorps, kicked off the ceremony with a video of the 2011 winning institutions. In addition to the medal, each would receive a $10,000 grant from IMLS, and the opportunity, in 2012, to record stories with StoryCorps.

Susan Hildreth, IMLS Director, read an excerpt from First Lady Michelle Obama, "Museums and libraries inspire us to stretch our imaginations, and play an important role in exposing Americans of all ages and backgrounds to fresh ideas. They teach our children new skills and ways of thinking, and even help to promote lifelong wellness."

(Hear! Hear! Well said, Madam First Lady!)

Keynote speaker Cokie (Roberts!) brilliantly entertained us, then highlighted a few museums and libraries, finishing with, "...and the Madison Children's Museum providing performance opportunities to a brain-damaged young man who was able to find work there and do performances that really made his life meaningful. So it is great that we are celebrating these libraries and museums."

When I heard her describe Ben without euphemism, I wondered what Ben thought. Later he told me, "I was impressed with her strong word choice. It's true. I didn't have any anger, I was dumbfounded at being selected, and she was using me as an example. I'm just a boy from a suburb of Madison, who got to achieve his goal – showing my employers I *can* do it. And it went beyond my thoughts, beyond my beliefs, to go to DC."

For each institution, Director Susan read the staff and community members' names. As each approached the podium to receive the award, she read the community member's summarized bio. MCM appeared several names down the list, and I listened carefully for the appropriate level of applause. These were libraries (shhh!) and museums, after all, not sports teams or rock stars. Much of the congratulatory applause seemed respectfully subdued. Until Director Susan announced the art museum from Erie, and a cadre of female noisemakers ululated, causing Cannon House to vibrate. I took my cue.

Director Susan read, "The Madison Children's Museum, Director Ruth Shelly and Community Member Benjamin Perreth."

(I clapped, whooped, 'n hollered politely, but oh, so vociferously.)

"Ben, who suffered a brain hemorrhage at the age of seven and has survived numerous surgeries and other medical challenges, began volunteering as a juggler at MCM. He now has what he calls his dream job working at the museum as a Visitor Services Associate."

I c'd, w'd, and h'd some more while staff took a formal picture of Ben, Ruth, Susan, and Cokie. Ben clasping the mammoth plaque, his unscathed hand to the side, his right hand laid, curling, upon the top. Then he warmly greeted Cokie (Roberts!) And I burst into tears.

IMLS National Medal Ceremony: Ruth Shelly, Cokie Roberts, Ben, and Susan Hildreth

Post-ceremony, for the next hour or three, I plead delirium. Right? That's defensible. For a woman glommed onto libraries and museums for her whole life, who never wanted things, but experiences, could there be a better motherhood award?

"You couldn't have chosen a better couple of people to be here to help you celebrate," I spurted to Director Susan, now that I knew the woman who sported the tasteful purple jacket. "I'm all over libraries and museums and have passed that love on."

Tongue-tied, I shyly handed Ms. Cokie a lavender sachet, and shook her hand, breathlessly, "I'm Katherine, Ben's mom." (Had she felt my creepin' eyes boring into her back throughout the evening?)

To quench my thirst from all the talkative excitement, I visited the sommelier. He'd run out of proper glasses, but poured white wine into a plastic tumbler, filling it to the brim. I swigged out of the short, fat cup as best I could with a face-splitting smile.

Frank, CEO of an award-winning botanic garden, approached, "We saw your tears of pride when your son walked up. We were watching you; it was so moving."

Yes, Frank, my tears of pride completely won out on this night of great joy. The colorful sea of congratulations, smiling faces, and warm handshakes solidified into pervading gratefulness.

Oh, Frank, and victory! Such great victory, for a Celtic Warrior Mother.

Monday - Night

Ben and I closed down the Cannon House joint, all but a handful of staff gone to their proper dinners. He playfully stomped his way through the white marble halls as I traipsed along behind, giggling and filming. Besides Buddy in *Elf*, I knew no one like Ben, so multifaceted in one day. Eloquently speaking for a video interview, then a mere seven hours later sending his footfalls echoing through the seat of US government. The same sound he'd made with his siblings for so many years, below the vaulted ceiling entrance of the UW Hospital.

Safely back in our hotel room, I grabbed my camera, filming myself in front of the full-length mirror, the camera blocking my face, "Okay, so this is Ben's mom, and Ben's mom gets to say, Yeah! Whoo! Yeah Ben! Go, Ben! Ben rocked the planet!"

(Complimentary kick-line.)

"So, I had two glasses of white wine, and oh! You can't see my face, I should look at me, well I'm not a videe-oh-ah-rg-o-gerpher, uh, vi-de-ah-gra-pher, I am a writer, and you cannot get a higher award than the museums (sniffle, choke) and libraries (sniffle, choke) national award, thankyouverymuch! And Cokie Freakin' Roberts! Ohmygosh, I need a double sniff of my lavender, and tai chi, right now!"

Sent airborne from Cinderella-Bendrenaline, and the glories of museums and libraries, I did not know one disposable plastic cup of wine isn't the equivalent of one glass. Yet, the excess wine only served to slightly ratchet up and release revelry.

Years ago a woman once accused me of being drunk in the middle of the day. I hadn't a drop of alcohol in my system, able on my own to regularly embrace poet Emily Dickinson's, "Inebriate of air am I, And debauchee of dew, Reeling through endless summer days, From inns of molten blue."

Summer, fall, winter, and spring, I can launch, lurch, and laugh in any season, intoxicated by life. On this winter night, from the ecstasy of being Ben's mom in this moment in time, came the victorious kick-line and my insistence that Ben film me, in my white, fluffy hotel robe, as I participated fully in the *Celtic Woman* PBS special.

"See, this is a Celtic woman," I yelled, flinging my arm toward the TV, "and I am a Celtic woman, and we are dancin' and singin' *The Circle of Life*, because...(sniffle, choke)...My. Mom. Is. Here. Oh lookit, I'm gonna do this! I can do this!"

We snapped our fingers and swayed, that PBS Celtic woman and I, while she hit the notes and I didn't.

"Oh, yeah, hit the drums, we need drums! Good. And I have my slippers on and my way cool robe, see? Oh, we're spinning. We're *spinning*! Me and the Celtic women!"

December 6 – Tuesday Early Morning

As I breakfasted alone at 6:00 a.m. a high school choir serenaded beautifully in the hotel lobby. Jazz@8 trilled scales and one song, bound for the White House. Would they be singing during our photo op?

To greet First Lady Michelle Obama, Ben wore his suit and Jerry Garcia tie, and I wore Classy Shoes and Stevie Nicks Dress: black, long tea-length, flowing, cotton, lace, velvet, demure-but-festive, and comfy.

(One summer, I'd rashly purchased the dress off an outdoor sales rack on my favorite kind of shopping outing, unintentional. While we'd waited for a red light, I'd jumped off my bike on State Street during one of Madison's Ride The Drive events, imploring Dan to "Wait just a sec!")

For warmth, instead of my mother's heavy, black coat I put on a borrowed velvet and chiffon jacket.

Ben and I shared a cab with Ruth, arriving at the White House gates 0715 hours. Dozens of others already stood lined up outside the gates. Who were all these people? The high school choir, gorgeously attired, headed in as a group, bypassing the line. Oh, so we must be going in as a separate IMLS group as well! Nope. Herded by Secret Service, they directed us to the back of the long line. Huh? Wasn't the White House closed for all tours? Wasn't this a private, IMLS, "very special" tour? Our IMLS Organizer of Logistics hovered, trying to corral the medal-winning participants arriving piecemeal. I hesitatingly asked, "So will we be seeing...?"

Thin-lipped, brow-furrowed, with pain in her eyes, she briefly shook her head once, saying nothing, communicating everything, crestfallen, apologetic, and grimly anxious. The poor woman! My brain threw on the brakes, pulled up sharply, and puzzled.

We're finding out now no First Lady is coming.
We're standing in line, what should Ben and I do?
Let our mouths hang open, our faces turn blue?
No photo op with Michelle the First Lady?
No bear hug, hot chocolate, or soy chai tea latte?
No First Lady-Ben Perreth left-righty shake?
No congratulatory muffins were baked?

Nope. I explained the sitch to incredulous Ben, grumbling for forty-two seconds, give or take a few. Then I stopped, recalculating like the Grinch, "Ben. Look where we are. You're in a suit, Jerry

Garcia around your neck. I'm in Stevie Nicks Dress and Molly's velvet, and we're going into *The Freakin' White House!*"

With a huge smile, Ben echoed, "The Freakin' White House!"

The line of White House visitors slowly shuffled forward. "My, don't you look elegant," complimented an elderly woman standing with us.

"Well, I don't get to do this every day, and my eighty-something fashionista, Molly, informed me, 'Velvet is permitted because it's the holidays.'"

"I need a Molly," the woman sighed.

Finally the line snaked past security, and we read a sign in surprise, "To celebrate the holidays, pictures will be permitted today."

Secret Service usually limited White House visitors to ID, cell phone, and, if raining, an umbrella. No purses, backpacks, cameras, lotion, tobacco, strollers, aerosol, pointed objects, guns, ammo, mace, stun guns, nunchucks, knives, fireworks, or blackberry jelly had read December's advance email warning.

The ripple of audible dismay spread as folks saw the sign. They'd obeyed. So had I. (Almost.) Along with my picture-taking cell phone in his pocket, Ben carried one lavender sachet and a card.

Once inside, the Jazz@8 choir angelically sang *Carol of the Bells, Silent Night, Joy to The World,* and other Christmas favorites, their voices adding to the magic. Ben and I wandered pinch-me-like through our national home. An abundance of fresh flowers adorned each room, as well as a variety of shapes and sizes of decorated evergreens. Ribbons on one proclaimed the season's White House motto, "Shine, Give, Share."

Rounding a corner, suddenly, there She stood! Firm, strong, regal, and drop dead gorgeous. The Official White House Christmas Tree from Wisconsin decked out in glory in the Blue Room. I greeted her formally, of course, with a wee curtsey. Whispering, "You betcha, ya dere hey," for good measure, as perhaps she felt homesick. But I did not attach my sachet to her branches.

Secret Service, stationed everywhere, answered questions, offered knowledgeable commentary, and prevented us walking away with the nation's silver.

"Last night a congressional dinner for 1,000 was held here," volunteered one SS woman standing in the doorway of the East Room, under George's watchful eye.

"Last night? Here?" The First Lady had played hostess to Congress only ten hours ago? But the place looked spotless! Not even a crumb remained for a mouse. (And you know how messy Congress can be.) She must've been up all night cleaning. Good grief, no wonder she couldn't manage a photo op right now, the poor woman. Betcha she could sure use one of my lavender sachets.

"Can you give this to the First Lady?"

"I'm sorry m'am. We're not allowed to take anything. But you can mail it to 1600 Pennsylvania Avenue."

Tuesday – Late Morning

Ben, Ruth, and I left the White House together, pit stopping briefly at the hotel to grab purse, camera, thank you cards, and sachets. Our cabbie then drove us to the heady seat of power, our nation's political lair. We trudged, mile after mile, where walls, floors, and ceilings blinded, as if reflecting sun on snow.

"Mom, it's very white in here. It reminds me of a dream I had."

(Which one, kiddo? In various states of awareness, you've been wheeled through so many incandescent corridors.)

Congresswoman Tammy Baldwin, a staunch supporter of Yahara House, and the Wisconsinite who had nominated MCM for IMLS National Medal consideration, spoke at length with Ben and Ruth. On her desk sat an animated President Obama at his desk, rapidly signing bills lefty. The Congresswoman's uncle had carved and mechanized the five-inch-high wooden President, hoping one day the leader of the free world would see it. With its tiny, pointy carved pen, would it ever pass through White House Secret Service?

Waving her ID badge like a wand, the Congresswoman's aide escorted us the sneaky way through brightly lit underground halls connecting various buildings with the US Capitol. Taking stairs to every level, we found statues, paintings, rich décor, and columns in abundance. She explained all. In the e pluribus unum rotunda, we paused for Ben to remove his AFO and readjust. The informative, kind, and lovely aide retied Ben's dress shoe. His AFO foot again afire, mine on a slow burn in Classy Shoes, we gladly took an underground tram for the last leg.

Senator Herb Kohl looked every inch a stately, kind, wise, and delighted grandfather. In the antechamber his eyes bored into mine, as he shook my hand,

"Katherine, so nice to meet you." Then turning to Ben, "Love you, love you, Ben."

(Standard politico-speak? I kept my mouth shut.)

"I love you too! I voted for you!" Ben shook the Senator's hand righty *and* lefty.

We followed as Senator Kohl led us back to the holy of holies, his personal office.

"Duh...duh...duh, duh, duh, DUH! Go, Pack, Go!" Ben cheered upon seeing Packers' paraphernalia organized shrine-like. As owner of the Milwaukee Bucks, the Senator had a few mementos of theirs scattered around too. His other Wisconsin family business? Kohl's department stores. His popular UW legacy? The Kohl Center.

(To my eternal credit, I did not yammer even one anecdotal tidbit about Kohl's. Not about coma-accessorizing tennies, or Ben's suit and tie, or that he'd once lived near the Kohl Center.)

After the photo op, an assistant ushered us out, "He was really excited to meet you. He read the newspaper front-page story on Ben yesterday."

Ah! That explained his sentimental greeting to Ben, and the warmth as he shook my hand, when he didn't so much use his vocal cords as his eyes.

The Senator gifted Ben a Bucks hat, and planting it firmly on his head, Ben sat in the Senator's reception area, airing his sore and red foot, readjusting his smiley-face AFO.

Tuesday - Afternoon

"Mission accomplished," declared Ruth, after the cab dropped us at the hotel.

Ben, trashed after two days of agenda, an early morning, and a boatload of walking, took to his bed at 1:00 Tuesday afternoon and didn't leave it until Wednesday morning. Free in DC, I spent the afternoon in a café happily tap tapping away on my laptop, after supplying Ben with food and drink.

In the 5:00 p.m. darkness on the Capitol lawn, I watched the lighting of our nation's Christmas tree, decorated with 3,000 handmade ornaments and 10,000 LED lights. Foresters had cut off the 108-foot-tall, 118-year-old fir at her waist before hauling her 4,500 miles. All the way from California's Stanislaus National Forest, just down the road from Summerville High School, home of the Jazz@8 choristers. For the third time that day, the choir sang sweetly for me.

California Senator Dianne Feinstein politely described the sixty-five-foot tree as "thin, tall, and narrow."

A woman next to me cut through the euphemisms, "That is one skinny-ass tree!"

That evening, Ben and I shared the remote control, switching between his cable TV treats and mine, *What Not To Wear*. A

Midwestern woman featured, nominated by her friends for her predilection for fixing clothing with duct tape. (Sister, I feel your pain.)

December 7 – Wednesday Morning

I packed our bags, twenty sachets of lavender lighter. Women, this round's on me: IMLS staff and video crew, Cokie Roberts, political aides, Congresswoman Baldwin, the hotel concierge, Ruth, and speech therapist Mary. We met Mary and her young son, another museum's community member, in the hotel elevator.

"Speech therapists are near and dear to my heart, Mary," I choked. "Thank you."

The last sachet I left with the tip for our hotel housekeeper; I'd worked that thankless job one summer. She received the sachet intended for the First Lady, a toss-up for which of the two women in DC needed it most.

First on our list of last-day sightseeing, the building whose dome we had seen from our hotel window. The 1897 Jefferson Building, part of the Library of Congress, pays tribute to knowledge. Since Ben's foot still ached, and I knew its service would be required all afternoon, I pushed him around in a wheelchair. Renting one with my driver's license, I explained we had only a short time.

"Go to the balcony to look down on the reading room, and don't miss the mosaic of Minerva, Goddess of Wisdom," the docent instructed.

Eavesdropping on a tour guide, I learned people mostly use the reading room for research, not for a day but for weeks or months. Books cannot be checked out, but at the end of the day the book is reserved. There are 225 desks, hardly any in use. He blamed it on the Internet.

"Since everything is digitized, people don't need to actually come here, but you miss the feeling. In fact, if I'm having a bad day, I grab a book and come here to read."

Stained glass windows represent each state. Statues honor those who made significant contributions to the knowledge of humanity. The guide pointed out the absence of women, noting that at least Madame Curie should be here. At the time of the building's construction, Einstein's fresh face barely sported peach fuzz, so he too was missing.

Inscriptions around the base of the dome proclaimed the great Western literary masters, composers, and origins of knowledge. Ben tried to read one aloud, but got stuck. "Mom, what does that say?"

"As one lamp lights another, nor grows less, so...nobleness... enkindleth... nobleness."

"Mom, why are you crying?"

"It's (sniffle, choke) what you do, kid."

In my mind, the Jefferson Building Library of Congress Reading Room, although only an infant in comparison, in some ways equals the Bodleian Library in Oxford and London's St. Paul's Cathedral. I found nourishment in all.

Wednesday - Afternoon

Our eyes dazzled by the tribute to knowledge, Ben and I had only one more place to visit in DC. People say you only need two hours in the International Spy Museum. But for whodunit, James Bond, Jason Bourne, *Mission Impossible*, and espionage history lovers, even five hours did not suffice. Upon arrival, we tacked on a late-afternoon additional experience, Operation Spy. To run it, staff required a minimum of four people to sign up. By 3:55 no others had, and Ben's face fell.

"He really wants to go on it, doesn't he?" rhetorically asked the ticket-seller. "Hang on, let me go check, maybe some of the staff can go."

Just then, three adults walked in, bought tickets, and another salesperson persuaded them to join our tour. "My peeps!" declared an excited Ben, making friends with them in sixty seconds.

I can't tell you what happened for the next hour, or I'd have to kill you.

"What just happened?" Ben yelled plaintively at the end. The others thought he joked. To cover his confusion, Ben joined the uproarious laughter, but I understood. The last few minutes had offered too much information too fast. As soon as we were out of earshot he hissed, "Mom, I understand what we did, but what was the last part?"

December 8 – Thursday

Upon our victorious return from DC, I first visited my imperceptibly recovering Beloved Aunt in the UW Hospital's ICU.

After decompressing with tai chi, I wrote a thank you.

Dear IMLS Staff,

I think you should know what you bought. Flying Ben and me to DC for the award ceremony cost a lot of money, but the outcome was priceless.

Ben, seeing pics of himself in a suit, has declared, "I look good!" People here report he has a glow about him, and is carrying himself with confidence and great self-esteem. They are so happy to see this, as am I.

DC did more to aid my broken heart than I could ever have imagined. Powerful healing took place during those 100 hours with Ben. For once, it was all about what is right with him.

After school Sarah asked, "So, how was it, Mom?"

Dozens of stories flooded my mind simultaneously, but I answered simply, "The opposite of finding my seven-year-old boy in a coma."

Some might say my boy is not right in his head. Ben, you are right. Just right. I saw it with my own eyes for four government-paid DC days in a row, your humongous heart in action, even larger than the reformed Grinch's.

No one can ever take that away from us, a gift on the taxpayers' dime. Thank you, Ben, for appointing me your care-giving companion to DC.

Thank you, citizenry of the United States of America.

In April 2012, Ben and I spent forty minutes together speaking into microphones, Ben, interviewee, his proud mom interviewer. StoryCorps archived our audio in the Library of Congress as part of the museum's IMLS National Medal award.

I had not expected the exquisite depth of our magical conversation. It was greater than the sum of its parts, neither Ben, nor I.

It was us. Like it's always been.

Ben wore his Snorg t-shirt that day, "If life gives you lemons keep them because, hey, free lemons!"

Chapter 29

Lambeau

Sunday, January 1, 2012 –

The Packers' game day hysteria began in Rosendale, population 1,063, sixty-seven miles southwest of Green Bay. Groups tailgated mid-morning along the village sidewalks, cheering the streaming line of tooting vehicles headed to worship at the temple of Lambeau. Even Dan honked, while the four of us flailed our arms and yelled.

Once parked in the stadium's disability lot, Dan knew better than to attempt to stop me from purchasing him a scalped ticket. My early morning adrenaline rush showed no signs of abating, and it spiked in the frenetic energy field surrounding Lambeau. The incoming sea of green and gold, punctuated with blaze orange, washed over everything. I swam upstream, but returned, ticketless. Dan would have to walk to a bar and watch.

We posed for pictures, Ben in his wheelchair, as I let out one of my loudest Elsa Snorts ever. Ben, with his faux fur, bison hood-hat horns stuffed through the holes of his cheese head ball cap. His bright yellow "After Further Review, The Bears Still Suck" t-shirt stretched over his brown, puffy winter coat. On his hands, a black mismatched glove for his left, and mitten for his curled right. Peacock-blue snow pants covered his legs, and he wore a Green Bay Packers' cloth around his neck, bandana-style. Ben's smile displayed a badly chipped front tooth; in the night, he'd fallen face first on the basement floor. (My first job January 2, trip to dentist.)

Determined to search one last time, I finally saw it, a ticket aloft, bobbing. "You selling a ticket?" I salivated.

"Just one," apologized the woman.

(Who'd wanna buy just one ticket to Lambeau? Oh yeah, baby!)

"All we need is one! How much?"

"$87."

"Oh, we don't have that much!" I meant cash, not that we couldn't afford it. One of our Rainbow Days, we'd planned to spend.

"Wait a sec. How much've I got?" I peeled off bills, counting $53. "Rats. I knew I shoulda brought the ten on the kitchen table."

Her face told me no sale, so I turned to go.

"Sell it to them for what they can afford," her husband implored, as they walked.

"But it's Mom's ticket!" the woman protested, stopping.

"Have you got $60?" the man called, just as I rejoined my family.

"Do we have $60? Kids, you got any money? I want us to keep enough for a hot chocolate. How much are they anyway?"

Dan stuck his chin out stubborn-like, sporting the look we call The Grim Reaper. The GR makes an appearance once every family vacation. It's tradition. "I don't wanna pay even $50 for sitting outside today –" he argued.

"Oh, yes you do! You come in with us." A definite order, what the hells'a'matter with the man? $60? Cheaper than what I'd paid for each of our four tickets.

"But we'd be separated, I'd have to sit by myself," he countered.

"I've done it, it's not so bad," chimed in the woman, finally figuring handing her mother sixty bucks would be better than zero. "Seat's on the forty," she added helpfully.

"Dad," the kids exclaimed, "That's a great seat!"

(Dan looked hooked.)

"Yeah, and we can try to have you sit with us," I suggested doe-eyed, glassy.

(Lined.)

He hesitated, wheels turnin' in his head.

(Sinkered.)

"C'mon Dad!"

"C'mon babe!"

(Landed!)

After taking a circuitous route into the stadium, and riding the atrium elevators, we settled Ben's wheelchair, placing our butts on the three accompanying chairs, two of us sharing one. I turned, beholding for the first time with my naked, undistracted eye the field before me. "Whoa Nellie. We're in Lambeau," I breathed in reverence. "Father Goodness, d'ya see this? Pinch me!"

A semi-official-looking man approached, explaining his authority over the disability seating, four people only per section, not five.

As I drew breath to launch into my hastily prepared, heartfelt plea for pity, the man beat me to it, "You're a nice family," he said. "You can stay. Not all five can stay here all the time, though. You'll have to walk around. Send the kids for concession runs."

Adjusting on the fly, as Life With Ben had trained me, I switched quickly between Dickens' characters. Only thinking Oliver Twist, "Please sir, you don't know what this family's been through. We're all skinny, we can share a chair." I actually spoke Pip, "Thank you so much, sir! This family has been through a lot of crap in the last sixteen years. Thank you for not breaking us up."

Smiling his "you're welcome," he conspiratorially beckoned me to follow.

"Just so you know," he murmured in my ear, "later I'm going to have a cop come and bust one of your kids."

"Oh, marvelous! Bust the girl. For being sixteen and sassy."

True to his word, soon enough, a cop came. "This one," groused my new hero, grimly pointing at my daughter.

"Wanna go outside?" the cop enquired pleasantly, leaning into Sarah's face.

"What did I dooo?" she wailed, laughing nervously.

"You wanna go outside and have a conversation?" the cop persisted.

"Noooo!" she whined, laughing, shaking her head.

(Could those baby blues get any bigger?)

"Do I havta putcha in bracelets, or what?"

Sarah, choked with confusion and laughter, shook her head, finally speechless.

"No?" the cop asked. "You wanna stay and watch the game?"

Her head nodded violently up and down.

"All right," he finished with a grin, patting her back.

"That was so mean!" she said, giggling, when he left. I would've chosen any number of different adjectives: clever, hilarious, perfect.

Filming the entire encounter for posterity, in my haste I'd banged into Ben's weak knee and leg. The ADA seating protected him from drunken fans, but failed miserably to shield him from his overexcited mother. Fortunately, no damage done.

My hero hadn't finished with Sarah. Over the course of four quarters he gave her fits, siccing Packers' personnel and yellow-coated security on her as well. Between that and the Pack, our minuscule section rollicked. Sam made as much racket as his siblings, hallowed ground, indeed. Like Ben, Sarah and Sam spontaneously thanked me numerous times, gave high fives to all and sundry, and even consented to polkaing with me after touchdowns, while Todd Rundgren's *Bang On The Drum* blared and the stadium bounced. The Packers' touchdown anthem, in my humble opinion, is the perfect polka.

That day, for playoff safety, quarterback Aaron Rodgers did not play at all. But his replacement provided a perfect polka balance, one for me and each kid (Ben's arm only), and three with Dan. Once, while holding each other after the song ended, Dan whispered, "Thank you. This day is like the Coldplay day."

Another Rainbow Day.

Coldplay, a band of four guys from the UK, accurately sing the souls of this family, five people ranging from teens to fifties. I'm not sure how they manage it, and maybe they aren't either. I once read, whether true or not, that they didn't know what *Yellow* meant after they'd written their first signature song. But my heart understood, and co-opted it as the national anthem of moms of special needs kids everywhere.

But, despite Packers team colors, Lambeau doesn't play *Yellow*.

The touchdowns kept us jumping and moving in weather urging us to do so. The cloudy, balmy-for-January, low-thirties weather was just cold enough to send snowflakes swirling. Driven by strong gusts, the snow added to the utopian day. But neither the whipping wind, nor the historic stat-breaking win, nor Sarah's repeated arrest, nor the cost of three hot chocolates caused my eyes to water. Fan population, 70, 294, had contained one more than expected in our tiny section.

Afterward, we traded picture taking with a family from Canada. The mom confided they'd always been Packers' fans, as the Edmonton Eskimos' football team wore green and gold too. On their first family trip to Lambeau, like us, they seemed beside themselves.

Ben, upon hearing "Canada," belted out *O Canada!*

Recent transplants to Wisconsin, the woman explained she worked at Gundersen Lutheran Medical Center in La Crosse. (You don't say. December's bizarre butt call number three pops up again.)

"The Canadian health care is so much better than here," Ben complimented.

"No!" she argued. "You've got great health care in the States. It's the access that's the problem."

"Do you see what she's saying, Ben?" I asked. "The doctors and nurses who saved your life gave super health care. But not everyone can get it."

In the land where self-evident truths proclaim citizens are "...created equal, endowed by their Creator with certain unalienable Rights, that among these are Life, Liberty, and the pursuit of Happiness...," access to health care – physical and mental – is not yet created equal for all.

Not quite yet.

Chapter 30

Let The Little Children

Marriage is always a stressful proposition, as it involves bonding two separate human beings. Much like soldering. Some say no other metal has the strength of Alloy 1090. Yet the process of annealing, where carbon steel is consistently subjected to very high temperatures, creates the hardest metal on the planet, strengthened steel. Our marriage, Alliance 1985, underwent annealing through the years 1990-2010. We stoked the fire by having one kid, moving to Japan, having another kid, returning to America, and then having a third kid. But the consistently high level of stress applied after Ben's brain blew in 1996 acted as a marital furnace, an inferno sure to please even picky King Nebuchadnezzar.

We moved to Japan after only five years of marriage, when I was unintentionally six months pregnant, and equipped only with an undiagnosed ADHD toddler, faith, trepidation, the numbers 1-100 in Japanese, and "Ikura desu ka?" (How much is it?) For two years, I remained mostly physically and emotionally isolated on a busy main drag in the large city of Nagasaki. Our 2DK room apartment, two tatami (woven grass) rooms and one linoleum room sufficing as dining room and kitchen, was really one long, narrow room with sliding doors dividing the three spaces. Two chairs in the entryway served as the living room. Ben ran laps.

Shortly after Sam's birth, my mom and dad sent nineteen-year-old Boo to Nagasaki. Her two-week stay to care for her nephew Ben probably saved his life. I know it saved mine.

Venturing out with Ben and baby Sam, we climbed 102 stairs to and from our fourth floor apartment. The "little dirt park" down the block was our usual destination, the haunt of the neighborhood stray cats, sandbox littered. Two wooden swings, one wooden slide (no slivers), one cement tube. The apartment was convenient, however, with a grocery store, post office, bank, bakery, and restaurants all on the same block. On Dan's weekly extra day off, I would grocery shop alone, while he took the boys. A woman once stopped me to ask what I planned to do with all that milk. I only had six liters, about a week's worth for children of a mother from Wisconsin.

The only nearby cheap transportation, city bus, displayed masses of kanji, Japanese language characters. One bus route I managed to decipher, relabeling megumi no oka (hill of blessing) as "spaghetti no oka." That bus wound its way up to the top of the mountain where Dan taught at a Catholic women's college, in clean air and with the adoration of hundreds of eighteen to twenty-year-olds. I stayed in the valley, understanding next to nothing outside my apartment door, and very little within. Japan or Ben. But by the third year I settled, mostly because Dan's contract was up, so we switched colleges and moved to another apartment, Ben attended yochien for five hours each day, and I had made friends. It also greatly helped that an American expat kept me well supplied with mystery books, her coping strategy for living overseas.

In both living situations, of an evening, Dan and I read and talked, read and talked, read and talked.

Our new apartment, across the lane from a Protestant women's college, had been built especially for tall Westerners. Rare in Nagasaki, it included an oven, a green-leafed branch outside my kitchen window, and a nearby parking space for a car, things taken for granted in the US. We lived on a virtual Hollywood set, smack on Oranda Zaka (Dutch Slope), near the "exotic" Western-style homes from the late 1800s. Whenever leaving our apartment, I checked for tourist groups, dodging out quickly to avoid gasps at finding live Westerners as props. Bonus: one kid with blue eyes and straight, straw-blond hair, the other with green eyes and curly, red hair. Once, a Japanese woman bravely asked if they had the same father. Nagasaki contained very few Westerners; we stuck out.

The overseas ESL teaching positions paid higher than Dan's age, as opposed to in the States (seriously), and we lived nearly rent-free. Food cost three times what it did in Wisconsin, and it was our largest expense. Our last year, Japanese friends gave us a car. We paid only the government fee for driving a car more than ten years old. Gas cost at least twice what it did in the States, but we rarely drove the car more than a few miles. Still, I found the car invaluable – my kids and I could be anonymous, out of the public's sightline. When we left, we gave it to another Japanese family.

Returning to the US felt easy in some respects, difficult in others. I missed tatami flooring and food, but, even more, the handful of Japanese women, Shinobu, Miki, and Rieko, who had salvaged my life almost weekly. Without them, and a few kind Japanese and Western expat families, I doubt I would've maintained sanity. As I had packed to return, my Japanese friends feared for my safety – America the land of guns. Back then I could assure them that since I did not intend to join a gang or deal drugs, I would be safe. Now?

When we left Nagasaki in 1993, we brought back a healthy bank account. Moving in with my parents, we planned to catch our breath until we found a place to live. Less than twenty-four hours after our arrival, Dad and Mom sat us down. They were selling the house. Did we want to buy it? We did. But we couldn't even try. Not until Dan's hourly

ESL pay solidified. Not until Mom and I cried, Dad agreed to drop the price, and Dan agreed to release most of our savings. Six weeks after our return, the night it all fell into place, the four of us beamed blurry-eyed at each other in the basement. Still, despite putting down half the home's value in cash, almost all we had squirreled away in eight years of marriage, we barely squeaked through qualifying for a special, first-time homeowner, low-income loan from our local bank.

Seven of us lived together for five months. Boo in her room, until she left for her first job post-college, Mom and Dad in theirs, Dan, the boys, and I squished in my old bedroom. We didn't mind at all, except for July when the boys tag-teamed chickenpox. The first three months, my parents owned the house, the last two, we did. My father has been gleefully telling that story for nearly twenty years: "We lived with my daughter and her husband until they kicked us out!"

Sarah's appearance in 1995 ramped up our lives in a beautiful way. For a year we felt almost like normal Americans. Dan, our bus-riding-sole-breadwinner, and me, our stay-at-home-penny-pincher, caring for two boys and a girl. Living the American Dream.

The dream had begun after we dated for 3 ½ years. Friday, March 1, 1985, Dan picked me up after work at my apartment to take me for a snowy, sunset picnic on the St. Croix River, the boundary between Minnesota and Wisconsin. We crossed the St. Croix, but did not turn off. Minnesota in our rearview mirror, we sped south on I-94. Only one place could the man be driving as a surprise. For only one purpose. Dan asked me to turn around and get something from the backseat of the car. A bouquet of my favorite flowers.

"I'm not moving to Japan, you know," I belligerently spurted. The summer before, he'd been in Japan for six weeks and returned with a cockamamie idea – to move there permanently.

To his credit, he did not turn the car around, but drove steadily toward his fate of faith, to Madison, to campus, up Observatory Hill, where we jumped out of the car and ran in the dark through the gelid March wind to the Sound of Music bench, where he got down on one knee, and spoke the words I'd longed to hear. Overcome with receiving the desire of my heart I could not answer. It wouldn't be the last time in my life I scared him.

Six months later, after I got behind his dream of teaching in Japan, we spoke in front of others, "With this ring, I thee wed...to have and to hold from this day forward, for better or for worse, for richer, for poorer, in sickness and in health, to love and to cherish until death do us part."

A few more details would've been helpful...

...in fights and in agreement, through confusion and clarity, in terror and in security, with empathy and with resentment, in sorrow and in jubilation, for growth or stagnation, through trouble and ease, in good moods and bad, during shouting and cold shoulders, in understanding and bewilderment, whether pensive or impulsive, in shock and in calm, through phases and changes, questionings and doubts, and fears and tears, and tears and fears.

But never boredom.

For twenty-seven years we've lived with complete and total mind-boggling variety, provided often by Ben, Sam, and Sarah. The variety made it tough to breathe sometimes, deep and awful, thrilling and exasperating, inspiring and infuriating, and ridiculously, addictively, joyfully satisfying.

Like a good curry, richly sweet, packing bite, tempered with the cool topping of a cucumber yogurt, the kids spiced up everything. Ben, deceptively sweet bell from the start, morphed quickly into jalapeno, blew through cayenne, hitting red savina habanero. He held his Scoville heat rating high, numbing, and burning. Sam, although beginning with a surprise conception, provided antidote to the intensity of Ben's burn, creamy and cool. Sarah's powerful cinnamon sprinkled liberally, creating the perfect topping to an irresistible dish. Hooked for life, I cannot imagine living with the absence of their potent combination.

Before their births, I never dreamed the variety to come. If I had, would I ever have done it?

The calendar year I christened "January 1, 2011 London, To January 1, 2012 Lambeau" kicked off the healing of my heart more than if I spent the rest of my life in lotus (as if), gazing softly upon all the calming Holsteins in Wisconsin. My Reverse Bucket List brimmed with things I never dreamed would happen during my Golden Jubilee celebration.

The year I declared, "Fifty is seventeen with brains!" The year I wallowed in my pleasure at not previously having killed myself, and buckled down in earnest to start writing The Book.

The year that showcased Ben. Well. Employed. Feted. He and I found a deeper home, our "win-win," as he calls it – life work that nourishes as we give our energy.

All a towering, three-tiered, double-decadence, chocolate cake.

The year I rambled through the White House, the First Lady presumably upstairs enjoying a well-deserved post-Congressional party lie-in, and cheered my voice gone in Lambeau, with QB Aaron Rodgers on the sideline.

Thick, chocolate, butter cream frosting.

The year I twice visited England. On the first trip, I chaperoned my trumpeting Rainbow Girl, and 110 other teens, in my alma mater's band. In London's New Year's Day Parade, marching down Piccadilly to Trafalgar Square, then down White Hall to Big Ben, it was utterly impossible to keep a marching game face. I exchanged delirious Happy New Year's greetings with the international crowd hundreds of thousands strong, waving my arm off, damaging my smile muscles, involuntarily resembling the Cheshire Cat.

On a calmer day that trip, sightseeing with the teens at Windsor Castle, I sauntered through St. George's Chapel. There, and at Westminster Abbey, centuries of entombed humanity surrounded, engulfed, and overwhelmed. In both places, suddenly pierced and weak-kneed, every cell in my body screamed, "Wrong! I was wrong!"

Wrong to ascribe enemy status to my Maker.

Dan and I flew to England less than six months after Sarah and I returned. For nine days we walked the streets of Oxford and London, for him seeing the sights, for me tracking the trails of my favorite literature, authors, and detectives.

Yet again, I wandered star struck through the home of one of the women I admire most. Her Majesty The Queen of England had grabbed my heart after declaring 1992 her "annus horribilis." (I hadn't been thrilled with my 1992 in Nagasaki either, Sam's life threatened in a hospital PICU.) As Dan and I toured the Queen's kickback, weekend castle, her standard waved above Windsor, the flag signifying she was in residence.

To be sure, during my Golden Jubilee Year, I did not see the inimitable Queen, our own stunning First Lady, or even our Wisconsin football hero, A-Rodg, when I visited their respective homes. But just because I hadn't witnessed their physical presence with my own eyes, it didn't mean they weren't there. On the contrary, I knew they were.

Just like Father Goodness.

Perhaps the Director of the Universe had not conducted a cruel science experiment, taking a woman of my sensitive disposition, subjecting her to repetitive brain-rattling trauma, shaking and stirring, just for the hell of it? Or even at all? Perhaps Love still loved? Perhaps, as I once heard a pastor proclaim, Love accompanied, did not afflict? Did not even demand I "do this right," as I'd pleaded in terror the night I'd found comatose Ben. Was there any other "right" way to do such a thing, except with love?

In 2011, I realized no matter how loud Love had shouted, I'd stopped hearing. The deafening roar of Ben's traumatic life had drowned out the multitude of angels who once proclaimed peace upon the earth and good will toward mankind. *Good* will. The kind the Man of Sorrows recommended we ask happen here, the kind done in heaven. In his early thirties, the guy spoke against arrogance and for love: of self, of others, of a Benevolent Being he called Our Father. Offering pretty decent hints his DNA was not strictly Homo Sapien, he taught we must become like little children to enter the kingdom of heaven.

I caught again the whiff of love from Someone speaking my language, Someone who placed life-enhancing beauty all around us. Someone stronger than the deafening cacophony of waves that had battered my shoreline, incessant and intense, hammering home their power. Accompanying those waves of life, I heard the whisper again, the unmistakable thundering backbeat of Someone always there, always there, always there.

Someone had journeyed with me, over the rainbow, to Somewhere Else.

During the healing, comprehensive writing of 2012, when my 5000-piece jigsaw puzzle of a heart was put together again, I rediscovered the unwavering, relentless faithfulness of Someone very interested in a whole Katherine: the glittering, ruby red cherry on top.

My cake is complete.

"Waiting for the morning," had read one woman's epitaph in an English church. Yes, sister. I will wait with you for morning, my faith a deeper, brighter hue of hallelujah. I am loved, body, mind, spirit, and soul by my Creator. And by myself. In my life, I wish to continually trade resentment, rage, and wrongful convictions for a different sort of 3Rs: reconciliation, redemption, and resurrection. Drawing healing breath, choosing to utilize what all humanity is generously equipped for, self-awareness and adaptation, as best I can I will manufacture peace and goodness while awaiting dawn.

A hoarder's home is filled to overflowing with the attempt to control, and I am guilty of stockpiling documentation, hard evidence of the life I did not want, and felt I did not choose. The life Ben definitely did not choose. My perfectionist, fix-it nature mistakenly thought if I could but understand what had happened beginning 10:10 p.m. on January 19, 1996, I could own it, and maybe even change it. Like a good detective, if I completely comprehended the facts, maybe I could unravel the why, and our life would make sense. Then, perhaps, we wouldn't hurt so much.

Sixteen-years' worth of Ben's medical reports, sometimes erroneous, and the heartbreaking, detailed annual calendars of our medical life fill file cabinet drawers in the basement. Flames will lick the starry, starry sky the night I bonfire cleanse those files. In my backyard of refuge, I'll toss a hefty batch of my own lavender to finish off the pyre, allowing tendrils of peace-inducing incense to float heavenward, setting myself free. A harvested stack of my 2012 lavender waits patiently to be burnt when this mother's heart lets go, when I hold in my hand a paperback copy of this manuscript.

Reframing the Whys from the negative, "Why on Sarah's first birthday?" and, "Why at all?" to the comparatively positive, "Why here, in my hometown and four miles from world class hospital staff?" and, "Why didn't Ben die when docs expected him to?" I have been enabled to accept that I know very little, understand even less, and the fallout from 1/19/96 will never make sense. The first step in relinquishing control, knowing the illusion, the second, speaking. (Or, as in my case, the other way around?)

I've needed help prying my fingers, mind, and heart loose from the black and white reams of hoarded evidence. Besides Dan, Ren, Phoebe, and my Hired Help, I've needed writers. Throughout 2011 and 2012, Group of Authors stepped up as my midwives, cheering me on as I wrote tens of thousands of words, then alligator wrassled them down, encouraging me through many Braxton Hicks false contractions, comforting me as I deluded myself time and again the summer and fall of 2012 with my weekly psychological ploy, "Done! I'm done writing The Book!"

My favorite moment in the August Olympics occurred just minutes before US gymnast Gabby Douglas nailed a routine, when her teammate gave her a pep talk. Gabby's anxious and doubting eyes futilely wandered. Her friend put her hands on Gabby's shoulders, squared up, and stared her down, commanding her full attention. You could see Gabby's eyes collect and focus as she listened to, and heard, what I imagined to be a firm declaration of belief: I know you. You can do this thing.

Group of Authors did this repeatedly for me.

I'm not the first writer to ride the neurotic teeter-totter, "Everyone read my book! Nobody read my book!" It doesn't matter, for I have figuratively grabbed The Spoon of the Perreth Clan, speaking my peace on these pages, entoming my voice. Don't bother looking, Dear Reader, you won't find "entome" in the dictionary. Making up words to suit, the only thing I have in common with The Bard. That, and understanding when life overwhelms in any direction, it helps to put it on paper. Since every word weighs between an ounce and 100 pounds, I know full well the intrinsic value in that.

And yet? The lightheartedness I felt after writing was replaced by a weight of anxiety and fear concerning what I'd written. Not many take a bullhorn and announce heart and soul, even if outspoken. Despite determining I could tweak this book every day for the rest of my life and never achieve perfection, I stalled with publication, lacking the courage to declare it "perfectus," (finished, in Latin). Dr. Puckette and Psychotherapist came to my aid. Ren, Phoebe, Chris, and Jill cheered me on. Mitzy told this Piglet to be brave. Leslie offered to be my book doula. Happy Psychologist advised I'd given the baby enough of my blood, I should let it now live on its own, and Father Goodness counseled, "It's time to bring to the birth and deliver. This is your spiritual act of worship."

And Dan, using his birth coach voice, gave me my focal point. We talked it through one last time before he gently placed his hand upon mine, and together we pushed "Submit."

Through the lingering and rapid months of 2012, while I wrote, and rewrote, and rewrote, life and death refused to remain static. For a short time, Beloved Aunt would regain life and laughter, even becoming well enough to write more letters for me to treasure. I visited her every month but one, following her from facility to facility, as she wrapped herself in the soft blanket I'd given her in December 2011.

And then the intense suffering returned.

The fall of 2012, as I raced to finish writing, she prepared to leave. I mailed her the last chapter of the manuscript, and on one of my last visits, she thanked me for it, saying it "helped." So did the blanket. She remarked she didn't know how people did it, without such a blanket.

One Saturday, while quiet on my yoga mat in Child's Pose, I sensed it was the day for Beloved Aunt to go. I don't know why. All day, as is not my custom, I answered the phone, expecting my father's voice to communicate death. He did not call.

Between 6:15 and 6:30 that evening, as I stood washing dishes after dinner, something never happening to me before, happened. A sense overpowered; the perception so strong it became an image.

For once, it was not from a triggered flashback. This was more a flashsideways.

Beloved Aunt lightly flew heavenward, borne on the wings of angels, one on each side. The angels carrying her flew as gently, translucently, and ethereally as floating milkweed, yet with great speed and purpose. Shooting through the windless dark, toward God.

Accompanying this image, my mind strobed a picture Beloved Aunt cherished, the smiling faces of her two sisters who had gone before.

My hands stilled in the lukewarm dishwater, in awe I silently wept – for the uncommon gift of the image, for "knowing" my mother's smiling face awaited her sister, and for Beloved Aunt's leave taking. Set free from suffering and tears, she flew, but we were left here, and selfishly, I'd just lost a friend.

Beloved Aunt not only reminded me of my mother, she had once described her relationship with my mom as that of twins. And she had become my close friend too. A friend separated by just over thirty years; I'd missed being born on her birthday by seven hours.

Within thirty minutes of my finishing the dishes, my father called. But it wasn't until my cousin wrote the following day that I learned the time of Beloved Aunt's bodily demise had coincided exactly with my image of angelic flight.

That night, staring at the slivered moon in the haze, I lay thinking. I knew the rest of the moon was really there, just not illuminated. Likewise, light pollution blocks from view 99.99% of the stars in my night sky. And stormy skies cover the always-existent sun. How hard it is not to see, how easy to forget.

Beloved Aunt's funeral was a day of thanks giving, and one of the most beautiful days of my life. Serenity pervaded, simplicity, and a grounding of deep love, all for the childlike woman who in her quiet ways had touched everyone gathered. A proper send off. I dressed to honor her, but instead of Sparkling Shoes, I wore my Dorothies.

Beloved Aunt had gone Home.

And my cousins made sure Beloved Aunt's soft blanket accompanied me back to Wisconsin; I write this now, wrapped in her love.

Love. Love. Wrapped in Love.

Julian of Norwich, a 14th century Christian mystic, wrote her insights from the Resurrected Son in *Revelations of Divine Love.* I believe, as she did, that "All manner of things shall be well." At the start and end of the day, but especially in the middle, I must believe Love watches, weeps, and laughs with us. Knees and pine needles, hopes and dreams. Sisters and brothers, near and far, holding hands, eyes, and hearts. Love did that.

The sky didn't have to be blue, the leaves green, and the rainbow all around us.

Epilogue

The fall of 2012, Ben moved into subsidized housing in downtown Madison. He waited for twenty months for a space to open. The large community is mainly composed of senior citizens and people with disabilities. Because of his volunteer days at the Madison Senior Center, and his connection to Yahara House, he already knew many residents. He's only a few short blocks from the Madison Children's Museum, an easy walk. The downtown Madison Public Library is one block away. From his corner room, his view stretches south and west across a tree-studded city, what he calls his "kingdom," looking over Lake Mendota.

The UW Hospital is in the distance.

Ben cannot believe his good fortune, and asked the manager on move-in day, "Can I live here for the rest of my life?"

"Ben, you can live here for one hundred years."

Children See

By Ben Perreth, December 2012

At the Madison Children's Museum where I've been for two and a half years, there's a sense of a new and higher appreciation for the children who come. I've seen children play like nothing, literally, is wrong with the world; spotted two just laughing at each other, licking Blue Moon Ice Cream.

Kids are making a giant impact on me every time I work at the museum. They're full of positivity, freely given in grateful honesty and integrity. Not only are they young at heart, I feel their spirits are much more alive in giving, expecting zero in return. They make me smile from the inside out, and I, as my job description shows me to do, I try to encourage them to do more discovery! What comes out is such a remarkable thing, for it's a win-win situation in my mind. The kids aren't discussing about money, taxes to pay, how to get the upper hand, no, they're enjoying life as it is at the moment, playing...just playing.

More often than adults, kids ask me, "What happened to your leg?"

I tell them, "When I was your age, I had a big owie in my head. It made my body go wacko and I had to take a 337-hour nap." For some kids, that's enough. Other kids want to know more, so I show them my two hands, "See my two thumbs? They're different sizes right? That's because of the big owie, but it doesn't stop me."

The Tortoise and The Hare is my favorite fable. I tell kids and adults I try to look at myself as the Tortoise – slow but steady, yet I win the race. Don't compare yourself to millionaires and billionaires, because in the end it's about whether you are at peace with yourself and others.

My wish is that more people take notice, and live at least half as much life as the kids are giving out to me, for that's what it's all about. And if we do, we will see the love between the people in this world we live in.

For that coming day when death takes me away, I sincerely hope that I gave more than what I got. When I do die, I do not want anybody to see me in a casket at a funeral, or even have a memorial service. I want to donate my physical body to science so they can better understand how I survived, and can apply it to similar people who have disabilities. I don't want people to be sad at my passing. Instead, I want people to celebrate 5% of my life and 95% of their own lives at the Madison Children's Musuem, because life is laughter.

Never give up.

Don't ever turn back.

And even though the path might be much harder than you thought before, please keep on going through that black tunnel, for I am in the black tunnel today, yet I have found light.

What You Can Do

Please support the global Clubhouse Model of mental health recovery by visiting International Center for Clubhouse Development (Clubhouse International) at: www.iccd.org. Please help launch a Clubhouse in your community, and support those that already exist.

Acknowledgements

This work is meant to be a love letter of gratitude and thanks to everyone on Team Ben and/or Team Katherine. A special thank you to those who allowed me to include their stories in mine. And to David and JoAnne, who gave me life. Thank you Mom and Dad for teaching me God is real, and to fly if I could, cry when I must, but above all, dance and laugh.

A very special thanks to those whose spirits enveloped, upheld, and offered courage when my feet suddenly froze: Dan, Leslie, Mitzy, Phoebe, and Ren, and all-for-one-and-one-for-all, Chris, Jill, and Sandra.

Author Contact

www.katherineperreth.com

Glossary of Annoying Acronyms Here (GAAH)

ADA – Americans with Disabilities Act; the 1990 act addresses accessibility.

ADHD – Attention Deficit Hyperactivity Disorder

AFO – Ankle-Foot Orthosis; a plastic leg brace, below knee to toe, to aid walking.

AVM – Arterio-Venous Malformation; a congenital defect of abnormal blood vessels lacking capillaries.

CDC – Centers for Disease Control; a federal agency promoting and protecting public health and safety.

CT – Computed Tomography; scan using x-rays to take pictures of internal structures. Also called a CAT scan.

EEG – Electroencephalogram; measures electrical activity in brain via electrodes placed on skull.

EKG – Electrocardiogram; measures electrical activity in the heart via patches on chest.

EMT – Emergency Medical Technician; often first responders to trauma.

ESL – English as a Second Language; non-native English speakers take these classes.

ICCD – International Center for Clubhouse Development; a non-profit and non-governmental organization supporting global mental health since 1994.

ICP – Intra Cranial Pressure; numbers measuring the pressure inside the skull.

IDEA – Individuals with Disabilities Education Act; federal law since 1975 ensuring services to children with disabilities.

IEP – Individualized Education Plan (or Program); by law, public schools must have these for kids with various extra challenges.

IMLS – Institute of Museum and Library Services; an independent US federal agency supporting museums and libraries.

IV – Intravenous needle placed in a vein (usually on hand) to deliver fluids or medicine.

KB – Katie Beckett program; a federal and state medical aid program for special needs children.

LLUMC – Loma Linda University Medical Center

MCM – Madison Children's Museum

MRI – Magnetic Resonance Imaging; a machine using magnetic fields to take pictures of internal structures. Shows different and more complete information than CT.

M-Team – Multidisciplinary Team; public school broad cognitive testing for kids with extra challenges.

NAMI – National Alliance for Mental Illness

NG tube – Nasogastric tube; a tube placed through nostril to stomach for feeding.

OR – Operating Room

OT – Occupational Therapy

PICU – Pediatric Intensive Care Unit

PT – Physical Therapy

PTSD – Posttraumatic Stress Disorder

SAMHSA – Substance Abuse and Mental Health Services Administration; a federal agency since 1992.

SSI – Supplemental Security Income; a benefits program administered by U.S. Social Security.

UW – University of Wisconsin

WESLI – Wisconsin English as a Second Language Institute

YH – Yahara House; a Clubhouse Model for mental health treatment and recovery in Madison, Wisconsin.

Book Discussion Questions

1. Do you think the title accurately reflects the text? Why do you think the author organized the chapters as she did?
2. Once the author figured out what her subliminal crystallized intelligence was up to, how did she incorporate the childhood motif? What other major and minor themes run throughout the book?
3. For each family member, what were some of the physical, mental, emotional, and spiritual ramifications stemming from Ben's hemorrhage?
4. What tools are in the author's coping strategies toolbox? Which coping strategies do you think were most helpful to her? When things in your life are hard, what coping strategies do you employ?
5. Why do we still stigmatize those who suffer from mental health challenges? What can be done to change the way we respond to mental illness?
6. What can be done to improve access to mental and physical health care/support?
7. The author alludes to personal paradoxes. For example, she backpacks intrepidly but also seems plagued by fear. What fears does she describe? What are yours? What other paradoxes do you find? What are your personal paradoxes?
8. What are some of the author's values? What evidence do you find that she embraces living "green"?
9. What are the constructive and destructive ways the author dealt with her anger?
10. "Be self-aware in loving care, or beware." What does the author mean?
11. Do you love shoes? Elaborate.

Made in the USA
Middletown, DE
26 April 2015